OBJECTS OF CULTURE

OBJECTS OF CULTURE

ETHNOLOGY AND ETHNOGRAPHIC MUSEUMS IN IMPERIAL GERMANY

H. Glenn
Penny

The
University
of North
Carolina Press

Chapel Hill
and London

2002

Designed by April Leidig-Higgins
Set in Monotype Garamond by Copperline Book Services
Manufactured in the United States of America

Earlier versions of some of the materials in this book have appeared in the following publications: "The Civic Uses of Science:
Ethnology and Civil Society in Imperial Germany," *Osiris* 17 (July
2002): 228–52; "'*Beati possedentes*': Die Aneignung materieller
Kultur und die Anschaffungspolitik des Leipziger Völkerkundemuseums," *Comparativ: Leipziger Beiträge zur Universalgeschichte und
vergleichenden Gesellschaftsforschung* 10 (May–June 2000): 68–103;
"Science and the Marketplace: The Creation and Contentious
Sale of the Museum Godeffroy," *Pacific Arts* 21/22 (July 2000):
7–22; "Fashioning Local Identities in an Age of Nation-Building:
Museums, Cosmopolitan Traditions, and Intra-German Competi-
tion," *German History* 17, no. 4 (1999): 488–504; and "Municipal
Displays: Civic Self-Promotion and the Development of German
Ethnographic Museums, 1870–1914," *Social Anthropology* 6, no. 2
(1998): 157–68.

The paper in this book meets the guidelines for permanence and
durability of the Committee on Production Guidelines for Book
Longevity of the Council on Library Resources.

Library of Congress Cataloging-in-Publication Data
Penny, H. Glenn. Objects of culture: ethnology and ethnographic
museums in Imperial Germany / H. Glenn Penny.
p. cm. Includes bibliographical references and index.
ISBN 0-8078-2754-1 (cloth: alk. paper)
ISBN 0-8078-5430-1 (pbk.: alk. paper)
1. Ethnological museums and collections—Germany—History.
2. Ethnology—Germany—History. I. Title.
GN36.G312 P46 2003   305.8'0074—dc21   2002007922

cloth   06 05 04 03 02   5 4 3 2 1
paper   06 05 04 03 02   5 4 3 2 1

For my mother and
in memory of my father

Contents

ILLUSTRATIONS

ACKNOWLEDGMENTS

During the Christmas holidays in 1999, I presented my family with a bound copy of my dissertation, on which this book is based. My niece Christie, impressed mostly by its weight, asked me with some suspicion if writing it had been any fun. She was, I think, somewhat surprised at my answer: it was a lot of fun and I am eager for more. Indeed, writing this book has taken me to places I never imaged while growing up in Colorado, and it has introduced me to people who have inspired me, angered me, challenged me, and shaped me in countless ways. It is with great pleasure that I acknowledge the individuals and organizations who supported this project from the beginning. Without them this book would never have been written.

I feel a great debt to the people who taught me the value of engaging the past. Barbara Engel, Robert Pois, and Lawrence Silverman kept me spellbound during their classes at the University of Colorado in Boulder. Indeed, it is hard to imagine more inspiring teachers. At the University of Illinois at Urbana-Champaign, I benefited greatly from having Peter Fritzsche as an advisor, perhaps the best advisor anyone could have. Richard Burkhardt, Harry Liebersohn, and Sonya Michel also assisted me in countless ways as I researched and wrote my dissertation, and they continued to support me as I began shaping it into a book. I am grateful to the University of Illinois and the Department of History for their intellectual and financial support.

The Council for European Studies at Columbia University financed my first venture into German archives. The Berlin Program for Advanced German and European Studies (supported in part by the Social Science Research Council) provided me with a year and a half to pursue my research in a variety of German cities. I received further support and a congenial place to begin writing this book from the Institut für Europäische Geschichte in Mainz. I am also grateful to the archives and archivists who welcomed and assisted me during my research. Much of this book was written while I was a James Bryant Conant Fellow at the Minda de Gunzburg Center for European Studies at Harvard University. That fellowship allowed me to draw on the exceptional holdings of the Tozzer library as well as the many talents of the other scholars who were in residence at CES (a special note of thanks is due to Abby Collins and George Cumming for their help with all the little things). My colleagues at the University of Missouri-Kansas City have provided me with a supportive environment in which to complete this project, and I am grateful to UMKC for providing me with a Faculty Research Grant during the final stages.

In many ways, it is easier to list the institutions that have supported my work than the many individuals who have assisted me. I have benefited greatly from conversations and correspondence with Celia Applegate, Andrew Bergerson, David Blackbourn, Rainer Buschmann, Sierra Bruckner, Martin Bruegel, Alon Confino, Alice Conklin, Susan Crane, Andreas Daum, Andrew Evans, Michael Geyer, Stefan-Ludwig Hoffmann, Sally Gregory Kohlstedt, Craig Koslofsky, Henrika Kuklick, Alf Lüdtke, Brent Maner, Kathy Mapes, Andrew Nolan, Marline Otte, Joe Perry, Till van Raden, Jim Retallack, James Sheehan, Lora Wildenthal, and, of course, Andrew Zimmerman. My ideas have also been shaped by many interactions at conferences, workshops, colloquia, and in meetings with people too numerous to list here. Matti Bunzl, however, deserves a special word of thanks for his support and assistance, and I am especially grateful to Suzanne Marchand and Lynn Nyhart. Their kindness, generosity, and sagacity seem boundless. I would also like to thank the anonymous readers for their comments on the manuscript. They were quite helpful.

Friends and family have given me incredible assistance along the way. This book would never have been completed if not for the garden house along the Rhine in Bonn at Gensemerstrasse 15a. In some ways it was Ingrid's *Erdbeerkuchen* that saw me through. My parents never wavered in their support, even if they sometimes wondered what on earth I was doing, and I only wish that my father could have seen this book completed. When I was about to leave graduate school in penury, Ian Witter sent me a check for no particular reason. He simply thought I was engaged in something significant and should not stop. Paul Shirkey constantly reminded me over the years that history is important, and he continually encouraged me to do more. Kimber Keagle helped me survive the last years of graduate school and my first years as a professor by supplying me with a (shockingly old) car. People, in short, have been incredibly kind. Beatrice Curio-Penny has never waved in her support of my decision to be a historian, even during the times when I worked too much and earned too little. Indeed, she was the best thing about my research in Berlin, my foremost discovery. The Timmer came into my world while this project was winding down. He brought with him perspective about the real successes in life, and for that too I am grateful.

OBJECTS OF CULTURE

By 1900, Germany's leading ethnographic museums had descended into chaos. A wild array of artifacts from all over the world pushed these museums well beyond their material limits: totems from Canada's west coast, porcelains from Peking, wooden bowls from Australia, Polynesian canoes, Eskimo clothing, Mayan alters, Benin bronzes, statues of Buddhist and Hindu gods, weapons from the Amazon (and essentially everywhere else), even collections of ancient pottery and Roman coins found throughout Germany were all there to see. These ever-expanding collections were crammed into exhibition halls, overflowing from display cases, and set out in "temporary installations" that remained for years in crowded entryways, walkways, and stairwells. Boxes brimming with artifacts that had been packed away for decades were stacked to the ceilings of basement rooms, storage sheds, and offices. By the turn of the century, the overwhelming disorder of things forced German ethnologists to cancel public tours, repeatedly delay publishing guidebooks, and engage in heated debates about the very nature and purpose of such collecting and display. These conditions forced ethnologists to recognize that they had reached the limits of their empiricism, and they encouraged a younger generation to abandon the project that had driven these institutions for over thirty years.[1]

Despite the disheveled condition of German ethnographic museums, ethnologists and museum directors across Europe and the United States continued to deem them the world's leading ethnographic institutions. With some chagrin, O. M. Dalton, a curator at the British Museum, jealously complained in 1898 that in contrast to the British, "Germans of all classes find ethnography of great interest," and he estimated that the collections in the Berlin museum alone were "six or seven times as extensive" as those in London.[2] Similarly, Northcote W. Thomas, the editor of a series on the native races of the British Empire, went so far as to maintain that in the last "twenty-five years the Berlin Museum has accumulated ethnographical collections more than ten times as large as those of the British Museum." In Germany, he wrote ominously, "the work of collection goes on incessantly." Yet England, "with the greatest colonial empire which the world has ever seen, lags far behind."[3] German colonies, he reminds us, were relatively modest, and German ethnologists' origins were even rather provincial. But their ethnographic museums set the standard for decades.

The ethnographic project that initially shaped these museums grew out of a strong liberal-humanist tradition in the German cultural sciences and a more general desire among many Germans to connect with the non-European world. Aspiring ethnologists such as Adolf Bastian, who directed Berlin's ethnographic museum from 1873 to 1905 and who became the leading ethnologist of the day, drew on the cosmopolitan character of the Humboldtian tradition to fashion their world views. Like Alexander von Humboldt, they sought global explanations in their studies of the natural and human sciences, and they shared a desire for comprehensive descriptions of the universe. They believed strongly in a unitary humanity, and they argued that only a comparative analysis of "mankind's many variations" would allow them to locate the most fundamental elements of "the human being" and use this knowledge to help them explore their own essential nature. Moreover, they also argued that this analysis could only be pursued in museums, where the empirical traces of human history could be brought together, and where theories about humanity could be generated and tested. They gained support for their project from upper- and middle-class Germans who eagerly consumed the travel literature generated by scientific "explorers" like Humboldt, and who were willing to extend their enthusiasm into the creation of these museums. These "worldly provincials" were enticed by the idea of participating in this international science, and they sought to use it to enhance and advertise the cosmopolitan character of their cities and themselves. In Hamburg, Berlin, Leipzig, and Munich, the cities at the center of this ethnographic project, scientists and their supporters created Germany's largest and most well-known ethnographic museums. These museums were closely connected to Germans' search for a sense of "Self," and this accounts for much of their success and the character of their displays.

Germans developed a future-oriented ethnology centered around large collecting museums, and they regarded their displays as working arrangements for exploring human nature, rather than static explanations about humanity and the world. These museums were created in conscious opposition to the wonder cabinets of an earlier age,[4] and they represented a determined attempt to move beyond curiosity and toward an empirically based science of human culture and history. They were also more ambitious than the museums we are familiar with today. Ethnologists presented their new museums as archives of interrelated visual texts, which, when complete, would function like thesauri of mankind. As Bastian envisioned it in the early 1870s, the ideal ethnographic museum would contain material culture from across the globe and throughout time. But it would not be constructed to articulate explicit narratives. Bastian favored open collections, in which objects were arranged in cabinets made of glass and steel, flooded by natural light from large windows and glass ceilings, and positioned in such a way that a well-informed visitor could move easily through the geographically organized displays, gain an overview of the objects from entire regions, and make mental connections between the material cultures of people living in different times and places. Such arrangements were fundamentally different than what one might find in art museums or even in the colonial museums and exhibitions that became so popular later in the century.[5] No particular object, grouping, or arrangement was suppose to stand out, or be emphasized. There were no developmental series of artifacts or evolutionary arrangements such as one would find in many British and American museums. Moreover, the museum's goal was not to instruct its visitors with didactic exhibits or project particular principles through its displays. These displays were meant to function as tools of induction and comparative analysis that scientists could use to locate and explore the elementary characteristics of a unitary humanity and the fundamental nature of "the human being."[6]

Regardless of the distinctive nature of this ethnographic vision and the praise heaped upon German ethnologists and their museums at the turn of the century, the history of nineteenth-century anthropology has been dominated for decades by the Anglo-American context. Indeed, German ethnologists and their museums have received relatively little attention in this historiography.[7] There are a number of different explanations for this absence, but primary among them is the trauma of National Socialism and German anthropologists' complicity in Nazi racial policies, which has made the history of late-nineteenth-century German ethnology difficult for historians to reconstruct.[8] The majority of scholars who have examined this period have generally focused on either locating antecedents to the racial and biological theories promoted by German anthropologists during the Weimar and Nazi periods, or they have sought to expose ethnologists' connections to imperialist desires and colonialist policies.[9] But they have not explored the appeal of ethnology in Germany, nor have they tried to explain why Germans, more than a decade before they began seizing colonial territories, created the world's largest ethnographic museum. Scholars have been unable to explain why German scientists like Bastian, who isolated themselves from the race debate, were energetically spearheading a worldwide effort to "save" the material traces of humanity. Indeed, despite Franz Boas's leading role in shaping American anthropology, and the fact that he gained his early training in Germany's large collecting museums,[10] no one has sought to understand what these museums were like, how they developed, why they grew so rapidly, or what their impact on the history of anthropology might have been. One can occasionally find references to nineteenth-century German ethnologists and their museums in the more general literature on the history of anthropology. We know from George W. Stocking's work, for example, that Edward B. Tylor in Britain was influenced by Bastian, and Curtis M. Hinsley has made it clear in his work on the Smithsonian Institution that Otis T. Mason's conceptions of museum display were shaped in fundamental ways by his visits to Leipzig's ethnographic museum. But for the most part, historians have paid surprisingly little attention to German ethnologists and their museums during the period in which they were arguably their most influential.[11]

Moreover, it is my contention that German ethnographic museums, like all such institutions, have to be seen as the sum of the forces that went into their making rather than the simple articulation of Bastian and his counterparts' ideals.[12] German ethnographic museums were arranged according to Bastian's essential principles, but there was a rich historicist tradition and a wealth of human interests tied up in these institutions that visitors could only glimpse in their displays. The Grassi-Museum in Leipzig, for example, was a monumental building that opened to the public with fanfare in 1896. It was filled with the thousands and thousands of artifacts acquired by its founding association over the preceding three decades. Its large majestic windows and central glass ceiling flooded the interior with natural light, and its artifacts were geographically arranged. As visitors entered the museum, they could move directly into displays from Indonesia and the South Seas on the first floor, or go up the central staircase to Asia on the second floor, Africa and the Americas on the third, or a small prehistory collection on the fourth. On any of these floors the visitor would encounter hallways and rooms furnished with Bastian's glass and steel cabinets, arranged in long rows and filled with an array of artifacts. Here were the working arrangements that invited visitors to make connections for themselves. On the second floor, for example, a visitor's movement through the rectangular hall mimicked a long circular journey through southern India and Ceylon, Persia, Tibet, Mongolia, China, Korea, and into Japan. In a single cabinet devoted to Persia, one could find colorful pieces of clothing, jewelry, embroidery, decorations for lanterns, amulets, drawings, lacquer ware, bows, arrows, powder horns and cartridge cases, as well as horns, whistles, and other musical instruments. From this case one could easily look across to those from China and Korea and see the similarly constructed reflex bows and the variations in religious icons and begin to contemplate the interrelated nature of these cultures as well as identify their particularities. Such similarities and differences were only rarely pointed out by guidebooks or labels; but the connections were there for the observer to see. Indeed, these were precisely the connections the museums' ethnologists were in the process of making, and they expected their visitors to take part in making them as well.

But each of these objects was not only part of an indigenous peoples' material culture. They were also artifacts of the worldwide cultures of collecting taking shape in the late nineteenth century and the localized cultures that shaped these museums. As such, every object also had its own story to tell about the international character of the ethnographic project being pursued in these museums and the variety of people who contributed to it. For example, on the first floor of the Grassi-Museum, in the section devoted to Australia, one of the cabinets contained a stone hatchet made of an elongated piece of greenstone and a thin piece of wood that was wrapped around the thicker end of the stone and bound together with human hair. This piece had been acquired by Amalie Dietrich, the daughter of a working-class family in Siebenlehn Saxony, while she was working as a collector for the Hamburg trading firm Godeffroy and Son from 1863 to 1872. After she acquired it in Queensland, Australia, it traveled along with other artifacts on one of Godeffroy's steamers to Hamburg, where it was received by the naturalist J. D. E. Schmeltz, the curator of Godeffroy's private museum, who later became director of the national ethnographic museum in Leiden. Doubles of any artifacts were quickly sold to other collectors and institutions. But this particular piece was placed in Godeffroy's collections and was one of the artifacts surveyed during the next decade by Bastian and other visiting ethnologists, described in Dutch, Danish, German, English, and Austrian scientific journals as one of the best collections of its kind, and fought over by the directors and supporters of German ethnographic museums when Godeffroy placed his collections up for sale in 1879. In 1885 it traveled along with other objects in the collection to its new home in Leipzig, where it was greeted with fanfare but left in shipping boxes for over a decade before being presented to the broader public in the newly opened Grassi-Museum.

But the greenstone's historical trajectory did not end as it was finally put on display. Its importance, its usefulness, indeed its very meaning continued to change. Its future was dependent on the shifting urban and institutional contexts in which it was located as well as larger national and international trends. The display, in this sense, did not constitute its subject;[13] that process of definition depended on many individuals' transitory points of view. Dealers and collectors of such artifacts, for example, immediately focused on the economic value attached to an artifact's unique character. Ethnologists thought first of its value for their science. Both saw these values change as new objects were acquired, similar objects disappeared, and scientific standards for collecting changed. For Bastian's generation, the greenstone hatchet was one more clue in their great ethnographic puzzle. But for a younger generation of ethnologists, it became a theoretical and pedagogical tool, a proxy in an emerging war of influence and ideas. Patrons and municipal sponsors, however, remained focused on its utility for their own projects, while visitors' reactions to it, regardless of how it was displayed, ranged from informed contemplation to curious fascination.

Most visitors, however, could not know all that, any more than they could know about the long and complicated stories of all the thousands of other artifacts on display or stuffed into the basement and storage sheds of this and other German ethnographic museums. Very few visitors could know why the founding of these museums began three decades earlier. Even fewer would be aware of the thick networks of communication and exchange that took shape around the museums, the international market in material culture that ensured the ongoing flow of artifacts, the imperative demands of the museums' sponsors, patrons, visitors, and scientists, and the ways in which all these were intertwined with the heated competition between collectors and the directors of the numerous museums being established across Germany, Europe, and the United States.

The displays, in other words, were only one small element of German museums, a shadowy reflection of the richness of these institutions and the array of human relationships and interests connected to them. The displays were and continue to be important, but the most exciting and informative aspects of these museums were often the dramas that played out in their back rooms and basements, in ethnologists' meetings with collectors, private supporters, and members of the local government, in ships on their way to and from the many reaches of the globe, and in the correspondence between the directors and ethnologists working in these museums. These working arrangements reveal how Bastian's ethnographic project initially took shape and why German ethnologists eventually abandoned their visions of themselves as part of a cosmopolitan scientific community and began championing their prerogatives as ethnologists who were self-consciously German. These arrangements help us understand why ethnologists shifted from a focus on acquisitions for science to possession for possession's sake. They explain why the directors of German museums eventually turned away from their open arrangements and toward the kinds of instructive, didactic displays that many of them openly deplored. And they help us to understand why wonders and curiosities never ceased, despite scientists' best efforts to move away from them.

No analysis of the displays alone could capture the multiple meanings tied to these museums or the ways in which market forces, the realities of collecting, the desires of local patrons, the professionalization of the science, and the changing demands of museums' visitors transformed German ethnology from 1868 to 1914. There are, of course, examples of scholars who have effectively used museum displays to analyze the social and cultural values of the groups who created and supported them. Donna Haraway is perhaps the best known. In her seminal article on the Akeley African Hall in the American Museum of Natural History, she did a masterful job of reading Carl Akeley's displays and locating the ways in which they were constructed to appeal to a eugenicist's vision of the world and legitimate the dominant social positions of the wealthy Euro-Americans who sponsored this museum. Animals were chosen and consciously arranged in a manner that reflected the Social Darwinist world views of "this great class of capitalists," and indeed, according to Haraway, as Akeley sought out, killed, recreated, and arranged these animals in the museum, he and his sponsors eagerly "made dioramas of themselves."[14] Haraway's argument that these displays articulated their sponsors' visions of natural hierarchy and order is convincing, and her article has since become standard reading for cultural historians. But she was able to make this argument because she was focused on one set of displays that were created in a fixed time and space, by a particular individual and a limited number of boosters, which articulated, and indeed which was intended to articulate, a pointed pedagogical narrative directed at a general public only a few years after the New York museum had shifted its focus toward instructing popular audiences. Her focus on a specific point in time, when a single group with a clear set of shared interests controlled the museum, made her analysis possible. What she fails to address while critiquing this "snapshot," however, is that even at such a moment, the state of any museum actually represents the sum of its history.

Because there was not a single individual or group controlling German ethnographic museums, and no clear one-to-one correspondence between the intentions of these museums' "creators" and the institutions that took shape (let alone the cultural functions of these museums), an analysis such as Haraway's would be difficult to pursue. There were simply too many groups and individuals involved in constructing these museums and helping to influence their changing priorities. The museums were conceived of initially by a limited number of scientists; but as they expanded, their ethnologists became increasingly professional and identified new goals. Their audiences grew larger, more socially diverse, and made their own demands. The museums' ties to the cities in which they were founded became stronger and more complex, which gave the municipal bodies who helped fund the museums more influence over what ethnologists could do. The number of people who had a hand in these museums' development increased with each year, and as a result, the science itself began to change. Between 1868 when the first museum was founded and 1914 when the war intervened, a project that began with attempts to locate the most essential elements of humanity ironically ended by articulating the fundamental difference between Europeans and peoples in faraway lands.

Yet for historians, the protean nature of these institutions is their greatest asset. The degree to which the realities of collecting, the capitalist imperatives driving the international market in material culture, and the desires and demands of patrons, officials, and visitors shaped the lives of these museums—the forms they assumed and their functions in their respective cities—illustrates the degree to which Bastian's ethnographic project quickly became a joint project. The museums were not simply the brainchild of a limited number of scientists with a history that corresponds to their intellectual development. Nor were they simply the tools of either a rising social class or colonialist lobbies. The ethnology pursued in these museums was driven by shifting configurations of scientists, patrons, officials, and visitors; and as these configurations changed over time, the science and the museums also shifted and changed. Tracing these changes is critical, because they give us profound insight into both the development of ethnology as a science and Germany's road to modernity.

The goals of this book are thus twofold. I am interested in identifying and analyzing the ethnographic project conceived of by Bastian and his contemporaries, and the ways in which scientists, collectors, visitors, boosters, and competitors both inside and outside of Germany pushed this project forward, reshaping and redirecting it over time. To show how these institutions and the science of ethnology were driven by a combination of social, cultural, and material forces, much of the book focuses on locating the motives and interests that propelled the German ethno-graphic project, examining the museum directors and their ethnologists, collectors, and supporters in action: Why did they scramble to the north-west coast of Canada in the early 1880s, and risk malaria in the jungles of central Africa and Brazil? What drove Germans to corner the market on Benin artifacts to the point that the Berlin museum alone contained up to eight times as many specimens as the London museum, forcing Dalton to travel to Germany to study objects that were initially captured by British soldiers in a punitive raid? What made German ethnologists change their collecting tactics in the late nineteenth century? What caused the shift in the organization of their displays, and what accounts for the rapid growth of these museums? These are the kinds of questions that guide my analysis.

At the same time, I argue that the motivations, desires, and actions of the museums' directors and supporters provide us with critical insights into a nation that had only begun to be created in 1871. The Germans who founded and supported Germany's largest and most well-known eth-nographic museums in Hamburg, Berlin, Leipzig, and Munich did so in four very different cities. Hamburg was a free-city and mercantile harbor, Leipzig a landlocked commercial center, Berlin the national capital and an important industrial hub, and Munich the capital of Bavaria, which the historian Veit Valentine termed "the 'classic state' of anti-national reac-tion."[15] Yet these Germans shared certain characteristics. They were con-sistently internationally as well as locally oriented. They were worldly de-spite their often provincial origins. They shared cosmopolitan outlooks, strong civic pride, future-oriented world views, and a powerful sense of optimism.[16] They evidenced a willingness to take control, challenge older institutional structures, and refashion their environments to suit their needs.[17] The actions and motivations of these worldly provincials reveal a Germany caught up in self-fashioning at the personal, local, and national levels. It was a Germany teeming with dynamic individuals and civic as-sociations who were eagerly embracing changes brought on by the second industrial revolution, growing population, and the rapid growth of their cities, and confidently viewing these changes as full of opportunities, something to be managed and negotiated rather than resisted.

The social life of these institutions also captures the tense interrela-tionship between regional, national, and international interests, as well as the avid intra-German competition that shot through Germany and the "German sciences" during the late nineteenth century.[18] Much of the his-tory of Imperial Germany and the German sciences has been based on analyses of actions and attitudes in Prussia and particularly in Berlin.

Given Prussia's dominant role in nation-building at this time, and historians' equally dominant interest in the origins and impact of World War I and what followed, the emergence of this Prusso-centric historiography is hardly surprising.[19] But the tendency to focus on Prussia when contemplating questions about Germany, German identities, or the German cultural sciences during the Imperial period has often obscured critical details about the development of modern Germany. It disguises the ways in which nationalism functioned as a stronger, more dominating form of particularism that ultimately proved much more stifling to Germans' cosmopolitan visions than their regional and local loyalties.

Moreover, these regional and local loyalties were hardly a drawback. They provided German science with much of its dynamism and verve. Despite the political and economic unification of Germany in 1871, the Reich Constitution left cultural affairs in the hands of the individual regions, and many of the people living in these regions refused to follow Berlin. Hand in hand with the concerted efforts at nation-building in the late nineteenth century, went the persistence of strong regional and international orientations and an energetic competition among the aggregate components of this young nation.[20] It was often this competition that drove civic societies to sponsor museums, continually increase their budgets, and support ever-greater expeditions in an effort to outdo each other. And in many cases, it was the scientists and their supporters in the provinces who were setting the trends—a fact the Prusso-centric historiography has left unexplored.

Indeed, a strong cosmopolitan orientation and competitive zeal were critical components in the drive to refashion the reputations and images of Hamburg, Berlin, Leipzig, and Munich during the Imperial period, and they constituted the chief orientation for the clusters of scientists and supporters who developed German ethnographic museums. They constantly compared themselves with their counterparts in other "world cities," and they took great pains to ensure that they were not only keeping pace with these other cities but setting that pace in scientific and cultural achievements.[21] In many ways, this competition on a world stage made these scientists much more worldly than they might have been. Their pressing desire to surpass the efforts of their counterparts and keep up with the latest international trends far outweighed any national interests behind the formation of these museums, and it continued throughout the period of this study to guide the efforts of their supporters in fundamental ways. Moreover, if we accept Alan Beyerchen's argument about competitive science and technology being hallmarks of modernity, then we have to recognize that these efforts were also explicitly modern even though they were not necessarily nationally oriented.[22]

This book is an attempt to explain the dynamics of the ethnographic project that dominated German ethnology from its inception in the late 1860s until the cycles of accumulation on which it depended were destroyed during World War I. What follows is neither an intellectual history of German ethnology nor a focused analysis of German relations with non-Europeans, but rather a materialist and social history of cultural institutions and their guiding concepts. It is a study of how the cultural and social as much as the intellectual interests and desires of scientists, civic associations, collectors, patrons, and visitors, as well as the force of a growing international market in material culture, shaped the science of ethnology and German ethnographic museums.

By focusing on the internal dynamics of the ethnographic project and Germany's road to modernity, I do not wish to slight the influence of non-Europeans on the developments within the international market that supported ethnologists and their museums or the impact indigenous peoples may have had on ethnology as a science. Collecting was a two-way process that involved indigenous peoples as well as Europeans, and there has been some excellent work on how the kinds of collecting I examine in Chapters 2 and 3 affected indigenous means of production, trade systems, exchange values, and the ways in which non-European peoples negotiated with Europeans and capitalized on Europeans' interests to serve their own ends.[23] I do touch on this topic during my analysis of collecting, but it is not the focus of my study. In this book I am primarily interested in the motivations and imperatives that drove German ethnologists and their supporters and what these can tell us about Imperial Germany.

At the same time, despite many historians' characterizations of ethnology as the "foundational colonial discipline," and repeated attempts to tie German ethnologists' efforts at museum-building to colonial aspirations and nationalistic desires,[24] this book provides more of an ironic commentary on imperialist acquisitions than a confirmation of these assertions. Indeed, it explicitly questions such assertions. Given the relatively weak enthusiasm for colonialist efforts in Germany during much of the Imperial period, it would strike me as misguided to assume that they could explain the creation and rapid growth of these museums.[25] If, however, we were to pursue this monocausal explanation, then simply the timing behind the founding of Berlin's ethnographic museum—by far the largest of its kind—should already give us cause to reconsider. The Berlin museum was envisioned before the creation of the German nation and founded eleven years before Germany became a colonial power in 1884. But this is only the first of many seemingly counter-intuitive facts. The second largest German ethnographic museum, for example, was not in Hamburg—Germany's major harbor city with its extensive connections to all corners of the globe—or Göttingen—where Georg Forster returned after his voyage with James Cook and where the term *Ethnologie* was coined in the late eighteenth century. Rather it emerged in the landlocked city of Leipzig, founded in 1868 by a local association comprised mostly of autodidactic physicians and businessmen, and supported throughout its existence as a municipal display rather than part of a national endeavor. Indeed, despite our historiographical preoccupation with questions of nation-building and colonialist expansion during this period, a closer analysis of German ethnologists' actions reveals that German ethnographic museums owed their creation and rapid growth to a combination of older, cosmopolitan interests in unveiling total histories of the world and a strong intra-German competition for status.

By making this argument I do not mean to deny ethnologists' complicity in colonialist projects, and it is not my intention to whitewash their actions. Clearly, ethnology took shape within imperial and colonial contexts, and ethnologists often became intertwined in colonialist agendas.[26] But this is hardly news. Stressing this single point would strike me as akin to running through an open door. And overstressing it would be an action that showed little appreciation for the complexity of colonial situations or the particular cultural and intellectual contexts in which German ethnology took shape.[27] There is no question that, as George W. Stocking has argued, colonialism was the "*sine qua non* of ethnographic fieldwork."[28] Colonial expansion expedited the very act of going into "the field" and provided many of the basic structures and conditions for ethnologists' experiences. But while the colonial context would prove increasingly important for German ethnology as the century drew to a close, we cannot simply transpose the British experiences that inform so much of our understanding about the relationship between colonialism and science onto German history. Nor can we lump all of Germans' interests and endeavors with non-Europeans under the loose rubrics of "colonial fantasies" or "imperialist ideals." To do so, would be to lose sight of other interests and motivations behind Germans' engagement with the wider world—motivations which I argue can tell us much more about the character of nineteenth-century Germany than a limited and predictable focus on the forces of imperialism and empire.[29]

When we examine the rhetoric and actions of German ethnologists and their supporters, there is much that could be attributed to imperialist ideals. Indeed, if we look for colonial connections we are sure to find them. One can certainly find explicit statements of support for colonialist efforts in most German ethnologists' writings. But one often finds repeated condemnations from the same people as well. A small number of the actors who appear in this study held clear, consistent opinions about colonialist efforts; but the majority had ambiguous relationships with the peoples they sought to study, the state's nationalist and colonialist policies, as well as other Europeans abroad.[30] Consequently, in attempting to understand ethnologists' motivations and identify the forces that guided and delimited their actions, I have tried to pay particular attention to whom ethnologists were speaking when they issued their most "revealing" statements about non-Europeans, and to understand the contexts of their actions before assuming that they are clear articulations of their beliefs and concerns. The relationship between colonialism and ethnology has been a popular focus for some time, and it remains a sexy topic.[31] But while colonial interests played a significant role in the history of German ethnology and the life of German ethnographic museums, that role was neither the dominant nor the most important factor in their development.

Moreover, when imperialism began to have a strong influence on ethnologists' displays, it was largely an imperialism that came from below, pushed into the museums by the increasingly broad and socially diverse audiences that began frequenting them around the turn of the century. These audiences arrived in the wake of efforts by municipal governments to link their scientific museums to more general trends in education and to use the museums' visual displays as the primary means of communicating with an increasingly large and diverse public. Because of their dependence on municipal funds, the directors of German ethnographic museums were drawn into these trends. But if a new collectivity was formed with the rise of visual culture around the turn of the century,[32] it was one in which the visitors to these museums, far from being "taught to see," channeled and shaped the meanings of ethnologists' displays and delimited what these scientists could do.

Indeed, as the ethnologists in Germany's museums became committed to the new educational efforts, they quickly realized that the meanings of even ostensibly straightforward and simple visual displays were difficult to control. Despite ethnologists' desires to place their science and institutions above earlier collections, wonder and marvel continued to dominate the responses to their exhibits and displays. Fascination, curiosity, and spectacle continued to intervene as audiences grew. Much to their dismay, ethnologists began to recognize that their visual displays were not only open to more interpretation and multiple meanings than the written word. They also depended on an intertextuality of experiences that, when spread across increasingly diverse groups of people, soon led to the oversimplification of the messages museum directors hoped to deliver with their new didactic displays, and in spite of their intentions, to the polarization between European visitors and the non-Europeans on display.

In the chapters that follow, I argue that the inspirations, motivations, and legitimacy for the creation of German ethnographic museums drew heavily on visions of a unitary humanity and the desire to sketch out a total, harmonic history of "mankind" along Humboldtian lines. But over the period of this study, these cosmopolitan ideals gradually combined with, and were eventually overshadowed by more modern, professional, and materialist concerns. I argue as well that despite ethnologists' increasing professionalization from 1868 to 1914, social demands and popular ideals continually reshaped their scientific efforts and priorities and, as a result, most of the fundamental shifts in ethnologists' orientations came largely from outside their professional circles. Throughout the book I stress that German ethnologists and their supporters were part of an international movement that began before the founding of the German Empire and continued until its demise. They participated in generating international discourses about the character of humanity, took part in an international movement in creating monumental ethnographic museums, and acted from local or regional centers.

Each of the chapters in this book is focused on a set of forces that helped shape German ethnology and German ethnographic museums from Bastian's initial vision in the 1860s until the outbreak of World War I. The study begins with an explanation of Bastian's vision, the different ways in which ethnographic museums appealed to established scientists, intellectual outsiders, amateur collectors, city officials, and other supporters, and the reasons why the four cities of Hamburg, Berlin, Leipzig, and Munich became centers for what Bruno Latour would call "cycles of accumulation."[33] It sets up a general argument, which continues throughout the book, that German ethnologists and their chief supporters drew on a modernist, future-oriented impulse in Germany—an impulse that affected many of their decisions and desires and helped drive their will to collect artifacts and create museums. It also begins an argument that I return to in the last chapters about the ways in which Germans involved in creating, supporting, and visiting these museums regarded these institutions as civic trophies and gained their enjoyment in a scientific manner that was only later, after the turn of the century, eclipsed by a more imperialistic concept of entertainment.

In the second and third chapters, the book turns to the networks of acquisition that took shape around these institutions, and the ways in which ethnologists identified their priorities, pursued their projects, and filled their museums. Chapter 2 is focused on the development of international networks, the ties between the shifting values of artifacts and ethnologists' professionalization, the tactics ethnologists favored, and their ever-expanding desires. It portrays the emergence of a powerful international market in material culture and the ways in which it was tied to ethnologists and their supporters' competitive verve, and argues that this market soon developed its own logic, one that contributed to the most fundamental changes in ethnologists' methods and goals.

The market dramatically influenced decisions by the directors of these museums, their supporters, and their collectors, but I argue in Chapter 3 that a general, international consensus about what constituted acceptable methods of acquisition and behavior also guided their actions and decisions. Here the focus shifts to the ways in which the cosmopolitan ideals that initially legitimated this project became intimately intertwined with the capitalist imperatives of the international market to shape the parameters in which ethnologists' decisions were made. These older ideals stemmed from a belief in an apolitical, international scientific community, which was focused on working toward a greater good and claimed a certain moral authority for its actions. I argue that the authority of this cosmopolitan science became a strong rhetorical tool, and that ethnologists continued to use it to legitimate their collectors' actions even after the realities of collecting caused them to act in ways that were opposed to the cosmopolitan character of their science and the liberal humanist ideals that had given birth to their ethnographic project. But the realities of collecting in an increasingly imperialist world also precipitated a fundamental shift in ethnologists' visions of themselves. They became increasingly politicized by their actions abroad, moved away from their apolitical rhetoric, and began championing their actions as the prerogatives of scientists who were self-consciously German.

The last two chapters of the book return from the field to developments within the museums during the same period. Chapter 4 demonstrates that the market mechanism functioned inside the museums as well, and it explores the dilemma that faced the museums' directors as they were forced to accept the demands of other scientists, patrons, educated elites, municipal governments, and, finally, more popular audiences along with their support. It shows that the kinds of visitors one could find in these museums varied from one city to the next, but that in each case, museums' audiences helped shape these institutions in fundamental ways, influencing their architecture, atmosphere, arrangements, the goals of their exhibits, and even their collecting policies abroad. Indeed, the most fundamental shift that occurred in the arrangements of ethnographic displays resulted in many ways from transformations in the urban contexts in which they were based, especially the changes in the composition of these museums' audiences and the willingness of their visitors to articulate their desires.

Chapter 5 then moves to a more general analysis of these museums as places that produced knowledge about both non-Europeans and the German "Self." It examines the relationship between the social and cultural forces discussed in the previous chapters and the changing character of the museums' displays. It argues that essential changes in the ways culture was consumed around the turn of the century had a critical impact on the shape and function of these scientific museums. It was largely the public receptions of the museums, and ethnologists' efforts to control them, that precipitated the shift away from Bastian's initial vision of open arrangements toward more didactic displays. Even then, however, as wonder, spectacle, and chaos continued to disrupt their efforts, ethnologists realized that they had not only reached the limits of their empiricism but that they would never gain control over the materials they had accumulated. They began to realize as well that they had little control over the cultural functions of their museums. As such, these realizations represented the logical conclusion of a project predicated on possession, unending expansion, and consumption—a project that began with attempts to locate the most essential elements of human unity, but which ironically ended by articulating fundamental differences between Europeans and their multiple Others.

ONE

MODERNIST VISIONS AND MUNICIPAL DISPLAYS

THE FOUNDING AND DEVELOPMENT OF GERMAN ETHNOGRAPHIC MUSEUMS

The ultimate goal of all ethnographic activities and with them the general purpose of ethnographic museums can only be: To contribute to the knowledge and understanding of ourselves.—Oswald Richter, "Über die Idealen und Praktischen Aufgaben der Ethnographischen Museen"

The degree of civilization to which any nation, city or province has attained, is best shown by the character of its Public Museums and the liberality with which they are maintained.—G. Brown Goode, *Principles of Museum Administration*

When Germany was founded in 1871 it possessed only scattered ethnographic collections, leftovers from princely treasure houses, forgotten items in curiosity cabinets, and the ill-gotten gains of adventurers.[1] Yet by the first decade of the twentieth century, a number of Germany's cities possessed internationally acclaimed ethnographic institutions, and the nation's capital boasted the world's largest, and according to contemporaries, grandest ethnographic museum. The rapid growth of these institutions was as unprecedented as it was surprising. Their appearance paralleled the creation and development of the German Empire, and they matured against the riotous backdrop of nineteenth-century colonialism. But the movement to create ethnographic museums was not driven by German nationalism or by a particular colonialist vision. City-building rather than nation- or empire-building provided German scientists with the support they needed to pursue ethnology with vigor.

Because ethnology only began to dawn as a scientific discipline in Europe in the late 1860s, German ethnologists benefited from the wave of civic associations that began forming after the Napoleonic Wars and especially the increasing numbers of natural scientific associations that were founded following the 1848 revolutions.[2] Scholars have calculated that by 1870, "one German citizen in two belonged to an association,"[3] and between 1840 and 1870, up to eighty new associations were founded devoted to the natural sciences alone.[4] This changed Germany's institutional landscape. Associations in the cities sponsored projects devoted to renewal, such as hygiene, welfare for the working classes, public health care, and they eagerly engaged in fashioning signs of their own cultural progress: art museums, natural history museums, opera houses, botanical and zoological gardens.[5] Many of the people involved in these associations, and many who would later champion ethnographic museums, were also inspired by the travel literature that began flooding Europe at this time. They were enchanted by Alexander von Humboldt's cosmopolitan vision, and many were eager to take up his challenge to pursue total histories of the world.[6]

German ethnographic museums owed their origins to a small number of aspiring ethnologists who seized on Humboldt's vision and were convinced that they could improve their knowledge of themselves by exploring mankind's extensive variations. But in many ways ethnology, and especially ethnographic museums, flourished in Imperial Germany because a range of different cities provided this science with particularly fertile ground for its development. Indeed, during the second half of the nineteenth century, German ethnology was an emerging discipline led by intellectual newcomers in cities caught up in the throes of change. It emerged as a science just as German cities were beginning a phase of uncommon growth, and a striking range of citizens in the largest of these cities embraced ethnologists and their institutions because they believed this new, internationally recognized science provided the city that possessed a significant ethnographic museum with a means for exhibiting its citizens' worldliness and thus for refashioning themselves.

The Shaping of German Ethnology: Adolf Bastian's Humboldtian Vision

More than anyone else, Adolf Bastian (1826–1905) shaped the development of German ethnology during the second half of the nineteenth century (Fig. 1). He established and directed Germany's largest ethnographic museum. He founded, contributed to, and edited a number of leading ethnological and geographical journals, and he was repeatedly featured in a number of popular magazines. He was a key player in Germany's foremost geographical society, the Berlin Society for Anthropology, Ethnology, and Prehistory, as well as several other scientific associations. He was also the first person in Germany to gain a university position as an ethnologist. By 1895, Bastian had over 230 publications to his credit, and by 1905 his books took up three to four feet of shelf space and included over 10,000 pages.[7] There were, of course, a number of other German scholars such as Friedrich Ratzel who also played important roles in the history of this science, and whose viewpoints differed in marked ways from Bastian's. But it was unquestionably Bastian who set the central trends in German ethnology from the 1860s through the 1880s as he sketched out his vast empirical project, established extensive international networks of collection and exchange, created an ethnographic institution that became the critical point of comparison for all others, and helped to train a number of Germany's first professional ethnologists and encourage them to harness this new science in pursuit of self-knowledge.[8] It was Bastian's vision that provided the initial framework for German ethnology and shaped the character of Germany's leading ethnographic museums.

Like many of his generation, Bastian was inspired by Alexander von Humboldt, the leading natural scientist of his age. Humboldt was renowned for his exploration of equatorial America from 1799 to 1804. He produced thirty volumes based on these journeys, which encompassed the botany, plant geography, zoology, physical geography, and political economy of the area. He also contributed to the sciences of anatomy, mineralogy, and chemistry, and he was keenly interested in the relationship between humans and their environment. His masterpiece was the five-volume *Cosmos* (published from 1845 to 1862), in which he attempted to write a comprehensive description of the universe and a complete account of the physical history of the world. Because of popular demand, the original edition of the first volume alone sold over 22,000 copies, making him one of the most successful authors of his day.[9] Humboldt's writings helped to establish geography as a scientific discipline, and his example influenced both the lifestyle Bastian embraced as well as the character and scope of his ethnographic project.[10]

Bastian dedicated his first major publication, *Der Mensch in der Geschichte*, to Humboldt, and in there he set out the essential parameters of the project he pursued for the next forty-five years.[11] Bastian argued during a speech he delivered in Humboldt's honor in 1869, that "world travel" rather than a limited contemplation of texts was the best thing for the

FIGURE 1. Adolf Bastian (1826–1905). The son of a wealthy merchant family in Bremen, Bastian spent over twenty-five years of his life abroad and became the father of German ethnology. (Bildarchiv Preußischer Kulturbesitz, Berlin)

"promotion of science."[12] Inspired by Humboldt's example, he undertook eight major excursions outside of Europe.[13] Indeed, he ultimately spent more than twenty-five years of his life abroad—gathering information, collecting for his museum, persuading well-placed individuals in other lands to assist him, and convincing talented young men like Karl von den Steinen to join in his project to unveil the total history of humanity in all its many variations.[14]

Moreover, much like his intellectual hero, Bastian's ethnographic project was governed by a set of methodological and political convictions rather than a single overarching theory. His reading of Humboldt's *Cosmos* had convinced him that the creation of universal theories about human history were secondary to the accumulation of knowledge about its particulars: "All systems-construction," he argued during his speech in honor of Humboldt, "remains mere metaphysical illusion unless knowledge of the details has been accumulated." For this reason Humboldt had posited no great theory, no general explanatory system in his *Cosmos*; nor, as far as Bastian was concerned, was one necessary. Such "systems," Bastian argued, "are ephemeral by their nature," but Humboldt's method (the development of a vast synthesis based on empirical induction) was "everlasting" and would eventually lead to scientific truths.[15] It was Humboldt's effort to fashion a total empirical and harmonic picture of the world that inspired Bastian's attempt to unite all knowledge of human history—ethnological, philosophical, psychological, anthropological, and historical—into a huge empirical synthesis and to abstain from issuing tentative explanatory theories.

This methodological commitment to careful, empirical research over "speculative theorizing" prompted Bastian and his counterpart in German physical anthropology, the well-known pathologist Rudolf Virchow, to shun Darwinian schemes of human history and isolate themselves from the race debate.[16] Virchow did argue in public debates that Darwinism was dangerous because of its possible association with Social Democracy; but his chief criticism always targeted Darwinism's speculative nature.[17] Bastian took the same position. While he admired Darwin's travels, he lamented the lack of "factual evidence" that might support his conclusions, and he compared Darwin's postulates about the "genealogy of mankind" to "fantasies" from the "dreams of mid-day naps."[18] But he found particularly offensive the efforts by Germany's leading Darwinian, Ernst Haeckel, to popularize these ideas. In his public debates with Haeckel, Bastian denounced these efforts as "unscientific forgery," lacking a sufficient empirical base for responsible presentation. As he noted, "Nothing is further from my intentions than popularization, because I know that my newly born science of ethnology is still too young for such a daring deed." While Haeckel strove "above all and with reckless abandon toward popularization," Bastian believed that only theories based on solid empirical evidence should be used to explain complex phenomena to laymen.[19]

In lieu of a definitive ethnological theory, Bastian had a set of specific convictions and a three-part plan of action. World history for Bastian was the history of the human mind. He argued, with a strong monogenicist

conviction stemming largely from his worldwide travels, that "human nature is uniform all over the globe" and that "if there are laws in the universe, their rules and harmonies should also be in the thought processes
of man."[20] Thus Bastian's first (and highly ambitious) goal was to engage
in a vast, comparative analysis of these thought processes during which he
expected that his second goal would ultimately take care of itself: empirical laws would eventually emerge. Once these laws were revealed, he believed that they could also be applied to his ultimate end: they could be
harnessed by Europeans to help them better understand themselves.

As Bastian wrote in 1877, "the physical unity of the species man [has
already] been anthropologically established." In consequence, his project
was focused on locating "the psychic unity of social thought [that] under-
lies the basic elements of the body social." The best way to do this, he contended, was not through subjective self-reflection on European cultural
history, but by bringing together and examining the physical traces of human thought, the material culture produced by peoples everywhere, which
he believed would reveal "a monotonous sub-stratum of identical elementary ideas" with which they could exfoliate the more general history
of the human mind.[21]

Bastian stressed that every group of people shared these "elementary
ideas" or *Elementargedanken*, even though they were never directly observ-
able. Having an "innate propensity to change,"[22] they always materialized
in the form of unique patterns of thought, or *Völkergedanken*, reflecting
the interaction of peoples with their environments, as well as their contacts
with other groups. *Elementargedanken* were thus hidden behind humanity's
cultural diversity—a diversity that was historically and geographically
contingent. Understanding the unique contexts in which each culture
took shape, Bastian stressed, was thus critical for gaining insight into the
universal character of "the" human being.[23] Indeed, it was largely Bastian's
interest in identifying these contexts that led Fritz Graebner to term Bastian the *Naturvölkers* "*Erwecker zu historischem Leben*," quite literally, the one
who brought natural peoples (or ostensibly primitive peoples) into history.[24]

In addition to Bastian's notion of *Elementargedanken* and *Völkergedanken*,
it was the idea of geographical provinces that formed the core of his
thought.[25] For Bastian, the *Völkergedanken* that characterized different
groups of people emerged within identifiable zones where geographical
and historical influences shaped specific cultures. Unique *Völkergedanken*,
like "actual organisms," fit within these particular geographical provinces,
shifting and changing as they came into contact with others. This interaction, Bastian emphasized, was the basis of all historical development, and

it could be observed most readily in certain geographical areas: on rivers, coast lines, and mountain passes, which he referred to as "*Völkertore*."[26]

Within Bastian's ethnology, the question of human difference played a critical role. On a basic level, humanity could be divided into two major categories, the *Naturvölker* (natural peoples) and the *Kulturvölker* (cultural peoples).[27] Having achieved literacy, the latter had a recorded past that historians and philologists could explore. This did not mean, however, that the former were without history or culture. Quite the contrary, Bastian believed that there were "essentially next to no peoples left on earth who were without historical influences."[28] The historical and cultural trajectories among the world's *Naturvölker* were in fact at the heart of Bastian's ethnological project. Indeed, what Bastian sought to explain were not so much the coincidences between conceptions among natural peoples, but the specific differences. It was these differences that held the key to historical development through the emergence of *Völkergedanken*.

To account for the general development of *Völkergedanken*, Bastian recommended investigations of the most isolated and simple societies. While "European cultural history" was "almost unmanageable due to its complex bifurcations," the cultures of simple societies could be readily contextualized. Using a botanical analogy, Bastian likened Europe to a "tree that grew for hundreds and thousands of years." Simple societies, in contrast, were similar to small plants. They "grow according to the same laws as the mighty tree," but their "growth and decline are easier to observe, since we are looking at a limited field of observation which could be compared to an experiment in a laboratory."[29]

Bastian did not believe that this analysis of simple societies would allow ethnologists to locate a normative sequence of cultural achievement of the kind proposed by British anthropologist Edward B. Tylor.[30] Rather than using ethnographic data to construct putative hierarchies, Bastian believed that a broad, comparative analysis of *Naturvölker* would help him identify a "set of seminal ideas from which every civilization had grown." This set of seminal ideas would in turn become the "methodological tool for unraveling more complex civilizations." Allowing the formulation of empirical laws regarding the effects of physiological, psychological, and social conditions of the human mind, Bastian's ethnographic insights could later be applied to Europeans.[31] In short, Bastian's quest to unveil the inner workings of simple societies was part of a conscious effort to help Europeans better understand themselves. And these introspective possibilities provided the central stimulus for his interest in ethnology and his desire to erect a monumental ethnographic museum.

Ethnology and the Museum Age

When historians think of museums, most of us draw on our own twenti-eth-century experiences, and we think of spectacle and display. This im-pulse has only been strengthened by scholars' recent attention to the sensa-tional worlds fairs around the turn of the century,[32] the "Victorian interest in mechanical inventions as symbols of broader cultural change," and the idea of progress—particularly in Britain and the United States—which was often articulated through technical advances displayed in the emerg-ing international exhibitions.[33] These observations have led some histori-ans interested in British anthropological museums, for example, to place the exhibitionary and instructive roles of museums at the center of their origins and development, to juxtapose the exhibition of contemporary material advances with the display of non-Europeans' material culture, and then to argue that, given the hierarchical undercurrents of these ex-hibits, "it is not surprising . . . that an emphasis on material culture—and its display in museum settings—became an important leitmotiv within the British anthropological community."[34] While this and other similar evaluations have helped to unveil the hegemonic potential inherent in ethnographic displays, it would nevertheless be a mistake to allow them to obscure the functionality and appeal of the museum as a scientific tool. Indeed, although an emphasis on hierarchy and progress also found their way into some German ethnographic museums after the turn of the cen-tury,[35] the initial attraction of museums as research institutions was ulti-mately the most significant factor in the genesis of German ethnographic museums.

Consequently, when we set out to imagine the birth of nineteenth-century German ethnographic museums, we have to think, at least ini-tially, in different terms. The aspiring ethnologists who founded these mu-seums did not initially conceive of them as "the scientific showcases of the age,"[36] or places for articulating different kinds of cultural and social messages, but as laboratories where they could explore the multiplicity of humanity. Moreover, these institutions were also part of more general sci-entific and intellectual trends: they reflected and promoted new ways of thinking about human history that were inspired by the insights of mid-century archeological discoveries. They were part of the more general trends in the sciences toward spatial and visual arrangements, and they were also a cogent response to the flood of new information and materi-als streaming into Europe at this time. All these factors combined with the particular needs of Bastian's ethnographic project to promote the creation and growth of German ethnographic museums.

Indeed, the impetus for creating ethnographic museums lay largely in a new way of thinking about human history and a new emphasis on the empirical value of material culture. During the second half of the nineteenth century, an array of newcomers in the fields of history, art history, and archeology turned to material culture as an alternative means of reconstructing the past. They quickly began challenging older paradigms built on written texts by using material culture as a means to explore areas of human history that had been neglected because of a dearth of written documentation. Within the German context, efforts by Freiherr Hans von und zu Aufseß to build a national history museum in Nürnberg threatened the narratives of the German past espoused in universities: they shifted the focus of historical inquiry from high art and culture to the material culture of everyday life, something that caused scholars such as Leopold von Ranke to react aggressively against Aufseß's efforts.[37] Similarly, a number of young intellectuals who stood outside the academic canon of classical studies began moving away from simply using artifacts from Greece and Rome to support arguments drawn from ancient texts, to producing theories based on direct interpretations of these objects. These new methods ultimately exposed the limits of philologically based historiography in the universities.[38]

In order to understand the powerful intellectual and cultural potential of moving beyond written texts to material culture, one only need think of the life of the German businessman Heinrich Schliemann. He shook up the world of classical humanists when he claimed to have discovered the site of ancient Troy during his excavations in Hisarlik on Turkey's Aegean coast. His discoveries cast doubt on the cultural dominance of professional philologists and their characterization of the ancient world as a somehow pure and singular cultural entity. This in turn unsettled the very authority of university-based specialists and contributed to the fall of humanist scholarship.[39]

In fact archeological efforts in general had a tremendous impact on the ways in which Europeans envisioned human history and facilitated the rapid growth of the ethnographic sciences in the last third of the nineteenth century (that is, those sciences like archeology, ethnology, prehistory, and art history that focused on material culture). The sensational discoveries of prehistoric tools together with the bones of extinct animals in Brixham Cave in 1858, for example, threw the Biblical time frame for human history into question and stimulated a general interest in the ethnographic sciences. These discoveries led the eminent British collector Henry Christie and many of his contemporaries to rethink human antiquity and redirect their research efforts, and they may well have contributed more to the growing interest in evolutionary theories in nineteenth-century Britain than the work of Charles Darwin.[40]

In short, the sensational archeological discoveries of the mid-nineteenth century gave the ethnographic sciences a tremendous boost. They helped convince many aspiring ethnologists such as Bastian that both the material culture of contemporary peoples and the material traces of earlier peoples could be read as historical texts.[41] Agricultural patterns could be unveiled through in situ analysis of artifacts and landscapes that could never have been discovered in ancient tomes. Lifestyles, even modes of thought, could be ascertained from studying everyday religious objects, weapons, and tools; and theories about the relationship between humans and their environments could be challenged or supported by studying the most simple things, such as how bowls were made out of reeds, grasses, clays, and metals. The recognition by individuals such as Bastian, that material culture was rich with historical significance and empirical value that would allow them to move beyond the limitations of written records, provided a critical impetus for the creation of Europe's large collecting museums.

At the same time, more general trends in the sciences as well as the practical necessities of working with "material texts" contributed to Bastian and his counterparts' interest in creating ethnographic museums. We should bear in mind that the institutionalization of ethnology as a science took place during a period in which many of the sciences were becoming increasingly museological. By the 1860s, a wide range of sciences, including medicine, the life sciences, geology, mineralogy, geography, and others, shared an emphasis on the collection, analytical classification, and comparison of specimens—living, dead, or inanimate—and a "notable synchrony between many of these new forms and their institutional bases."[42] This international trend in methodology provided a critical backdrop for ethnologists' decision to work in museums.

There was also the practical question of space. Because the ethnology of the 1860s and 1870s was predicated on the broadest possible comparison of material culture, the physical space it required made museums vital to its very existence as a science. Bastian's commitment to inductive methodologies and his conviction that one needed to know the whole and its parts simultaneously, necessitated both the collection of specimens—

in this case material culture from all areas of the globe—and the ability to bring them together.[43] Once these specimens were assembled, ethnologists could begin comparing them, looking for similarities and differences in their forms, materials, uses, and meanings, and generate and test more general theories about human development. Without the physical space afforded by museums, this task would be impossible.

Moreover, the veritable flood of new information about the variety of humanity that was flowing into Europe and the United States at this time made Bastian's goals appear increasingly imperative. As many scholars have noted, the ever-growing number of traveler's tales about new and bizarre peoples and cultures, and the wave after wave of weapons, articles of clothing, sketches, official reports, unofficial rumors, and published accounts about the different peoples and cultures one might encounter abroad undermined Europeans' confidence in their own belief systems and led many to feel as if the "world had been turned upside down."[44] Indeed, the artifacts arriving in European harbors—colorful headdresses and stone weapons from the Americas, wooden masks and statues from Africa and the Pacific, and the Buddhist and Hindu idols from the East—as well as the stories being reprinted and passed around during the second half of the nineteenth century that focused on strange and spectacular places and peoples were not just curious. The sheer number and variety of these artifacts and stories could be puzzling and even upsetting.

Of course neither the influx of information and artifacts from abroad nor Bastian and his counterparts' desire to place them in museums were unprecedented. Information about the indigenous peoples of the Americas and the Pacific was also arriving in Europe during the eighteenth century, and here too museums functioned as a means of taming and ordering much of the information that threatened older schemes of knowledge.[45] Yet in the latter part of the nineteenth century, the stakes were raised considerably as rapidly expanding international trade and the continual, steam-powered movement of ever-growing numbers of people around the globe—military personnel, diplomats, explorers, colonists, tourists—transformed a trickle of information into a flood.

During the period 1864–73 alone, over one million people left Germany for a life somewhere else, many of them traveling overseas. The 1880s saw even more intense waves of emigration; 86,000 Germans moved to Brazil alone during the second half of the century.[46] During these same years, numerous scientific organizations, such as the German Association for the Exploration of Equatorial Africa, were created, and they continually sponsored a range of expeditions abroad. From 1873 to 1900, for example, 150 different expeditions were sent to Africa—an average of 6 per year. Similar associations were focused on other areas of the world, and all of them generated travel reports and biographic accounts of their "scientific heroes," which contained stories of the "new" places, peoples, and customs they had encountered. This new information continued to call into question contemporary views of the world.[47]

These reports about "new" cultures, "primitive peoples," and "unique civilizations" could be both menacing and exhilarating. Europeans faced a formidable task as they attempted to expand their historical imagination beyond the biblical time frame, rethink the relationships between classical antiquity and the rest of the world, and integrate under the rubric of "humanity" the varieties of peoples, religions, cultures, and races portrayed in popular, official, and scientific reports. These often overwhelming tasks heightened uncertainties about the modern age as older paradigms were continually thrown into question; yet at the same time, this new information also held out the promise of greater knowledge about humanity and the world.

The challenge for ethnologists was thus to find a way to make sense out of this information, and here, too, ethnology and ethnographic museums seemed to offer the best means to this end. As Bastian himself argued, in a rapidly changing world in which fundamental beliefs and once "natural" orders were constantly unsettled, "ethnology seemed to offer a ray of hope . . . that we might finally find a solution to the contemporary situation in which our world view is both unsure and fragmented. Ethnology seemed to offer the best chance to put the science of man on that same solid base of actual proof as we find now in the natural sciences."[48] In a time rationalized by positivist thought, the promise of natural science was both a stronghold against the growing insecurities of the modern age and the point from which Germany's aspiring ethnologists could gain control of this new information and put it to use. In particular, inductive empiricism promised to provide the basis for bringing the chaos of new beliefs and customs into a comprehensible order. Bastian even predicted that these "inductively reached proofs in ethnology," would allow them to "create a set pattern, a tool, with which to give judgment, exactly and definitively, on any social and religious problem."[49]

Bastian argued this point in his earliest writings on the museum,[50] and he continued to press this position throughout his life. Shortly before his death in 1905, he wrote again that ethnological institutes should function not only like archives and libraries but as laboratories in which ethnologists worked to "decipher ornamental and allegorical symbols from their hieroglyphics into readable text."[51] He stressed to visitors in the guide-book to his museum that these institutions "bring before our eyes the vivid embodiment of the growth process of an intellectual organism" that "blooms" in the "thought processes of humanity."[52] And he repeat-edly emphasized that "the new direction [in the study of humanity] will not arise through theoretical considerations, [but] rather through practical work in museums."[53] What museums, and only museums, afforded, he contended, was "a bird's-eye view" of these human growth processes, a place in which the diversity and wholeness of humanity could be re-assembled for observation and comparison, and where they could de-velop and test ethnological theories.

By the early 1880s the greater ethnographic project as envisioned by Bastian was widely embraced throughout Germany and the museum had become the institution of choice for ethnologists. This general conviction is perhaps best captured in a memorandum issued in 1883 by the directo-rial committee of the Leipzig ethnographic museum: "It is clear, that as soon as one enters the way of inductive research in order to progress from the singular to the general, and as soon as one recognizes that a sys-tem will only first emerge as particularities are brought together, then one must also realize that museums are a *conditio sine qua non*, and must be there from the beginning."[54]

Kultur, *Bildung*, and the Modernist Moment

The museums that Bastian and his counterparts in other German cities demanded were quickly created and almost immediately overfilled. To a certain degree, this growth can be explained by ethnologists' ability to take advantage of the technological advances of the late nineteenth century—the faster and more reliable communications and transportation, and the establishment of worldwide networks of Europeans—which eased the accumulation, preservation, and transportation of scientific specimens. Businessmen in Singapore helped museums acquire Bata clothing off Su-matra; government officials in Sydney provided Aboriginal weapons from Australia; steam-powered ships delivered Haida and Bella Coola masks from America's northwestern coast; and telegraph lines and efficient mail services kept the museums in continuous communication with their con-tacts and collectors abroad. Yet ethnologists' desires and the increasingly favorable conditions alone do not account for the breakneck pace of ac-quisitions and the incessant call for ever-bigger museums. Rather it was these scientists' recognition of the paradox that the very technological advances that facilitated the location of an array of previously "unknown" peoples—and thus the "empirical evidence" ethnologists needed to complete their project—were also contributing to the rapid destruction of these peoples and their material culture. This moment of realization, which one could call the modernist moment in ethnology, caused many ethnologists to believe that matters were urgent, that opportunity was fleeting, that knowledge—about the world and oneself—would be glimpsed, but not obtained, if they did not act fast.

Ethnologists throughout Europe and the United States acknowledged the ephemeral nature of the "natural" world; but this realization had a particular resonance in Germany. German ethnologists recognized themselves—socially, culturally, and professionally—as living in a time characterized by flux. World views had become noticeably "fragmented," and their own social and cultural orientations were under question. Even the concepts of *Bildung* and *Kultur* were open to challenge as scientists began using the material culture of non-Europeans as a means for locating the essential nature of the human being, and establishing museums that not only threatened the universities' monopoly on the production of scientific knowledge but also provided professional opportunities for a range of newcomers who were eager for intellectual and social change.[55] These ethnologists realized that "natural peoples" were evanescent, and they understood that their own social and cultural positions could shift or be quickly refashioned. Yet what made this moment of recognition among German ethnologists modernist was not simply their awareness of a rapidly changing world and the insecurity of their positions—something they shared in many ways with their British and American counterparts—but the ways in which German ethnologists viewed these changes as full of opportunity and something to be managed and negotiated rather than resisted.[56]

Spurred on by a conviction that they had to stay one step ahead of the homogenizing power of European "civilization," these ethnologists, in a desire to—as the young Franz Boas put it, "strike while the iron is hot!"—focused on locating and collecting as much material culture as possible while arguing in their private correspondence, academic journals, and more popular publications, that they had to act quickly.[57] A jargon of authenticity soon dominated their discussions, and a pointed desire to locate peoples whose material culture showed the fewest traces of mixing or change became their most pressing concern.

Already in 1872, in a letter from the Berlin Society for Anthropology, Ethnology, and Prehistory (BGAEU) to the Prussian Cultural Ministry, Bastian and his associates justified the need to collect widely and to create an ethnographic museum by arguing that an array of cultures were threatened with extinction and that entire groups of "natural" people were "perishing before [their] eyes under the rapid advancement of civilization." "Our time," they wrote, "which through steam power and electricity has unlocked the farthest reaches of the globe, simultaneously destroys there the original characteristics of the anthropological provinces, mixes racial physiognomy, thwarts the creative styles shaped by specific local influences, and suppresses through the superiority of civilization, the spiritual and mental creations in which the images of the peoples' souls [*Volksseele*] are characteristically reflected."[58] The spread of European "civilization," they stressed, was destroying the boundaries of difference almost everywhere and obscuring the "elementary ideas" Bastian and his colleagues hoped to find: "The Indians of North America," they exclaimed, were "vanish[ing] . . . like snow before the rising sun of civilization," many African societies were noticeably loosing their stability, and an array of Australian peoples had already been destroyed. Each loss was irreversible. Every failure to act contributed to the "disappearance of another unique group of people from the earth," and the destruction of another "witness to the primitive life of mankind."[59] Arguing that it was their "duty" to gain and preserve the "records of human development" that these different cultures seemed to possess, they called for the creation of a new type of museum, an institution that would allow them to "save" the clues to the inner workings of "human culture" and the "history of mankind."[60]

Ethnologists' urgent call for action was never limited to such project proposals, nor was it simply a funding ploy meant to secure support for their museums. The tone and rationale of the BGAEU's letter was echoed again and again in ethnologists' scholarly and popular publications. Bastian repeated these same assertions during the meetings of scientific associations and in a number of scientific journals ranging from the *Zeitschrift für Ethnologie* to *Globus*. His call for action also played an important part in the guidebook to the Berlin museum, in which he explained to a broader public the urgency of the museum's mission: "So many favorable opportunities," he wrote, had "already been irretrievably lost for all time through the disappearance of the original primitive tribes or their transformation under new influences." What visitors to his museum saw around them were the few things ethnologists had managed to "save," and it was imperative, he assured them, that they act immediately to "salvage" what was left.[61]

The recognition of fleeting time and ethnologists' calls to action were also not unique to Bastian and Berlin. They were internationally generated and avidly championed by a range of ethnologists in their published reports and in the correspondence surrounding Germany's other museums.[62] For example, when the Museum für Völkerkunde zu Leipzig was placed under the city's auspices in 1896, Karl Northoff, the chairman of Leipzig's ethnographic association, wrote to inform the city fathers that the most fundamental building blocks of the ethnological sciences were only momentarily available, and that they must obtain them immediately: "According to the unanimous judgment of all ethnologists and scientific travelers, the last moments during which ethnographic objects can still be saved stand before us now. The progressive and powerful colonization everywhere, which quickly levels out everything in its wake, will have suppressed the unique culture of the *Naturvölker* within the next one or two decades. It is thus necessary to quickly save what can still be saved from the ethnographic artifacts of the *Naturvölker*, in order to collect and secure the material out of which science can proudly erect the knowledge of the totality of mankind."[63] Their argument was based on the "unanimous judgment" of an international group of experts, who believed that time was short, and who agreed with their counterpart Karl Hagen in Hamburg that: "each day not taken advantage of by a Völkerkunde museum can be counted . . . as a day lost to it,"[64] and with Georg Thilenius, who wrote just shortly after becoming the director of Hamburg's ethnographic museum in 1904, that ethnologists must act "without delay," because they were "living in fact in the twelfth hour, as Bastian already stated years ago."[65] Action without further contemplation was simply the ethnological mantra of the day.

Although this discourse of urgency often contained a sense of apprehension and repeated warnings about the dangers of inaction, the disillusion sometimes voiced by these scientists should not be misread as a type of cultural pessimism or a rejection of modernity. In the same breath in which these men—from different generations and with different degrees of professional training—expressed anger and concern over the devastation of cultures and criticized the destructive nature of modern expansion, they also embraced its possibilities and reveled in their ability to obtain ever-larger collections. Moreover, their efforts were rational, calculated responses to information they received from countless observers abroad, such as Pater Joseph Meier in New Guinea, who answered a request for assistance from Karl Weule, director of the Leipzig museum after 1906, by saying that he would be pleased to help the museum with its collecting and studies, but that almost everything of scientific interest in his area had already vanished. Writing in 1904, he stated: "Things that you have before your eyes on a day-to-day basis in your museum, have long since disappeared from view here, in fact have never again been seen by me, although I have been in the Archipelago for the last five years."[66] Kept informed by their sources, ethnologists made sober evaluations of the international landscape, moved quickly from one fleeting opportunity to the next, and attempted to make their collections as complete as possible while they still had time.

Because many historians of Germany might regard the modernist quality of ethnologists' attitudes as most fitting among a younger generation of scientists around the turn of the century, and the general sense of urgency most typical of the Wilhelminian period, the rather long intellectual pedigree of these attitudes should be born in mind. Just as Bastian could argue in 1872 that "the Indians of North America vanish . . . like snow before the rising sun of civilization," and his successor as director of the Berlin museum, Felix von Luschan, could adamantly state in a letter to the General Administration of the Royal Museums in 1903 that "ethnographic collections and observations can either be made now, in the twelfth hour, or not at all,"[67] so too did Richard Thurnwald—later called the father of German functionalism[68]—remind his readers in 1912 that ethnographic items from throughout the world should be collected before they are "forever swept away before the storm of modern, homogenizing culture streaming out of Europe and North America."[69] Despite generational and theoretical shifts, the modernist moment and the stress German ethnologists placed on the twelfth hour or the final chance lasted for over forty years and fundamentally shaped both ethnographic museums and the science of ethnology in Germany.[70]

Several reasons account for the modernist moment's longevity. To begin with, the concept of "natural peoples" and the belief that the most "authentic" cultures were those not yet touched by Europeans never wavered, and thus ethnologists' goals remained essentially consistent as well. At the same time, the ethnographic project conceived by these scientists was immense. Not every area of the globe was simultaneously accessible, and it was simply impossible to collect everything at once. The process of collection was relatively modest at first, but as new technologies developed and new techniques of preservation, acquisition, and storage took shape, the ethnographic project grew rapidly, acquired momentum, and quickly became self-perpetuating as the changing character of the world continued to be confirmed and new and ever-greater possibilities appeared repeatedly on the horizon. This momentum was only curtailed by the advent of World War I, which simultaneously eliminated the museums' financial (and often human) resources and disrupted the international acquisition networks on which they relied.

Of course a concern with the rapid change inherent in modern conditions was largely universal among European and American cultural scientists, and non-German ethnologists engaged in this sort of "salvage anthropology" as well; but German ethnologists displayed a particular willingness to embrace these changes and explore their possibilities. In his analysis of the motives behind Anglo-American anthropology, for example, Curtis M. Hinsley has argued that "students of anthropology in England and the United States were engaged in a strenuous effort to *contain* the exploding diversity of the human world within the explanatory frame work of the Mosaic account [my emphasis]."[71] Thus their museums "embodied imposed order," and were meant to function as "an important defense against racing change, social turmoil, and a world of more human variety than was previously imagined or, one suspects, desired."[72] In his opinion, anthropologists working in the Smithsonian from 1880 to 1908 believed that "by displaying order in the tangible works of man through all ages and places, they would *confirm* cosmic purpose. The consequence of this stance was an anthropology that was constraining rather than expansive, classificatory rather than exploratory. The anthropologists of the early National Museum sought to contain the world within walls and categories; *they sought old verities, not new truths* [my emphasis]."[73]

Hinsley's observation reveals a fundamental difference between the motivations driving Anglo-American ethnologists and those driving the Germans. While ethnologists in late-nineteenth-century American museums were "containing," their German counterparts were creating—believing that "new truths" about the fundamental nature of humanity could indeed be learned, if they could only tap into this human diversity before it was eliminated. Their perhaps conservative-sounding challenge "to save what can still be saved" was never constraining, but both progressive and creative, driven by the conviction that "knowledge is power," and a strong belief that the individuals and groups who took on this challenge could and would attain a better understanding of humanity's pasts and presents through a comparative analysis of "mankind's" variations.[74]

Unlike evolutionists in Britain and the United States, Bastian and his counterparts in other German cities did not "take [their] own culture as the absolute standard of comparison," against which the characteristics of other peoples could be "meaningfully interpreted." Nor did they arrange their museums hierarchically, teleologically, or attempt to produce a particular narrative with their displays.[75] Rather, they drew on nascent ideas of cultural pluralism while setting their goals and fashioning their institutions. As Ivan Kalmar reminds us, Franz "Boas may have been the first to use the word 'culture' in the plural, *in English*. But not in German. In Germany, the term *Kultur* was used in the plural (*Kulturen*) as early as the 1880s and not just by cultural pluralists [his emphasis]."[76]

In short, German ethnographic museums took shape within an intellectual milieu that quickly rejected synoptic or genetic models of cultural development in favor of cultural comparisons and analyses. Consequently, Bastian and his German counterparts organized their museums according to geographical principles, with open displays that required each visitor to make his or her own connections, rather than fixed systems of cultural progression such as those found in the Smithsonian Institution or the Pitt-Rivers Museum in Oxford.[77] Indeed, the fundamental disparity between these models of organization (and the conceptions of what constituted good science that lay behind them) was starkly profiled in 1887 when Boas, shortly after arriving in the United States, drew on his own experiences in the Berlin museum to attack the Smithsonian's developmental arrangements as "missing the whole point of post-Darwinian natural science."[78] Americans, he stressed, had failed to realize that they should not simply be engaged in ordering materials in a preconceived system. They should be trying to understand cultural developments by locating them in their complete historical and social contexts.[79] Thus while both German and Anglo-American ethnologists produced ethnographic museums, they did so with different sets of motivations and radically different goals.

[margin note: W. G. as future-oriented]

Several sociological factors also contributed fundamentally to German ethnologists' greater willingness to embrace exploratory science, to search out new truths, and to view "the exploding diversity of the human world" as an opportunity rather than a threat. To begin with, Germany on the eve of World War I has been characterized as a "starkly future-oriented" and "modernist nation," filled with an array of political and social groups bent on the process of self-creation, and distinguished by a general willingness to accept ongoing changes.[80] The population of Germany grew from 49 million in 1875 to 69 million in 1913, and it shifted from living primarily in rural areas to urban settings. Two-thirds of the population, in fact, had moved into cities by 1914.[81] German cities also increased radically in size: Berlin grew from a provincial capital to a city of over two million people. The populations in Hamburg and Munich increased five fold, and Leipzig's population of 63,000 in 1850 grew to nearly eleven times that

[margin note: Ekstein]

size by 1910.[82] Most of these people were new urban dwellers. Many of them were part of the new white-collar class, and all of them were living in worlds that were quickly shifting around them in the wake of rapid technological advances. They were also bombarded by political pressure groups and interest parties that were actively engaged in trying to rework the entire political process, an effort that ultimately led to the staggering elections of 1912 in which one out of every three Germans voted for a socialist candidate. German ethnographic museums took shape within this political and social context, in which even the most conservative classes increasingly regarded "newness" and "change" as "inevitable."[83] These conditions facilitated, and perhaps even encouraged, a proactive, future-oriented ethnological science in Germany.

Many of the individuals involved in creating ethnographic museums were also motivated by another kind of self-fashioning. They were part of an intellectual counterculture, an alternative to the classically oriented *Bildung* of nineteenth-century educated elites. Prior to the 1870s, an exclusive group of academics, closely linked to classical education and the universities, dominated the cultural sciences in the German-speaking areas of central Europe.[84] Scholars' recognition in the 1860s that material culture supplied them with another kind of "text" gave a range of young, enthusiastic scientists the opportunity to develop an expertise that could challenge the philologically based knowledge of the universities.[85] And while this new science of ethnology gave them the intellectual means, ethnographic museums furnished them with a new culturally respectable space—an alternative institution that they quickly harnessed for the production of knowledge.[86] From this position, a new generation of intellectual outsiders began to challenge the academic canon, to create professionally respectable identities for themselves, and to destabilize the *Kultur* of educated elites.

The modern concept of culture appropriated by German ethnologists was itself a powerful alternative to the elitist idea of *Kultur*.[87] This concept of culture, as "patterns of thought and behavior characteristic of a whole people," became a central component of several new academic disciplines and the base for several increasingly separate bodies of social theory in Germany during the middle of the nineteenth century.[88] These intellectual currents led most German ethnologists to reject anthropological theories with a biological focus in favor of cultural comparisons and analyses. This move not only provided them with an alternative to the biologically oriented developmental concepts prevalent in Britain, but also introduced the possibility of redefining the elitist idea of *Kultur*, of destabilizing its exclusiveness, and perhaps even showing that cultivation does not have to come from classical studies, but could also be attained through new disciplines—all of which had a particular resonance with individuals and groups on the academic fringes.

In the 1860s and 1870s, new professional opportunities in German museums coincided with ethnological opportunities around the globe, both of which attracted a generation of Germans who—despite their provincial origins—shared a strikingly cosmopolitan view of the world. The life of Moritz Wagner, who became curator of Munich's ethnographic collection in 1862 and the first director of their ethnographic museum in 1868, captures the international orientation of these adventurous individuals from land-locked German states.

Born into a schoolteacher's family in Augsburg in 1813, Wagner traveled extensively, produced a veritable mountain of journalistic and scientific publications, but nevertheless consistently faced difficulties finding a place among German educated elites. Shortly after completing his training as a businessman in Bavaria, he was sent to work in Marseilles, where he soon developed an avid interest in North Africa. After returning to Bavaria in 1835, he began studying natural history in Nürnberg and Erlangen, and in 1836 he became part of a scientific commission attached to French troops near Algiers. From there he wrote extensively for an array of different German journals and newspapers, and following his return to Europe in 1838, produced a three-volume account of his travels and observations that was well-received among natural scientists.[89]

Wagner became an editor for the *Allgemeine Zeitung*, spent time studying in Göttingen, and made contacts with Alexander von Humboldt and Carl Ritter, who helped him gain the support of the Berlin Academy of Sciences for his travels in Africa, Persia, Russia, and southeastern Europe in the 1840s. Disenchanted by the 1848 revolutions, he followed thousands of refugees to the "new world" in 1852, where he studied the flora, fauna, and the Americans he encountered as he traveled across the upper half of New York, west into the German settlements in Wisconsin, down through the southern United States, and then further into Central America before returning to Europe two years later to produce more volumes on his travels and observations. In the mid-1850s he gained the support of Maximilian II, the king of Bavaria, to travel to South America in order to investigate the potential for Bavarian immigration abroad and to conduct his own research. This final venture, which he regarded as bringing him especially close to Alexander von Humboldt, lasted from 1857 to 1859 and took him through a war between Peru and Ecuador, violent encounters with local populations, and bouts of disease, after which he returned "tired, sick, half-blinded and financially at his end."[90]

Despite his extensive travels and numerous publications, however, Wagner returned to a tenuous professional existence. His health partially ruined and terribly in debt, he repeatedly attempted to secure a regular university position. But because he lacked the necessary credentials, this proved an impossible task.[91] Indeed, although he ultimately influenced Friedrich Ratzel's theories of *Anthropogeographie* and the field of natural history in Germany,[92] Wagner continued to be regarded as a mere journalist and a dilettante rather than a legitimate scientist by German educated elites, and he complained until his death in 1887 that the "armchair scholars" in the universities never took him seriously.[93] With his appointment as curator of Munich's ethnological collections, however, he gained a certain intellectual credibility and an otherwise unattainable institutional base from which he could participate in academic discussions about humanity and its variations. A permanent university position was impossible for him to obtain; but the arrival of ethnographic museums on central Europe's institutional landscape provided him with a solid position from which he could contribute to discussions about the relationship between geography and human development.[94]

Not all of the individuals involved in the genesis of German museums were able to travel as extensively as Wagner. But they generally shared his enthusiasm for Humboldt's cosmopolitan vision and his fascination with ever-widening natural and human expanses; and they too used their respective museums as a means to circumvent the universities and take part in exploring these new fields. Thus Hermann Obst, a physician from Leipzig who dreamed of going abroad but was denied the chance to take part in expeditions to the North Pole and East Asia in the 1860s, found his intellectual niche and gained social stature and institutional power by directing the Leipzig ethnographic museum, which quickly became the second largest of its kind in Germany. He was a founding member of the association dedicated to maintaining this museum, a group that consisted of businessmen, journalists, and others who were essentially an intellectual grade below Germany's educated elites, but who shared Obst's enthusiasm for ethnology. They recognized the cultural capital of this international science, and they used their museum to carve out a new cultural territory among educated elites that they could occupy without university degrees.

Most ethnographic museums took shape outside the universities, and they were often directed and supported by individuals with a particularly self-assured pride in their endeavors, but with only tenuous connections to academic elites or the nineteenth-century "temples" of high art and culture. Even when connected to universities, ethnographic museums were built around a different canon of knowledge that drew on a different set of authorities and methods and continued to offer opportunities for newcomers. Bastian, for example, despite his connection to the Berlin university, remained an enigma among academics. He not only spent twenty-five years of his life abroad; he also looked beyond the wisdom of classical thinkers to a different intellectual heritage. Naturalists and travelers such as Humboldt and Adelbert von Chamisso appear as often in his notations as more classical scholars such as Johann Joachim Winckelmann or even Johann Gottfried von Herder.[95]

Of course, German ethnographic museums became professionalized around the turn of the century, replacing their self-educated directors with scientists holding the highest university degrees. But ethnology remained dependent on different authorities and a method grounded in the accumulation and comparison of material culture that was obtained abroad. Thus it continued to offer opportunities for mavericks such as Leo Frobenius, who, despite his lack of university degrees, slowly carved out his own position among German scientists and created his legitimacy among academics through a series of exceptional expeditions through equatorial Africa. These expeditions ultimately endowed him with an unrivaled expertise that made university-trained academics turn to him.[96]

Ethnologists' new and unstable identities thus provided another critical layer to the modernist element pushing the German ethnographic museum movement. These ethnologists were tied to new source material, to institutions that stood outside of the university system, and to a new science that demanded quick and precise actions and which promised to help them refashion their world views. Consequently, German ethnologists had practical as well as theoretical and methodological reasons for embracing "new" information and recasting their understandings of the world. As they were working to "salvage" the last traces of "natural peoples" and fashion alternative institutions for the production of knowledge, they were simultaneously engaged in creating themselves—professionally, socially, and culturally.

Municipal Displays

While ethnologists' motivations provided the impetus that initiated the rapid founding and unprecedented growth of German ethnographic museums, such massive projects—simply because of the financial commitment involved—required much more than scientific dedication or professional enthusiasm to survive.[97] The kinds of supporters each museum could attract and the character of their respective cities played critical roles in the museums' institutional development and the forms they ultimately assumed. Thus, despite the more general cultural contexts discussed above, and the fact that German ethnologists shared certain desires and motivations, we must be careful about trying to locate a unitary "German" vision behind these institutions. It is important to bear in mind that dissension and competition among Germans was often the secret to their more general scientific success. German universities, for instance, overtook the leading position of French universities in the nineteenth century largely because they were *not* centralized and were often at odds with each other.[98] Much like the universities, German museums not only remained decentralized during the period of this study (and indeed until today), but the same types of museums did not appear everywhere at once, nor did they always appear in the most obvious places. Not all of Germany was simultaneously seized by a desire to discover "the Other," and not all cities were interested in sponsoring ethnographic museums. Local elites in Germany's largest cities supported these museums for many of the same reasons they supported the art museums, theaters, opera houses, and other public institutions being built at this time. These museums had a role to play in civic and regional self-promotion. They contributed to fashioning local reputations by functioning as municipal displays.

Historians generally characterize late-nineteenth-century Germany as a site of avid nation building, and during the last two decades, scholars in Europe and the United States have expended considerable energy exploring the links between German museums, monuments, and exhibitions and national image-making.[99] It has become almost commonplace to argue that these projects were initiated and supported out of a desire to contribute to "strengthening a national identity."[100] Unfortunately, it is often forgotten that many of the most successful "German" projects—museums or otherwise—were regionally or locally initiated and supported, while examples of nationally oriented projects that never came to fruition are generally side-stepped or lost in the historiographical shuffle. Yet these regional successes and national failures are critical for understanding what makes or breaks such institutions, and for explaining the large number and relative success of German ethnographic museums. Ultimately, they reveal that during the height of European imperialism and in the midst of fervent efforts at German nation-building, older, cosmopolitan ideals, municipal loyalties, and a strong intra-German competition for status drove the development of these museums much more than any nationalist or colonialist visions.

An obvious candidate for helping to "imagine the nation" was the "national ethnographic museum"—which was never built. This museum was based on an idea that was as old as the nation. Ethnologists repeatedly suggested its creation. There was strong agitation in its favor at the turn of the century, but the idea was never endorsed by the state.[101] The history of this project is worth telling. The suggestion to devote a section of Berlin's ethnographic museum to the material culture of German-speaking peoples was included in original proposals for the museum.[102] This section was never created, however, because of space limitations. By the time the new museum building opened in 1886, it was already too small to hold all the non-European acquisitions accumulated during the previous decade, and the European section had to be left out.[103]

Attempts by the Berlin museum's ethnologists and supporters to create a separate museum devoted to Germans' material culture continued throughout the last decades of the nineteenth century. But they failed to gain any national response. After years of discussion, Rudolf Virchow and others decided to create a privately funded *Volkskunde* museum to house these European collections, following the surprising success of a *Volkskunde* exhibit in Louis Castan's Panoptikum in 1888.[104] Virchow's *Volkskunde* museum was initially opened in the Hygienische Institut in Berlin and took up one large and six smaller rooms in that building—all of which were overflowing with objects by August 1889.[105] From the outset, Virchow and his associates attempted to gain more space and governmental funding for the museum. Yet despite numerous speeches in the museum's favor by Virchow and Prussian cultural minister Gustav von Gossler, and the sensation raised in Berlin by the opening of a similar, but nationally supported museum in Vienna, their efforts to strike a chord with the competitive, nationalist spirit of the age fell on deaf ears.[106]

Even their use of an explicitly nationalist rhetoric brought little notice from the Imperial government. And after Virchow's death in 1902, the state continued to show little interest in the project regardless of the fact that the association supporting it began to collapse.[107] It was only when Justus Brinckmann, the director of Hamburg's Kunst- und Gewerbemuseum, made a strong bid to purchase the *Volkskunde* museum and spirit it off to Hamburg, that the new director, James Simon, was able to gain the kaiser's attention, secure the museum some state support, and have it incorporated into the Prussian state collections in 1904.[108] But this move was not inspired by "national" interests. Where arguments about national imagery had created little stir with the Imperial government, the threat of regional competition provoked a Prussian reaction.

As early as 1893 there was also a movement underway to combine the *Volkskunde* and prehistory collections in Berlin to create a separate "German National Museum."[109] And over the next fifteen years, ethnologists and their supporters made repeated attempts to generate interest in this project by lobbying the General Administration of the Royal Museums and the national government, and even stressing the "propagandistic potential" of such a museum in the popular press.[110] Despite such calls for this national and nationalist institution, however, the proposals were consistently rejected, and Wilhelm von Bode, the director of the Royal Museums, even argued in a published report that such "national" collections would actually do more good and have greater appeal if they were left in the provinces.[111] While there may be some validity to the accusation that Bode, trained as an artist, did his best to undermine the creation of a national museum in order to reserve a greater proportion of the Prussian museum budget for his own projects, Bode alone cannot be held responsible for this proposal's fate.[112] This nationalist project, despite its "propagandistic potential," was never able to stir strong interest with the state, and its potential for contributing to the formation of a national "Self" was not sufficient to ensure its creation.

A second and perhaps even more noteworthy example is the virtual failure of the German Colonial Museum. This museum was founded by a private association following the success of the Colonial Exhibition at the Berliner Gewerbe-Ausstellung in 1896.[113] It drew largely on ideas for a *Reichshandelsmuseum*, which had been circulating in Germany since the 1870s, as well as earlier discussions within the government about the possibility of creating a museum for the collections of colonial items flowing into Germany during the last decade of the nineteenth century.[114] From the outset, the Colonial Museum was created for propagandistic purposes. Its mission was to stimulate broad interest in the colonies' potential among Germans of all classes, as well as to promote the economic interest of its supporters.[115] Colonial magazines and newspapers openly stressed that the museum should be less a scientific institution than a means for communicating to the general public.[116] To facilitate this, the museum's director harnessed the most modern techniques of spectacular display, bringing together a mosaic of panoramic settings with photographs and life-groupings, and an ongoing series of lectures and slide shows. The museum's supporters also championed it as a critical nationalist endeavor and tried desperately to gain national support. They solicited the kaiser's endorsement and presence at the museum's opening, and they encouraged the government to help the museum create special arrangements with the schools. Entry fees for students were drastically reduced, special tours were set up, and huge numbers of children and teachers visited the museum.[117]

Despite these auspicious beginnings, the museum never lived up to its original conception. Its reception among scientists was mixed. Its ability to gain significant state funding was limited. Its backers gradually lost interest, and it never managed to develop beyond its initial creation in the Lehrter Bahnhoff—an old train station in Berlin. Already in 1905 (during the colonial heyday!) the museum's director began trying to sell the collections because he was so short of funds,[118] and although these negotiations were suspended after he received a brief windfall from the original sponsors, conditions in the museum hardly improved. It continued to subsist over the next decade on meager, short-term grants from the association that founded it, and in 1914, it was up for sale again.[119]

The point of this short excursion into the history of two failures is not to try to debunk the idea that nationalism happens, that national identity was being formed in these years, or that ethnographic museums contributed to this process. Many nationalist projects were obviously also successful, and to a certain degree Berlin's ethnographic museum, despite the fact that it was a Prussian institution, was essentially *the* German ethnographic museum. At the same time, however, it was also a regional museum on a municipal stage, and its continued development hinged on its being able to function on these, as well as several other, levels of representation. Moreover, for this and other museums to be consistently successful, they had to contribute to these processes in ways that appealed, and neither scientific enthusiasm nor nationalist/imperialist potential alone could ensure a museum's success or survival. Consequently, the most important displays were often the museums themselves, as municipal displays of status: the support of ethnology as a science rather than simply a spectacle imparted international standing and the expression of worldliness, and many Germans regarded the creation of a significant ethnographic museum as a means to securing *Weltstadt* (world city) status—something neither the national museum project nor the Colonial Museum could really do.[120]

As local elites, municipal governments, and civic associations in Hamburg, Berlin, Leipzig, and Munich set out to refashion their cities and themselves, they did so with an eye toward international developments and focused increasingly on becoming *Weltstädte*. During their efforts, the citizens of these cities looked outside as well as inside their new nation for confirmation of what this might entail. It was not just about size. The conventional definition of a *Großstadt*, or large city, was one that contained at least 100,000 people.[121] But this term also connoted "comfort, sophistication, and cultural amenities,"[122] while the term *Weltstadt* suggested a certain cosmopolitan character that might set a city like Hamburg or Berlin on a plane with London, New York, and Paris. The high numbers of foreign students in German universities, art schools, and academies certainly helped increase the cosmopolitan character of the cities hosting them.[123] But so too did the possession of scientific institutions that could claim to be setting the pace in an international science, especially a science that showed a connection with the wider world.[124] Such institutions, and particularly those that could be opened to the public, functioned as exceptional municipal displays that allowed a city to exhibit its sophistication and raise its cultural value.[125] This was precisely the appeal of ethnology and ethnographic museums: ethnology was a new, international science that took in the world, a science in which the *Weltstädte* of the United States and Europe were also actively engaged. It was an unrestricted, international field ready to be captured. And as a science that was not yet established in the universities, and which many argued was best pursued in museums, it was open to an array of individuals with an eye on the future rather than a grip on the past.

By the end of the nineteenth century, ethnology had made its appearance in one form or another in most major European cities, and in many cases its presence or absence was regarded as indicating something about the character of the city that possessed it. For example, the arrival of *Völkerschauen* (exhibitions of exotic peoples) in Basel was greeted by the local papers as a sign that their city was no longer a *Kleinstadt* (provincial city) but a cosmopolitan center with an interest in peoples from all over the world,[126] while in the *Großstadt* (major city) of Hamburg, the presence of *Völkerschauen* was considered to be fitting for this harbor city. It was from here that the entrepreneur Carl Hagenbeck organized his famous "people shows," which toured throughout Germany in the late nineteenth and early twentieth centuries; such exotic displays seemed to have a natural place in the local milieu.[127] But for the *Großstadt* to be regarded as a *Weltstadt* at the end of the nineteenth century, Hamburgers needed much more than a bustling harbor, extensive trade networks, and a familiarity with the exotic. They needed to show an appreciation for the arts and sciences, to communicate that they understood the value of scientific and cultural endeavors, and to express their commitment to participating in

the international projects that created them. For the harbor city of Hamburg, however, governed by the narrow-minded businessmen portrayed by Richard Evans, this was no mean feat.[128] The movement toward creating significant scientific institutions really began only in the late 1880s. <
Even then, the process moved forward sporadically, and few of the leading members of the government seemed to understand the need for this particular type of conspicuous display. Nevertheless, as the century drew to a close, the value of scientific institutions for Hamburg became increasingly clear, as both citizens and visitors rejected the city's image as a crass, single-minded center of trade and called for changes.

The commotion raised by the Danish ethnologist Kristian Bahnson in Hamburg provides a particularly instructive example. When Bahnson published his well-known article on European ethnographic museums in 1887, which surveyed the growth of ethnology in Europe over the last half-century, he strongly criticized the state of Hamburg's museum. He lamented the limited space given to the arrangements, the disorganization of the collection, and the fact that "to a certain degree the ethnographic principle, which initially structured the ordering, was not consistently followed." Most importantly, he chastised Hamburg's city fathers while noting that the German city with perhaps the greatest opportunity for producing a major international ethnographic institution had not even attempted to reach its potential.[129]

The reaction in Hamburg was quick and strong. Newspapers reprinted Bahnson's evaluations and comments about the sorry state of Hamburg's museum. Some took his criticisms further by portraying the museum as one in a state of chronic disrepair. None of the papers reproached the museum's director; rather they all blamed the city. They complained about the stain on Hamburg's image, and one critic pointedly warned that if Hamburg's leading citizens continued to behave like "philistines," placing their business ahead of everything else, then they would "perhaps remain an important trade and manufacturing city," but they would "also sink to the level of a provincial city, a fate from which Hamburg should remain protected!"[130]

This public accusation that Hamburg's citizens, despite their economic success, remained short-sighted provincials, quickly gained the attention of the city government. Governmental reports in the next week termed the author of these criticisms a "competent judge," and the *Senat* agreed that something had to be done. As a result, they quickly reevaluated the museum's budget, moved for the museum's reorganization, and transferred it to a location that would accommodate a wholesale rearrangement.[131] This expeditious action by the city government reflected an entirely new attitude toward ethnology and their ethnographic museum, and it initiated a series of actions that would lead to the museum's explosive growth around the turn of the century. The public outburst, in other words, forced the city council to realize that the fate of this scientific institution was closely tied to their own reputations.

Over the next decades the city's honor and reputation continued to play a fundamental role in the *Völkerkunde* museum's development; at the same time, the museum continued to be regarded as a means for refashioning the city's image. With this in mind, Senator Werner von Melle began a campaign to revamp the museum and other scientific institutions in the last decades of the nineteenth century,[132] and major decisions governing large acquisitions or changes to the museum were consistently based on their importance for the city's image. This trend was articulated quite clearly, for instance, during a heated governmental debate over the acquisition of a Burmese collection in 1907, when one senator argued: "We citizens of Hamburg have recently demonstrated, by creating the so-called Hamburg scientific foundation, that we surely know to honor and promote art and science in our *Vaterstadt*. We have here once again a fitting opportunity to demonstrate to others, that Hamburg is not only a *Handelsstadt* and a city of material gains, but that we are also willing to nurture and cultivate art and science inside the walls of our *Vaterstadt* and therefore I beseech you again to pass this motion!"[133] According to the records, the *Senat*'s reaction was a resounding "Bravo!" Clearly, creating and supporting such a museum made a statement. It expressed, in clear, material language that needed no translation, that the city supporting it was willing and able to participate in an important international endeavor. This form of communication functioned because of the powerful symbolism of science and scientific institutions in the late nineteenth century, and because the creation of such institutions involved participation in a process of municipal self-fashioning during a period in which self-creation was not only encouraged but expected by both residents and visitors.

Moreover, while the desire to glean prestige from international science was a fundamental motivation for creating and continuing to support ethnographic museums, the tremendous growth of these institutions was also closely linked to an avid intra-German competition and a desire not only to emulate other world cities but to overshadow their German counterparts. In each of the cities discussed here, the rationale for supporting their own museum combined emulation and a general discussion of the internationally recognized virtues of science with staunch local pride and a strong competitive desire to exceed other cities' achievements.

The Berlin museum, for example, was linked to that city's image as the capital of both Prussia and the young German state. The Prussian government was motivated to exceed any efforts in the Austrian, British, and French capitals, while carefully ensuring that they stayed ahead of any efforts in other German cities as well—reacting immediately to any notable expansion or acquisition in either Hamburg or Leipzig with renewed efforts of their own. In 1879, for instance, when the ethnologist Feodor Jagor complained to the Prussian Cultural Ministry that the new museum building that they had been promised six years earlier had not yet been built, he not only stressed that the international movement was leaving them behind but also warned that even the citizens of many lesser cities, not to mention the capitals of other nations, had already recognized and acted on the need for such institutions: "Everywhere ethnographic museums are being founded, existing collections completed, and the currently accepted scientific standards fittingly established. In France they have founded an ethnological museum of the greatest scale, one equipped with everything current scientific standards require; in Vienna, the most famous architects of the land are erecting a splendid building . . . in a short time Leipzig, and probably also Hamburg will build their own museums for this purpose."[134] The actions of these cities alone, he argued, "should suffice to show that it is high time for us to take practical steps as well to join in this movement and to develop the Berlin collection in a manner fitting to the capital of the German Reich," and "if the collections of the Royal Museums are not imperial collections," he added, then "it is an *Ehrenpflicht* [point of pride] for the Prussian state."

Such arguments were effective, and the Berlin ethnologists soon gained their museum building. Yet even after Berlin founded an ethnographic museum and it became the leading institution of its kind, arguments such as Jagor's continued to be made about the importance of maintaining their position—of continuing to lead, rather than follow, the scientific stream—because these were the arguments that ultimately gained ethnologists and their museums the most support.[135] Even in Berlin, in other words, where the connections between museum and university were closest, the support the museum received had little to do with the utility of science, and everything to do with honor, image, and prestige.

In Leipzig as well, discussions of the museum often focused on questions of image and honor, and arguments about utility saw much less success. Their museum's exceptional status in the international community of science was regarded in Leipzig as an accurate measure of their importance as a leading university city, a site of international trade, and a place crafted by self-made men. Consequently the museum's ethnologists and supporters not only made concerted efforts to maintain this reputation by pursuing ever-bigger and more coveted acquisitions, but repeatedly attempted to usurp Berlin's leading position while playing on their own exceptional status.

In a newspaper article from 1874, for example, one author made comparisons similar to those stressed by Jagor in Berlin, but changed the nature of his evaluation to favor the particularities of this Saxon city: "There already exist today in Berlin, Vienna, London, Paris, St. Petersburg, Copenhagen, and other world cities rich anthropological and ethnological museums; but dependent as they are on the governments that founded them and the state support they receive, most of these only represent— if perhaps also in a splendid way—certain sides and particular tendencies of cultural developments, while the Leipzig Museum für Völkerkunde, through its, as it were, international organization, will be in the position to bring together an overview of the nature and products of all of humanity from all of time."[136] Leipzig rather than Berlin or one of these other world cities, he argued, should be leading this science because this cosmopolitan idea could best be realized in a city "lying in the heart of Germany, yes, of civilized Europe," with its "ever-growing connections, with its position in world-wide trade," its "rich and extensive transportation networks and it multifarious intellectual and material power," and most importantly, its university. Leipzig's worldly character, he stressed, made it the natural place for such an important international institution.

Moreover, just as ethnology could be made to conform to the self-proclaimed goals of Leipzig's educated elites or the aspirations of the businessmen in Hamburg's *Senat*, so too could it be appropriated to help ordain Munich, Germany's self-proclaimed cultural center. Here too the fate of the museum was closely tied to civic society, international trends, and the city's self image; yet in Munich these factors came together in a much different way. Munich's museum was one of Germany's oldest, but because it did not initially meet the interests or needs of a city engaged since the national unification in an aggressive struggle with Berlin over artistic reputations, it was essentially ignored during the last three decades of the nineteenth century.[137] This all changed abruptly, however, with the growing international interest in non-European and exotic art during the first decades of the twentieth century. As a result of this movement, Munich's powerful artistic community developed a sudden interest in ethnology and their ethnographic museum, which became an asset for the city almost overnight. Its fate quickly changed. The local government immediately hired Lucien Sherman, a university-trained expert on Asian and Oriental arts, as its new director and gave the entire museum a complete makeover; its budgets and acquisitions grew exponentially.[138] In one year, 1907, Sherman was able to procure more artifacts for the museum than his predecessor had obtained in the previous decade, and during his first ten years as director he acquired over ten times as much as the royal family had collected in the previous 400 years, allowing Munich to gain a special place among ethnographic museums because of its peculiar concentration on non-European art. Because the emphasis lay on the possession of exotic art rather than international science, the intersection of international discourses about ethnography with intra-German competition and local interests was different here than in other German cities, but the reason for the museum's explosive growth was the same: once it was firmly linked to the city's image it began to boom.[139]

Most striking in all of these examples is how limited a role the rhetoric of "nation" and "empire" played in the promotion of these museums. Indeed, the nation was not "self-producing" in this cultural realm. Instead, the rhetoric and actions surrounding the creation of these museums demonstrates that ethnologists' call to act quickly elicited such a powerful and long-lasting response in Germany because it served multiple purposes: intellectual goals, professional desires, and intra-German as well as international competition for status. The movement to create and continuously expand their museums was closely intertwined with three concerted efforts at self-fashioning—the construction of a new history of humanity by ethnologists, the creation of social identities by an intellectual counterculture on the rise, and efforts to enhance cities' images by refashioning internationally recognized scientific institutions into municipal displays. This movement found its most profound expression in Germany because of the modernist, or future-oriented, context in which Germans in a variety of cities were operating, because of the high number of these individuals who shared a strong cosmopolitan vision of the world, and because the polycentric nature of Germany at this time promoted an ardent and ongoing competition among cities, regions, and clusters of scientists that made their desires to excel beyond their competitors (and thus to expand their museums and collections) essentially insatiable.

TWO⊙

THE

INTERNATIONAL

MARKET IN

MATERIAL

CULTURE

We call those objects valuable
that resist our desire to possess
them.—Georg Simmel,
The Philosophy of Money

As Germans committed themselves to the ethnographic
project, they became champions of "salvage anthropology." Their central goal was to rescue as much
material culture as possible from the onslaught of European expansion, and their "guiding principle," as Adolf Bastian stated
quite plainly, was to "collect everything."[1] But not everything could be collected, not everything could be saved, and from the artifacts that were sal-
vaged, there were seldom enough to satisfy everyone. Moreover, almost
immediately after embarking on their mission, German ethnologists faced
fierce competition for artifacts and collections from other scientists, private
collectors, curiosity dealers, missionaries, and eventually from indigenous
governments as well. Ethnologists soon found themselves entrenched in
an international market of material culture in which a discourse of scarcity dominated their acquisitions and market forces redefined "scientific
value."

The market was based on international networks of communication and exchange. These networks emerged alongside existing trade systems and diplomatic connections. But ethnologists also reshaped and extended them as they drew on the cosmopolitan character of their science and museums to gain assistance abroad. Each German museum became inextricably linked to this international system of communication and exchange, each competed on the market for its share of the spoils, and each helped to continually heighten the competition. The market fed on modernist urgings to action, the promise of technological and theoretical advances, and the prestige of possession, which required that each acquisition be more important than the last. It gained its momentum from ethnologists' quest for comprehensive collections, and it transformed the ethnographic project at its most basic level: capitalist imperatives usurped the primacy of their Humboldtian visions.

Possession

The ethnology pursued in German ethnographic museums began with possession. As Adolf Bastian explained to Leipzig's lord mayor in the early 1880s, "*Völkerkunde* is an inductive science, and as such it requires the greatest possible pooling of materials from which to draw conclusions, because these conclusions gain more certainty and value as the number of observations on which they can be based increases."[2] But if more evidence was considered better, less evidence was understandably worse, even threatening to the ability of this science to fulfill its mandate; thus limited collections of material culture could lead to equally limited conclusions. The chief repercussion of this connection between possession and knowledge was that ethnologists quickly prioritized locating and acquiring ethnographic artifacts over all other efforts (such as classifying and ordering their collections). This policy became known as salvage anthropology, and it quickly led ethnologists to place the highest value on those objects that were the most difficult to obtain.

The discourse of salvage anthropology was perhaps the most powerful force shaping nineteenth-century ethnology and the development of both German and non-German ethnographic museums. It combined feelings of urgency, loss, and possibility with scientific competence to create a sense of purpose that demanded extraordinary sacrifices to possess cultural artifacts. Ethnologists repeatedly wrote in their scholarly journals, private correspondence, and official reports about the need to act immediately and to save what was still salvageable. But as early as the 1870s, this rhetoric also appeared in popular publications about the missions of the museums, and government officials as often as the scientists themselves harnessed this discourse to legitimate museums' goals. Not only did Leipzig's lord mayor embrace Bastian's cause, but officials in other cities repeated his argument as well. Princess Therese von Bayern, for instance, championed the cause in her travel writings on Brazil. And just as she used the rhetoric of salvage anthropology to argue that Munich's ethnographic museum should turn to a focus on *Naturvölker*,[3] suggestions that *Völkerkunde* museums in general might limit their acquisitions to representative pieces were shouted down again and again by their supporters.[4]

Yet salvage anthropology—as either persuasive argument or influential discourse—did not work its wonders alone. Rather, the tenets of salvage anthropology combined with the prestige of possession to transform acquisition from a means to an end. The ethnographic project, as envisaged by Bastian and his contemporaries, was not only massive but also expensive, and although the theoretical argument in favor of salvage anthropology could be convincing, ultimately someone had to pay for it. Ethnologists quickly learned that the most effective way to gain support for their project was to offer their patrons something for their efforts, and their most potent currency was often the ethnographic objects themselves. In exchange for monetary support, their city acquired objects with an internationally recognized value that was created through the authority of science and the fact that the most prestigious possessions are generally those that other people cannot have.[5] This relationship, however, had far-reaching consequences for ethnologists and their science: it led both ethnologists and their supporters to focus their most intense efforts on items from those areas where no collectors had been, where the artifacts, and the cultures that produced them, appeared to be disappearing at the most rapid pace, or where ethnographic objects were the most difficult to obtain. By the end of the 1870s a doctrine of scarcity emerged that fed a growing desire for irreplaceable artifacts among ethnologists and their supporters in a variety of cities and lands; it quickly led to a fierce competition on an international scale. This competition transformed almost immediately into a collecting frenzy that lasted well into the twentieth century, attracting a range of new competitors to the objects most coveted by the ethnologists in museums. Once this movement gained momentum, it became almost self-perpetuating and only increased ethnologists' need to privilege acquisitions over all other concerns.[6]

The Market

In order to pursue their ethnographic project and obtain the "greatest possible pooling of materials," the directors of ethnographic museums had to be able to effectively negotiate the market in material culture. They had to understand the value of artifacts when they came on the market, anticipate how that value would shift or change, convince their backers to support their purchases, and compete with their counterparts in both Germany and abroad. There are countless examples of ethnologists competing for exceptional collections during the late nineteenth and early twentieth centuries. But perhaps the most instructive example is the contentious sale of Johann Cesar Godeffroy's private museum in the early 1880s. The struggle over this museum illustrates how scientific standards, prestige politics, and market forces combined to fashion the value of ethnographic artifacts and collections. It also reveals that this value did shift and change, and indicates the degree to which ethnologists had to be cognizant of this process if they hoped to be effective players on the international market of material culture.

The Godeffroy museum contained artifacts collected in the 1860s and 1870s by the ships' captains and naturalists employed by the Godeffroy trading house in Hamburg, and it was generally recognized across Europe as the most complete collection of natural and man-made artifacts from Australia and the Pacific islands. The museum contained botanical, zoological, and mineralogical collections, but its ethnographic section was especially prized because it had been assembled prior to the most destructive "europeanization"—the term ethnologists used to refer to the worst cultural effects of colonization and the rapid expansion in international trade. The "primitive" weapons and religious objects crafted out of wood, shell, and bone from Micronesia, the curious masks from Fiji, the idols from Samoa and Tonga, as well as the assorted Australian artifacts—the stone knives with sheaths of animal skin sewn together with human hair, the necklaces made of reeds and water plants, and the rings fashioned out of braided sea plants or carved from the shells of nuts—were without equal in any other museum. Ethnologists in the 1880s regarded these items as containing the only clues to cultural practices, indeed to an entire religious world, that had just disappeared. The breadth of Godeffroy's collections, their relative completeness, and ethnologists' convictions that the indigenous cultures in these areas were largely "decimated" by Europeans in the 1880s, made the contents of his museum unique and irreplaceable.[7]

Moreover, because most of Godeffroy's collections had been assembled and organized by "trained naturalists," his museum had an excellent reputation in the scientific community. Godeffroy's collectors were a cosmopolitan mix of individuals from an array of different backgrounds, who, much like Moritz Wagner, had gained an interest in exploring the wider world and shared some degree of scientific training and a desire to spend long periods of time abroad. These included people such as the Swiss medical doctor and naturalist Eduard Graeffe; the Polish political exile Johann Stanislaus Kubary; the American Andrew Garret, who left Vermont at the age of sixteen for a life at sea; and the now highly acclaimed Amalie Dietrich, who initially supported and then quickly outdistanced her husband's élan for natural history and became famous for her work among Aborigines in Australia.[8] These individuals all turned to Godeffroy as a means for traveling abroad and pursuing their own scientific (and other) interests. In exchange for free passage on his vessels as well as scientific instruments, weapons, and other supplies, they committed themselves to sending him natural and man-made "objects" for his museum. These artifacts were meticulously cataloged by J. D. E. Schmeltz, the self-educated carpenter-turned-naturalist who later became director of the national ethnographic museum in Leiden,[9] and the combination of the objects' rarity and the care given to the collection led Adolf Bastian, among others, to describe it as "one of the most magnificent of its kind."[10]

Godeffroy put his collection up for sale when he began dissolving his trading house in 1879. From the moment this collection came on the market, a heated competition to obtain it ensued among Germany's major museums.[11] Letters raced back and forth between Godeffroy's associates and the directors and supporters of Germany's various museums, negotiating prices, exchanging information, and attempting to reach a consensus on the collection's value. Bastian and the directors of several other sections of the Royal Museums immediately traveled to Hamburg to evaluate the collections. Leipzig sent their representatives as well, and local scientific associations and committees in Hamburg attested to the high quality and singular importance of Godeffroy's museum.[12]

Once the collection's scientific importance was confirmed, the directors and supporters of the various museums began private negotiations and public agitation to gain a competitive edge. They quietly solicited information about their competitors' intentions, negotiated among themselves in an attempt to find compromises, turned to brokers for help while negotiating with Godeffroy, and tried to whip up support among members of their local governments. Debates about the need to possess this museum also broke out in local papers and nationally distributed magazines, and as the competition became public, efforts to acquire the collection became tied to local reputations, debates became fervent, and competitors passionately argued that "what other cities can do, we should do as well."[13] Consequently, when Godeffroy's ethnographic collection was eventually sold to Leipzig in 1885, the Hamburg press erupted in condemnations, local elites expressed shock and dismay, and the *Senat* quickly moved to acquire Godeffroy's natural history collection in order to save face.[14] At the same time, newspapers in Leipzig gleefully reprinted the lamentations of the Hamburg press,[15] and local officials celebrated their city's good fortune, while outside observers shook their heads at Leipzig's coup, with the head of the German commission at the 1885 World's Fair in Antwerp calling it a "laughable price."[16]

While these events appeared emotional and frenzied, many of the decisions were, nevertheless, quite deliberate and businesslike. Bastian, for example, was simultaneously negotiating a number of different deals while bargaining with Godeffroy, and the fact that he did not acquire the Godeffroy collection at this time can hardly be seen as a failure. At most it was a calculated loss based on cost-efficiency. Despite his relatively large budget, Bastian was still operating with limited funds, which he sought to use as effectively as possible, and between 1881 and 1885, as new opportunities opened up elsewhere, the expensive Godeffroy collection, priced at 300,000 Marks, lost some of its allure. Bastian had collections flowing in from a variety of different lands, including objects from the Pacific that were not represented in the Godeffroy collection.[17] Most prominent among his concurrent acquisitions was the now-famous Jacobsen collection from the northwest coast of Canada and the United States, which had already required the formation of a special committee to raise funds for the venture. Jacobsen's year-and-a-half-long trip to "save" cultural traces of the "still untouched" coastal peoples from Vancouver to Alaska was a sensational success and produced a collection of beautifully carved masks, stone and bone weapons and tools, clothing and decorations, totems, canoes, and even examples of dwellings, which remains unparalleled to this day. This collection was at least on a par with Godeffroy's, but considerably cheaper. Moreover, Bastian had been purchasing doubles from the Godeffroy museum since the 1870s and recognized that the acquisition of the entire Godeffroy collection would leave him with a large number of duplicates during a period when his museum had not yet been completed and his storage facilities were already bursting with objects. While these factors alone never inhibited Bastian from acquiring a collection, they nevertheless encouraged him to calculate out the exact loss-gain potential for this acquisition.[18] Moreover, for Bastian, who was also attempting to centralize the efforts of German ethnographic museums, his most critical concern remained keeping the collection in Germany, where he could at least have access to it whenever needed. This led him to rethink the value of possessing this particular collection, contemplate alternatives, and even suggest joint purchases.[19] Ultimately, Bastian appears to have let this acquisition go and turned his attentions to areas where he could get more for his money, indicating the degree to which the "value" of these artifacts hinged on the market rather than the intrinsic "worth" of the collection.[20]

Similar kinds of calculations were in the minds of Hamburg's city fathers as well, but despite their reputations as successful businessmen, they lacked Bastian's knowledge of this particular market and consequently they failed to retain the collection. The major factors that prevented the city of Hamburg from purchasing the collection were the inability of the Hamburg *Senat* to recognize the symbolic importance of such a collection and their preoccupation with making the best possible deal. Godeffroy had initially argued that his collection must be placed in its own museum, an expense the city's fathers were unwilling to consider, and they argued that the price of the collection itself was estimated as simply too high. Burgermeister Kirchenpauer and the *Senat* calculated as well, however, that the price would also be too high for everyone else, and they ultimately expected that "Dr. Godeffroy, a man swimming in money, would decide to donate the valuable collection to his *Vaterstadt* in one form or another."[21] While in many ways this was not an unreasonable speculation, it was nevertheless a critical miscalculation for Hamburg's *Senat*—in terms of both the potential monetary investment at hand and the powerful symbolism inherent in either losing or gaining this possession. Several different articles appearing in Leipzig's newspapers in 1882 foretold the future. One argued that "the sacrifice, that one makes at this moment will bear ten times the fruit." Another argued that the collection's "value will grow from year to year, but even now it will be a precious, irreplaceable treasure for visitors." A third author noted that the failure to acquire this collection would be a "blow . . . , that could never be made good again."[22] In each case these predictions came true—and all to Hamburg's disadvantage.

Immediately after this collection was sold to Leipzig, Hamburg's city fathers began to recognize their mistake. The topic quickly became public as local papers ran articles denouncing the city's failure to act. One author wrote that he and other Hamburgers "could not believe," that "the *Bürgerschaft* would have refused demands in this direction," and he vehemently complained that "many in the nation's interior will again violently criticize

Hamburg's artistic appreciation and, as it appears to us, with good reason."[23] Moreover, their miscalculation was not forgotten with time but returned to haunt them again and again. During the controversy surrounding the publication of Kristian Bahnson's article in 1887, critics held up the loss of the Godeffroy collection as the "shining example" of the city's inability to recognize the potential and importance of science.[24] This sore spot also became an effective tool of persuasion, which Georg Thilenius, director of the Hamburg museum after 1904, later turned to his advantage when arguing for a radical increase in acquisitions and the support of a major expedition. During his discussion of the ever-rising prices of ethnographic objects in a budget proposal in 1905, for example, Thilenius reminded the *Senat* that the value of the artifacts in the Godeffroy collection had indeed increased by ten, and in some cases, as much as twenty times.[25] And in proposals for his 1908 South Seas expedition, he repeatedly stressed that he was offering the *Senat* a chance to make up this old loss of face and "to win back the place held by the Museum Godeffroy in Hamburg a generation ago."[26] Thilenius's assertion clearly struck a chord with the city fathers. As Senator Werner von Melle noted in his reflection on why he favored this particular expedition, "the chance to make amends for an old wound," or what he later referred to as a "colossal failure," appeared to him, "in the interest of Hamburg's intellectual [*geistigen*] reputation, to be especially desirable."[27]

As Hamburg's city fathers eventually realized, creating a significant ethnographic museum meant being able to successfully negotiate the marketplace in which the material culture of other peoples was eagerly collected, traded, bought, and sold. It meant being able to bargain and contend with other museums, as well as an array of other competitors ranging from private collectors and dealers, to young scientists, missionaries, and adventurers, all of whom became more numerous as the collecting frenzy at the end of the nineteenth century picked up momentum and spread. The motives of these different players were varied, yet in each case they worked through a common currency of exchange, an understanding of the value of these artifacts, which they themselves helped to fashion on the international market of material culture. Negotiating these values was often difficult, but as Thilenius eventually made clear to the Hamburg *Senat*, if they were going to be players, then they were going to have to learn to play the game.

[handwritten margin notes: "① World's fair / V-selia as site of exchg < Key to FL @ CH / Unlawfl)"]

As an international market in material culture took shape in the wake of rising competition, museums emerged as the largest and most influential consumers. Their directors and supporters participated in fashioning the emerging markets of exchange, through either their ongoing negotiations with the owners of existing collections or their organization, support, and direct participation in expeditions and other collecting ventures. In order to optimize their resources, they developed strategies to negotiate this market and compete most effectively with private collectors, dealers, and other museums. World's fairs soon began functioning as centers of distribution—sites for procurement as much as places for display or intellectual exchange—and networks of shifting alliances between an array of players quickly took shape. These networks, strategies, and alliances became increasingly important for successful acquisitions as the market and number of competitors grew. Successfully navigating this market required directors to know their competitors and have a keen understanding of how to do business with both rivals and friends. Once the museums became well established, they gained a certain legitimacy through the size of their collections as well as their connections to science, which in turn compounded their advantages over smaller competitors. From this powerful position, the directors of successful museums often attempted to control the market and dictate the value of the ethnographic commodities being exchanged.

International and colonial exhibitions were natural meeting points for people interested in ethnology as either a rigorous intellectual endeavor or an occasional vocation. A number of scholars have focused on the importance of nineteenth-century exhibitions and posited a series of useful arguments about the ways in which ethnographic exhibits at these fairs could function to promote ideas of racial superiority and heighten local, national, and class identities.[28] But in addition to being sites of display, these fairs were also critical sites of material exchange. Museum directors and their assistants commonly visited such exhibitions, often traveling at considerable expense to exchange ideas, review the latest activities of their counterparts, and ferret out new acquisitions. Museums of all sizes took advantage of these meetings, and during the last decades of the nineteenth century several German ethnographic museums gained some of their most significant collections through exhibitions. The *Völkerkunde* museum in Leipzig, for example, acquired large collections at the 1874

World's Fair in Vienna, the 1883 International Colonial and Export Exhibition in Amsterdam, and the 1900 World's Fair in Paris.[29]

Acquiring collections through such exhibitions was particularly attractive. Not only were they already assembled, the collections were generally of high quality and usually quite cheap. Representatives appointed by different nations to organize their states' various exhibits were a major source of these transactions, because they often had no personal stake in the collections. But sometimes these artifacts also came from other museums, which had displayed collections of duplicates and preferred to avoid the costs of shipping them back to their institutions. During the 1874 exhibition in Vienna, for example, Hermann Obst was able to gain donations for his recently founded institution from both kinds of sources, including the Royal Museums in Berlin, the Association for Anthropology and Ethnology in Moscow, the ethnographic museum in Leiden, the Smithsonian Institution in Washington, D.C., in addition to collections from a number of national consuls.[30] The directors of the larger museums took advantage of these opportunities as well. Bastian and his representatives, for instance, were particularly well known for trawling the exhibitions throughout the world, convincing various parties to donate their collections to the Berlin museum or setting up arrangements to purchase collections they could not otherwise obtain. As the kaiser was informed with regard to Eduard Seler's visit to the St. Louis World's Fair, Seler not only attended it for his own education but also to "make valuable acquisitions for the Museum für Völkerkunde" as well as to "form influential connections."[31]

However, one had to be quick to pick up the best deals. Such a large number of representatives from different museums generally led to competition over the collections available for donation or offered up for sale. As the Deutsches Committee at the 1885 World's Fair in Antwerp explained to Obst in response to his request for information, despite their general willingness to assist him, they were "unable to send him good news," because a representative of the Museum für Völkerkunde in Berlin had been to the fair "a few days earlier and had acquired practically everything that was of any interest through either purchase or trade."[32] Although Obst had snatched up a Sumatran collection from under Bastian's nose during an exhibition in Amsterdam two years before, he had not moved fast enough on this occasion.[33]

Similarly, one had to be savvy to make these arrangements work. As the well-known collector Adrian Jacobsen reported from the 1893 Chicago World's Fair, even established ethnologists and old acquaintances could be found waiting in the wings, hoping to snap up collections from participants for only a fraction of their market value. Jacobsen, for example, arrived in Chicago in charge of collections belonging to Karl Hagenbeck and the trading firm Umlauff, as well as artifacts from his second trip to the northwest coast of America. From the beginning he had hoped to turn a profit by selling these collections at the fair, and he was initially pleased that they drew considerable attention from a number of ethnologists. Yet while many were interested in learning about his collections, none of the ethnologists wanted to purchase them until after the fair had ended. According to Jacobsen, Franz Boas and the director of the fair, Frederic E. Putnam, waited calmly until Jacobsen and the owners of similar collections began preparing to leave—and became desperate for funds—before making him and others extremely low offers for their collections. Although Jacobsen and Boas had known each other since Boas's earliest years at the Museum für Völkerkunde in Berlin, Boas had no qualms about offering to purchase Jacobsen's collection for only a quarter of its estimated value. Jacobsen was incensed and wanted to refuse the offer. Yet, much to his chagrin, his associates felt obliged to accept it, rather than pay the costs of returning the collections to Europe, where it would take an indeterminate amount of time to sell them. Boas and Putnam simply out-maneuvered Jacobsen and the others, and thus the "Yankees," as Jacobsen called them, gained a "brilliant collection for a pittance"[34] The collections acquired here by Boas and Putnam became the basis of the Chicago Field Museum.

Negotiating for collections at international exhibitions in either Europe or the United States could lead to "brilliant" acquisitions, but most ethnologists preferred to get their collections directly from their places of origin. Thus in addition to taking part in the "ethnographic trade-shows" at world's fairs, the directors of German museums spent considerable time creating worldwide networks of communication that helped them gather both artifacts and information. Berlin was understandably in the best position for networking, because even before the beginning of German colonialism in 1884, Berlin's ethnologists were able to draw on the nation's diplomatic corps and military vessels to help solicit aid from Germans in foreign lands. They were also able to use the German foreign office to coordinate their searches and collect information. In 1881, for example, Richard Schöne, director of the Royal Museums, wrote to the Prussian Cultural Ministry asking them to contact "the ambassadors, envoys, resident ministers, and general consuls," and update them on the museum's needs. He noted that a previous circular from 1870 had been very productive, and that these connections had been critical to the museum's initial success. He argued, however, that conditions had changed considerably in the last decade and asked that a new circular be sent out to German officials. He also asked that in addition to information about artifacts produced by indigenous populations, officials be instructed to send the museum information about existing collections, copies of catalogs, yearly reports, or other pertinent publications from ethnographic institutions or associations, and to immediately inform Berlin when any governmental or private expeditions were undertaken in their areas. Moreover, this circular was not only distributed to faraway places such as Peking, Lima, Santiago, and Yokohama, but also to the capital cities of western nations, such as Paris, Lisbon, Madrid, and Washington. The ethnologists in Berlin wanted to be informed of everyone's actions.[35]

The directors of Germany's other museums did their best to tap into official structures as well. Hermann Obst in Leipzig was particularly good at targeting German officials and soliciting their support for his museum. In 1879, he launched a campaign to try to harness Germany's official international connections. He distributed reports on his museum to 100 German consulates throughout the world, which included descriptions of the museum's purpose as well as instructions about how one could join in their international endeavor by becoming a member of this association. In addition, he sent personal letters to thirty-two of these consuls, asking them to become *Bevollmächtigte* (official representatives) of the museum. He also targeted ships' captains and officers scheduled to travel to the Americas, the Far East, Australia, and other potentially rich ports of call.[36] These efforts were quite successful and usually resulted in officials either accepting the position or recommending that one of their associates be given the task.[37]

In searching out potential contacts Obst never limited his efforts to either Germans or governmental employees. He cast his net wide and sought assistance from a variety of people, associations, and institutions in a number of different lands. The campaign began almost from the moment the Leipzig museum was founded. He asked similar institutions for donations of artifacts, especially for duplicates from others' collections, and initiated exchanges of yearly reports, catalogs, and other publications. The efforts of Obst and his associates were exhaustive. They contacted large institutions such as the major ethnographic museums in Berlin, London, and the United States, as well as smaller, locally oriented institutes such as the Verein für Naturkunde in Fulda and the Davenport Academy of Natural Sciences in Iowa. Moreover, they persistently continued these efforts during the nineteenth century, sometimes losing touch with a few associations, but generally increasing their number of contacts each year.[38] These tactics did not always pay off, and occasionally the bombardment of letters from the Leipzig museum could even become overwhelming or annoying, leading an assistant at the Smithsonian to write in the margins of one letter: "Dr. Obst wants more specimens. He is the King of Beggars."[39] Nevertheless, despite the occasional upset, networking was critical to Leipzig's successful acquisitions.

A common sentiment or feeling of brotherhood among nineteenth-century scientists also played a crucial role in facilitating Leipzig's tactics. The cosmopolitan nature of their efforts attracted an array of naturalists and explorers who exhibited an unbridled willingness to take part in this self-proclaimed international endeavor, and often went out of their way to be helpful. The well-known German explorer Georg Schweinfurth is a good example. He was born in Riga in 1836 to a German businessman and the daughter of a local handworker. He began studying natural sciences at the university in Heidelberg in 1857, went to the University of Berlin for two years in 1860, and deposited his doctoral thesis in Heidelberg in 1862. The study was based on collections of African plants from two different German expeditions. He eagerly consumed the travel literature produced by the array of African explorers during these years, closely followed the first German expedition into inner Africa, and already in 1863, set off on a three-year African venture of his own. In 1868, sponsored by the Humboldt-Stiftung der Akademie der Wissenschaften, he embarked on a second expedition into "the Heart of Africa," after which he produced the two-volume travel report that made him famous as the "discoverer" of pygmies, cannibals, and the Uelle River, a tributary of the Congo.[40]

While living in Cairo and helping to build up the Société Khedivale de Géographie, Schweinfurth was contacted by Obst in 1877 and asked to join their association and help them secure collections for their museum. Schweinfurth greeted the chance with enthusiasm and vigor. He wrote that immediately upon being appointed a *Bevollmächtigte* of the Leipzig museum, he had taken it on himself "to turn to the Germans of this land with a request for collections," and to create a circular that explained the importance of the project for science, including a list of the wide variety of human products that could be sent to Leipzig, and argued that every house in Cairo was sure to have "one thing or another . . . that would be a welcome contribution to the Leipzig museum."[41] It was precisely this sort of ebullient commitment from individuals who were easily caught up in their cosmopolitan project that allowed Obst to build his networks and rival Berlin.

A desire to contribute to a "greater scientific project" also led a significant number of Germans and non-Germans to go to great efforts to support a museum they had never visited and would probably never see. Hermann Herrings, for example, a well-known collector living in the Dutch colonial areas around Sumatra, agreed during the 1883 Colonial Exhibition in Amsterdam to give Leipzig a "unique" collection from the "unknown Batas" valued at 14,000 Marks, despite the fact that he had never visited the museum. Similarly, another potential supporter, Gerhard Rohlfs, exclaimed in his letter from Zanzibar after being contacted by Obst: "How unfortunate! I have never been in the halls of your museum," but he was nevertheless delighted that Leipzig had contacted him; and he wrote that he considered it a "tremendous honor . . . , to be counted among the *Bevollmächtigte* of the Museum für Völkerkunde."[42] Moreover, the great distance between Leipzig and many of the individuals who became members of the ethnographic association did not prevent new *Bevollmächtigte*, such as the collector Paul Eugen Wolff in Australia, from quickly referring to it as "our Society" and "our museum."[43] Writing from New Zealand in 1891, W. B. Andrews summed up many of the sentiments shared by these men in both his actions and words. Although he noted that the college where he was teaching had its own museum and that Maori items were increasingly difficult to obtain, he assured Obst, "I shall always be glad to do anything to help my brother scientists," and immediately began contacting friends and associates about collections from the area and sorting out duplicates from his museum.[44] The feeling of joint purpose was in some cases extraordinary.

Yet perhaps even more important for the success of Leipzig's networking than the scientific enthusiasm of the museum's contacts was the prestige—real or imagined—associated with supporting the museum. From the beginning, Obst and his associates set out to create a reputation for their museum and use this reputation as a means for gaining support.[45] The more supporters they attracted, and the more important they were, the easier it became to perpetuate this process. Leipzig's earliest letters to the Smithsonian, for example, not only offered its director membership in Leipzig's ethnographic association and explained the importance of Leipzig's institution as one which had "the best prospect for . . . becoming truly cosmopolitan," but also *showed* its importance by noting that it had already received "promises of assistance from East India, China, Japan, Australia, Africa, etc.," and that the administration of the Royal Museums in Berlin "has ordered the transfer of all the duplicates of the Royal Ethnological collections" to their museum in Leipzig—an effort they termed "a gift of the highest value in itself, and one that may induce followers."[46] Such letters consistently received positive reactions and often brought new collections to Leipzig, but the key to Obst's prestige industry was actually his ability to solicit the support of influential individuals. Obst's success in obtaining the king of Saxony's backing prompted many Saxons to support the museum, and his ability to convince several foreign monarchs to accept the status of "protector" allowed him to attract even more powerful patrons.[47] In return for their support, these men received one of a series of titles and their names were listed accordingly in the yearly reports under "Representatives," "Honorary Members," "Sponsors," and "Patrons."[48] As was immediately made clear to Herrings, Rohlfs, Wolff, and many others, any German or non-German could find himself listed alongside these famous men in exchange for collections or other assistance.

Through the museum's association with well-known scientific institutions and prominent individuals, Obst and his colleagues essentially created a reputation network that extended around the world. Some of his contacts contributed to this network simply by joining, while many others took an active hand in exchanging prestige for money or collections. Wolff, for example, understood Obst's methods quite well. He made a point of inviting prominent individuals in Australia to join the Leipzig ethnographic association, including W. J. Clarke, whom he termed a "leading millionaire" who could probably be convinced to give "a certain sum towards the construction of a respectable building for our Museum at Leipzig." Wolff also advised Obst about how they could make this happen: "the thing can easily be worked, provided an *Orden* [decoration] from the court of Saxony be placed in his way, more so as Lady Clarke is very ambitious, the latter procedure would certainly lead to something good." Wolff was also quite calculating about whom he approached, noting "that it is not advisable to name members in the colonies not holding a position or being scientific men, as otherwise distinguished men such as the governor, Sir W. Clarke and others would not appreciate the honor of membership."[49] Yet most of Obst's contacts did appreciate this honor, as a letter from the vice-consulate in Chile in 1893 illustrates: "Confirming the receipt of your honorable lines from the first of this month, I thank you kindly for the friendly delivery of a second copy of the document, which I have placed under glass in my private office."[50]

The effectiveness of Obst's methods did not escape Bastian and the directors of other German museums, nor were these methods limited to

Obst and Leipzig.[51] Bastian made establishing these connections a priority and often argued, as he did in an 1881 report on the state of the museum, that "the first task lies in the need to win through correspondence supporters in the different areas of the globe, who are prepared to use their general knowledge of their local areas to make acquisitions in accordance to instructions sent to them."[52] He and his assistants had quickly moved beyond any dependence on governmental networks and, like Obst, they were also predisposed to give out honors and medals in exchange for collections or assistance—especially when they thought that an individual could be of further assistance. Following the donation of a Peruvian collection valued at 6,000 Marks, for example, the governmental "master builder" Plock was nominated for a Königliche Kronenordnen 4. Klasse. The reasoning was made quite clear: "As technical director of the trains he has extensive and influential connections in South America and would easily be in the position to further enrich the collection. Based on the current evidence, the General Administration also has no doubt that he will exert himself in this sense. They would, however, wish, by granting him an award, to obligate him to the museum and tie him that much closer to its interests."[53] Similarly, after returning from one of his own collecting ventures in 1880, Bastian quickly had a long list of names forwarded to the *Königlichen Direktor* of the Münz-Kabinett, asking for official letters of thanks and decorations for people who had assisted him.[54] In fact, Berlin's networking was so widespread that it was not at all uncommon for Obst (or the director of another German museum) to receive replies from potentially good contacts stating that they would have been quite willing to assist him, but that they were already working with the Berlin museum.

By the time Thilenius took over the Hamburg museum in 1904, these methods had become a common and recognized practice, and building networks became a director's main priority. Consequently, Thilenius immediately insisted in an early report to the *Senat* that he and members of his staff be given leave to attend conferences, visit expositions, and travel to look through other museums. He stressed that "the first priority" was to build up and maintain "personal relationships" between himself and "the directors of other museums," and noted that they not only needed to maintain "inquiries and answers addressed to dealers but also the ongoing communication with other museums," as well as a wide "correspondence with authors of scientific articles and essays" both of which would enable them to gain new representatives and even "small collections." Thus he insisted, almost immediately after arriving at the museum, that he needed a typewriter, copy press, and secretarial help so that he could efficiently produce multiple copies of letters and keep up with this ongoing exchange of communications.[55] He also immediately posited a method of harnessing local merchants' worldwide connections for acquisitions,[56] and he even accepted the position as general secretary of the German Anthropological Society because he believed that he could obtain "useful connections for the museum, which otherwise would have required much more effort to achieve."[57]

As central organizational points in these networks, directors of German museums soon began acting as both distributors and consumers on the international market of material culture. In some cases museums functioned as distribution centers, helping to parcel out goods to other museums. In 1898, for example, after Felix von Luschan, head of the African section of the Berlin museum, had purchased large quantities of Benin artifacts in the wake of the 1897 British "punitive expedition," he began organizing and distributing Benin collections to other museums. He put together a "series" for George A. Dorsey in Chicago, who—although he had never met Luschan—was expected to purchase them sight unseen, as well as for several German museums, such as Graf von Linden's museum in Stuttgart.[58] In other cases, museums functioned more like large trading houses, buying collections that contained a high number of duplicates, and then either selling the duplicates for profit or trading them for other collections.[59] As Karl Weule made clear while lamenting the special arrangement between the New Guinea Company and the Museum für Völkerkunde in Berlin, Berlin's ethnologists "most likely purchase everything, in order to sell [the pieces they do not actually want] later," and in this way make the most of their resources.[60] If a museum could gain control over a unique collection or monopolize a part of the market, then they could use this as bargaining power in further transactions. Moreover, such monopolies limited what other museums could possess, they manufactured scarcity, and they gave the possessors some control over the artifacts' value and encouraged the directors of other museums to create monopolies of their own.

As major consumers and distributors, the directors of ethnographic museums held privileged positions from which to do business, and in some instances this allowed them to circumvent normal trading, arrange to keep collections off the market, or control the bids made for particular collections. In 1904, for example, while Luschan was engaged in trying to secure a collection from the ethnologist Leo Frobenius, he used his position to make secret arrangements with his main competition, the private dealer Heinrich Umlauff, so that bidding would be reduced to a minimum and he could secure the collection from Frobenius at the lowest possible price. In other instances museums' positions simply gave them a tremendous advantage over collectors or dealers. As Bastian once explained to Obst regarding a collection from the traveler H. Ribbe: "In general, the decisive factor in purchasing [a collection] remains, not the price that the owner demands, but rather that, which the museum can pay. . . ." Because unless there is avid competition for a particular collection, Bastian argued, an owner's demands could be easily refused, and given the limited buyers to whom the owner could turn, the owner would quickly realize, "if not immediately then in any case soon afterwards . . . during calm contemplation," that he "will have to accept a rational offer."[61] In this case Bastian was right. Ribbe replied to Obst that the offer he had been made was much too low, criticized how German museums did business, and exclaimed that it was "no wonder" that so many German collectors were "forced" to sell their collections to foreign museums, since "a German operation is *never* supported [his emphasis]." Despite these protests, however, Ribbe was compelled to do business with the museum and continued to sell them collections for years. The power of being one of the only customers able to purchase a large collection was thus immense, and in some cases allowed museum directors simply to dictate value and name their price.[62]

The directors of museums often applied their entrepreneurial methods to friends as well—and sometimes in a rather brutal manner. In 1899, for example, Oscar Mengelbier, a *Bevollmächtigte* of the Leipzig museum since January 1898, began dealings with Obst over a collection of silver artifacts he had acquired while in Chile.[63] As was often the custom, the collection had been sent to Leipzig for inspection, and Obst began looking for a patron who would be willing to purchase it for the museum. Mengelbier, however, had made the mistake of confiding in Obst that he was forced to sell his collection because he had been in Spain "as the big stock market crash hit Berlin," had lost vast sums of money, and was now desperate for cash. Consequently, Obst stopped actively looking for a patron shortly after the collection was in his possession and began waiting for Mengelbier's desperation to increase. However in this case Obst overplayed his hand. Mengelbier had initially offered to sell the collection for 20,000 Marks. Soon afterwards, however, he explained that although the collection had cost him between 8,000 and 12,000 Marks, and the freight from Chile another 1,000 Marks, he was in such a dire need of funds that he would accept 15,000 Marks if they were unable to pay the full twenty. A short time later he reduced his price further to 10,000 Marks.[64] Despite the fact that he had already commissioned a set of cabinets for the collection for the price of 1,300 Marks, Obst told Mengelbier that he was only able to offer him 5,000 Marks for the whole collection or pay him the value of the silver. Mengelbier was incensed. He asked for his collection to be returned, was further enraged when he was charged for postage, and berated the museum for their actions. He noted that "the price was well-known to you from the beginning," reminded them that they had taken it into their museum ostensibly to help him find a buyer who would then donate the collection to the museum, and wrote that their offer of 5,000 Marks was "a direct insult to which I will give you no answer." After declaring that "before I will sell the collection for *a single Pfennig* under 10,000 Marks, I'll burn it [his emphasis]," he exclaimed: "As to your offer to pay the *Schmeltzwerth* [price for the melted-down silver] for the silver items, I decline to answer, because it seems every bit as ridiculous to me as your last offer of 5,000 Marks. Any Jew would pay me the *Schmeltzwerth* for the silver. When you say that you would not have profited through this collection, that may well be. Until now I have always regarded museums as scientific institutions and not as businesses that are out for profit."[65] Unfortunately for Mengelbier, regarding museums as scientific institutions rather than businesses was his mistake. As Obst and the directors of other successful ethnographic museums had long since realized, on the international market of material culture, museums were not simply scientific institutions. They were major consumers and distributors of scientific goods, directed by ambitious entrepreneurs attempting an immense task with limited funds, pressed to keep one step ahead of the competition, committed to making and breaking connections as they served them, dominating exchanges, and excelling in their trade. Nevertheless, despite the powerful bargaining positions museums often obtained, their directors were never able to gain complete control of the market. The value of ethnographic objects was too mutable for that.

Value

None of the objects collected by ethnologists or purchased for their museums had absolute value. The value of each artifact was, like most commodities, protean in nature, shifting from one context to the next. Moreover, an artifact's value was never singular; it was made up of scientific, aesthetic, economic, and other factors that combined to render its ultimate value within each particular context. As the earlier discussions of the Godeffroy collection and other acquisitions have made clear, the market value of ethnographic artifacts often influenced scientist's attitudes toward particular objects and collections and clearly had a significant impact on what and how they collected.[66] At the same time, however, just as the monetary value of an object can influence its importance for scientists, so too can the aesthetic quality of an object influence its economic or scientific worth, or the scientific importance of a collection its economic value. Consequently, ethnologists' scientific desires could never be insulated from the marketplace or the interests of other, nonscientific collectors.

In the nineteenth-century world of ethnographic collecting, scientific interests, aesthetics, and the marketplace were tightly intertwined. As the historian Douglas Cole has noted with regard to the Jacobsen collection from the northwest coast of America, "nearly everything of ethnological interest on the coast, from large sculptures to small charms, from finely crafted masks to fishhooks and arrows, was ornamented in some way. This feature made Northwest Coast material showy and desirable"; thus the aesthetic quality of the artifacts enhanced and perhaps even ensured their high scientific and material value.[67] At the same time, the economic value of an ethnographic collection was often dependent on the decisions and attitudes of scientific authorities, which greatly affected how traders such as Heinrich Umlauff treated his collections and delimited the prices he could demand. It was precisely for this reason, for example, that although Umlauff's firm was primarily a trading house rather than a scientific institution, collections were "preferably not broken apart, rather only taken in [or sold] as a unit, because well documented pieces naturally increased their [the entire collection's] value"[68]—"value," in this case, being scientifically defined and economically realizable.

The exact relationship between economics, aesthetics, and science for the creation of an object's value, however, is difficult to identify or generalize, because value as such is fundamentally situational. Even within the context of particular transactions, estimations of artifacts' worth will often conflict. Therefore, the multiple determinants contributing to any particular estimation of value must be carefully weighed, and scholars cannot afford to forget additional factors such as the prestige a collection may have because of its association with a particular person,[69] or the personal attachment an individual or group may have to a given object. The point to bear in mind, however, is essentially that the aesthetic, economic, and scientific value of artifacts are neither mutually exclusive nor interdependent. They are potentially interdependent; they have the ability to influence each other, and that is what allows us to locate the market's impact on ethnologists' attitudes toward specific collections and to show

how it influenced the kinds of collections that entered German museums.

The shifting value of ethnographic artifacts allow us to trace these "things-in-motion," to use their "social lives"[70] to analyze the transactions and attitudes around the distribution of artifacts. In this way we can unveil the central impulses and motives guiding and determining the collection process at the turn of the century, as well as the essential human contexts in which they took place. The reactions of ethnologists and others to the arrival of the Benin bronzes and ivory carvings on the international market of material culture in the late 1890s provides perhaps the best illustration of the protean and contextual nature of the value of ethnographic artifacts and the ways in which their scientific, aesthetic, and economic values were so closely intertwined. But these transactions and the fluctuating worth of the independent pieces also throw light on ethnologists' own needs and desires and illustrate the extent to which the possession of any given artifact or collection could only provide them with a fleeting sense of satisfaction.

The arrival of the Benin artifacts on the international market of material culture began with a whisper, grew quickly into a roar, and then after a time, died down to a murmur. Benin artifacts made their appearance in Europe following Britain's brutal "punitive expedition" to Benin city in February 1897. More than 2,400 artworks were removed from the city— many pieces literally ripped with bayonets from the palace walls—by members of the British forces,[71] and a vast number of these artifacts eventually found their way into German museums through British ivory merchants and dealers in antiquities.[72] The Benin artifacts were truly one of a kind. The British returned with large, intricately carved ivory tusks that portrayed animals, warriors, the royal court, and many other scenes in careful detail, which were of a much higher quality than anything ethnologists had seen from this part of Africa before. They also seized an array of bronze castings: plaques in which individuals such as musicians, priests, royalty, warriors, and even European soldiers stood out in stark relief, alters decorated with an array of figures; bells that were carefully detailed, and large snakes' heads, roosters, and leopards were perhaps the most notable (Figs. 2, 3, 4). Moreover, the bronze castings, many of which had been created during the sixteenth century, were later designated as far superior in craftsmanship to anything made in Europe at that time. This realization effectively threw a wrench into evolutionary theories, and caused varying degrees of consternation or enthusiasm among European and American ethnologists.[73] For the British government, however, the Benin "treasures" were war booty rather than invaluable artifacts, and upon their

FIGURE 2. Benin bronze casting. More than 2,400 artworks were seized from Benin by British troops in 1897. The main staircase to the British Museum is still adorned with a collection of such castings; the majority, however, made their way to Germany. The themes on the bronze plaques varied widely, including scenes with musicians, priests, royalty, warriors, animals, and Europeans. This particular casting portrays a warrior, his three companions, and in the top corners, two Europeans drinking. Many of these plaques were damaged when British soldiers used their bayonets to tear them from the palace walls. (From Felix von Luschan, *Die Altertümer von Benin*)

FIGURE 3. Benin bronze casting. Bronze memorial heads of royalty, such as this one, also became common fixtures in European and American museums. The bronzes were praised by Europeans for the high quality of the workmanship, which many argued (some with surprise) surpassed anything produced in Europe at the time. (From Felix von Luschan, *Die Altertümer von Benin*)

FIGURE 4. Benin bronze casting. In addition to the plaques and memorial heads, the museums assembled "sets" of bronze figures, altars, bells, and animals, especially snake heads, roosters, and leopards. This particular piece portrays a king holding a scepter and a stone axe, with two kneeling companions, two leopards, and two decapitated men at the base. (From Felix von Luschan, *Die Altertümer von Benin*)

arrival in Britain they were treated as such—with the consequence that they moved quickly from the soldiers' hands to the merchants and dealers' warehouses and then onto the open market.[74]

These artifacts' initial value would be difficult to determine precisely, but it is perhaps best illustrated by the fact that the British government sold off a number of the bronzes with no second thoughts in order to help finance the new African protectorate, and many of the carved ivory tusks which later caused such a commotion among ethnologists were initially slated to be sold for little more than the price of the ivory (Fig. 5).[75] The British attitude toward these artifacts left German ethnologists somewhat baffled, since they regarded the Benin objects as incredibly important on several different levels. Hans Meyer, head of a large publishing house in Leipzig and well-know patron of German ethnology, for example, wrote to Felix von Luschan with regard to some Benin items he had just managed to acquire: "It is actually a riddle to me, that the English let such things go. Either they have too many of them already or they have no idea what these things mean for ethnology, cultural history, and art history." Nevertheless he was exceedingly pleased. As Meyer also noted: "whatever the case may be, the main thing remains, that *we* have these magnificent specimens."[76] Luschan and Meyer—immersed in the ethnographic project and avidly collecting for years—immediately recognized the potential of these objects even if the British did not.

As ethnologists on the continent became aware of what the British had acquired, the Benin artifacts quickly became a sensation. For many it was simply unbelievable that such a huge quantity of extremely high-quality African artworks could suddenly appear. It was as if the gates of Eldorado had been opened. This enthusiasm is captured, for example, in a letter written by Luschan in July 1897 to Assistant Director Albert Grünwedel at the Museum für Völkerkunde in Berlin. Luschan wrote excitedly that he had just received a curious visit from a representative of a local ivory firm who informed him "that in the second week of August in London supposedly 600 (six hundred!!!) *Zentner* [600,000 kilograms] of ivory will be brought to auction, which the English seized in *Benin*, all of which consists of huge tusks covered with ancient engravings and carvings of men, riders, animals, etc. etc." Full of enthusiasm but also somewhat taken aback, he explained that he had shown the representative a photograph of one of the large ivory tusks currently in the museum's possession, "which is not to be sneered at," and was immediately told that the majority of the tusks were "bigger than our biggest tusk (Umlauff 3,000 Marks) but carved in the same manner as our most expensive goblet." In amazement he

FIGURE 5. Ivory tusks from Benin. German ethnologists were astounded by the intricately carved ivory tusks that came on the market following the British punitive expedition of 1897. Equally surprising to them was that initially these tusks were slated to be sold for the weight of the ivory. Once at auction, however, prices shot up rapidly; a tournament of bidding ensued. (From Felix von Luschan, *Die Altertümer von Benin*)

noted that the items must be "of almost immeasurable worth," but that even "the largest of the tusks would only cost 600–1000 Marks." Somewhat disoriented by the shocking revelation but equally determined to gain possession of part of this "treasure," he stated resolutely: "What should happen now? In my opinion we must acquire as many of these tusks as possible *at all costs*—if they really are as outstanding, as they appear to be [his emphasis]," and he recommended they solicit the wealthy geographer Hans Meyer's support in this effort.[77] Grünwedel immediately approved Luschan's proposal. Meyer responded to his inquiries by deeming his report "certainly a colossal story, even if only half of it is true," and Luschan's expectations were quickly confirmed.[78] After seeing a photograph of some of the tusks being placed on sale, Luschan immediately wrote back to Meyer that they "exceeded" his "highest expectations."[79]

Once ethnologists on the continent realized what was taking place, they threw immense energy into staking their claims. A virtual flood of letters whipped back and forth across their networks soliciting information from the traders and auction houses offering Benin artifacts for sale, and securing promises of monetary support from their governmental and private patrons. Luschan, among others, quickly left for the first auction in London.[80] Dealings began small, and Luschan initially tried tracking down several individual pieces upon hearing of their existence. He quickly wrote to Justus Brinckmann, director of the Kunst- und Gewerbemuseum in Hamburg, for instance, to argue that the pieces Brinckmann had recently acquired "unquestionably belong in an *ethnographic* museum [his emphasis]." He noted that the Hamburg *Völkerkunde* museum would almost certainly be unable to afford them, and then voiced his enthusiasm and desire to have them moved to Berlin, stating: "I have not seen the objects myself, but I am completely convinced that hardly any sacrifice would be too great to acquire these two pieces." Sight unseen, Luschan was willing to make great efforts and go to huge expense to possess these items.[81]

Neither the size of acquisitions nor their costs remained small for long, and Luschan's willingness to make any sacrifice recognizably changed as prices became daunting. Through the last months of 1897 and the first months of 1898, auctions of Benin artifacts became common in London. These "tournaments of value" sent prices soaring as the directors of ethnographic museums on the continent clamored for acquisitions, their supporters committed vast sums, and the owners of Benin artifacts sensed their desire. Equally important were the dealers. W. D. Webster, a "Collector of Ethnological Specimens, European and Eastern Arms and Armour" in England, became particularly influential, channeling a vast number of Benin artifacts to continental museums. Berlin and the other museums began dealing with him in early 1898, and soon afterwards were appalled at the prices he could command. Yet the finite number of items available on the market, their singular quality, the destruction of the city where they were produced, and the desire of ethnologists to acquire them while they still could, all sent prices out of control. As Berlin issued a complaint about the rising prices in April 1898, Webster responded by explaining that he was "perfectly aware that Benin specimens are expensive but everyone wants them so prices have gone up considerably," and then added he would immediately "give nearly double the money for specimens I sold soon after they were brought over," because "it is quite impossible to get any more as Benin was cleared out and everything brought to this country."[82]

Although the authority ethnologists gained from their institutional and academic positions allowed them to define Benin artifacts as scientifically "valuable," they had no control over the "value" these objects took on in the eyes of many academic and non-academic competitors once they were released on the open market. The economic "value" simply followed the laws of supply and demand. After only a few months, for example, Webster began refusing the offers made by the directors of continental museums, stating firmly, "I . . . am sorry you think the prices too high for you to buy—but I am convinced that they will go still higher and that you are making a great mistake in missing anything you have not got." He then quickly added that prices were rising so quickly that "there are a good many Benin specimens which I sold at first which I should be pleased to give a good profit on to secure them again." While Luschan later termed the prices Webster demanded "completely absurd," Webster quickly explained to Luschan that he had *"conveniently got[ten] a few things when they first came over,"* when the officers did not know their value [his emphasis]," and that conditions had changed so rapidly that it was now Luschan who was ignorant of the value of the objects he possessed.[83] The truth of Webster's assessment became vividly clear to Luschan upon visiting yet another auction in London in 1899, after which he exclaimed with surprise to one of his supporters, Arthur Baessler, that "at such prices our current Benin collection would bring well over a Million!" Baessler could only respond by terming the prices currently demanded at the last auction "enormous."[84]

Despite the acquisition frenzy, however, the run on Benin items eventually subsided. As the museums acquired their sets of artifacts, their directors became quite particular about what they still needed, and what they were willing to acquire. Some items—the rarest—continued to be desirable, but the more numerous lost their allure, and many pieces that would have been snapped up a year or two earlier were designated "inferior" to what the museums already possessed and became difficult to sell.[85] In 1911, when the German ethnologist Leo Frobenius claimed during his latest expedition to have discovered bronze castings that he suspected were from Benin, the *Daily Graphic*, sarcastically noted that "Benin Bronzes are nothing new."[86] Once a sensation, their novelty had worn off; they no longer generated the same excitement.

The Benin artifacts were not only unique in their composition; their arrival as a finite number of artifacts on the international market was unprecedented in many ways. This exceptional situation made ethnologists aware of these objects' status almost from the beginning and allowed them to quickly gain a good understanding of the variety this group of artifacts had to offer; they could then collect accordingly. By 1911 Benin bronzes were not so much "nothing new;" rather ethnologists and others believed that nothing could be new about them. Scientists had surveyed the landscape, created representative sets, and the rest were leftovers, "inferior," and essentially disposable. As was the case with all collections, once they were possessed, the international market and the desire to "collect everything" encouraged ethnologists to turn quickly to new projects and interests. With Benin, however, the anticlimax that could accompany this tendency was particularly acute because the artifacts' unitary identity was so quickly known and everything essentially hit the market at one time. Thus, after an intense feeding frenzy, things quickly died down. Successful ethnologists emerged with tidy sets and turned elsewhere. Benin had been consumed.

The Doctrine of Scarcity

As the international market expanded and grew, relationships and goals altered as well. The networks established by the directors and supporters of German museums constantly shifted and changed. Competition for artifacts and haggling with independent collectors continued, yet by the mid-1880s, cornering the market no longer meant simply taking possession of the Godeffroy collection or one of its well-known counterparts. Special events such as the arrival of the Benin artifacts continued to occur, but in general the field of competition extended well beyond the European setting as ethnologists increasingly shifted their attention toward sending their own collectors into the field to extract detailed information about the origins and cultural functions of artifacts as well as the objects themselves. There were two major reasons for this change. The first is that the professionalization of ethnology as a science led to a more rigorous definition of the relationship between material artifacts and the cultures that produced them, and therefore the context of artifacts' origins became an increasingly important part of their value. The other reason was simple economics. Directors of museums quickly realized that by sending their own collectors out to assemble artifacts, they could acquire better collections at cheaper prices, extend their resources, and ultimately obtain much, much more. Despite these changes, however, certain characteristics remained salient. Decisions on what and where to collect continued to be tremendously influenced by market forces, and the doctrine of scarcity continued to govern the shifting hierarchy of value. The prestige of possession, of course, never faltered, even as the objects of desire changed over time.

Scarcity has many shades. The never before seen, the extremely weird, the incredibly old, the difficult to have, the seldom acquired, all fall under the rubric of scarcity. They all arouse a certain curiosity or interest which perhaps explains Jean Baudrillard's assertion that "an object only acquires its exceptional value *by dint of being absent* [his emphasis]."[87] Many scholars interested in the history of anthropology or the history of museums have argued that a significant change occurred in the nineteenth century, stemming from a desire to move away from the strange and the curious to well-ordered systems of definition—a transformation during which, ideally, a fascination with the extreme gave way to an interest in the typical. David Jenkins has pointed out, for example, that among earlier collectors, "the rare, abnormal, bizarre, and the old were especially valued," while in contrast, nineteenth-century ethnologists were primarily interested in sorting "the world systematically into drawers, glass-fronted cases, bottles and filing cabinets" in an effort to move beyond "fragmentary collections." He argues that ethnology during this period "represented a shift from delighting in the world's strange offerings and the appeal of subjective involvement, to an attempt to master and control the world's diversity through new forms of conceptualization."[88] While in some ways this assertion is quite true, we should nevertheless bear in mind that the "shift" toward order did not take place quickly, uniformly, or unproblematically, and that the "delight" in the world's strange offerings never disappeared —nor did they lose their privileged place in the hierarchy of desire.

Many of the characteristics generally attributed to "earlier collections," for example, remained prominent in the scientific collections of the late nineteenth century. Based on his familiarity with early modern collections, Krzysztof Pomian has argued that "if one wanted to be more faithful to the text, one would in fact talk about the hierarchy of rare things, given the predominance of the words 'rare' and 'rarity'" in the descriptions of many early modern collections. But, as he also notes, the prominence of rarity "is not simply a question of words," because the owners and viewers of early modern collections not only commonly described objects as "curious, rare, very ingenious, greatest . . . ever seen," but also identified "the weirdest, strangest, most spectacular offerings" in many of the actual collections as well.[89] While Pomian's characterizations would certainly agree with most historians' appraisals of early modern collections, they are also applicable to many nineteenth-century collections. Despite the hegemonic position of positivistic science, scarcity—in the form of the rare, the odd, the old, or the strange—maintained a prominent role in the selection of artifacts and the designation of their value.

Kristian Bahnson, for example, in his 1887 survey of European ethnographic museums, championed the shift described by Jenkins, yet often relied on methods of description discussed by Pomian. In his article, Bahnson set out to discuss not only the state of Europe's ethnographic museums but also their history and their goals for the future. Early in the article he stressed the new nature of collecting and display that should guide the efforts and development of ethnographic museums, arguing at one point, "it is no longer the rare and outstanding things, which one preferably wishes to preserve, although they consistently retain an entitled place in collections;" rather collections must focus on the "often apparently unimportant things . . . which explain the *Niveau* [level] and characterize the progressive developments in different areas."[90] Despite this assertion, however, the "most rare and outstanding things" continued to claim their "entitled place" in his own descriptions. The Jacobsen collection, for example, quickly took pride of place in Bahnson's discussion. He especially lauded its "exceedingly rich material," which was "of that much greater value, since it would be terribly difficult to ever acquire another collection that was equally complete." In other words, Bahnson stressed that the value of this collection lay in the fact that it was one of a kind and essentially irreplaceable. He stressed as well that the importance of the individual objects in this collection stemmed from their ensured rarity, since "on the West coast as well, contact with Europeans had brought the original industries into ruin, and good products from such industries are becoming increasingly rare."[91] Similarly, even within his discussion of the particular items in the Jacobsen collection, he gave special attention to "a dance house from eastern Vancouver," which he described as both "one of the most note-worthy things that one can find in the North American collections in Europe," and one of "the most interesting of the Berlin museum's acquisitions."[92] Despite his desire to champion the typical, his continual return to the exceptional gave away his deference to the doctrine of scarcity.

An affection for the exceptional over the typical also guided collectors' choices and influenced the kinds of artifacts that would reach European museums. Neither Jacobsen's selections, for example, nor those of many of his contemporaries remained focused on the "apparently unimportant things." Rather, particular attention was often paid to the unusual, the strange, the old, and the rare. Jacobsen, we know, intentionally focused on collecting very old items while in Canada, especially stone or bone weapons and implements.[93] He had a particularly good eye for attractive pieces, and he based many of his choices on aesthetic criteria (Figs. 6, 7, 8). Indeed, it was largely this conscious selection process that accounted for the tremendously positive reception Jacobsen's collections received in Germany.[94]

By the same token, it was also Jacobsen's ability to procure things that

FIGURE 6. A Bella Bella (Heiltsuk) canoe acquired by Adrian Jacobsen in 1881. This rare photograph also portrays the North American exhibits in the Berlin museum in 1894, with the tall iron and glass parallel cases cluttered with a variety of objects that had become so typical by that time. Equally important, and in some ways unique, are the paintings by George Catlin on the back wall that show a rare instance in which more popular images were mixed with the material culture assembled in this scientific museum. It is unclear if similar images might have been found in other areas of the museum. There is no reference to such paintings in either the museum's guidebooks or in records. I am grateful to Peter Bolz for sharing these photos of objects from the Jacobsen collection. (Staatliche Museen zu Berlin, Ethnologisches Museum)

FIGURE 7. Nootka eagle mask, collected by Jacobsen in 1881 during a visit to Barkley Sound. It illustrates the astounding beauty of the objects assembled by Jacobsen that so captured Berliners' imaginations when they were first put on display. (Staatliche Museen zu Berlin, Ethnologisches Museum)

FIGURE 8. Kwakiutl mask of the crooked beak. Collected by Jacobsen in a Newitti village on Hope Island, it is among the oldest of its type in existence. One of the keys to Jacobsen's success as a collector was his inclination (without much instruction from ethnologists) to acquire objects that were exceptionally beautiful and very old. (Staatliche Museen zu Berlin, Ethnologisches Museum)

other collectors had been unable to obtain, together with assurances by many "experts" that the collection could never be repeated, that created his reputation as a collector and ensured the value of his collection. As Richard Schöne, director of the Royal Museums, noted, "If one considers that these objects are for the most part not only new to Europe, but are also only seldom found in the large American collections, and that they represent a culture caught in the throes of quick extinction, then the importance of the acquisition cannot be misjudged."[95] Clearly, Schöne was extremely pleased to have acquired something that no one else possessed or could ever obtain; especially since this also included the Americans, to whom he implies it most naturally belonged. Given his enthusiasm for the singularity of this collection, it also seems clear that he would have been less enthusiastic if the Jacobsen collection consisted of things everyone could have—and in fact a second collection that Jacobsen procured from the area brought much less attention.[96] Most important, the doctrine of scarcity consistently inundated the rhetoric of the Danish ethnologist, the Norwegian collector, and the director of the Prussian Royal Museums.[97] In each case, regardless of national origin, educational background, or political position, their interests remained the same.

Moreover, with regard to the practice of collecting, as well as the value of ethnographic artifacts, the most fundamental shift that took place in the later part of the nineteenth century was the degree to which the value of an object became linked to the quality and amount of information a collector obtained about its origins and its function in the culture that created it. In the 1870s, as Bastian launched his appeal for an ethnographic museum that would enable him to assemble the material culture of humanity into a catalog of sorts, ethnographic objects were seen as clearly readable signs, parts of a world system of things. The objects themselves were sought after as the representative parts of this system, and as the fundamental building blocks for recreating it in miniature; information about artifacts was also considered desirable, but the objects remained the primary objective. Over the next decades, however, information about the cultural context in which objects were produced and functioned became increasingly important, and artifacts brought back to Europe or already in Europe that lacked this information dropped accordingly in scientific and economic value.

One of the Jacobsen collection's limitations, for example, was its scanty labeling, and for this reason it can be seen as a transitional collection. The Jacobsen expedition of 1881–83 was one of the first major collecting ventures launched specifically for the purpose of salvaging everything possible from a particular geographical area, and it was initially deemed a major success. But the usefulness of Jacobsen's acquisitions were later regarded as limited by the fact that he had not recorded all possible information about the objects in his collection.[98] Franz Boas, among others, recognized these limitations while working with the collection in Berlin;[99] his experiences with the Jacobsen collection led him to argue for the need to record exact information about objects while collecting. He insisted that all collectors include an object's name in the local language, its geographical origin, its lineage, and "its associated 'story' and song"—criteria which were becoming standard among ethnologists by this time.[100] Boas argued that such information was critical for understanding the meaning of the object within the culture that created it, and warned his fellow ethnologists, during a debate over the organization of American museums in 1887, that "by regarding a single implement outside of its surroundings, outside of other phenomena affecting that people and its productions, we cannot understand its meanings."[101] It was therefore with great enthusiasm that Boas later retrieved some of the stories explaining Vancouver Island artifacts in the Jacobsen collection, after meeting some of the Native Americans from whom Jacobsen had purchased artifacts a decade earlier at the 1893 Chicago World's Fair.[102] This information helped raise the Jacobsen collection back up to standard.

Stressing the importance of exact information about the objects in collections became an ethnological mantra by the turn of the century and remained so through 1914.[103] Ethnologist Richard Thurnwald summed up the essence of this relationship in an article in *Museumskunde*, in which he sought to clarify why ethnologists collected much differently than art collectors by explaining that the value of ethnographic objects actually lay more in their representational qualities than in their physical form: "Their value also does not lie, as in the case of art objects, in the single objects themselves, rather they have *representative* meaning. It depends on their position and relationship to the entire life [of the culture from which they come], on the functions, that they have to fulfill, on the needs, out of which they were created, on the foreign influences, which they or relatives brought, on the changes, to which they were exposed."[104] The key implication of Thurnwald's explanation is that without the proper information about the objects, ethnographic artifacts became unreadable texts, pieces that could never be fit into the bigger puzzle. The acceptance of this attitude quickly affected the relationship between collectors and museums, as well as redefined the acceptable methods of collecting. It led, for example, to ever more precise instructions for collectors, and eventually to contracts between collectors and museums that held the collectors responsible for obtaining exacting details about their objects and often for providing the museums with catalogs that carefully described all artifacts in the collection.[105]

Moreover, the economic value of objects was reassessed along with their scientific value. As Leo Frobenius explained during his discussions with the Hamburg museum about the price he should receive for the objects he obtained, the size and appearance of the object should make no difference to its value, because the physical characteristics were ideally of secondary importance: "The straw, iron, and wood that I hand over to you represents absolutely no value." Rather, "the value is first given to it through the historical and developmental-historical relationships that bind these materials to our science."[106] Thus collectors such as Frobenius who conformed to the new standards could easily appropriate current scientific discourses to argue about the material value of their artifacts,[107] while those who failed to adhere to the new principles could not expect to get paid. Once the critical characteristic of a desirable artifact was redefined as knowledge about the relationship between the object and its history, a new level was added to the hierarchy of value, one which made "good" collections even harder to find.

As the largest consumers on the international market, ethnologists' wishes had a significant effect not only on how things were collected but also on who could do the collecting. One of the central ramifications of the shift toward an emphasis on information was that the "best" collections were now particularly difficult for untrained individuals to obtain, and the ability to recognize a "good" object—or rather to create a good object through accumulating the proper information—became increasingly limited to an ever-smaller number of people. Indeed, because the dynamics of the marketplace were intimately connected to those of the professionalization taking place at this time, the value of each collector rose and fell along with his or her collections.

Trained collectors had, of course, always been preferred. In the early 1870s, for example, official reports regarding the founding of the Berlin museum stressed that its director must be an "educated expert" who could properly coordinate and guide his collectors, while the "personal competence and sufficient preparation of the travelers" was regarded as quite "naturally a primary requirement [*Hauptbedingung*] for the entire operation."[108] The fact that they were not always well trained was also lamented in the museum's first guidebooks. In 1877, for example, Bastian wrote, with regard to a Mexican collection that had been considered the richest of its kind when it was assembled in 1858, that "unfortunately, all the objects are without exact notations about their origins, and with the owner already deceased, the possibility of gaining further information was removed," and that although "an exhibition was recently held based on the collection's primary components . . . the scientific utilization of this still untilled field" was terribly hindered by these "very disorganized materials."[109] Similarly, in 1887, Bahnson stated that "we understandably owe the most valuable material to the specialists," noting that the majority of collections came unfortunately from interested but unprepared parties, aided only with the inadequate written instructions and limited preparation; and he pointed out that "the older collections often suffer from a lack of reliable descriptive information, as well as information regarding the uses that gave rise to the creation of the objects."[110] More stringent criticism was evident as well, and during the same decade, Virchow, the geographer Eduard Pechuel-Loesche, and others termed "completely useless" many collections created by even well-known amateurs such as Hermann von Wissmann, the first European to cross equatorial Africa.[111]

By the turn of the century ethnologists were agreed that only educated, well-prepared collectors would do, because amateur collectors, regardless of their enthusiasm and best intentions, were simply not up to the task. As Thilenius later remarked:

Daily experience in museums confirms that the layman only collects what attracts his attention, even when he goes about his work with the best intentions. He is neither able to distinguish the things that are important for a culture, from those that are unimportant, nor to oversee the many new questions that come up with every unknown piece. Only the *Fachleute* [specialists] are able to guarantee success, because they approach the task with complete knowledge of the general questions and the currently available results from one or the other area, and at the same time they alone have the technical skills at their disposal that are necessary for the avoidance of failures and the safeguarding of results.[112]

In the face of such attitudes it is hardly a surprise that less-educated collectors began losing their ability to compete with the "specialists," as some of the playing rules shifted.

Adrian Jacobsen's personal history is worth returning to briefly as an example of how this shift determined who could participate in the ethnographic project. As noted above, Jacobsen was celebrated for his first collection from the northwest coast of North America. After returning from the expedition, he worked closely with the ethnologists ordering the collection, was present when the collection was opened to the public, and accompanied Bastian as he presented it to Kaiser Wilhelm I. Jacobsen also undertook two other major expeditions for the Berlin museum. Soon after finishing his work with the American collection, he led an expedition to Siberia in 1884–85, and another to Indonesia in 1887–88. In between these trips and for some time afterwards, Bastian was able to keep Jacobsen tied to the museum by paying him the low monthly wage of 100 Marks in exchange for his assistance with preparing and ordering his collections.[113]

Jacobsen's true aspiration, however, was to gain a permanent position with a museum, and he lobbied for it repeatedly. He discussed the possibility with Bastian, with the head of the *Hilfscommitté*, J. Richter, and with Prussian cultural minister Gustav von Gossler,[114] and he sent a personal letter to Kaiser Wilhelm II. He explained that he had always hoped that in return for the 16,000 items he had acquired for the museum—which he estimated was one-sixth of their entire holdings in 1890—that he would gain a permanent position there.[115] But despite the praise heaped on him by ethnologists in their private correspondence and in professional and more popular publications,[116] he was consistently refused a permanent position of any kind. His collections had been received with fanfare in the mid-1880s, but by the end of the decade, as the emphasis shifted from the object to its information, his usefulness for the greater ethnographic project was already starting to wane. His reputation and experience still allowed him to be employed as a collector, but the idea of giving the poorly educated Jacobsen a permanent museum position was unthinkable during this increasingly professional age.[117] In the early 1890s Jacobsen helped set up displays at two international exhibitions, but the sporadic nature of this sort of work continued to wear on him. In 1895 he gave up on his chosen occupation and began managing hotels and restaurants. His time had essentially passed and he faded from the scene.[118]

Historians and cultural critics generally claim that two central factors led to the kind of professionalization that drove Jacobsen from a career in ethnology. The standard argument posited by many cultural historians and historians of anthropology is that the professionalization of ethnology was directly related to the self-creation of the ethnologists, in that objects and experts were united in museums where "one justified the other," or where artifacts and ethnologists were "reciprocally" defined.[119] As with the "owner" of any collection, the trained ethnologist has been portrayed as engaged in extending and defining him- or herself through the process of collection, as well as through the exclusion of non-experts.[120]

The other argument is that the shift from amateur to professional collecting in the late nineteenth century was tied to broader social changes. Henrika Kuklick, for example, has convincingly argued that in order to understand British anthropologists' transformation from "armchair anthropologists" to professional researchers working in "the field," historians must look outside of the discipline of anthropology, and indeed beyond the academy. Kuklick stresses that this movement into the field swept through all the natural history sciences in Britain at the end of the nineteenth century and stemmed largely from "widespread social trends that affected specialists no differently from many of their contemporaries."[121] She links armchair scholars' tendency to rely on other's fieldwork with Victorian conceptions of gentlemanly proprieties, and the younger generation's desire to get their hands dirty with middle-class ideologies that effectively "inverted the prestige hierarchy of the gentleman naturalists." For Kuklick, the movement of these "self-styled 'practical men'" is one that followed a general shift in British society, rather than simply the internal dynamics of British academics.[122]

But in Germany, this shift in collecting tactics and the increased number of ethnologists who went into the field was directly tied to the market mechanism. Social pressures played a role, but it was not simply a middle-class need to dirty their hands that drove ethnologists into the field. Rather, aspiring young ethnologists' desire to distinguish themselves from their counterparts while competing for a limited number of permanent positions made them eager to go abroad. Theirs was an effort, in essence, to increase their own value in an increasingly competitive job market.[123] Moreover, as noted above, the idea of sending experts into the field did not originate with this younger generation. Bastian, for example, spent over two decades of his life outside of Europe in a long series of collecting voyages;[124] Karl von den Steinen took two extensive collecting trips through Brazil in the 1880s before settling into museum work;[125] and while young men such as Boas certainly championed the need to send experts into the field, this tenet was already written into the original discussions of the Berlin museum before Boas had attended his first university lectures, and it was supported by Virchow and other members of his generation as much as by Boas himself. Yet despite this older generation's desire to send well-trained collectors into the field, their ability to do so was hindered by the limited number of qualified candidates. As these candidates became available, however, there was an increasing and general call to have them dispatched—a call not limited to the younger generation, and one that was primarily fueled by concerns over the quality of the empirical evidence being brought into ethnological institutions.[126] Thus Jacobsen was not only excluded because of his lack of academic credentials, but also because of the radically increased number of candidates from whom the directors could chose.

Moreover, the movement to send better-trained collectors into the field—despite being facilitated by different kinds of changing social conditions in Germany and Britain—was neither German nor British. It was international, and the market mechanism played a significant role in this shift.[127] Essentially, once a few museums began sending educated researchers and collectors into the field and gaining a higher quality of evidence, other museums, both inside and outside of Germany, were forced to do the same or lose their mantle of scientific legitimacy.

In 1906, for example, Weule argued in a report to the Leipzig city council concerning Leipzig's first expedition, that museums in Berlin, Vienna, Bremen, St. Petersburg, New York, and Washington had already sponsored significant expeditions, and that Leipzig needed to support similar efforts so that they would not be left behind.[128] In 1909, he returned again to the same types of comparison and drew specifically on the recent efforts of other German museums in order to highlight Leipzig's relative inaction. He argued that "the formation of this type of expedition is quite usual for us nowadays," and stressed that "even such a small museum as that in Lübeck has managed a year-long undertaking in equatorial West Africa." At the same time he noted that the museum in Berlin "is simultaneously directing an array of operations in the most different areas of the world," and that "Hamburg has even sent out a large ship in 1908 for a thorough ethnological exploration of the South Seas." Leipzig had sponsored a few smaller expeditions by this time, and Weule, pointing to these initial successes and the examples set by other museums, argued for a substantial increase in the city's commitment to expeditions, and stressed that the results promised to be "scientifically extraordinarily valuable."[129] To do otherwise would have been to allow the Leipzig museum to fall from its place as the second most important ethnographic museum in Germany. Once the stakes had been raised, in other words, Weule and the directors of other museums had little choice but to follow suit, and therefore increasing numbers of museums sent trained researchers and collectors into the field, and their ethnologists planned ever-larger expeditions.

While this sort of reaction and emulation might seem commonsensical, the point to bear in mind is that the market mechanism consistently encouraged the search for newer and better collections, and that in many ways the shift toward professional, university-trained collectors and ever-bigger expeditions was a natural extension of the fundamental impulses that had initiated the quest for possession several decades earlier. In 1873, when the Berlin museum was initially founded, any collection was sensational. A number of places on the globe offered equally rewarding finds. By the end of that decade this was already no longer the case. The landscape was changing, many private collectors had become involved, competition for limited goods increased, while some areas had already been picked clean of everything remotely indigenous. The search for "salvageable" objects thus became increasingly refined to focus on areas not yet touched by other museums or freelance collectors. This desire led to the frenzy over the Godeffroy purchase. It accounts for the Jacobsen expedition setting the standard for emulation in the early 1880s. And a similar impulse was responsible for shifting the focus to an even more refined, focused type of gathering by the 1890s, leading to the American-led Jesup North Pacific Expedition by the end of that decade. The professionalization of ethnographic collecting, indeed of ethnology in general, was tightly intertwined with this pressing desire to obtain and possess the "best" collections, an impulse still governed by the doctrine of scarcity.

Moreover, as standards continued to be pushed, they necessitated increasingly large investments and created expectations for ever-greater returns. In the 1870s, the amount of money invested in ethnographic expeditions launched during the first decade of the twentieth century would have been unfathomable to ethnologists and their supporters, largely because the desire to obtain and possess the "newest" and "best" collections did not yet demand such sacrifices; in 1870, the "best" things were still relatively easy to get. But over the next two decades, as large sums of money became involved, the numbers of interested competitors grew. And as participants increased and definitions of scientific value were refined, prices continued to soar. By 1905, Thilenius stressed in his budget proposal that the dramatic increase in the number of museums sending professional collectors into the field had resulted in "an extraordinary competition and an enormous rise in prices," which sometimes priced other museums right out of the competition. European museums, he argued "must, for example, completely abandon the competition with American museums for lack of sufficient funding." Yet it was precisely the American's attitudes which he argued should be emulated. The Americans, he pointed out, had invested over 700,000 Marks in the Jesup expedition to ensure its tremendous success. If Thilenius's supporters in Hamburg wanted to be equally successful, then this was a commitment they must be willing to match.[130] The market, in other words, fundamentally influenced how ethnologists would collect while abroad.

Once in the field, directors of ethnographic museums might maintain their privileged place as the market's largest consumers, but they could no more control the exchange value of the objects in forests or jungles than they could in auction houses or at world's fairs. As Weule argued in his 1909 budget proposal:

> This competition is especially bad in the ethnographic area; when one attempts to contact the owners of ethnographic collections with a request to bring the price to some extent into accord with the actual value, one will hear in 8 out of 10 cases today: 'If you do not accept what I want, then there is always space in America, and no one bargains over there.' In addition, as a further aggravating element, the directors of American museums today charter an array of ships, with which they sail to the most interesting ethnographic areas, such as Melanesia, Micronesia, and parts of Polynesia, and purchase everything there for any price that is asked.[131]

In fact, Weule complained that in all areas of the world prices were being pushed up "two- to three-times," while at the same time researchers and collectors were spreading across the globe "in an until now never heard of scale."[132] Nothing was being left in their wake, and collecting was taking place at such a pace that ethnologists were helping to fulfill their own prophesies about the quick end of indigenous cultures. "In a very few decades," Weule added, "even the South-American Indians from the interior will be using Swedish matches and shooting breechloaders. Among the Nigers today, for the most part, it is already so."[133]

As expeditions grew in size and intensity, ethnologists and their actions often contributed fundamentally to the wholesale disappearance of native material culture from the regions they visited and thus helped to perpetuate and substantiate the doctrine of scarcity. Ethnologists essentially ensured the rarity of what they acquired by taking all the "original" artifacts and replacing them with the common and mundane. As Thilenius remarked in a 1906 budget proposal, ethnologists inevitably had an impact on the cultures they visited, particularly cultures that were still "free" of European influence. Therefore "*the first collection out of such an area is at the same time not only the best but also the only reliable one.* Whoever comes as second to an area, may still find one or another old, good piece. The vast majority of his objects, however, will be newly created with new tools, or, what is even worse, created for the express purpose of trade. *The museum for which the first acquisition was possible, attains through this effort, a never again to be repeated lead over all others* [his emphasis]."[134]

He supported this statement with an example from a recent expedition by the Berlin museum, which, by emptying an area of artifacts, had significantly increased the value of their acquisitions: "As the Raum expedition arrived at the Ramumünde station in New Guinea in 1898, they found the inhabitants of the village without any knowledge of iron. The expedition acquired every accessible object and the collection was successfully returned to the Museum für Völkerkunde in Berlin. A participant in the expedition had the opportunity to put together a small private collection, and today he can demand any price he chooses for it, because he introduced iron [to the village in New Guinea] and nothing more will be produced with the old, beautiful, but strenuous techniques."[135] As can already be seen by the tone of this evaluation, Thilenius greeted the recognition that ethnologists left irreversible change in their wake less with a concern for the impact ethnologists had on these cultures, than with the conviction to be the first to strike.[136]

As Thilenius arrived in Hamburg in 1905, he was given the assignment of raising the reputation of the museum up to the highest possible level. His method, as he explained in a report to the *Oberschulbehörde* several years later, was simple. His goal became "the acquisition of large collections, which essentially exhaust [empty out] an area." The exact origins of the collections were immaterial to him; what was important was the condition of the cultures from which they came. It was for this reason, he noted, that he had lobbied for the purchase of the Hellwig collection from the Bismarck Archipelago; although the collection would not be completely unique because the Berlin and London museums both had small holdings from these areas, it would still give his museum possession of "the most complete and largest collection from both the islands of Wuvulu and Aua," a position it was guaranteed to maintain, "because on both of the small islands the last trace of the old culture has been exterminated [*vernichtet*] for some time."[137] His plan for a South Seas expedition was equally calculated. As he stated in his 1907 proposal:

> The concern [of this expedition] will be to choose a population currently exposed to Europeanization, so that on the one hand, all of the important elements of the culture are still present, yet on the other hand [it] is already far enough along in the process of Europeanization that a resurgence of the old culture would be out of the question. In this case the expedition would be able to return home with a complete picture of the culture including its most fundamental characteristics, without having to fear, that an expedition to the same area, undertaken at some later time by another museum, could obtain equally valuable results.[138]

Thus the primary goal of this scientific expedition was to "corner the market" in one area of material culture by gaining a collection that would retain its value and contribute to the prestige of Hamburg and its museum—a collection that was sure to never be reproduced by a culture guaranteed to perish.

Thilenius's strategy reflects the realpolitik of ethnographic collecting by the turn of the century, the natural extension of the acquisition escalation that began in the 1870s. The collecting frenzy that dominated ethnology by the turn of the century dovetailed with the riotous colonial energies of those decades. But these aggressive enthusiasms were not its cause; rather, the large expeditions, the professionalization of the science, the creation of monopolies, and the ever-greater desire for possession built directly on the enduring modernist project as conceived in the early 1870s. From the beginning, ethnologists eagerly pursued the "best" collections—one after the other, and often simultaneously. Their needs were endlessly expandable and their desires, like those of most consumers, unquenchable; their willingness to possess was heightened by their professional needs, pressures from their patrons, and their competitors' actions, and it was only curtailed by their financial and technical limitations. As these limitations gave way to technical advances and stronger supporters, the projects continued to grow. The fires of desire were fanned to ever-greater extremes by the ongoing competition and the doctrine of scarcity, reaching their greatest height in the years just prior to World War I.

Throughout this process, the most valuable objects remained those most difficult to obtain or those that were the last of their kind. A desire for unique individual objects grew into a desire for sets of objects, to better sets with more information, and further to unrepeatable sets from particular regions, which ethnologists ensured could never be duplicated. Desires simply grew as resources expanded, and if each piece found its way into the greater collection of the museum, a feeling of completion remained at most a fleeting sensation that quickly gave way to an urge for more as the set of sets continued to grow.

THREE

THE CULTURES OF COLLECTING AND THE POLITICS OF SCIENCE

It is self-evident that I will drop Frič as soon as he compromises our museum in any way.—Georg Thilenius to Wilhelm von Bode, 14 May 1907

The collecting frenzy during the late nineteenth and early twentieth centuries was not a complete free-for-all. Salvage anthropology, combined with the passion for possession, often legitimated radical excesses in both the amount of collecting that occurred as well as the methods employed by ethnologists and others. Yet there were also limitations. Collectors were forced to operate within parameters created through a combination of political, academic, financial, cultural and "moral" factors. In essence, an unwritten system of rules and regulations shaped by both older cosmopolitan traditions and pressing practical and professional considerations created a consensus about what constituted acceptable methods of acquisition and behavior abroad.

By the end of the nineteenth century, the cultures of collecting that emerged around German ethnographic museums also underwent a critical transformation. Bastian's generation of ethnologists owed much of their legitimacy, and their scientific authority, to their belief in an international community of science. There was a moral imperative behind much of their work, and gentlemanly ideals of progressive, apolitical science facilitated the creation of their acquisition networks. Many of the ethnologists who went into the field drew on their belief in a progressive, international scientific community to insulate themselves from the reality of their actions in an imperialist world. But for many more, the contradictions between the realities of collecting and the rhetoric of international, progressive, science became both clear and acceptable by the 1890s, and the legitimacy and justification they employed for their actions abroad soon shifted from the higher goals of international science to utilitarian calls for immediate action.

Coupled with this transformation was another critical shift. A younger generation of ethnologists came to the fore around the turn of the century. Trained during an age of aggressive nationalism and imperialism, and caught up in a wave of professionalization, they began rationalizing their actions as an expression of their own prerogatives as the self-proclaimed leaders of the ethnographic sciences and as ethnologists who were self-consciously German.[1] This younger generation never abandoned the older gentlemanly ideals; indeed, they continued to maintain them as a means to publicly legitimate and explain their collectors' actions. But by the turn of the century these ideals ceased to play such a significant role in ethnologists' understanding of themselves or in the goals of their ethnographic project. The realities of acquisition and the professionalization of the science changed everything.

The Authority of Science

Ethnologists in Imperial Germany consistently drew on the authority of science in order to fashion their professional identities and legitimate their collecting ventures. They justified their behavior, supported each other's efforts, and often condemned the actions of nonscientists based on a belief that their own efforts served a higher purpose, and that nonscientists' interference might hinder these greater goals. They championed their own collecting as part of a broad intellectual project, which promised to raise general levels of knowledge about the "multiplicity of humanity" and the "history of mankind." Their methodologies were ostensibly geared toward understanding, and they developed under the auspices of an international community of science that attempted to set its own goals and regulate collecting standards. They were quick to criticize nonscientists who did not meet these standards, often morally condemning individuals who collected ethnographica for profit, made careers out of trading on the international market in material culture without regard for the ethnographic project, or mistreated indigenous peoples while abroad. Yet these were actions that ethnologists themselves might, under different circumstances, accept or employ. Indeed, the authority of science could both condemn and justify. It gave those groups and individuals endowed with it the power to define the acceptable, and it provided ethnologists with a means for controlling other collectors' actions, as well as for legitimating equally rash actions by the scientists themselves.

Before 1914, most ethnologists believed that they belonged to an international community of science. Their identities were steeped in a conviction that science operated on a higher plain and that scientists worked for a greater good, and these convictions functioned simultaneously to help define and legitimate their collecting efforts.[2] Despite national and colonial rivalries and the ongoing competition for artifacts, this powerful sentiment led many ethnologists to share information, invite other scholars to work in their museums, and aid each other's projects—at least during those times when they believed that their counterparts' actions would not threaten their own immediate goals.

An ongoing exchange of publications, catalogs, artifacts, unpublished papers, and information about different regions and cultures was fundamental to the greater scientific project, and something to which most ethnologists eagerly contributed. For this reason, Spencer Baird, the director of the Smithsonian Institution from 1865 to 1891, enthusiastically endorsed and maintained an active exchange with German and other foreign museums.[3] The American ethnologist William H. Dall willingly provided Adolf Bastian with information about how best to trade with the inhabitants of the northwest coast of Canada and the United States.[4] And Bastian argued for the creation of a standing system of exchange between scientists and tried to create a publication that would keep all ethnologists informed about what had been collected and what still needed to be secured.[5] In short, as a result of their convictions about the international character of science, the information they gathered flowed freely across an array of political borders both within and outside of Germany.

Bastian, for example, welcomed other ethnologists' efforts when he believed they would contribute to the greater ethnographic project. He supported the founding of the Museum für Völkerkunde zu Leipzig from its very first years,[6] and he physically embraced Karl Weule when he learned that Weule would be leaving the Berlin Museum for a better position in Leipzig. He exclaimed that although Weule was going over to his main

German competition, he always regarded it as a cause for celebration when an ethnologist obtained a solid institutional position.[7] Similarly, he greeted the closing of Mexico's borders to traffic in ethnographica in the 1890s with a mixture of disappointment over the lost opportunities for acquisition and enthusiasm for Mexico's efforts to establish its own museum—an institution that he felt would contribute positively to the greater scientific project.[8] Regardless of their active competition, most ethnologists agreed that the larger project was ultimately the important one, the one to which all scientists should be contributing, and the one that ultimately justified their actions.

Affiliation with the internationally sanctioned sciences thus endowed individual practitioners and institutions with a certain legitimacy; nonaffiliation, however, was suspect. Just as a collector's membership in the scientific community could legitimate his or her actions, his or her independence from this community or unwillingness to follow its standards could easily lead to censure. Much of the work on the professionalization of the sciences in the late nineteenth century has made this point quite clear. Henrika Kuklick, perhaps the foremost scholar of the professionalization of British anthropology, has argued that in general, as a "disciplinary community becomes a coherent group," its members look "primarily to their peers for confirmation of the merits of their efforts" and endorsement of their standards, and they legitimate their actions and efforts through their inclusion in these communities.[9] Individuals unwilling or unable to maintain the standards of collecting around the turn of the century, however, often found themselves excluded from both the community and its umbrella of legitimacy regardless of their generation or national origin. These scientific communities were thus "disciplinary" in more than one sense. Failure to conform to their standards could lead to exclusion from the credibility of science, and collectors whose intentions were other than "scientific" were often left with illegitimate projects.

In many instances collectors' intentions became the critical factor in establishing their legitimacy. Amateur collectors who could not maintain the rigorous scientific standards demanded by the ethnological canon during the late nineteenth century were not held in the highest esteem by the scientific community, but their willingness to contribute to the scientific project and their recognition of scientists as authorities precluded banishing them from association with the discipline. Such supporters, were in fact welcomed and needed, if encouraged to remain among the rank and file.[10] Their intentions, in essence, were good, even if their abilities were not up to standard. By the same token, a collector with ability but improper intentions could run into difficulties. Adrian Jacobsen, for example, whose 1881 expedition to the northwest coast of America and Canada under the auspices of the Museum für Völkerkunde in Berlin was a tremendous success, faced incredible difficulties selling a second collection he obtained with his brother from the same area only a few years later. To a certain degree these difficulties were due to the fact that the collection was not a new sensation, rather a second serving of something German ethnologists had already seen and a smaller one at that. But it also received a cold reception among ethnologists because the second collection had been assembled purely for profit, not for science.[11]

Ethnologists' self-proclaimed affiliation with internationally recognized scientific projects, and the distance they attempted to maintain from economic schemes, helped them to fashion their identities in opposition to collectors who were out for profit, or individuals who operated without an understanding of ethnologists' achievements and goals. Indeed, while justifying their own positions and berating those of wayward nonscientists, they often seemed to regard themselves as occupying high moral ground. Bastian and Virchow, for example, drawing on their liberal backgrounds and belief in a unitary humanity, participated in an ongoing campaign against the inhuman treatment of "inferior races," often championing the "equality and human dignity of all cultures."[12] They repeatedly condemned Europeans' persistent characterizations of other peoples as "savages" and chastised their treatment of indigenous cultures in colonial territories. Bastian, for instance, argued in the 1870s, that "in our own European civilization . . . we would most certainly find a form of mental barbarism that not only equals that of the African or American Indian, but surpasses in stupidity any savage society."[13] Such moral objections were adopted by succeeding generations as well, and appeared again and again in ethnologists' popular and academic writings. Thus several decades later, Felix von Luschan continued to condemn the "white savages . . . who indeed think and act like savages," and castigated the "misguided" colonial policies of Germans and other Europeans, which contributed to the mistreatment and quick death of so many colonized peoples, policies that he, the young Georg Thilenius, and an array of other ethnologists condemned for both moral and practical reasons.[14] Elements of Bastian's cosmopolitan vision, in other words, remained a critical part of the ethnographic project and the ways in which German ethnologists viewed themselves in the world during the late nineteenth and early twentieth centuries.

Despite ethnologists' willingness to denounce others' actions from this high moral ground, their own relationships with non-Europeans were generally rather ambiguous. Theft is one case in point. Many scholars have pointed out the willingness among even well-known ethnologists' and anthropologists' to bend the rules of acquisition and resort to deception and theft in order to obtain what they wanted. Frank Hamilton Cushing, whom some have termed the first professional American ethnologist, was not adverse to stealing from burial sites while leaving a village—actions that were anything but exceptional for ethnologists of his age;[15] Franz Boas "collected hundreds of bones and skeletons" by digging up Native American burial sites during the night and against the will of a number of different tribes; Adrian Jacobsen attempted to secure skulls and religious objects by climbing into grave sites in trees; and George Dorsey gained renown for his plundering of burial caves—all actions conducted under the cloak of scientific legitimacy.[16] A number of scholars have also recounted how ethnologists on Thilenius's South Seas expedition, from 1908 to 1910, pursued a policy of "anonymous purchase"—leaving tobacco or some other form of payment in place of objects taken while their owners were not present, and they have stressed that the scientists on this expedition sometimes turned to more violent methods of intimidation and deception as well.[17] There was often a striking contradiction between ethnologists' pretensions and their actions.

Moreover, ethnologists' relationships with their subjects were not only ambiguous, fluctuating with time and place, but inconsistent on several levels. As ethnologists engaged in theft and deception, they not only went against their own moralistic and practical arguments about the importance of respecting, understanding, and treating decently other cultures, they also violated the essential tenets of professional ethnology, which placed so much value on the information surrounding artifacts.[18] The ethnologists who engaged in these tactics participated, in fact, in actions that they were quick to condemn when undertaken by either amateur collectors or dealers in ethnographic artifacts, and they did so with relative impunity and without much fear of condemnation from their counterparts.[19] There was, of course a chance for censure, and ethnologists could find themselves in legal difficulties or even physical danger if they were caught in the act of stealing artifacts.[20] But in general there appears to have been an unwritten policy that when locals were unwilling to cooperate with collectors, subterfuge and theft—legitimated by the needs of science—were acceptable means of acquisition. Ethnologists' association with a project geared toward contributing to the "greater scientific good" thus played a critical role in legitimating otherwise reproachful actions.

Not everyone, however, could pillage burial sites and monuments without eliciting protests. Indeed, without the legitimacy of science, plundering could easily lead to censure by scientific and political bodies. In 1900, for instance, the German Foreign Office received a memorandum from the British embassy regarding ethnographic items from Burma in the possession of a "Mr. W. Thomas Gillis," who, they believed, might have offered to sell these objects to the Berlin museum.[21] Gillis was accused of "illegally" removing "cartloads of religious artifacts" and "frescoes" from Burmese temples while posing as an agent of Berlin's ethnographic museum. In response to this warning, the German consul in Calcutta wrote to Reichskanzler von Bülow and the Museum für Völkerkunde in Berlin and urged them "in the interest of German honor" to report to the Indian government if Gillis had any connections with German institutions as well as to break any ties that he might have had with the museum.[22] After making inquiries, the Prussian Cultural Ministry determined that Gillis, whose name was actually Thomann-Gillis, was the son of a Bavarian doctor and a Greek woman but that his own nationality remained unclear. The ministry also reported that although Thomann-Gillis had attempted to sell some of these "stolen" artifacts to the Berlin museum, they had not been purchased because his prices were too high. Most importantly, they also condemned his actions in Burma, stressed that his plundering had been a private venture, and quickly distanced themselves from him by pronouncing that they had neither given him any monetary assistance nor engaged him through an official contract—assuring the Foreign Office that any contact that their museum might have had with Thomann-Gillis had been broken.[23]

Thomann-Gillis, who could only feign scientific credentials, was censored for his plundering and blacklisted among European museums, while similar acts of theft by "real" scientists were often excused or justified.[24] This censure took place because although his actions were similar to those of the ethnologists discussed above, his intentions and the contexts in which his actions took place were different: unlike Boas, Cushing, the ethnologists on the South Seas expedition, and even Jacobsen, Thomann-Gillis had no affiliation with a scientific institution and was not protected by the authority of science. His actions could not be rationalized or legitimated by the greater scientific project, and indeed his actions were even regarded as threatening this project and the authority of science because he was motivated by profit—a motivation that was deemed as wholly unscientific. At the same time there were other complications. He had not only stolen from indigenous peoples but from Britain's colonial subjects, which meant that he had transgressed political as well as moral boundaries. And, because he was operating outside the auspices of international science, his actions were easily viewed from within the context of colonial politics, in which they were uncontentiously regarded as theft by all concerned parties. The contexts in which he had operated, in other words, defined his actions.

In many ways it was also in ethnologists' best interest to distance themselves from individuals such as Thomann-Gillis. Because the authority of science rested on scientists' participation in a project that was ostensibly above political and economic concerns, interacting with individuals who were unwilling to respect (or unable to recognize) these divisions was inherently dangerous, because it could potentially contribute to eroding these distinctions, to upsetting the authority ethnologists gained as scientists, and ultimately, it threatened to inhibit their efforts at fashioning professional identities for themselves. As a result, ethnologists and their supporters were quite willing to take part in policing the distinctions between "scientific" and "nonscientific" collecting, in "disciplining" individuals who threatened to undermine their authority, and in distancing themselves from nonscientists who traded in ethnographica. However, in their willingness to disdain collectors operating outside the authority of science and champion their own positions, ethnologists were often seemingly unaware of just how thin a line separated themselves, their attitudes, and their actions from many of their nonscientific competitors—especially the dealers.

Dealing with Dealers

The dealers, who, like Bastian, solicited agents to procure whatever they might think valuable during their travels, or who quickly went abroad themselves during exceptional periods of activity, received rather negative evaluations in ethnologists' correspondence and official reports. Unlike ethnologists, the dealers' intentions were suspect because they—like Thomann-Gillis—were engaged in an *open* game of profit. According to Bastian, they snapped up scientifically valuable artifacts before ethnologists were able to get them, and then demanded "exorbitant" or "fantasy" prices that museums were too often "forced to pay."[25] Their unashamed activity in the ethnographic market as a means of financial gain, he argued, threatened ethnologists' pocketbooks, their principles, and ultimately the ethnographic project as well. Yet the working relationships between dealers and ethnologists were actually quite strong, and there was a marked disparity between ethnologists' rhetoric about the dealers and ethnologists' actions with them—a disparity that corresponded to the gap between the ideals and the realities of acquisition.

When one reads ethnologists' reports on collecting and acquisitions, and even their private musings, dealers are often set up in opposition to the "scientists," portrayed as unscrupulous, and generally regarded as undermining everything the ethnologists were trying to do. Thus Max Buchner, director of Munich's *Völkerkunde* museum from 1887 to 1907, characteristically responded to an offer of Fijian items by the independent collector P. E. Wolff by writing to the directors of the city's scientific collections: "Herr P. E. Wolff appears to be a dealer, like many whom I came to know in Australia and Oceania, and who thus awakens no feelings of trust."[26] Much of the daily private correspondence between ethnologists portrays the dealers as not only untrustworthy but also predatory, and the act of doing business with them as somehow distasteful. A statement by Thilenius in a private letter to Luschan, for instance, illustrates this attitude quite well. During a discussion of arrangements with the Hamburg-based dealer in ethnographica, Heinrich Umlauff, Thilenius stated: "I have also, by the way, decided with a heavy heart to acquire the old . . . feather box that Umlauff offered; we have so little from New Zealand that I have to do this painful injury to myself."[27] Given the rhetoric of these and other exchanges, as well as the many conflicts between dealers and ethnologists during the frenzied collecting actions like those that followed the fall of Benin, one could easily gain the impression that ethnologists worked with dealers only reluctantly, and generally only in extreme circumstances—when desperate for a certain type of collection and thus "forced to pay."[28]

The close working relationship between scientists and dealers in ethnographic artifacts, however, was as old as the museums and it continues today.[29] It was never limited to exceptional circumstances and, despite the professionalization of ethnology around the turn of the century, did not alter significantly before World War I. In many cases, the purported division between ethnologists and dealers was more a function of the rhetorical strategies ethnologists used to maintain their own self-images and retain their authority, rather than a reflection of actual conditions, and in general, their working relationships simply became more intense as the museums' budgets grew. The official reports issued by the Leipzig museum, for example, list not only the names of Adolf Bastian and Spencer Baird among the museum's "supporters" but also Karl Hagenbeck, the well-known dealer in exotic animals and organizer of *Völkerschauen*—the displays of exotic peoples that traveled throughout Germany and Europe.[30] Many scholars have pointed out the relationship between German ethnologists and anthropologists and the organizers of these popular shows and have stressed the reciprocal benefits of their working arrangements.[31] Hagenbeck and other organizers of *Völkerschauen* frequently invited scientists to visit their shows, deliver speeches, and write reports and reviews of the exhibits for local papers, in the hopes of gleaning legitimacy from their scientific authority. Scientists in turn were often eager to attend these events. Virchow in particular was an enthusiast who saw these shows as unprecedented opportunities for anthropologists to study living subjects and gain empirical evidence without being forced to travel abroad.[32] And Bastian and other ethnologists regarded the *Völkerschauen* as excellent opportunities for securing ethnographic collections accompanying the shows through purchase or donations.[33] On occasion, participants in Hagenbeck's shows were even invited to the museums to discuss the objects from their homelands and provide ethnologists with more information about the artifacts in their museums.[34]

Hagenbeck's connection to the museums, however, as well as that of dealers such as the Umlauff family, were not limited to their overlapping interests in *Völkerschauen*. Not only does Hagenbeck's name appear as a supporter in the earliest reports from the Hamburg and Leipzig museums, but both he and Umlauff contributed to these museums' earliest acquisitions and remained long-standing sources of collections and displays.[35] As the museums grew and gained a larger financial base, and as the science of ethnology was professionalized, the museums' relationships with dealers such as Umlauff simply became stronger and later acquisitions through these dealers only became more frequent and larger.[36] Already in 1877, for example, J. F. G. Umlauff sold the Leipzig museum one of their largest collections to date, a collection that was celebrated as one of their "best" early acquisitions.[37] As late as 1907, his son, Heinrich Umlauff, put together a *Sonderausstellung* (temporary exhibit) in the Hamburg museum, which consisted of figures and structures as well as house pets, pack animals, and camels from Kazakhstan—introducing one of the first life-groupings of this kind to the Hamburg museum.[38] Moreover, the Umlauffs' influence on the museums was not simply a matter of supplying these institutions with different things. In most cases they put together the collections, made the arrangements, commissioned the figures, and then either sent them off to museums or, as with the Hamburg display, set them up themselves. They then offered to sell the collections and displays to either the host museum or one of its competitors. The point, then, is that much of what could be seen in these museums was not collected, cataloged, or assembled by scientists at all. These scientific institutions, and what a visitor might encounter in them, were often as much the product of efforts by Umlauff, Hagenbeck, and other freelance collectors as those by Bastian or Thilenius.

Of course, the scientists retained their authority. Museum directors continued to set the standards and claim the power to authenticate or reject collections. In one case, for example, Weule wrote to Umlauff that his "bushmen look like boiled corpses," and explained that he expected something more from Umlauff's artists. And, while this concerns artistic representations rather than collections, the working relationships revealed in the following critique makes it worth quoting at length:

> Dear Papa Umlauff,
>
> I have no use for your Adaman grouping; the ethnographica on them are real and authentic, in contrast to the completely untenable posture of the large man shooting a bow, as well as his disposition. Even the old Salomon islander was positioned in such an unbelievably incorrect manner for a marksman that we stuck him in the deepest dungeon of our museum several months ago. The Ainu marksman will also not escape this fate one day. When you come here again, I want to give you a friendly lesson over this art; in the meantime I would ask you to look at the small opus of a certain Weule, "Kulturelemente der Menschheit," Stuttgart, 1911, which you can obtain in any bookstore for one Reichsmark. Beginning on page fifty-two you will find something on hand positioning, especially the right one. Concerning the left, I think that there is no Naturvolk that lays the arrow on the outside of the bow; where should the arrow gain its support? It slides much more cheerfully on the left side of the bow, through the finger.[39]

As this quoted passage makes clear, Umlauff and Weule not only engaged in a business relationship in which Umlauff often visited Weule's museum and provided him with a variety of objects and some of their earliest figures and life-groupings, but they were on friendly enough terms that Weule felt comfortable calling him "Papa Umlauff," joking and teasing with him about the mistakes he and his artists had made. In short, Weule and Umlauff were in close and frequent contact. Moreover, Umlauff had similar, if less humorous, relationships with the directors of the other German ethnographic museums as well as ethnologists in many other nations.[40] Umlauff had no scientific education, but he was well-versed in the international market of material culture. He drew his authority from pos session rather than science. He was not a member of the scientific community, but he was certainly an important part of the cultures of collecting, and despite his open quest for profits, ethnologists worked closely with him and his family for decades.

How then can we account for ethnologists' efforts to distance themselves from some nonscientists like Thomann-Gillis, who collected for profit, while they continued to associate, indeed even work closely with, others who made the collection and distribution of ethnographica their profession? To begin with, we have to acknowledge that the ambiguities and apparent contradictions were part of a system in which actions (and relationships) were situationally defined. At the same time, we also have to identify the functions that ethnologists' rhetoric about the proprieties of science ultimately fulfilled. Ethnologists were less concerned with collectors' methods of acquisition or even the dealers' and other collectors' motivations than they were with maintaining control over the field of collecting and their own social and cultural positions. As long as ethnologists' positions remained unthreatened, and the artifacts they obtained made the grade, almost any action by themselves, their collectors, or the dealers was acceptable.

As a result, there were certain unwritten rules and regulations that governed the arrangements between dealers and ethnologists, as well as between the museums and their collectors, which most of the participants seemed to understand and be willing to follow. Museum directors would work with dealers—buy from the dealers, accept figures, collections, and life-groupings created and arranged by the dealers, but only in the most exceptional circumstances would they sell objects or collections to dealers.[41] Selling to dealers legitimated their quest for profits and could sully ethnologists' reputations and thereby undermine the authority of science and, eventually, ethnologists' social positions. In a similar way, ethnologists could buy from a wide range of collectors, with little regard for the way they collected as long as they maintained ethnologists' scientific standards. Ethnologists themselves could break their own tenets of morality if it was for the greater good, and they could create close working relationships with merchants in ethnographica if it was for the good of scientific research. As long as the contradictions that were inherent in this system were not openly discussed, it functioned to the benefit of dealers and ethnologists alike.

Imperialist Opportunities

At the same time that Berlin's ethnologists and politicians were absolving themselves of any connection to Thomann-Gillis and denouncing his actions, they were also preparing to capitalize on one of the bigger plundering campaigns at the turn of the century: the radical seizure of Chinese cultural artifacts in the aftermath of the Boxer rebellion. The efforts of Bastian and his associates to take part in this action are worth exploring in detail for several reasons. To begin with, we know that museums of all kinds have benefited from wars, rebellions, punitive raids, and acts of imperial aggression and violence. Of the events that occurred during the late nineteenth century, the plundering of Benin has seen the most scholarly attention, much of which has emphasized the brutality of the military action. Yet as events surrounding the Boxer rebellion illustrate, such actions were not limited to *Naturvölker*; Europeans eagerly applied these tactics to "civilized" peoples, or *Kulturvölker*, as well. Indeed, ethnologists' actions during the aftermath of the Boxer rebellion reveal a learning curve of sorts, in which ethnologists appropriated the lessons of Benin and recognized Britain's punitive raid in Africa as a precedent that opened up new opportunities wherever indigenous governments fell to Western military forces.[42] Ethnologists' actions during this incident also show the ways in which the rhetoric of scientific authority was not just a strategy meant to keep up the public face of an ethnographic project with a darker side. It was often a lived idea, one that helped many ethnologists make sense of the contradictions between their actions and their ideals when they moved out of their museums and into the chaotic world of in situ acquisitions, and found themselves participating in imperialist opportunities that ran contrary to their cosmopolitan world views.

Shortly after the outbreak of violence against westerners in China and the quick response by a joint expedition of Western military forces in the summer of 1900,[43] ethnologists and other collectors and dealers recognized the Boxer rebellion as a rare opportunity for procuring valuable ethnographica. Only a month after the conflicts began, Bastian wrote to the General Administration of the Royal Museums in order to call their attention to the discord in Peking and stress the opportunities it presented to science. In this initial plea, Bastian pointed to earlier precedents, earlier mistakes, and more recent policies. He drew on the general history of museum acquisitions and stressed, for example, the importance of Napoleon's military campaigns for enriching Parisian museums. He argued that "if the victors had not later reclaimed their property," then "the art museums of the city on the Seine would have been liberally enriched by the Corsican conqueror's campaigns." He also warned the administration that the last opportunity for acquiring large numbers of Chinese artifacts had been overlooked, and argued that "European museums would currently be decorated with precious rarities from the history of Chinese art, if [they] had not failed to take advantage of the opportunities offered by the occupation of the Summer Palace during the 1860 campaign." Moreover, their previous failure to act in a timely fashion had put scientists in an uncomfortable position, because the small amount of "booty [*Beutestücke*] which was brought back to Europe ended up in the hands of dealers," who later sold it at "exorbitant prices." The precedents for action, in other words, had already been set. Tremendous opportunities for acquisition were created by the military occupation of foreign cities, and the strong competition from nonscientists was reason enough to act quickly.

Moreover, Bastian reminded the administration that a policy that endorsed using the military to enrich their museum's acquisitions already existed—one which tied together the imperatives of the ethnographic market with imperialist opportunities and ethnologists' scientific claims. The ethnological section of the Royal Museums had already received several rich collections in the wake of "military expeditions that ensued from colonial-political causes," and for this reason the Imperial Naval Office had issued instructions to its officers "that during punitive expeditions, the forfeited property of the guilty parties [*der Schuldigen*]"—or rather those who had evidently forfeited their property along with their human rights through conflicts with Western powers—"instead of being destroyed should be handed over" to the Berlin museum where they could be "preserved for the purpose of scientific study." Bastian stressed as well that although these regulations had been written regarding areas populated by "savage tribes" [*Wildstämme*], the situation in China was actually quite similar. It was therefore imperative, he argued, that German military contingents in China be reminded of the cultural importance of their mission "in order to avoid being affected by accusations of negligence, if they were too late to act."[44]

After receiving reports from German officials in China, however, Bastian's initial call for instructions to the German military quickly turned to agitation for ethnologists' direct participation in the plundering, as he recognized that other nations had beaten their military to the punch and that the greatest opportunities had already passed. In October 1900, the German Imperial diplomatic minister in Tientsin, Freiherr von der Goltz, painted a grim picture of events in the royal city. Describing the destruction by both Chinese and Western forces, he lamented that it was probably "already too late" for the Berlin museum to "salvage" much of anything. He wrote that the "Han lin Academy, with its extremely valuable library and handwriting collection, was set on fire by the Boxers and completely destroyed," and then went on to describe how Europeans quickly snatched up anything the Boxers might have missed:

> Immediately after the capture of Peking the participating troops — Japanese, English, American, and Russian — began systematically plundering the Imperial Palace, the residences of the princes and other imperial notables, the Imperial Ministries, temples, pawnshops, and stores. The Russians in particular have distinguished themselves through their ingenuity. They have taken control of all valuable objects such as silk embroidery, bronzes, porcelains, jades, etc. etc., which had not already been stolen by the palace servants, in the residential palace of the Emperor and the queen mother in Peking, as well as in their Summer residences in Wan-shau-shau and J-ho-yuau. Only the empty glass cabinets, stands, and wooden cases remain behind. Indian troops have been billeted in the wide grounds of the temple of the sky, the great sanctuary of Chinese theocracy, and have certainly taken away everything that was not nailed or screwed down. The genealogical tables that were stored there . . . have also been taken, and have evidently been appropriated by the British Museum.[45]

He noted as well that the British military was exceptionally well organized, declaring all items taken by their officers and soldiers governmental property, while objects procured by other forces were being auctioned off daily in Tientsin and other cities. "Most of the valuable objects," he emphasized, were already in boxes of "Chinese curiosities on their way to Europe and America."[46]

Goltz's reports prompted Bastian to lobby aggressively with the General Administration of the Royal Museums, the Prussian Cultural Ministry, and the German Foreign Office to immediately send German ethnologists to China. His rationale was three fold: he stressed the exceptional gains for science, the threat of freelance dealers cornering the market, and the practical political and economic advantages this action could bring the German nation. In a letter to the General Administration of the Royal Museums, he claimed that the interests of the Berlin museum could be "terribly damaged" if they did not act quickly, because items that were not swept up by the "competing museums" would — as they had in the 1860s — quickly find their way into the hands of "antique dealers" who, he reminded them, had already "established themselves along an entire street in the plundered capital."[47] Sending their own people to Peking would give them an opportunity to circumvent the dealers who would demand "exorbitant" prices, and allow them to cut out the middle men with whom they had been forced to do business following the sack of Benin.

Bastian, in fact, connecting his immediate economic rationalization with a scientific one, held up Benin as one of the central examples of how this sort of military expedition could be incredibly important for science:

> That military campaigns can bear fruit for scientific fields of research and can be *exploited* [my emphasis] for this purpose, is evidenced by multiple examples—recently again through the results of the conquest of Benin—and already proven most sensationally during the earlier French expedition to Egypt, which (through concomitance of a staff of 120 academics, artists, technicians, and engineers) laid the groundwork for the magnificent blossoming of Egyptology following the discovery of the Rosetta stone, the key to decoding hieroglyphics, which threw a flood of light onto the grayness of prehistoric times.[48]

There was, then, a long and repeatedly proven precedent that should continue to be followed. Teaming up with military expeditions, indeed, "exploiting" the opportunities that they—and imperialism in general—appeared to offer up to Europeans, he argued, was a proven way of making extraordinary gains for science.

But in addition to contributing to the greater scientific project and undercutting the dealers, Bastian also stressed a practical reason for governmental action, which went beyond the museums' economic and scientific concerns, and which distinguished this action from those that took place in other colonial areas. An ethnological expedition to Peking, he pointed out, could provide Germany with a critical advantage during the "peaceful international competition" over trade privileges with China, which was sure to become increasingly important in the coming "decades and centuries." A knowledge of "China's relevant organizational structures" in both the past and present, he argued, would give Germans a significant edge in future economic and diplomatic dealings. Science in general, and ethnology in particular, would provide the German nation with a decided political advantage in the years to come.

There was, however, another reason for action, one perhaps even closer to Bastian's personal motivations, which he revealed in a letter to Goltz: "While the American, English, French, and Russian museums will find their Chinese collections brilliantly endowed with trophies," Bastian wrote, "the Germans have come away empty handed." Although they were slow to act, he hoped that by taking advantage of China's weakened condition during the peacemaking process they could make up for the missed opportunity, and catch up with other Western museums.[49] Bastian was impressed with, and somewhat jealous of, what these museums had been able to obtain, and it is clear that given the opportunity, Bastian would have gladly participated in the wilder moments of plundering and forceful acquisitions.[50] The ends in this case more than justified the means.

In February 1901, the Prussian Cultural Ministry contacted Bastian and informed him that he had convinced them to send an ethnological mission to Peking.[51] F. W. K. Müller, an Asian specialist from the Berlin museum, was chosen as their representative.[52] He quickly left for China with instructions to collect as many antiquities, manuscripts, and ethnographic artifacts as his budget would allow,[53] and he was encouraged to try to set up relationships with Chinese and European diplomats who could assist him in going outside of Peking to obtain things from areas as yet untouched by other museums. In this way they hoped to make up for their lost opportunities and turn their late appearance to their advantage.

Müller's reports to Bastian reveal a genuine and optimistic conviction about the goals of his mission, and illustrate the ways in which the rhetoric of international science and the cosmopolitan ideals behind the ethnographic project allowed believers such as Müller to make sense of their actions in a chaotic world in which scientific specimens were bartered like tomatoes on the streets, and palaces that were once temples of material culture lay in ruins. Müller spent most of his time making contact with authorities in charge of different sections of the city, almost all of whom he found extremely cooperative. He acquired artifacts from a variety of sources and let his scientific training and his eye for scarcity guide his decisions. "Regarding acquisitions," he wrote, "the operative standpoint for me was, where possible, to only acquire those things that were absolutely unobtainable or very difficult to obtain under the usual conditions."[54]

Müller sought to use this chance to fill out his section of the museum, both for the good of the museum and for the use of scientists in general, and his enthusiasm for furthering the greater scientific project drove his efforts. Indeed, while the opportunism apparent in ethnologists' actions—both in this case and many others—is sometimes astounding, it should be borne in mind that although Bastian was willing to use governmental employees to buy up whatever they could, he preferred to send Müller or other ethnologists to the scene for a better, more systematic, and thus more scientific acquisition. Moreover, Müller, despite suffering from an illness during his trip, was nevertheless "running about daily from dawn until dusk" by foot, by horse, or with his wagon, attempting "to save what can still be saved for our museum."[55] His efforts were extensive, his conviction unswerving, and his intention clearly to work for an international science. Indeed, when we reflect on the context of the phrase "to save what can still be saved," which he wrote in a private letter to Bastian, not in a public declaration or an official report in which he might be trying to justify his actions, it is clear that this was not merely the use of a worn-out cliché. Müller sincerely believed that he was salvaging these items for the greater good and recognized a qualitative difference between his own actions and those of the dealers and other collectors motivated by personal gain. Moreover, the power of his conviction is given further testament by the willingness of officers from a number of different nations, with little or no prompting from him, to donate artifacts in their possession to his museum.

The fact that Müller's intentions were clear for all to see is particularly important, because it illustrates the ways in which the authority of science was much more than a rhetorical strategy that allowed him to cross political lines. Müller, the Berlin ethnologists, and the other Europeans in China, regarded his efforts as morally correct and believed that he was contributing to "salvaging" these "rare" material texts. The way in which he was able to internalize these beliefs allowed him to make sense of his actions in the streets of Peking. The destruction and pillaging of the city, in which he unquestionably played his own small part, was certainly in opposition to Virchow, Bastian, and Luschan's moralistic musings about European abuses abroad. This contradiction, however, and the fact that it played no role in their calculations, simply gives further testimony to the ambiguous relationships between ethnologists and their subjects, and the rather curious combination of humanitarian feelings and harsh scientific utilitarianism that a number of scholars have noted was so typical of the time.[56] Müller's story helps explain how the two coexisted.

Colonial Complications

Germany's emergence as a colonial power in 1884 brought both advantages and disadvantages to German collectors. On the one hand, German ethnologists could look to the colonial and economic associations as well as the national government for economic and logistic support. By providing colonial officials and colonists—especially the directors of plantations or other large projects relying on indigenous labor—with "knowledge" about the colonized subjects and cultures, they could link their efforts to colonialists' goals, make their science "useful," and gain increased support for their projects in German colonial territories.[57] On the other hand, colonialism also created new difficulties. It introduced governors, bureaucrats, and other officials who had to be appeased, rules and regulations that had to be followed, and borders that had to be crossed. Moreover, while colonial authorities could offer scientists a certain amount of added security in some situations, their presence also led to uprisings among indigenous populations, which subjected scientists to new dangers.[58] All of these factors inhibited collectors' movement and thus their ability to acquire artifacts for the museums.

Internal contention also resulted from the fact that not all German ethnologists and museums benefited equally from the German colonies, or from Germany's imperialist actions in places like Peking. Soon after Germany became a colonial power, a federal law was passed in 1888 that became known simply as the *Bundesratsbeschluss* among ethnologists. This law required all items collected in the colonial territories by government officials or by expeditions that were supported by any governmental funds to be sent to Berlin. Ethnographic items were supposed to be delivered to Berlin's *Völkerkunde* museum, sorted, and the doubles distributed to other German museums. In practice, however, little was redistributed. The Berlin museum became a stockpile for ethnographica from the colonial territories, and the bottleneck it created led to a remarkable lack of colonial materials in other German museums—a fact that shocked and dismayed a young Karl Weule when he arrived at the Leipzig museum in 1899 and realized the effect this law had had on its collections. This situation led him, Thilenius, and the directors of other German museums to join forces in an attempt to "break Berlin's monopoly." Their efforts eventually led to the creation of a coalition of non-Prussian museums and repeated public confrontations with Berlin's ethnologists and the federal government. This fight continued unresolved until 1914.[59]

Moreover, since the collection of ethnographic objects was meant to encompass the entire globe and museums were meant to be filled with artifacts from all corners of the world, colonialism's most important impact on the ethnographic project was the ways in which it made collecting in many areas of the world difficult or impossible. The creation of colonial territories and the establishment of many new non-European nations limited ethnologists' movements, reduced the traffic in artifacts, and made it almost impossible for German museums to obtain objects from many other nations' territories. As Europeans' possession of colonial territories was extended to the material culture of their colonial subjects, scientific missions became conflated with nationalist actions, leading to repeated conflicts between German collectors and officials from other nations.

By the last decade of the nineteenth century a number of new nations had passed laws regarding the sale and distribution of their historical and cultural artifacts. Mexico, for example, made the export of such artifacts illegal, essentially closing its borders to collectors in the 1890s. Bastian's attempts to get around this difficulty were repeatedly frustrated, because his usual tactic of offering to trade duplicates in his museum for duplicates in another were hindered by the fact that the Mexican government passed this law before building a museum of their own, leaving Bastian with no counterpart. His connections within Mexico were also unable to assist him, and in some cases they faced their own difficulties. As one contact in the Yucatan explained to him, he could occasionally smuggle out a few pieces, but not entire boxes of collections, and in fact he was himself a little concerned, because in order to get his own collection through the check points, he "would have to wait for a very special opportunity."[60]

Such actions not only frustrated ethnologists and forced them to develop new collecting strategies, they also had an immediate impact on the international market of material culture. These closures essentially manufactured scarcity and thus radically increased the value of any artifacts from these areas that were already in circulation. The collections assembled by Hermann Strebel in Mexico during the last quarter of the nineteenth century, for example, increased substantially in value after Mexico closed its borders, and when he began to sell these collections one at a time, German museums clamored to obtain them.[61]

Moreover, as ethnologists searched for new collecting tactics in an effort to maneuver around political constraints, they were forced to change their standards regarding the kinds of people they were willing to employ. Indeed, the very definition of what constituted a qualified collector changed in ways that ran directly counter to the professionalization taking place around the turn of the century. In 1904, for example, the Berlin museum hired H. von Zengen to work as a collector in Borneo. Zengen had no university education and hardly fit the new profile of the professional ethnological field worker that was becoming prominent in the first decade of the twentieth century. His technical qualifications were limited to a short education as a taxidermist at the natural history museum in Berlin and his experiences on an African safari. But his limited technical and professional credentials were sufficient for working in the Dutch colonial areas because he also possessed the two things that most German ethnologists did not—Dutch citizenship and a purported understanding of languages indigenous to Borneo.[62] As Albert Grünwedel at the Museum für Völkerkunde in Berlin stressed in a marginal notation on Zengen's application, Zengen's language abilities made him a strong candidate, but "especially favorable is the fact that the traveler has become a citizen of Holland, and as such should be able to easily procure permission to enter areas that would remain forever closed to a foreigner."[63] The constraints created by colonial borders, in other words, directly affected who could work with and for the museums, radically altering the priorities that normally governed their choice of collectors and undermining the process of professionalization.

The biggest change brought on by these new borders, however, was that collecting in general became more politicized as ethnologists increasingly found themselves crossing political borders in pursuit of their goals. Colonial politics cast doubts on scientific imperatives, and colonial administrators, officials, and colonists began regarding German ethnologists as first and foremost foreign nationals rather than members of an international scientific community. And, after a time, the younger generation of ethnologists who were focused on acquiring these collections also began thinking of themselves as such. Their world views shifted away from the cosmopolitan visions of Bastian's generation; they embraced their national characteristics, set aside their rationalizations about their contributions to the greater good, and began championing their prerogatives as ethnologists who were self-consciously German.

One conflict between Leo Frobenius and British colonial authorities in southern Nigeria provides an excellent example of the ways in which the ideals about the international community of science became reduced to empty rhetoric as museum directors abandoned their cosmopolitan visions in favor of their newfound rights as German scientists. Frobenius, whom many scholars regard as the first German field worker of note,[64] led a series of different expeditions into Northern Africa during the decade preceding World War I.[65] During his travels in Nigeria in 1911, Frobenius came into direct conflict with British authorities concerning his collecting policies in what has come to be known as the Olokun Affair.[66] This incident developed following complaints by inhabitants of Ifé, the "sacred capital of the Yoruba country" in southern Nigeria, that Frobenius had mistreated and deceived them, and had taken away religious objects without their consent.[67] The principle item of dispute was the bronze head of the god Olokun, which Frobenius claimed to have "discovered" in a grove outside the walls of Ifé, but which the town's inhabitants accused him of stealing. As a result of these complaints, which followed Frobenius's departure from the city, British authorities summoned Frobenius back to Ifé, brought him before an improvised British court, and eventually forced him to return many of the items he had acquired from the area.

British accounts of the incident describe Frobenius's behavior as uncooperative, dishonest, and at times childish. Their reports stress that, in the interest of "science" (and here they mean a sort of apolitical international science that commanded a certain moral authority), their agents had accommodated Frobenius from the beginning. In response to his requests for assistance, the British sent two hundred copies of ethnographic questionnaires ahead of him to British governmental officials in the area and instructed them to assist him in his efforts. Frobenius, however, "abused" this "courtesy" by "removing certain ancient stone monuments and other objects of value against the wishes and without the consent of the Oni [king]," and by refusing to cooperate with the British official in charge, the district commissioner Charles Partridge, who responded to the protests by native peoples. The British stressed that Frobenius instructed his assistants to hide many of the most valuable objects, claimed ignorance of their whereabouts, and then professed that he had "forgotten about them" or that "he knew nothing about it" when "sacred 'fetish' objects" were discovered in boxes concealed in the roof of the house he was occupying and "hidden under the ashes of a fire in a shed adjoining the kitchen." The British report also stated that according to the testament of the *Oni*, members of his family, the policemen who had accompanied Frobenius, and Frobenius's clerk and interpreter, Frobenius treated the priests "very roughly," forcing them to take money and whisky in exchange for the Olokun, and then "handing them a certificate written in German." The British also reported that Frobenius later apologized to the *Oni* after the proceedings were over and told Partridge, "'I admit that I went too 'wide' in getting the 'Olokun'"; he later confessed "'that he had not had enough respect for the people.'" The British foreign office, however, was particularly incensed, claiming that Frobenius had not only mistreated the people in Ifé and lied to Partridge, but that he had also written "absolutely erroneous and misleading accounts of the facts" in articles that appeared in the *Berliner Tageblatt* and other German newspapers, articles in which Frobenius claimed Partridge was forced to apologize to him—something the British government adamantly denied.[68] Frobenius, in short, had offended both their scientific and their moral standards of behavior.

Frobenius, however, portrayed this conflict in his private correspondence, newspaper accounts, and travel reports much differently. He cast this conflict as one between a German representative of the international community of science on the one hand, and British national and political interests on the other. Frobenius, in other words, much like the British in their own reports, used the authority of science to place himself rhetorically on moral high ground. According to Frobenius, the entire incident resulted from a mistranslation by one of his assistants[69] and the jealousy and maliciousness[70] of Partridge, whom Frobenius accused of committing "one of the greatest brutalities that was ever inflicted on the scientific body."[71] Indeed, if we are to believe Frobenius's charges, this was an action precipitated by British jealously and the inability of British anthropologists to keep up with German collectors.

Frobenius portrayed his party as the well-meaning and hapless victims. His written accounts stressed his fairness and the degree to which he tried to accommodate the wishes of the people of Ifé. He claimed that he always made sure that his sporadic excavations were not offensive, pointed out that he had often returned items when he learned that they had been stolen by another party, and also complained that residents of Ifé stole things from him which he had purchased fairly.[72] He explained events, in other words, in terms that would be readily acceptable to his readers, because they conformed to the ideals of international science.

While he had acted "properly," he argued, the English had been the true aggressors—intimidating the people under their administration, mishandling him and his employees, and mixing personal, political, and scientific goals. In many cases, he insisted, his efforts were hindered by the local people's fear of the English government, which, he was told, had exerted their authority over the material culture of peoples under their jurisdiction and forbidden the sale of many artifacts—effectively hindering his legitimate scientific project.[73]

Moreover, Frobenius claimed that Partridge had "done everything to make the trip impossible for us," allegedly hindering their permits and their attempts to hire porters, and supplying them with misinformation.[74] He condemned Partridge's treatment of his employees once the quasi-legal proceedings began,[75] implying that Partridge intimidated the city's residents, and he accused Partridge of carting away many of the items Frobenius had been forced to return.[76] But he also later bragged that he had outwitted Partridge on several occasions and had managed to keep some of these items out of British hands.[77] Most important, he accused the British representative of a great assault against science, stating that Partridge had "brutally torn apart and confused" a delicately assembled "net" of "scientific research" that would be impossible to reconstruct "in the near future."[78]

Both the German national government and the museum directors who hired Frobenius reacted immediately to the incident, but their responses were fundamentally different, and neither the government nor the directors acted out of a concern for the integrity of this international science. On the one hand, the German government was terribly upset with Frobenius, found the incident embarrassing, and as a result the German Foreign Office began to pressure Wilhelm von Bode, the director of the Royal Museums, to withdraw his support from Frobenius and leave him financially adrift. On the other hand, for Weule and Thilenius this incident was more an inconvenience than a serious concern, and because they were not directly tied to the national ministries, the question for them was less one of British-German relations, or even the integrity of Frobenius's actions, than of eluding the difficulties that accompanied colonial politics and ensuring that Frobenius continue his work in the field.

Indeed, Weule and Thilenius's actions during this affair make it clear that they had long since abandoned any concerns about how their collectors procured objects, or any need to justify these actions by relating them to a greater good, a cosmopolitan vision, or an international science. In fact, there is little evidence that the directors of these museums believed Frobenius's version of the incident. Nor was the "truth" of either British allegations or Frobenius's tale their chief concern. At issue for them was not so much the Africans' rights or Frobenius's collecting methods, but rather his attempts to effectively negotiate the obstacles placed in his way by the inhabitants of Ifé and the British colonial administration, and his ability to gain possession of good artifacts.

Consequently, the directors of the German museums rose to his defense, and despite the international incident and pressure from the German Foreign Office, neither Weule nor Thilenius was willing to withdraw his support from Frobenius or condemn his behavior. Although both admitted that he could be personally abrasive, and Thilenius noted that Frobenius's actions had certainly not been "unobjectionable," they quickly rationalized and legitimated his behavior based on his success as a collector, what they perceived as British incompetence, and Germans' authority as leaders in the ethnographic sciences.[79]

Weule, in fact, regarded the idea of returning artifacts or collections as completely out of the question, and he considered Frobenius's deception and uncooperative attitude toward the British as fitting to the situation. In his letter to the Leipzig city council in July 1911, for example, Weule defended Frobenius on all counts and condemned both British actions and the German government's misplaced concerns. Stating that neither he nor Thilenius regarded the complaints from the British foreign office as "tragic," he argued that "every resolute traveler endeavors to retain what he has acquired." "These cunning characters," he explained, "regularly use every opportunity to their advantage," and when an opportunity appears for one of them, as it had for Frobenius, to acquire more than the British ever have, "one cannot be surprised when [the British] retrospectively regard such purchases as invalid, indeed as impudent plunder." But, according to Weule, Frobenius's actions, even as described by the British, were completely justifiable and typical of the necessities involved in collecting. In his estimation it would be naive to expect either Frobenius or another collector to behave differently, since the goal of their efforts remained, ultimately, to gain as much as they could through whatever means possible.[80]

Moreover, Weule and Thilenius argued that the problem actually stemmed from the British, who did not understand *Völkerkunde* or the value of the material culture under their jurisdiction until after it was shown to them. A week after Weule defended Frobenius in Leipzig, they wrote to Bernard Ankermann, their counterpart in Berlin, in an attempt to induce him to convince Bode, the director of the Royal Museums, that Frobenius, despite his transgression, was really too valuable to abandon. Stressing that both he and Thilenius had already appealed to their local governments, and repeating many of the same arguments he used to convince their local supporters, Weule urged Ankermann to "take his excellence Bode aside" and explain to him the situation. As Weule saw it:

> The English government's letter of protest should be seen in Berlin as what it really is, the petty malevolence of jealous *Auch-Gelehrten*,[81] for whom the *somewhat careless action* [my emphasis] of a German offered a welcome occasion to discredit *das Europäertum* 100% in the eyes of the blacks. Why then have the good Englishmen not concerned themselves with the ethnography and archeology of their territories before this? And what sort of crazy short-sightedness motivated him to expose a member of the white race before the black pack in such a way? Moreover, between us, don't you agree that it is a bad collector who returns what he has already obtained?[82]

Frobenius, he argued, was effective because he knew how best to collect, and in Weule's mind the British were simply jealous of Frobenius because he had achieved what they had not even thought to do. Of course Frobenius had been "somewhat careless," forgetting, perhaps that he must proceed more cautiously in areas controlled by the British, but his methods were essentially effective and good. And who after all, he wanted to know, were the British to criticize Frobenius's tactics or the tactics of any other German collector when it was clearly the Germans who were spearheading this international science? "Especially we Germans," he wrote, "with our contributions to *Völkerkunde* have the least reason to eat crow before a people [*Volk*] who possess 31 million square kilometers of colonial territory and whose combined ethnographic collections still do not amount to so much as a single section of your Berlin museum. Speak again with Bode in these terms."[83] As Weule made clear, the importance of Frobenius's achievements were given testament by the effectiveness of his results, an effectiveness which legitimated his (and other German collectors') methods and threw British complaints into question, even as their evident incompetence in the realm of *Völkerkunde* undermined their authority to judge him. The most acceptable methods among people in tune with the culture of collecting ethnographica, Weule clearly argued, were those that produced results, and the Germans more than anyone else knew what those methods were.

Moreover, as Thilenius reminded Ankermann, Frobenius was a tested and highly successful collector, he was gaining artifacts that would soon be impossible to acquire, and Bode and Ankermann would be making a grave mistake if they disassociated themselves from him, because he was clearly the best candidate for the job and the only one who could take advantage of the present opportunities. "Who among German ethnographers," he asked, came even close to Frobenius's "command" and understanding of "this area of west-African culture," and "who is in a better position to do the collecting than Frobenius?" Frobenius could easily be offensive and tactless, but that "says nothing, absolutely nothing about his scientific [qualifications] or anything about his qualifications as a collector." Moreover, he stressed, the timing alone justified Frobenius's actions: "train lines are being laid out or planned everywhere, and you know the devastating results that will follow as well as I. Under these conditions there is no question whether and to what extent I will support Frobenius, so long as I have the money." Regardless of whether Frobenius's behavior was right or wrong, and despite the protests and the sensation in the press,

Thilenius argued that the important point to bear in mind was not Frobenius's actions during or after the incident, but his achievements.[84]

The contexts of Frobenius's actions remained the critical factor for their evaluation and the kinds of rhetorical strategies each group chose to adopt. From the British perspective, his actions were contemptible because they stemmed from a German scientist operating within British territory, and his behavior had threatened their authority. British accusations, of course, were not formulated in exactly this way; rather they focused on Frobenius's treatment of Africans, and the British defense of their rights. Yet considering the British's own record in Benin, and the fact that some of the artifacts Partridge retrieved from Frobenius did actually end up in the British Museum, their attempts to evoke the moral high ground ethnologists often claimed and the argument set forth by C. H. Read at the British Museum, that "Mr. Partridge is to be commended and England congratulated on his prompt action in preventing the sacred places of natives under our rule from being pillaged," still rings somewhat hollow.[85] At the same time, accusations by German ethnologists that the British were engaged in a defensive reaction to an encroachment on their areas cannot be discounted; such reactions were typical for the time. Equally typical was the German ethnologists' complete abandonment of any desire to take up a moral position in this context and their assertions that scientific success legitimated harsh or extreme measures, that the ends essentially justified the means. The directors of German museums recognized that their collectors should attempt to move a bit more "carefully" in other nations' colonial territories, but the concern revolved around negotiating the political power of these colonial authorities, not respecting the rights of the colonized peoples. Indeed, Weule's language makes it clear that he was less concerned with respecting "the black pack" than with keeping Africans in their place.

The controversy surrounding the Olokun Affair and the language used to describe the events thus illustrates how rationalizations and standards of acceptability changed from one context to another. Frobenius, for example, spoke much differently about the affair in his private correspondence with Weule than he did in his travel writings or news releases, and Weule's arguments about respect for other cultures fell to the wayside when discussing acquisitions for his museum and British attempts to hinder one of his collectors.[86] Moreover, while the international controversy had focused on collecting methods and attitudes toward native peoples, the scientific discussion remained centered around priorities, revealing the different faces of ethnology during this period and providing us with insight into the degree to which the directors of German museums had abandoned their vision of a cosmopolitan community and embraced their own particularist goals. The ideals of international science with which Müller had rationalized his actions were no longer necessary in a world in which any action is legitimate and the only justification needed is its utility. Weule's recognition that anything goes, that "these cunning characters regularly use every opportunity to their advantage," expresses the essential standard of behavior which placed the priority on possession rather than actions.

However, Weule's recognition that Frobenius had also been somewhat "careless," or Thilenius's comment that Frobenius's behavior was not "unobjectionable," reveal how the public face of science required slightly more polished standards than the realities of collecting in a chaotic world might allow—a fact which savvy collectors wisely bore in mind when operating under the scrutiny of another power that might use the contradiction between actions and image to their political advantage. Frobenius's account of the incident in his travel reports, which stressed a respect for local people, emphasized fair dealings, and called for international cooperation, actually provides us with a portrait of how ethnographic collecting might be conducted in a world where cosmopolitan visions guided collector's actions, and a view of ethnology which ethnologists continued to use to fashion scientific legitimacy. At the same time, the British accounts and the defensive statements of the museum directors illustrate the contradictions between the myth of proprieties and the realities of collecting.

Colonial politics thus added an extra element of complexity to the process of acquisition. Ethnology was pursued in a world that was divided by political borders and boundaries that complicated the pursuit of artifacts and knowledge. These borders inhibited ethnologists' ability to create complete collections and fill their museums with the material culture of peoples from all areas of the world. Political divisions helped transform museums founded on cosmopolitan principles into national institutions, and they contributed to the uneven distribution of artifacts in German museums: Mexico was out of bounds, the Dutch colonies were closed, and the German colonies were now the sole domain of scientists in Berlin. Moreover, the division of the world into colonial empires transformed Germans' ethnographic project at the conceptual level. German cultural scientists abandoned their cosmopolitan visions and embraced their identity as Germans. They became increasingly particularist in their orientations, and willing to use their self-proclaimed position as leaders in the ethnographic sciences to justify their actions. They began to accept, even celebrate their participation in a Conradian universe in which the ethnographic project had been reduced to assembling whatever they could acquire by any means possible, and in which the apolitical nature and cosmopolitan ideals of their science had become a thin veneer, useful for opening doors abroad, or as justification after the fact, but not as a guide for collecting.

"The Case of Frič"

The wide range of individuals who made careers out of collecting ethnographica for European museums acted in liminal zones between empire and indigenousness. The corruption of the ideals that gave birth to the ethnographic project were difficult to overlook in these "contact zones,"[87] where the slippage between utilitarian actions and the rhetoric of an apolitical, cosmopolitan science began taking place, and where, by the turn of the century, it was often difficult to tell scientists from charlatans.[88] Yet despite the growing willingness of the museums' directors to accept the realities of collecting, the public face of ethnology could not be abandoned. The museums and the contact zones were in many ways two different worlds that called for two sets of ideals, and ethnologists' professional identities required that the division between these worlds be maintained. Yet, as the case of Alberto Vojtěch Frič demonstrates, these two worlds could easily collide. The more people museums sent into the field, the less control they had over their actions, and the greater the risk that these collectors might engage in activities that could undermine ethnologists' efforts and reputations. And the more the museums' collectors used the authority of science as a rhetorical tool, the more it was open to abuse, and the more ethnologists ran the risk that the disparities between the real and the ideal might be brought out in the open and the authority of science called into question.

In September 1906, Alberto Vojtěch Frič arrived in Buenos Aires carrying letters of introduction and papers identifying him as a representative of the ethnographic museums in Hamburg and Berlin. Frič had no ethnological training and only limited academic credentials. This was, however, his third trip to South America, and during his last excursion in 1904, he had assembled an ethnographic collection that was good enough to convince Karl von den Steinen and Eduard Seler, the directors of the American section of the Berlin museum, as well as Thilenius in Hamburg, to send him back to South America to collect for them.[89]

Frič's collecting efforts immediately after his arrival were fairly successful, but he soon ran into problems. His credentials as a representative of two German museums helped him secure the assistance of the German consulate in Curitiba, who supported his first major expedition into the jungles of Argentina. During this initial excursion he was able to assemble a collection of artifacts from the "Sambaquicultur," which he was convinced no German museum could equal.[90] But he also contracted malaria and began running short of funds, and soon after he returned from the forests, he began bombarding Thilenius with requests for more money and suggestions that he alter his original plans and, among other things, travel south to collect in Tierra del Fuego or visit the Spas in Uruguay for a few months of convalescence.[91] Frustrated that Thilenius refused to send him more money or let him alter his original plans, he began looking elsewhere for new associations and soon became affiliated with the "patriotic league for the conversion of the Indians," or simply the "Liga," an organization pledged to fight for the protection of Indians in Brazil.[92]

Soon after he joined the Liga, Frič's actions degenerated from being somewhat unorthodox to utterly bizarre. Proclaiming himself "Pacificador dos Indios," Frič began writing a series of articles for South American newspapers condemning the treatment of Indians at the hands of the Brazilian government and German colonists.[93] Soon afterwards, he traveled to Blumenau, a German-dominated city in the Brazilian state of Santa Catharina, where he openly and aggressively denounced its citizens.[94] He condemned their participation in "punitive expeditions" against the Indians, accused them of supporting bands of Indian hunters, reproached them for condoning a clandestine slavery, and claimed that many local priests had even taken a leading role in perpetrating these inhumane crimes.

An uproar quickly followed, and a flood of questions, condemnations, and demands from private individuals, nationalist and colonialist organizations, and various government officials in Germany and Brazil were directed at the German Foreign Office, Wilhelm von Bode, Thilenius, and the ethnologists in the Berlin museum. Most damning were the long, detailed letters from Dr. Hugo Gensch, a resident of Blumenau, who explained that while he had long opposed abuses against the Indians in Brazil and initially welcomed the Liga's decision to take on an "Indian researcher" to assist them, he had quickly become incensed after Frič's arrival in the city.[95]

Gensch drew on his authority as a doctor, a long-term resident of Brazil, and someone familiar with scientists and the local Indians to question Frič's intellectual abilities, his scientific qualifications, and his mental stability, and to strongly condemn his moral character. Gensch described Frič as "a somewhat shabby person who wore a loaded revolver on his belt and carried a small camera in his hand with great ostentation," and who, as he arrived in Blumenau, was filled with an arrogant self-importance because of his letters of introduction and a request from the governor that the city support his efforts at their own cost.

The bulk of Gensch's accusations were drawn from a meeting with Frič in the doctor's home. Gensch explained that Frič had no understanding of the Indian problem and posited "fantasy plans" for relocating groups of Indians. Gensch wrote as well that Frič became absurdly excited by a rumor that one of the Indian women captured during a recent raid had become pregnant thirteen months after being delivered to a local mission, and boasting of his earlier exploits and his willingness to use his revolver to threaten such perpetrators, discussed leading an investigation to the mission.

However, the conversation quickly changed from "ridiculous" to disturbing when Frič asked to examine the twelve-year old Indian girl Gensch had taken into his home, and revealed a "certain perversity" that he "as an old experienced doctor" had already sensed in the first moment he saw him. Gensch described Frič's improprieties in detail: Frič asked for the girl to disrobe so that he could take pictures of her, but the doctor forbade this, claiming that too many photos of this type already existed. Frič then asked "in the presence of [the doctor's] wife," if the girl was still a virgin, and not only suggested that the doctor examine her while she slept but posited that he would find signs of abuse, "probably from a priest." After this "shocking" series of inquiries, Frič began with an "absurd" attempt to determine the girl's tribal affiliation through a language exam which, Gensch argued, immediately revealed the weakness of Frič's own abilities as he attempted to speak to the girl using words written in a small notebook, "few of which he actually understood," and numbers that he consistently confused and mispronounced.[96] Gensch explained that as an "indecent inspection of the arms, breast," and other areas followed, the doctor tried to end the discussion, claiming to be tired, at which point Frič suggested that the doctor bring the child to his hotel room the next day and leave her with him for several hours so that he could take "anthropological measurements" of her features. Gensch was appalled by this suggestion and argued that given that "his entire equipment consisted of his camera, a small stereoscope, his small notebook . . . and a book (probably a volume of v[on] d[en] Steinen's travel report)," he felt that Frič had other, less honorable intentions.

In addition to listing Frič's improprieties in his home, Gensch also described Frič's actions in the town as dangerous and bizarre. He discussed how Frič "accosted" many citizens in the most "uncomfortable way." He related how Frič was thrown out of the offices of the *Urwaldsbote*, the local German nationalist paper. He explained how nativist elements were using Frič as a foil against Germany and that Frič was seen at an anarchist conference. And he described how Frič created a scandal by appearing before the "courts" and demanding that police accompany him to the local mission—spurring the "Superior of the Franciscan mission" to travel to the capital and lodge a personal complaint with the governor. In the end, as the "discord" in Blumenau turned particularly ugly, and Frič—according to Gensch—was in danger of "receiving a beating," he was placed in a "pitiful farm wagon" by the city government and essentially run out of town.[97]

Frič, of course, adamantly denied Gensch's accusations about his moral character and the more bizarre aspects of his behavior; but none of this actually concerned Thilenius or his counterparts in Berlin. His great ostentation and overbearing attitude, the grandiose statements about his revolver, even the stories about the photographs he carried of himself and Indian women together naked in the forests,[98] or Gensch's allusions about his perversity, were all part of the weird corruptness of these contact zones that museum directors had already acknowledged they could not control. No eyebrows were raised, no shocked statements were released, and, in fact, these stories received almost no mention in the directors' correspondence with each other. They all simply agreed that they had never considered Frič to be "completely normal,"[99] and that his character was no more an issue than the fate of the Indians or even the fact that Frič's supposedly wild accusations about the savage abuse visited upon Indians by German colonists and Brazilian authorities—if mistaken in many of the particulars—were essentially true.

However, Frič's willingness to engage in local politics while representing two German scientific institutions, and, indeed, his willingness to use his authority as an "Indian researcher" to allow him to become involved in these politics, was another matter. These actions threatened to undermine ethnologists' authority and reputations, and led to his almost immediate dismissal. Moreover, Frič's arguments that his trip to Blumenau had been necessary because he had felt morally obligated to try to stop what he regarded as heinous crimes by the German colonists, and his exclamation that his position in the "service of German science" should not require him to let "criminals of German descent" simply "walk away" were not effective.[100] In fact they were not even mentioned in the directors' correspondence with each other, and they did nothing to dissuade Thilenius or Bode from violating their own contracts and dropping him once he had compromised their museums.

Frič's actions in Blumenau enraged the German Foreign Office, which demanded that Thilenius and Bode terminate Frič's contracts. But the directors' decisions to do this were not simply a response to the demands of the Foreign Office. Rather they were a reaction to Frič's willingness to mix science with politics and his inability to produce first-rate collections. The Foreign Office could be ignored, and indeed, in the case of Frobenius, Thilenius had no reservations about defending his collector's tactless behavior and ignoring its demands. But whereas Frobenius produced exceptional collections, Frič's abilities as a collector were unclear, even under suspicion. Because despite the fact that Seler had found Frič's 1904 collection "astonishingly well-preserved,"[101] the artifacts Frič sent Thilenius from Brazil arrived poorly packed and poorly organized, several of the pieces were broken, and the catalog was not in good order. Moreover Thilenius had reason to believe that part of it had been purchased in Blumenau, and consequently he regarded it as having little scientific value.[102] Thus Thilenius had little reason to support Frič against the wave of accusations or to risk his own reputation in the hope that Frič's next collection might be better.

Moreover, the risks were significant. The rhetorical division between politics and science was one ethnologists carefully guarded, despite their own understanding of the realities of collecting and the fact that they had come to accept the politicized nature of their actions. This division was critical for maintaining their scientific authority, their professional identities, and their ability to gain support from a range of individuals both at home and abroad. Indeed it was the ostensibly apolitical nature of their interests and actions that allowed them to build up their acquisition networks and cross as many borders as they did. But politics that dealt with the treatment of indigenous peoples were particularly sensitive, because these had the potential to expose the disparity between ethnologists' cosmopolitan visions, their purported liberal humanism, and the realities of collecting in a colonialist world. Frič's actions threatened to bring scrutiny to bear on ethnologists' roles and responsibilities in the contact zones of South America, and for this reason as much as because of the quality of his last shipment of artifacts, Berlin and Hamburg quickly terminated his contracts, and Frič was left penniless and without resources in South America.[103]

Indeed, when Frič revisited his charges against the Brazilian government and German colonists a year later at the Sixteenth International Congress of Americanists in Vienna, the division between "science" and "politics" quickly became the center of debate both in the lecture halls in Vienna and the public newspapers in Berlin.[104] The immediate effort by all parties to salvage what was left of the veneer of their apolitical science in the face of Frič's accusations vividly illustrates the importance this division had for ethnologists in general. According to the *Neue Freie Presse*, when Frič turned his presentation on Brazilian Indians into a forum for denouncing abuses against the Indians and the termination of his contracts, a heated debate immediately ensued among members of the audience until Eduard Seler "firmly declared . . . that absolutely no political questions should be touched upon during the congress." Frič, however, responded that "if political questions spill over [into scientific areas], then they must also be discussed." At which point Karl von den Steinen called out that "political questions must be kept absolutely separate," and Professor Ambrosetti from Buenos Aires, who was chairing the meeting, began "clanging the bell" and calling the session back to order.[105]

Frič's outburst in Vienna received considerable coverage in Berlin's most important dailies,[106] and during this coverage, Frič was denounced as a Czech nationalist, explained away as a fanciful idealist, and criticized for "meddling in things that did not concern him." But no one supported his argument that scientists must address political or humanitarian issues when confronted with them while abroad, or his insistence that ethnologists, as the people in Europe with the best knowledge of the Indians, should take it upon themselves to publicly protest such abuses. Rather, there was a general agreement in all the dailies that, as von den Steinen argued, "the colonial-political absolutely does not belong in the forum of this congress,"[107] and that even during the pubic discussions in Berlin, "two aspects must be kept separate: Herr Frič's relationship to the Berlin museum and the Indian question in Santa Catharina, which for their part are to be divided into scientific and colonial or ethical questions." Indeed, the *Berliner Tageblatt* even responded by issuing an editorial that explained what they assumed was common knowledge: ethnologists could, like everyone else, have political opinions that were critical of a state's actions, but because of their association with the international scientific community, these opinions could only be expressed in certain ways: "If [Frič] wanted to accuse the German settlers of inhumane acts against the indigenous peoples, [he] should have taken these charges to the Brazilian government, or included his assertions objectively in the report over his research trip."[108] Scientists, then, could certainly voice political or moral opinions, but they should be expressed in private letters to local governments, or in travel reports—as Frič had earlier done in his initial publications—and which very few people ever read.[109]

As Frič blurred the border between politics and science, he also jeopardized the authority of "science" on which so much of ethnologists' professional identities were based. For this reason, von den Steinen strongly emphasized—despite his own references to experiencing a kind of "paradise" among the Indians of South America and his epithet as a "warmhearted friend of the Indians"[110]—that the division between politics and science must be maintained. Any breach of this tenet was threatening, because if collectors became political critics, then the willingness of local authorities to allow collectors in their midst or to support their efforts would, in many cases, quickly diminish. Similarly, if a scientific conference became a political forum where nonscientific questions could be fielded and entertained, then these forums would be opened up to nonspecialists, and the privileged spaces of science invaded. Scientists, in other words, would lose control over their own meetings and their authority over their fields of "knowledge" if they did not strictly maintain control of the topics and the means of discussion during their meetings. Consequently, because the division between science and politics preserved as well as limited their authority, it was in the scientists' best interest to respect and reinforce this division. The politics of their science made it clear that maintaining these rules of separation worked to everyone's advantage, and everyone seemed to understand this—everyone except Frič.

By the early twentieth century, ethnologists' ambiguous relationships with the state, their subjects, and the excesses of imperialism were well-known secrets—but secrets best left unspoken, nevertheless. The great challenge for the new generation of museum directors thus became to achieve a balance between the older cosmopolitan traditions that provided them with much of their cultural authority, and the modern, capitalist, and increasingly nationalist character of their professional pursuits. This effort had a tremendous impact on their decisions about collecting and even the goals of their science. Their new imperative became to sustain their scientific project by negotiating power structures in ways that would allow them to maintain their apolitical, moral, and professional public images while continually pursuing ever-greater acquisitions by whatever means possible. This new imperative governed the ways in which they coordinated their collectors and the ways they themselves acted in the field. In the end, it left them operating in a gray zone in which the priorities of their science overshadowed their concerns about the treatment of colonized peoples, and their actions as ethnologists in pursuit of collections contradicted their vehement condemnations of European abuses as the bearers of scientifically substantiated "truth." This new generation of ethnologists eagerly embraced the realities of an often bizarre, Conradian universe of collecting, in which the ideals that gave birth to the ethnographic project were best left at home. They accepted that they were working in the debris of the postcontact moment, and they continued to fill their museums beyond their capacity. But this action now found its greatest justification in itself.

FOUR

THE AUDIENCE
AS AUTHOR

MUSEUMS IN PUBLIC

Ich will mich *hier* zu deinem
Dienst verbinden,
Auf deinem Wink nicht rasten
und nicht ruhn;
Wenn wir uns *drüben* wieder-
finden,
So sollst du mir das gleiche tun.

[I'll bind myself to be your
servant here / And tireless in
your service I shall be; / If
when there in the yonder we
appear, / You will do the same
by me.]—Goethe, *Faust*

German ethnologists faced a Faustian dilemma almost immediately after establishing their museums. The expense of building and running these institutions required the directors to turn to local elites, wealthy patrons, and municipal and state governments for assistance, a step which allowed these groups to influence ethnologists' efforts both inside and outside their museums. The scientific legitimacy of the museums rested on maintaining the standards expected by the international community of science, but their social legitimacy required the directors and their assistants to meet both these scientific standards and create institutions that their supporters found useful and pleasing. Successful directors proved incredibly adept at juggling their scientific and social commitments, but the networks and alliances they created to ensure their success came at a price: by the first decade of the twentieth century, and largely due to external pressures, ethnologists began shifting their focus from creating reliable scientific institutions to fashioning popular displays.

The critical link between the museums' social and scientific legitimacy was their audiences. These audiences can be broken down into four essential groups, each of which influenced the museums in fundamental ways. Members of the international scientific community visited each others' museums, scrutinized their architecture, holdings and displays and, when displeased, pronounced cogent judgments that quickly initiated change. Patrons called for immediate modifications of museums' organization and exhibits, but not necessarily for scientific reasons. Local elites questioned ethnologists' arrangements based on their own understandings of this science. They demanded that the museums' atmosphere and aesthetics meet their standards for public institutions and, by the turn of the century, they began calling for ethnologists to pay more attention to the educational roles of their museums. Perhaps most importantly, the increasingly broad and, as many ethnologists referred to them, "uneducated" elements of museums' audiences, gained critical influence with the rise of mass politics and culture in the late nineteenth century.

Because of these cities' different characteristics, the museums in Hamburg, Berlin, Leipzig, and Munich attracted a different combination of visitors from these four "ideal" groups. But in each case, there was a diachronic development between the museums and their audiences, a mutual transformation of science and civic society. Indeed, in many ways the variations in the museums' audiences account for the chief differences in these museums' historical trajectories. In each museum, social demands channelled and shaped ethnologists' scientific efforts and priorities, they pushed reforms in the museums' organization and displays, and by the turn of the century, they drew ethnologists away from their initial vision and changed their most essential goals.[1]

The International Community of Science

German ethnographic museums were constructed under internationally fashioned (and sanctioned) standards, which were often maintained through the disciplinary power of visiting ethnologists' "scientific" gaze. Indeed, an international community of science set the most basic standards and parameters that guided the development of German ethnographic museums. Whether ethnologists or their supporters were planning new buildings, creating new displays, or rethinking their intellectual and pedagogical methods and goals, German ethnologists—like most of their non-German counterparts—relied heavily on contact with other museums to help set their agendas and solve their problems. This was true for all aspects of the museums, ranging from ethnologists' methodological and theoretical concerns to the most mundane problems of day-to-day operations. They exchanged tips on where and how to collect, about methods of observation, and on tactics of acquisition. They debated the pros and cons of different kinds of cabinets, shelves, hallways and rooms, discussed different kinds of organization and lighting, different means of storage and preservation, and they argued about the best types of arrangement and display.

Even the physical spaces within "German" museums were envisioned and created in the midst of international comparison, emulation, and exchange. Each time a new ethnographic museum was built in Germany it began with excursions: The architects and members of the museums' staffs went abroad to visit other museums, note the advantages and disadvantages of particular architectural styles, study their methods of organization, and mine other institutions for inspiration about how to build "the best possible museum."[2] In 1908, for example, Georg Thilenius and his architect produced an extensive report on the state of European museums, and based their recommendations for a new museum building on "observations of over 100 museums."[3] And in 1912, as Berlin was planning another new building for its *Völkerkunde* museum, Wilhelm von Bode, director of Berlin's Royal Museums, took it upon himself to tour the different ethnographic museums in Europe and the United States for precisely the same reasons.[4]

Of course, ethnologists visited their counterparts' museums at other times as well. They went to work with particular collections, stopped by on their way to conferences and exhibitions, and took trips abroad simply to survey the institutional landscape and evaluate the state of the field. These visiting scientists were a key component of the museums' audiences, and ethnologists and their sponsors throughout Europe generally welcomed them. Foreign scientists' interest in a given museum confirmed its importance; positive evaluations enhanced its reputation; and the directors of most European and American museums usually sought to emulate any aspects these visitors praised in their published reports.[5] At the same time, ethnologists were often dismayed if their museums were overlooked during a foreign scientist's tour. Both Hermann Obst in Leipzig and A. B. Meyer in Dresden, for example, wrote distraught letters to George Brown Goode in 1883, when they realized that their institutions had not been included in his report on European museums. Of course, they would have been even more distraught if they received negative evaluations.[6] Strong criticism by such visitors, in fact, often resulted in immediate changes to the museums they had toured.

In Chapter one I discussed how the Danish ethnologist Kristian Bahnson's published criticisms of Hamburg's ethnographic museum in 1887 sparked public debates that essentially forced the city government to revamp the museum's budget and move it into a newer, better location. This was in no way an isolated incident. Only a few years earlier, for example, Professor Erico Hillner Giglioli from Florence published an equally influential critique of Leipzig's ethnographic museum in an Italian journal following his own 1880 tour of European museums.[7] In a manner similar to Bahnson's, Giglioli lauded the extent of the museum's collections, its director's endeavors, and the support it received from its members. But he also condemned the conditions in which the collections were stored, the completely "inadequate space" set aside for displays, the museums' total "lack of order," the inability of the museum to keep pace with currently accepted "scientific standards," and, according to him, the surprisingly limited support this scientific institution received from the government of this "well-known university city."

Giglioli's criticisms of the museum's conditions added the influential voice of the international community of science to a scandal that was already brewing around the inadequate conditions in the museum and the lack of attention it received from the university and the city.[8] This scandal peaked the following year and ultimately led to a renewed pledge of support from the city, increased funding for acquisitions, a commitment to purchasing the expensive and well-know Godeffroy collection,[9] and a 1,400,000 Mark award-winning new building.[10] The Leipzig city council, pushed into motion by the evaluations of outside visitors like Giglioli as much as by their own ethnologists, agreed that losing this museum would be an unbearable blow to the city's reputation as a center of learning. As Oberbürgermeister Otto Georgi put it, "one would certainly never understand, either in our city or outside of it, if Leipzig—a primarily trade and university city—did not want to maintain an institute that appears to so clearly complement these activities and interests."[11]

Visiting scientists thus had tremendous disciplinary power: Their praise could greatly enhance or even secure a museum's reputation, while their critiques could undermine its very legitimacy among scientists and laymen alike.[12] Because ethnologists and their supporters depended on these evaluations to ensure and enhance their reputations, both native and foreign scientists were consistently regarded as one of the most important components of ethnographic museums' audiences, even as these audiences grew increasingly broad and socially diverse during the first decades of the twentieth century.

Patrons

It is no secret who the great patrons of Germany's ethnographic museums were; their names were found throughout the museums' publications, and one can still see them carved into entryways or etched into brass plaques adorning walls. Several pages of the introduction to the 1887 guide to Berlin's *Museum für Völkerkunde*, for example, were devoted to listing and paying thanks to the museum's patrons. Organizations such as the Königliche Akademie der Wissenschaft, the Humboldt-Stiftung, the Afrikanischer Gesellschaft, and the museum's famous Hilfskomitee were prominent among them. Well-placed individuals like Geh. Reg.-Rat Dr. Werner Siemens and wealthy enthusiasts like Dr. Hans Meyer, heir to the Meyer publishing house in Leipzig, are placed alongside adventurers like Hermann von Wissmann, the nationally celebrated African explorer, and governmental ministers in foreign cities, such as the Minister-Resident von Bergen in Guatemala, Consul Sahl in Sidney, and Consul Kellner in Natal—all arranged according to social and military ranking, with only the most celebrated explorers such as Wissmann usurping the order. At the end of the list the reader finds an array of well-known and once-aspiring ethnologists whose donations and efforts helped fill the museum, and a special place is given to the Prussian Crown Prince, members of the royal family, the admiralty, and the ships' captains who so often assisted the museum. All these names can be found in other sections of the guide book as well.[13] They were woven into the descriptions of collections. Many were inscribed on the cabinets and cases containing their donations, and many of the labels attached to the artifacts on display bore their names.[14] The museums' patrons were constantly present, intimately tied to the artifacts and publications, and prominently displayed.

These patrons were also critical members of the museums' audiences, engaged in surveying and critiquing the museological landscape based on their own, particular visions of propriety and order. Indeed, ethnologists recognized that they were operating under their patrons' gazes while creating "their scientific displays." Because of their debt to their patrons, the directors of these museums were forced to constantly negotiate their divergent motives and interests.

Almost all of the gifts German ethnographic museums received, for example, came with strings attached. This was true of the large donations from people like Heinrich Schliemann, who defied ethnologists' methods when arranging his collection in the Berlin museum, as well as the smaller collections and individual objects from travelers, explorers, businessmen, and others. Schliemann's celebrated collection of artifacts from what he claimed was ancient Troy, for example, was considered an exceptional treasure, and securing this collection for the Berlin museum was regarded by Rudolf Virchow and others as a point of national pride.[15] Consequently, Schliemann's conditions—that his collection be kept together in rooms bearing his name—were readily accepted,[16] and Schliemann himself was allowed to arrange the displays.[17] While doing this he often showcased individual items in a manner common to art museums, but which actually went against ethnologists' efforts to create an open structure and de-emphasize individual pieces. Like many other patrons, Schliemann regarded the collection as his own creation, eschewed a systematic arrangement, and demanded that his "best" pieces be given pride of place. Because of their desire to possess these prestigious collections, the museum's ethnologists and supporters felt forced to accept his conditions despite the fact that his displays did not conform to their standards. This patron, in other words, not only influenced these exhibits, he created them with little regard for the museum's scientific mission and demanded they be left unchanged.

The owners of other extensive or singular collections often had a similar amount of direct control and influence. Alphons Stübel, for example, who was born in Leipzig and later became a resident of Dresden, was well-known in the 1880s and 1890s for his extensive travels and ethnographic research with Wilhelm Riess in South America. In 1891, Stübel offered to donate a large collection of drawings, paintings, photographs, and maps of Ecuador to the Leipzig *Völkerkunde* museum to be included in its monumental new building as a section devoted to *Länderkunde*. While certainly less famous than Schliemann's collection from Troy, Stübel's was nevertheless celebrated in the scientific community. It also promoted a particular scientific interpretation of human development: linking geography and ethnology closely together, it delivered a clear message that variations among humans were closely tied to environmental conditions.[18]

The museum's ethnologists immediately accepted this well-known "treasure" as well as Stübel's conditions—namely that the collection be kept together and be given a particular amount of space. He required the architect Hugo Licht to rethink his plans for the building in order to accommodate these interests,[19] negotiated with the museum's director several times for more space,[20] and ultimately chose where in the museum the collection would be placed. In fact when he discovered that the third floor of the right wing of the new building, which was meant to hold a prehistory collection belonging to the local history association, would be better suited for his collections than the rooms he had initially chosen, he pressed the director to allow him to set up his displays on the third floor. Moreover, the second floor of this wing, which had previously been allotted to his *Länderkunde* collection, was not given to the history association in exchange. Rather Stübel was able to have it held in reserve for the future expansion of his collection, while the history association was promised a place in a proposed future expansion.[21]

Once the museum was opened in 1896, Stübel continued to control the collection, the rooms' atmosphere, and the displays. Soon after the opening he had the lighting changed, complaining that the viewer could see "the red roofs of neighboring houses and buildings in the glass" covering many of the pictures, and that this "evil" (*übelstand*) had been noticed by "other experts" as well.[22] As new pieces were added to the collection, he instructed the curator where they should go—new maps next to, but not too close to, the portrait of Alexander von Humboldt, new photographs of volcanic regions in a particular corner.[23] He helped design and paid for a printed guide to the *Länderkunde* collection which came out a decade before a general guide to the museum,[24] and when the museum received a new African collection from Hans Meyer, another well-known patron of the museum, Obst felt obligated to ask Stübel's permission before setting it up temporarily in the rooms Stübel had yet to fill.[25] As with Schliemann, Stübel was more than influential. In exchange for his financial commitment and coveted donations he was allowed to reshape this scientific museum.

While Schliemann and Stübel's authority over their collections was extreme, their demands and their ability to influence museums' arrangements were hardly exceptional. In 1885, the New Guinea Company, a trading concern that had been given exclusive rights to collecting ethnographica in German New Guinea, offered to contribute their unparalleled collection of ethnographic artifacts to Berlin's *Völkerkunde* museum immediately before its opening in 1886, but only on the condition that it remain undivided, completely accessible to all visitors, and in its own rooms.[26] In 1902, Willy R. Rickmehrs, a Bremen merchant with interests in Central Asia, offered the Berlin museum a collection of rugs and other items from the Caucasus and Bucharest "under the condition that the collection would be set up immediately, remain open to the public," and that the

Bucharest items never be divided.[27] And in 1899, Arthur Baessler, a steadfast patron of the Berlin museum, felt comfortable demanding that his collections not only remain together and open to the public, but that he also be given the right to arrange them—conditions quickly agreed to by the museum director and section leaders.[28]

Initially, collections donated by powerful patrons were eagerly accepted because this was the only way ethnologists could possess them; but because of the conditions attached to them, they often became a problem. Patrons regarded their collections as static entities, but Bastian's ethnographic project required museums that functioned as working arrangements. These static collections could not be moved, and the artifacts in them could not be redistributed as the geographical arrangements within the museums shifted and changed. Newer items from a particular region could not be easily integrated into a patron's displays, so that the geographic distribution was disturbed and comparative analysis, the cornerstone of the ethnographic project, was hindered. Moreover, despite the fact that the more systematically assembled collections created around the turn of the century by trained ethnologists were generally regarded as having a higher scientific value than the collections created by travelers and laymen, the collections donated by powerful patrons often remained prominently displayed for decades despite theoretical shifts or the importance of new acquisitions. These collections, in other words, maintained their dominant positions in the museums' exhibitions as much because of the names of their suppliers as any sort of "scientific" consensus, and they hindered ethnologists' abilities to effectively use the space in their museums.[29]

Even collectors who donated smaller collections or individual items demanded their immediate presentation and would complain loudly if their donations did not gain a prominent position or were moved or placed in storage to accommodate other, perhaps more (scientifically) significant artifacts. For the museum's ethnologists, this aspect of patrons' expectations was a particular problem. Already in 1879, Rudolf Virchow and others argued that one of the central reasons local history museums were more likely than the larger state institutions to receive donations of prehistory collections was that contributors realized that the smaller museums were less crowded and better able to offer their "treasures" a prominent position in their exhibits. In fact, Virchow noted that many disgruntled donors would even ask for their collections to be returned if they were not displayed to their satisfaction, and that a second donation was unthinkable if a patron felt his or her gifts had been slighted in presentation.[30] Thirty years later, and despite the professionalization of ethnology as a science, this tendency had hardly changed. As Karl Weule lamented in 1909, in addition to the practical problems of overcrowding in most *Völkerkunde* museums after the turn of the century, ethnologists were faced with the "wrath of the collectors and donators," who demanded to know why their pieces were not placed in their own cabinet or why their collections could not be placed in a room that was given their name.[31]

Patrons, in other words, often kept a watchful eye on their donations, defending their rights and scrutinizing the ethnologists' treatment of their collections years and even decades after they were donated to a museum. When, for example, H. Göring in Berlin realized that the Chinese porcelains and Javanese objects he had given the Leipzig museum were not labeled to his satisfaction, he subjected Hermann Obst to his "wrath." Exclaiming to Obst that the museum had not kept its word, he wrote emphatically *"I was promised, that every single piece would be properly labeled as belonging to me,"* and demanded that this oversight be rectified [emphasis is his; italics were underlined twice].[32]

Similarly, the ship's doctor Herman Schneider, who had donated a collection of artifacts acquired during his voyage to the South Seas to Munich's ethnographic museum in 1869, wrote a scathing reproach to the Bavarian Cultural Ministry in 1886 (seventeen years later!) complaining that his collection was no longer being kept under the conditions promised to him when he donated it to the museum. He wrote that Moritz Wagner, the former director of the museum, together with several Bavarian ministers, had convinced him to donate the collection as a patriotic gesture, and that he had only agreed to this under the conditions that it would be kept together, given its own place in the displays, and be adorned with his name, all of which had met with immediate approval. He had recently learned, however, that these conditions were no longer being maintained, and after visiting the museum himself, realized to his dismay that his collection was not being displayed in its entirety and that many of the pieces that were on display were no longer credited to him.[33] The artifacts in his collection had been redistributed and combined with other artifacts in order to conform to the museum's geographical arrangement. But the prominence of his name as well as the unity of his collection had been taken away as the principle of geographic arrangement had replaced that of patron privilege, and the impudence of these actions in the name of science infuriated him.

Schneider's protests prompted a series of circulars, inquiries, and pronouncements between Bavarian ministries, eliciting a trenchant retort from Max Buchner, the museum's current director. Buchner reported that in the first place, he "could find no written confirmation of the conditions" Schneider mentioned, so he could not be certain that such an agreement had even been made. More importantly, however, he exclaimed that "an ethnographic museum cannot be a hall of glory [*Ruhmeshalle*], divided up according to the names of donors."[34] "These names," he noted, were included "where possible, . . . but not every single piece can be marked in this way." If they were to follow such a policy, he complained, everything in the museum "would soon be covered over with labels." He pointed out that Schneider's contributions had not disappeared but had been redistributed geographically as the museum acquired new things and argued that the museum "cannot be returned to the way [it was] 17 years earlier," especially since "the collections have grown, but the rooms have not."[35] In this particular instance Buchner was able to successfully defend his position because of the time that had expired since the museum had received the collection, the fact that a record of the initial agreement could not be found, and the collection itself had declined in value. Such successes, however, were more the exception than the rule.

As all of these examples illustrate, many of the patrons who supported German ethnographic museums read their arrangements in ways that had little to do with ethnologists' goals. Indeed, for many patrons, collections of artifacts represented the people who donated or paid for them as much as the people from whom they were obtained, and as they viewed a museum's collections, they perceived hierarchies that reflected directly on themselves. In exchange for contributing their collections to a museum, these individuals expected to become part of a municipal display that they had envisioned; and when they believed that changes in a museum's arrangements inhibited this goal, they drew on written and verbal agreements to protest the manner in which "their" collections were displayed. In most cases, the ethnologists were forced to comply, because they had entered these agreements freely, even eagerly, in order to maintain the flow of artifacts. Such arrangements were closely tied to the market mechanism that governed ethnologists' acquisitions, and they were a critical part of their Faustian dilemma: Because of their agreements, ethnologists' own ideas about the goals and purposes of their museums and the organization of their displays were forced to incorporate, and often compete with, those of their patrons and other visitors.

One did not have to be a powerful patron or member of the international scientific community to influence the development of German ethnographic museums. Other members of the leisure classes had an impact as well. Indeed, the well-educated and propertied classes in German cities, individuals whom I have grouped together under the rubric "local elites," came to these museums with their own expectations about what these institutions could do for them and what kind of experiences they should have within their walls. These visitors often wanted more than monotonous rows of spears or crowded cases meant to facilitate a comparative analysis. They demanded an aesthetic many of them had grown accustomed to in art and art history museums: quiet halls for their contemplation, organized in a way that would allow for their easy movement through the displays, and which would satisfy their spectatorial gaze.[36] While Bastian and his counterparts wanted to create laboratories for the study of mankind, a place for exploration and experimentation, many of these visitors expected a place for their edification, but also a space that was simply pleasing to visit during their leisure time. When the museums conformed to their visions, these visitors could be quite laudatory, but when their expectations were not met, they were more than willing to voice their objections—even exploding on occasion with trenchant critiques about the overcrowding, the organization, the visiting hours, the other visitors, and issuing adamant demands for change. During these moments of reaction they often wrote letters to the museums directly, to the local governments, and to the press, and by engaging in this process of reception and reaction, local elites took part in a dialog with the directors and supporters of German ethnographic museums through which they helped shape these institutions in a variety of ways.

As in many art museums across Europe, local elites' complaints about opening hours, admissions policies, and visitors' dress forced the directors of German ethnographic museums to better regulate this public space.[37] Arguments by parents, for instance, that children should be allowed to roam the museums freely and never be excluded from exhibitions, were fielded along with complaints by other visitors that children disrupted the environment, disturbed their contemplation, and that because of children's tendency to engage in "silliness" and "horseplay," they should be barred from the museums altogether. In 1890, for example, E. Prölss wrote to the General Administration of the Royal Museums from the well-to-do suburb of Steglitz complaining that his son and some school friends had been denied entry to the museum because they were not accompanied by an adult. Somewhat disenchanted by the treatment his son had received, he demanded to know why the museum was there, "if not to visit," and asked for an explanation of their policies.[38] In 1909 a similarly distraught father in Leipzig wrote a critical commentary in the local Leipzig papers when his eight-and-a-half-year-old son, despite his "*lebhaft* (lively) interest in all aspects of natural history and ethnography," several previous visits to the museum, and a "close familiarity with travel literature," had been denied entry to see a special exhibit of a giant mammoth set up in the Leipzig *Völkerkunde* museum because of his age. While this father agreed with the administration that unsupervised children might create problems, he found any concerns about children accompanied by adults unfathomable, and like the father in Berlin, demanded a precise explanation.[39] Such appeals forced directors to rethink their goals and the purpose of their museums, justify who could make up their audiences, and create firm admissions policies that designated whom they sought to serve. They were pressed to list precisely the age limits, the minimum requirements for visitors' dress, and make the museums' opening hours conform to the hours that best corresponded to the generally accepted hours of leisure time.[40] Through a process of reception and communication, in other words, these visitors helped shape the atmosphere in scientific institutions and significantly affected the museums' public operations and policies.

More importantly, local, well-educated visitors voiced their opinions about museums' contents and helped initiate changes in both ethnologists' collecting practices and the nature of their displays. At times, these opinions were expressed rather harshly, as Max Buchner, director of the Munich ethnographic museum, realized in 1891, when he returned from a collecting venture in the Pacific to find that the aboriginal weapons and Buddhist idols he had brought back did not strike his public's fancy. "What," wrote one critic, "do we want with these jagged sticks and [this] desert idol junk? That belongs in some *tingeltangel* [honkey-tonk] suburb of Hamburg."[41] And although lay opinions were not usually so crassly stated, these voices also influenced ethnologists' efforts in the field. In 1909, for example, Karl Weule, the director of the Leipzig museum, wrote to ethnologist Leo Frobenius that he had received complaints about the monotonous character of Frobenius's collections of African weapons, explained that he had removed these items from public exhibition, and urged Frobenius to vary his choice of artifacts more widely; such collections simply did not appeal to their visitors' spectatorial gaze. Moreover, while Weule noted that he appreciated Frobenius's attempts to collect thoroughly and recognized the scientific "value" of Frobenius's choices, he also agreed that the complaints about the collections were "not so terribly incorrect," or "at least not from the layman's point of view"—a layman with whom, he reminded Frobenius, "the director of every museum has to contend, much more than the scientist in him would like."[42] The collector as well as the director must bear in mind the aesthetic appeal ethnographic collections should have for their visitors.

In some cases, public voices led to more dramatic changes than altering collecting strategies and removing objects from display. Not too long after the Leipzig ethnographic museum moved into a monumental new building in 1896, its ethnologists received local criticism for neglecting to include Europe in its displays and for banishing European pre-history and German *Ur-Volkskunde* to an "insecure and poorly lit existence," in "a tiny basement room."[43] Ethnologists' initial response to this criticism was to deny that these collections had been purposefully neglected, to argue that they had planned to put Europe in the museum from the beginning, and to claim that Europe was only excluded because of space limitations and because of the internationally recognized scientific necessity of immediately collecting as much material as possible from the many "primitive cultures" disappearing in the wake of European expansion.[44]

Nevertheless, despite these official statements about the lack of space and the needs of science, local visitors' outcries were enough to convince the museum's ethnologists that, ultimately, they would need to rethink their priorities. As a result, Leipzig's ethnologists designed and set up a "temporary exhibition" of European material culture, and it was so well received by visitors that, despite the ever growing number of artifacts from non-European peoples, and a museum building that was still described by its director as literally bulging at its seams, a prehistory section was soon opened in the Leipzig museum amid public pronouncements by its director Dr. Karl Jacob that these collections had indeed been neglected.[45] Leipzig's ethnologists, in other words, recognized that their visitors had preferences and demands, and that despite their "scientific objectives," it was in the ethnologists' own best interest that these demands be met. In this case, local elites' influence was strong enough that they were able to put Europe into a museum that had become dedicated to "non-Europeans."

The "Uneducated Public"

From 1868 to 1914 museums' audiences grew increasingly broad with the rise of mass culture, mass politics, and commercial consumer culture. This shift did not take place everywhere at once nor did it follow a precise pattern. But in general, by the first decade of the twentieth century visitors to German ethnographic museums had grown substantially in number and social diversity, and the directors of these museums—like most of their European and American counterparts—were eagerly seeking to include "less-educated" or even "uneducated" people in their audiences.[46] Individuals such as clerks, seamstresses, teachers, and even workers became increasingly common in museums' galleries and halls, and this shift had notable consequences. At the same time that German ethnologists were caught up in the process of professionalization and working to improve on their museums' scientific standards, civic leaders were demanding that they refocus their attentions on public education and follow the international trends in this direction.[47] As ethnologists attempted to serve both of these callings, their tasks were forcibly bifurcated, and the imperatives of serving their rapidly expanding audiences gradually usurped the "scientific" project that had spawned these museums. Moreover, as these "popular" elements became a significant component of museums' audiences, they also became partners in the process of reshaping these scientific institutions and, ultimately, in the production of knowledge that took place there as well.

One small debate over the presence of children in Hamburg's *Völkerkunde* museum captures the shifting attitudes about the cultural functions of scientific museums around the turn of the century and foreshadows some of the changes that would take place in Hamburg and other German cities only a few years later. In 1904, a physician named Fritze wrote a trenchant letter to the Hamburg museum, complaining about the presence of children in its halls and rooms. He explained that he had visited the museum at three o'clock on a Sunday afternoon in the hopes of studying the collections, but that this "had been simply impossible" because of the "swarm of children," some "as young as three or four years of age," who he was sure had "no interest in the artifacts on display." According to him, these "children only used the museum as a playground," they "storm[ed] between the visitors and the objects, practice[d] jumping from the steps, stir[ed] up dust, and made as much noise as possible." In many ways this letter captures a vision of impropriety against which the two fathers I noted in the previous section were forced to argue—unsupervised children did not belong in a place of quiet contemplation. Yet there is also a critical difference. While the fathers I mentioned above were writing to defend the rights of their children—future members of the local educated elites—to participate in the self-cultivation taking place in these museums, the children who were the target of Dr. Fritze's complaint were from Hamburg's *Volksschule*, from the city's working classes.[48]

Because Hamburg's *Völkerkunde* museum shared a building with the Museum of Natural History at this time, Fritze received responses from both of these museums—responses that also happened to be diametrically opposed. Dr. Karl Hagen, who became Thilenius's assistant only a few months later, was temporarily in charge of the ethnographic museum when the letter arrived, and he agreed with Fritze's complaint. Hagen wrote that while he was always overjoyed, "when school classes under the direction and supervision of their teachers" visited the museum, he also found children without supervision to be inherently problematic. He noted that a small number of these children "certainly" came to the museum "with the intention of enriching themselves," but he also agreed that most of them were oblivious to its potential and used it as a "playground" in which to "practice horseplay of every kind." Because he too regarded the museum as "primarily a place of higher learning [*Bildungsstätten*]," he agreed that the presence of these children should be curtailed.[49]

Professor Carl Gottsche in the Natural History Museum, however, who felt strongly that Fritze's complaint "concerned his museum as well," responded quite differently. He wrote that with the opening of the building in 1891, they had posted an official policy at the entrance which stated that children would only be allowed into the building when accompanied by an adult. But he also pointed out that both "the public and the museum's directors" found this exclusion "rather severe," and that for years the overseers had been advised that they should only enforce this policy when "the children were very small or uncleanly dressed." He explained that the number of children had risen in the museum in part because arrangements had been made with the schools to provide their students with tickets (*Controlmarken*) that would allow them to come to the museum. And while he acknowledged that "horseplay is seldom absent where children are concerned," he argued that there was generally plenty of room for both the children and the other visitors, that these children did respond to the overseers, and that Fritze probably would have gotten "satisfactory results" from the children and been able to change their behavior had he "appealed to them properly." Most importantly, he argued that the museum was providing these children with particular opportunities and experiences which he refused to deny them simply because they "occasionally engaged in silliness." As he explained it:

> The Natural History Museum is rooted much more than any of the other museums in the wider classes of the population; our public has neither understanding for French *Plaketten* nor Japanese *Faiencen*; but for that which crawls, and flies, and sings outside they have not only understanding but also love. It is so touching to see how the boys come to us with the treasures they have collected, and how proud they become if they are able to discover their names. And almost all of the children who gain this pleasure from us are [male and female] students of the *Volksschule*, that means children who at the age of fifteen go into the working world. This short period of time, during which they can come to us, cannot be shortened even more; the enthusiastic among them should not be denied entrance to the museum because on a given Sunday the father must continue working in order to provide for his family.[50]

This second response is particularly revealing. It illustrates a recognition among scientists such as Gottsche that scientific museums can serve multiple publics, that they are not simply bastions of "elite knowledge," or places for quiet contemplation. It shows a willingness to use the museum for several levels of education and a desire to link them to the schools, something that was becoming increasingly common among natural scientists in the last decade of the nineteenth century.[51]

It is also quite fitting that this strong opinion was voiced by the representative of the Natural History Museum and in such stark contrast to that of Hagen, the ethnographic museum's curator. Natural history museums set the trend among scientific museums toward public education, and they began creating *Schausammlungen*—didactic displays meant for a more popular public—decades before ethnographic museums began to follow suit.[52] As new ethnographic museums were being planned and older ones refurbished around the turn of the century, however, priorities began to change. Ethnologists found themselves pushed by local governments, private supporters, and scientists alike to follow the natural scientists' lead and begin reshaping their museums to accommodate a much broader public. Not long after Fritze issued his complaints, for example, members of Hamburg's local government and representatives of its ethnographic museum began debating the plans for a new museum building.

From the outset of these discussions in 1904, there was general agreement among members of the museum commission, the local government, and the scientists alike that this new museum's "primary goal" would be to serve the "education of the general population." As one senator defined it, this "broad public" would not only include the local elites and foreign visitors, but people from "all of Hamburg's classes," "from the area around the city, the people from the countryside, small villages, and the suburbs."[53] This point was never challenged during these discussions; rather the most heated debates revolved around the question of which location would be the most accessible to the schools and the general population, and thus which of these would best serve their "primary" obligation.[54] Even Thilenius, despite his own professional ambitions and his commitment to creating a first-rate research institution, agreed wholeheartedly with these convictions and set out to design a museum that could serve multiple purposes and publics.[55] Of course, given his dependence on Hamburg's city fathers and the powerful international trends, he had little choice but to accommodate these desires. As the definition of the museum's audience began to shift, the museums' most basic principles of display were forced to change as well.

By the turn of the century, in fact, the creation of *Schausammlungen* were paramount in the minds of ethnologists and the directors of German ethnographic museums as they sought to keep up with international trends toward public education as well as their own visitors' demands. These new displays were a radical departure from the museums' more "scientific" arrangements. Instead of exhaustive collections of material culture— rows of Bantu spears, a "complete" collection of Benin bronzes, or an entire "set" of "prehistoric" pottery from a particular German region— these new displays were based on "representative" artifacts that allowed easy comparison, a few "life groupings," plenty of empty space, and a clear message or narrative.

There were, then, two opposing philosophies of display with two different sets of goals and conceptions about why the museums were there. Many ethnologists, such as Bastian, deemed the new *Schausammlungen* "unscientific" and thus "inadequate" for the pursuit of their ethnographic project. Yet because of the new emphasis on public education, other ethnologists—particularly younger ones such as Oswald Richter in Dresden who were more interested in their national responsibilities than Bastian's ethnographic project—argued that these more easily-digestible displays were the only means with which they could communicate with the "laity" and participate in educating the broader public.[56] The old-style displays, he contended, had been mere curiosities for the general public and taught them little or nothing.

For Bastian, however, this public was incidental, even superfluous. He stressed that ethnographic museums were first and foremost research institutions, and he adamantly refused to "reduce" his standards to accommodate a curious laity; rather he expected both the "public" as well as his counterparts to "rise" to them. The essential problem, according to Bastian, was that the move toward *Schausammlungen* presupposed that these museums could be reorganized to deliver "a message," or impart a particular "truth." But as he had repeatedly argued throughout his life time, these museums were never meant to instruct visitors or provide them with easily digestible, pleasing, or entertaining displays. Rather they were conceived as a means for assisting ethnologists in discovering elementary human ideas and the essential connections between human beings. Reorganizing their museums as tools of instruction would undermine the most fundamental principles of the ethnographic project.[57]

Despite Bastian's warnings, the directors of German ethnographic museums felt compelled to accept this new kind of display, and during the first decade of the twentieth century they all began moving beyond the museums' patrons, scientists, and local elites to address a more general audience. Even in Berlin, where Bastian stood adamantly opposed to rearranging his museum and adopting *Schausammlungen*, the virtues of these displays were being hotly debated by the turn of the century and the pressure to follow this controversial international trend continued to rise. By the late 1890s, pressing space limitations initiated discussions among the Berlin museum's ethnologists about dividing the collection into two separate displays—one for public consumption and the other for scientific research—as many natural history museums had already done.[58]

Initially, most of the museum's ethnologists argued strongly against any division of the collection. But only a decade later, the relentless overcrowding combined with the fact that other German museums had begun following this international trend made the change seem inevitable. Indeed, despite protests by George Dorsey and other American scientists, efforts to revamp museums in the United States greatly impressed some German ethnologists and, in 1909, when Richard Thurnwald returned from New York endorsing the radical changes in the ethnographic arrangements in the American Museum of Natural History in New York City, American ethnologists were brought into the Berlin debates.[59]

In response to Felix von Luschan's request for their evaluations of the efforts in the American museum, both Dorsey and Franz Boas strongly denounced its arrangements.[60] While Dorsey characterized its director's attempts to "popularize the science of ethnology" as a "vulgariz[ation]" of the science, Boas acidly exclaimed that the New York museum "caters only to the sensational appetite of the uneducated public," and that its director had "sacrificed . . . all attempts at scientific accuracy, truthfulness, and efficiency to the popular clamour for striking exhibits."[61] Luschan harnessed these testaments from American authorities to dissuade Berlin's museum administration from endorsing radical measures, from following actions so extreme that American scientists had washed their hands of the results when the director of the New York museum brazenly cast aside all scientific goals.

But the movement toward *Schausammlungen* in general, and the new focus on the "uneducated public" in particular, had arrived in Berlin, and they were there to stay. Luschan, in fact, began publicly endorsing such arrangements as early as 1905, and he was prevented from implementing a wholesale rearrangement of the museum after Bastian's death only because he was engaged in designing an entirely new museum building—a project that was not completed until after World War I.[62] Despite the Berlin ethnologists' initial convictions and their commitment to "scientific arrangements," any strong position against displays aimed at an "uneducated public" became essentially untenable by 1914, and after the war, a return to the more "scientific" collections was unthinkable.[63] In their new museum, exhaustive displays would be replaced by representative objects. Berlin too was forced to conform.

Most importantly, as the directors and supporters of these museums joined their counterparts from other nations in the search for a new organizing principle, they often turned to their newer, broader publics for direction. Weule in Leipzig excelled at this effort. Unsatisfied with his museum's geographical arrangement of artifacts but unwilling to embrace the kind of *Schausammlungen* found in natural history museums, he began experimenting with different kinds of comparative displays. When his initial efforts with individual cabinets met with an enthusiastic response from visitors, he set up a series of temporary exhibitions focused on particular comparative themes such as methods of transportation or modes of industry among ostensibly primitive cultures.[64] One of Weule's displays, for example was a straightforward comparison of the kinds of animals people used for transportation in different areas of the world and the different kinds of bridges and vessels they built with materials at hand and that was meant to illustrate the relationship between geography and technical innovations.

During these events, Weule paid careful attention to public responses, discussed his methodology with visitors, and used this information as a guide to refine his methods. In a 1909 report to the local government, for example, he noted that so many of the visitors he spoke with lauded his efforts and used them as a vehicle to criticize the museum's permanent exhibit, that the desire for the entire museum to be reorganized along these lines "ran like a red thread through each of these private discussions." In the local papers as well, the temporary exhibition was publicly praised for being "accessible," in a way that the "unclear," "unexplained," "poorly labeled," and "overcrowded" permanent display was not. These public responses confirmed his conviction that he was moving in the proper direction—away from what the public regarded as curiosities and toward didactic displays.[65]

Strong public responses also impressed Leipzig's city council, and as a result, Weule paid particular attention to the number and kinds of visitors his new displays attracted when discussing these projects with members of the city government. He also repeatedly stressed that both he and his supporters regarded the displays' wide spread popularity as proof of their success. In his report on the first of his temporary exhibits, for example, he emphasized that the attendance grew "greater and stronger with each day,"[66] becoming "just enormous" in the last weeks, and he took pains to differentiate among visitors in order to show the variety of people that attended. He pointedly detailed the number of guides they distributed and the interest his exhibit stirred among local associations and visitors from out of town. He stressed that the number of school children who came to see the first exhibit was so "unexpectedly large" that they had to limit their arrangements with the schools because they could not "fit any more classes in their exhibition hall."[67] While reporting on the lecture series that followed, he included tables that listed the numbers of visitors according to social classes—22% teachers, 17% university students, 28% businessmen, 4% bureaucratic officials, 6% school children, 18% workers, 5% private persons—and argued that "the composition of listeners from all circles of the population, from the most simple worker to the highest official, [wa]s the best indication of the necessity of [these] courses."[68] The social breadth of his audience as well as the sheer number of people who came to these events legitimated his project in his eyes as well as those of Leipzig's city fathers; thus his assistant Fritz Krause wrote with some pleasure in his report to the city council that during the temporary exhibit in 1910, 386 school classes, 400 teachers and a total of 13,400 students attended in only 42 days.[69]

Such numbers, however, not only impressed Weule and his supporters, but ethnologists in general. Following these experiments, Weule declared at the annual meeting of the German Anthropological Society in 1910 that these exhibits were instructive in more than one sense. He explained that he and his associates had "recognized what our museum was lacking" by observing the "great enthusiasm" with which the "public" studied these new displays, and he reported that his audience had "shown [him] the direction [ethnologists] should take." Weule posited a combination of a broad, geographically organized permanent exhibit, with rotating comparative exhibitions and lecture series as the best means for communicating with a range of different publics.[70] The volume of attendance at his exhibitions and his visitors' apparent "enthusiasm" legitimated his methodology for both Weule and his counterparts; his talk generated a wave of excitement among ethnologists, and even prompted many to visit his museum in the hopes of gleaning from his efforts.[71]

German ethnologists were enchanted by Weule's results and eager to join him in his pursuit of the broadest possible public. Yet we should not regard Weule's success simply as one which allowed him and other ethnologists to spread their "elite" knowledge among an ever-broader public, nor should we think that the communication taking place between the ethnologists and their audiences flowed in only one direction. These changes took place as part of a shift in an international consensus about the roles of museums. German ethnologists were motivated to follow these trends in part because of internationally-generated conversations among scientists, but also because of the insistence of local elites who were interested in keeping up with these trends. This combination of forces caused even the most reluctant ethnologists to begin turning toward a broader public that included secretaries and workers as well as teachers and school children. But as these new visitors began attending exhibits by Weule and others, showing their pleasure and displeasure with different kinds of displays, they also became implicated in the changes that followed. Their "uneducated" opinions began to carry considerable weight, and as a result, they became effective co-producers of these new museums, affecting ethnologist's methods of display and delimiting the kind of exhibits that could be in these "scientific" institutions. Indeed, they helped to totally reorient ethnologists' goals.

Who's Being Served?

Clearly, the ethnologists in charge of German ethnographic museums operated in anything but intellectual or cultural isolation, and it would be a mistake to think of ethnographic museums' audiences as homogenous groups that can be set off in opposition to the museums' ethnologists and their closest supporters. Each of the groups discussed above contributed to shaping German ethnographic museums, but there were also significant variations in the composition of these museums' audiences from one city to the next. Identifying and contrasting the different ways in which these groups came to influence the individual museums is particularly important. It not only sheds light on the different cultural and social stratifications in Hamburg, Berlin, Leipzig, and Munich, it also tells us much about the ways in which the market mechanism continued to function inside of these museums and affected ethnologists' decisions about their scientific displays. These comparisons illustrate that many of the particularities in these museums' histories and displays had as much (if not more) to do with the variations in the institutions' financial status and the demands of their respective audiences, as with the personalities and scientific goals of the museums' directors and their assistants.

At the same time, comparing and contrasting the relationships between ethnologists and the different visitors in these cities can also tell us much about the variations in the kinds of people who contributed to this "German science." They show us, for instance, that the developments in Berlin were anything but a microcosm of what went on in the rest of the nation, and that "German science" should not be too quickly identified with Prussian endeavors. Because of its secure financial status, the Berlin museum was in many ways an anomaly. Its ethnologists were able to pursue their ethnographic project in relative isolation from the social and political changes that were affecting other German museums around the turn of the century, and consequently, it was not the Berlin ethnologists who led the movement toward serving more popular audiences and creating instructive displays. This fundamental shift was spearheaded by the directors of the more "provincial" museums, and it was only later that Berlin's ethnologists began following them.[72] Indeed, it was largely the interaction between ethnologists and their audiences in these other German cities that redirected German ethnology, not the intellectual innovations of ethnologists in Berlin.

The Munich ethnographic museum was the oldest of the four museums in this study, and its connection to the Bavarian government both ensured and limited its existence. The museum was founded in 1868 as one of the Royal Collections; it received its budget from the state, and its directors were only responsible to the Bavarian monarchy and its ministries. The museum was opened with fanfare and public pronouncements, and local newspapers discussed its educational goals in a manner not unlike that reproduced across Germany some forty years later. The Bavarian Cultural Ministry, in fact, initially sought to set aside "special days" for people who wanted to use the museum for "scientific studies," especially anyone from one of Munich's "numerous schools."[73] This initial connection to a more general public, however, was short-lived, because there was little "public" or private interest in the museum as a scientific institution. Its first two directors also lacked the financial resources and governmental support to expand their activities, and as a result, they were unable to realize the museum's "educational potential" and it quickly drifted to the fringes of Munich's society.

While the museum's first two directors made some efforts to alter their institution's fate, both of them ultimately became resigned to working in veritable isolation on projects that had little appeal in their city.[74] Moritz Wagner, the first director, paid careful attention to scientific developments among his counterparts in northern Germany, worked closely with the well-known geographer Friedrich Ratzel, and expressed the desire to create an important scientific institution.[75] Wagner, however, was unable to connect with the people of a city in which, as one newspaper put it, "ethnological literature is probably nowhere else so little respected, read, and purchased."[76] His acquisitions were seldom greeted with enthusiasm by the governmental ministries, his displays sparked little interest among faculty at the university, and after its well-heralded opening, the museum gained almost no notice in the local papers during the rest of his tenure as director.[77] Similarly, Max Buchner, the seasoned Africanist who took over the museum after Wagner's death in 1887, was "unable to bring his vision of an ethnographic museum into harmony with that of the artistically-oriented city of Munich."[78] As in Wagner's case, Buchner's efforts "suffered under the strong lack of interest of the population,"[79] where, according to him, even his assistants had a "love of the classics," and "despised ethnology."[80] His attempts to expand his collections and make changes in the museum along lines pursued by ethnologists in the North were hindered by the museum's meager funding, while his efforts to increase the museum's financial state were curtailed by the fact that "the misery of the ethnographic collection was only a reflection of the torturous existence under which all the scientific collections of the artistic city of Munich existed."[81] Consequently, both Wagner and Buchner worked in a small museum that served an equally small public, and what audience their museum did have, was limited to local and visiting scientists, a modest number of patrons, and the state.[82] After working against these conditions for a time, and watching other German museums surpass their own in almost every respect, both of these men ultimately conceded—Buchner quite bitterly—that they could not recreate this institution themselves. Change, it became clear, would have to come from somewhere else.

When changes did arrive, they did so seemingly in the hands of Lucien Sherman, who replaced Buchner as director of the museum in 1907, and who quickly began increasing the museum's collections at a dramatic rate and completely refashioned its displays. He thinned out the otherwise cramped exhibits by storing artifacts in different locations around the city. He used this extra space to prominently display particular objects, placing them on different colored backgrounds, or creating free-standing exhibits that would increase the aesthetic appeal of the displays. He used mirrors to light the backs or interior of larger pieces, transferred the collections from overcrowded tables to the vertical space of cabinets that would provide better viewing,[83] and called on Munich's local artists to help him conceptualize the new arrangements in the museum's permanent display as well as its temporary exhibits (Fig. 9).[84] His efforts were not only discussed in the local press, they were also well received by the public, and ever-greater numbers of visitors soon began frequenting the once-isolated museum.[85]

These changes were so abrupt that it would be easy to locate their source in Sherman himself, and to portray the museum as one that was neglected by two somewhat interested, but not particularly motivated, directors and later reinvigorated by an enthusiastic individual who vigorously reshaped the museum and brought it up to international standards.[86] Without taking anything away from Sherman's abilities, however, we should bear in mind the degree to which these changes, and in fact Sherman's very presence in the museum, were a response to the demands and interests of the museum's supporters and audiences. It was no accident that Sherman became director in 1907. He was carefully chosen from a field of nine candidates because his background in Indian and East-Asian art and cultures made him the most likely to bring this museum into line with artistic interests in the city.[87]

During the first decade of the twentieth century, ethnology in Munich was given a shot in the arm by Princess Theresa of Bavaria.[88] She supported vigorous efforts at "salvage anthropology," had herself been on collecting ventures in South America, and became a powerful patron of the Munich museum. She essentially spearheaded the conception and creation of a large, temporary display of Peruvian artifacts in the Bavarian National Museum in 1906. Her interests clashed with those of Buchner's,

FIGURE 9. Indian exhibit, 1912. An example of Sherman's effort to move toward less cluttered, more aesthetic displays. (Staatliches Museum für Völkerkunde, Munich)

who soon felt compelled to retire. But she found a close associate in the *Generalkonservator* and president of the Bavarian Academy of Science, Karl Theodore von Heigel. Heigel reasoned that since the museum's strength had always been its Asian collections, and because the museum should better serve Munich's artistic interests, that they must replace Buchner with a director who would build on these strengths.[89] His convictions, and later Sherman's endeavors, were further supported by many of Munich's art critics, artists, and leaders in other scientific disciplines who, because of the rising international interest in non-European and "exotic" art, gained a rather sudden appreciation for the museum.[90]

Thus by the time Sherman took charge of the museum, the general attitude in Munich toward the science of ethnology was already shifting, and the museum was well on its way toward gaining an interested audience made up of influential patrons, local and visiting artists, and art critics such as Wilhelm Hausenstein, who was connected to the artist Paul Klee and the well-known group of modernists who made up the Blauen Reiter. The point is that while Sherman did indeed reshape Munich's museum almost overnight, he did not achieve these changes single-handedly; and while his own creative energies were certainly responsible for much of the momentum with which the changes took place, he followed a direction already sketched out by patrons and members of Munich's local elites who were interested in seeing the museum flourish. He created *Schausammlungen*, much like those being created by ethnologists in Northern Germany, but he did so in an attempt to raise the museum's aesthetic appeal more than its educational potential, and with the intention of serving an audience in which the international community of science and the uneducated public played much smaller roles than they did in the North. Both his presence in the museum and his efforts as director were a response to his particular audience's traditional interests in high art and to their more currently developed interest in the art of "exotic" peoples.

In stark contrast, the directors of the Leipzig ethnographic museum were forced from the outset to pay more attention to public interests and demands because their museum lacked any strong state support and suffered from tenuous finances. A private association created the Leipzig museum in 1869 without the benefit of a secure state budget.[91] This association relied on contributions from its members, entry fees paid by visitors, and donations from an array of patrons. From the beginning, its directors and members sought out a broad public base of support both inside and outside of the city. The museum's creation was followed by a series of promotional lectures, which ranged from presentations on "fire and its role in societies" to the "great roads of world transportation," all of which were reviewed in local papers.[92] Once the museum was opened, detailed discussions of donations, acquisitions, memberships, and visitors remained a central part of the museum's yearly reports until the city took over the institution in 1904.[93] Moreover, almost every significant action taken by the museum's supporters—large and small acquisitions, new displays, the opening of new rooms, movement to new buildings, visits by the King and Queen of Saxony—were discussed in local newspapers.[94] In short, from the first days of its existence the Leipzig museum maintained an uncommonly consistent and even exceptional public profile, its directors and supporters went to great lengths to sell their endeavor to an array of individuals, and they committed themselves to serving a broad audience with varied interests and desires. Indeed, the history of this institution's relationship with its visitors helps to explain why Weule took such a leading role in introducing *Schausammlungen* in German ethnographic museums and why he so willingly engaged the general public while rearranging his displays.

The Leipzig museum's remarkable public presence was due in no small part to the fact that it required funding from private sources and public events to survive. From 1874 to 1881 the museum was located in a rented building owned by the city, and the museum association supported the institution through membership dues, donations, and entrance fees.[95] After the association's 1881–1884 confrontations with the city, which ended with Oberbürgermeister Otto Georgi and the city council's strong statements of support, the museum was given rent-free accommodations by the city until their new building was finally opened in 1896. Yet until 1904, when the association turned over control of the museum to the city council, this organization alone was responsible for funding all other aspects of the museum, including its acquisitions, which made up the overwhelming majority of the museum's budget and provided the museum with its legitimacy as a scientific institution. After 1904 the museum's finances were secured by the city's commitment, but even then the director was required to come to the city council with requests for money when he was interested in major renovations, large acquisitions, or support for expeditions. And in order to gain these funds, he could not afford to be too introspective or too focused on creating a research institution, because he had to be able to show that his museum continued to provide a service for Leipzig and its citizens. Hence the director and his supporters' ongoing desire to maintain broad public interest in their museum.

During all three phases of the museum's history—as it moved from no governmental support, to partial support, to a city institution—each of the different groups outlined at the beginning of this chapter were being served. Their relative importance, however, did shift to some degree as the museum's relationship to the local government and the city's needs changed over time. International scientists constantly provided the Leipzig museum with legitimacy and remained an integral feature of the museum's audience from 1868–1914. Wealthy patrons were consistently important for gaining new acquisitions and maintaining the museum even after it became a city institution, although smaller patrons' influence did begin to wane after 1904. Local elites continually dominated the association's membership and were the museum's most regular visitors. During the entire forty-five year period, the "uneducated public" maintained an important presence as well; yet as the museum's audience expanded in size over time, this group in particular grew in importance, changing the dynamics between the institution and its audience and pushing ethnologists toward popular displays.

This shift in the "uneducated public's" importance was due in part to the international movement toward education discussed above. But it was also closely tied to the museum's increasing dependence on the local government and the director's need to illustrate the broad appeal of his institution in the city. As in Sherman's case, this need led to a reconfiguration of the museum's displays and the creation of *Schausammlungen*. Weule sought a new kind of display that would allow him to carefully balance his museum's commitment to international science and his desire to communicate with a broader public, while Sherman sought more aesthetic arrangements that would appeal to patrons and local elites—two seemingly different goals. Yet both men were largely motivated by financial considerations and a desire to secure their museums' positions in their respective cities. Just as Sherman needed to serve his city's artistic needs, so too was Weule forced to maintain his commitment to broader education once his museum was firmly established—and financially supported—as a civic institution. Both directors, in other words, took part in an international movement toward creating new kinds of ethnographic displays out of an interest in making their institutions "useful" by meeting particular local needs.

The Hamburg museum's origins were akin to those of the Leipzig museum, and as a result, they shared a similar pattern of development that stemmed from the kinds of public interest they initially generated and their primary sources of funding.[96] Like the Leipzig museum, the Hamburg museum was initially set up by a group of Hamburg's citizens with an interest in ethnology.[97] During the middle of the nineteenth century, Hamburg boasted only a smattering of disorganized ethnographica that ultimately came under the auspices of Hamburg's Natural History Association in 1867. From 1867–1871 these artifacts were reorganized into a small ethnographic collection that was located in the city library and supported by the Natural History Association. Acquisitions were only possible through donations, and the collection suffered from an almost complete lack of funds.[98] In 1871 the city began to contribute a small sum to the maintenance of the collection, which, as in Leipzig, was initially proclaimed a cultural history museum. This museum first gained its own location in a new school building only in 1877, and it was reopened as the Hamburgisches Museum für Völkerkunde in 1878. Carl Wilhelm Lüders, a local merchant and self-educated ethnologist who had traveled to North and South America and had served on the museum's board since 1873, was named its director the same year, and his salary and the museum's budget were paid by the city.[99] The movement from independently sponsored institution to city museum was somewhat quicker here than in Leipzig, but the pattern was essentially the same.

Once the Hamburg museum was firmly established, however, its development was in many ways closer to that of Munich's museum. Much like the initial directors of the Leipzig and Munich institutions, Lüders was not a trained natural scientist, but an autodidact, who, like Wagner and Buchner, largely gained his legitimacy through his travels.[100] He too quickly found himself in charge of a scientific institution in a city where scientific endeavors stirred little public interest, and in this case, a city that did not even have a university. Like Obst, he was forced to rely on donations and patronage networks for acquisitions, but like his counterparts in Munich, his salary and his institution's existence were secured by the city; after a short period of time he also withdrew into his own humble projects, even more content than his counterparts in Munich with his small museum and his equally limited audience. His institution received scant notice in the local papers during his tenure, except for the Bahnson incident, and in this and every other case of significant changes to the displays, real innovation only came from outside the institution. Indeed, when one compares the histories of these three institutions it becomes clear that the innovation of their respective directors and the size of their respective audiences were inversely proportional to their financial security. Ethnologists in an institution with a strong financial base could ignore public demands and focus on their own projects, but ethnologists in an insecure institution were forced to make it appealing to groups that would give them money, and this affected what they could put in their museums and how they could arrange their displays.

As in the case of Munich, the most profound changes appeared to arrive in the hands of a new director, Georg Thilenius, who took charge of the museum in 1904. But, just as in Munich, the director was chosen for his particular abilities, and set about reforming the institution in a manner that had already been largely sketched out by Senator Werner von Melle and his associates, who hoped that they could use the museum to refashion the city's self image. Just as Sherman revamped his museum to serve Munich's artistic sensibilities and respond to new interests in non-European and "exotic" art, so too did Thilenius refashion Hamburg's museum into a leading scientific establishment, one that became the stepping off point, as von Melle had hoped, to creating Hamburg's Colonial Institute, and later, its university.[101] In both cases Sherman and Thilenius used their particular abilities to respond to the equally particular needs of their cities, and in order to achieve their goals, each of these directors focused on distinctly different kinds of materials. While Sherman moved quickly to fill his museum with collections that were primarily from Asian and Indian *Kulturvölker*, Thilenius moved even faster to obtain artifacts from an array of rapidly vanishing *Naturvölker* in Africa, South America, and most notably, the Pacific. Each individual set out to refashion his institution according to shifting interests in his city, and each sought out the materials most fitting for the publics being served—*Kulturvölker* for the art city of Munich and *Naturvölker* for the trading center of Hamburg. As a result, the people who visited these museums entered two fundamentally different worlds represented by two different kinds of *Schausammlungen*—one filled primarily with porcelains, silks, Buddhist and Hindu carvings, and steel weapons, and the other dominated by hand-hewn Micronesian canoes, African masks, and weapons tipped with sharks' teeth, bone, stone, and shells.[102] In both cases the social and cultural contexts in each of these cities dramatically affected what ethnologists could do.

In this cast of German institutions, the Berlin museum was ultimately the exception. Its financial security allowed its ethnologists to focus on their scientific projects for decades while ignoring most public demands. Unlike the other museums in this study, this institution had a large and consistent budget from the moment of its creation in 1873. It also had a range of extremely wealthy supporters who provided its ethnologists with surplus funds for major acquisitions, and its director was the most well-known ethnologist in Germany. Bastian and many of his assistants had advanced degrees and taught classes at the Berlin university, while none of the museums' directors in the other three cities had similar credentials or were closely affiliated with their cities' universities until after 1904—and in the case of Hamburg, Thilenius had to wait for his position to be created along with the university in 1919. After 1889, the Berlin museum had a federally decreed monopoly on all collections originating in German colonial territories, a restriction that made such collections noticeably scarce in other German museums. The Berlin museum had a much closer working relationship with the German Foreign Office, the German military, and the admiralty, and the prestige of being the largest museum of its kind gave it a special position within the international community of science. The Berlin museum's secure funding and ample resources allowed its ethnologists to persistently create magazine-style arrangements, eschew the creation of *Schausammlungen*, remain focused on "elite science," and essentially ignore a broader public until so many other European and American museums had moved in this direction that even the scientific community expected them to follow suit.

Consequently, Germany's largest ethnographic museum served a group of visitors that was *less* socially diverse than audiences in Hamburg and Leipzig. It continually played host to international scientists, its patrons could have considerable influence, and local elites frequented the museum. But while Thilenius was busily creating an institution that would serve "all of Hamburg's classes" and Weule was conceiving of new types of displays, the Berlin museum's ethnologists rarely considered the "uneducated public" and were much less willing to allow them to be implicated in reshaping their displays. The Berlin museum had been conceived from the beginning as a scientific tool rather than a vehicle for public display— the equivalent of a first-rate research institution rather than a public library—and for decades Berlin's ethnologists paid only scant attention to the needs of any but the most well-educated visitors. For this reason the language in their guidebooks and other publications was not so different from that found in contemporary scientific journals, and although a new edition was prepared almost every other year, it was only in 1900 that the interests of a broader group of "laymen" were considered in the guides or were seriously entertained in ethnologists' ongoing discussions.[103] Much as in Munich, in other words, Berlin's "uneducated public" was not consciously being served because the museum's secure financial situation allowed its ethnologists to essentially ignore the "uneducated" until that group of potential visitors became an issue for the international community of science, which opened the doors to their presence in the museum, and eventually their influence.

By the turn of the century, then, the rise of mass culture and politics saw their counterpart in the mass consumption of science in German ethnographic museums. Ironically, after forty years of professionalization— and despite growing links between the cities' universities and their museums, and the increasing number of directors and assistants with advanced degrees—these museums became less "elitist," less focused on specialists and well-educated visitors, and less "scientific" as they moved further and further from the promise of their initial edeavor. In many ways, the market mechanism, the museums' increasing reliance on local governments, and most ethnologists' need to show the broad appeal of their institutions forced them to secure allies, seek out larger audiences, and continually attempt to sell their science to more and different kinds of people. Once ethnologists in the weaker museums began turning toward broader audiences and fashioning popular displays, ethnologists' more general conceptions about the fundamental goals behind their museums began shifting. By the first decade of the twentieth century, what had begun largely as a financial practicality became a generally accepted necessity as international trends combined with local desires to displace Bastian's ethnographic project.

mUSEUm CHAOS

SPECTACLE AnD ORDER In GERmAn ETHnOGRAPHIC mUSEUmS

Kommt Zeit, kommt Rat! Was man hat, hat man, und kann später besser untergebracht werden! [Time will tell! What one has, one has, and later it can be better accommodated!]
—Ludwig I of Bavaria, in response to accusations that there was no place to put the ethnographic collections he had recently purchased, 1842

n 1877 Adolf Bastian argued in his guidebook to the Berlin museum that acquisitions must be given priority over the comprehensive ordering and display of artifacts and that the museum's current limitations should not be allowed to restrict the accumulation of objects. He stressed that in order to "save what can still be saved" it was imperative that artifacts "be quickly collected and secured in museums," even if they could "only first be stored in magazine-like arrangements." Such temporary conditions would soon give way to better displays and exhibits once they built museums that could properly house them, and their immediate focus on collecting would ensure that these future exhibits would be that much more comprehensive and "instructive."[1]

Yet only four years later, as Bastian reflected on the state of his science and the condition of his museum, he prophetically wrote that while he and his contemporaries had been "enticed" and even "entranced" by the promises of ethnology and had eagerly pursued them, "these daring intentions soon began to crumble to dust as we looked into the more intricate depths of the materials so copiously accumulated, and as the mountain of publications [and collections!] grew to an awesome height." Consequently, he wrote, "we must abandon the aim, indeed the very idea, of achieving one comprehensive and comprehensible whole from all the materials thus far presented to us." His generation, he exclaimed, "must" continue to accumulate and preserve these artifacts, but it was the task of some future generation to bring them into order and create the kinds of museums and displays he had initially envisioned.[2]

There is a typical narrative that informs the history of most museums in the late nineteenth century, a whiggish rendition of their progressive march forward: they became more professional, more scientific, more comprehensive, and more comprehensible. Order and utility began to reign. The history of German ethnographic museums can also be written in this way; indeed, it often is. But already in 1881, Bastian indicated that there are other sides to this history, other ways to understand the internal dynamics of these institutions as well as their cultural functions. Where there was change, there was also stasis, and where there was progress there was also a persistent paradox: order, it turns out, was fleeting, chaos ubiquitous, and the museums consistently failed to function as their creators intended.

First Walk-Through: A Whiggish History of Development and Display

In 1953 Alfred Lehmann, the director of the Leipzig museum at that time, began a commemorative essay on the history of the museum with recollections from his first childhood visits. As a boy, he had been enticed by the glimpses he caught of the huge Baining dance masks and the Aztec and African stone sculptures as he first entered the building, and suitably impressed by the "frightening grimaces" carved into the faces of the large wooden Japanese guardians on either side of the vestibule. These initial moments provided him and other visitors with a "foretaste of the treasures that awaited in the museum" and the "wonder after wonder" they would see as they strolled through its halls. Lehmann included these memories to illustrate the impact the museum had on many of its visitors and to explain the origins of his own ethnological interests. Such introspection is exceptional for this kind of essay, but the rest of his account is typical of the kinds of institutional histories written about these (and other kinds of) museums. He stressed the many difficulties the museum's different directors faced: the problems between the city government and the association that founded the museum, the frustration of moving into a new museum building in 1896 to discover that it was already too small to hold all their collections, and the strong personality conflicts between Hermann Obst and Karl Weule. Yet like most of these histories, his story was generally one of constant progression and positive institutional development, painted against the background of the ever-growing numbers of collections that made this "Germany's second largest museum," and punctuated by major acquisitions, new buildings, funding increases , and changes in command. As with most of these histories, Lehmann's narrative is unashamedly whiggish, portraying steady, if at times arduous, growth and improvement based on objective facts and statistics—a museological development with purpose and direction.[3]

Twentieth-century museum directors are not the only ones who tell such whiggish tales. In many cases their institutional portraits essentially reiterate and extend the "histories" written by nineteenth-century predecessors.[4] Moreover, the same kinds of accounts continue to be reproduced in the more general historiography on nineteenth-century museums.[5] The trope of moving from antiquarian interests to scientific study, from a focus on curiosities—objects difficult to classify—to scientific objects that could and should be classified, consistently dominates these museums' histories.[6] Scientific progress not only forms the backdrop of these tales but continues to provide historians with their central metaphor: the scientist who abandons "fragmentary collections" in favor of attempts to "sort the world systematically into drawers, glass-fronted cases, bottles and filing cabinets." The emergence of this hardy individual ultimately represents for many scholars "a shift from *delighting* in the world's strange offerings and the appeal of subjective involvement to an attempt to *master* and *control* the world's diversity through new forms and conceptualization [my emphasis]."[7]

The Pitt Rivers Museum in Oxford is the quintessential example of such efforts, a scholastic favorite that appears again and again in the scholarship on nineteenth-century museums as the pinnacle of planned development. This "orderly illustration of human history," which was "no mere miscellaneous jumble of curiosities," is often represented as characteristic of nineteenth-century ethnographic museums and their scientists' goals—despite the fact that it was an anomaly among these museums.[8] Yet as the apex of purposeful organization, with clearly stated intentions and methodology, it effectively illustrates the whiggish visions of museum development in which progress is judged by degrees of order and control.

Indeed one can read the histories of German ethnographic museums from a whiggish perspective as well, by focusing on the efforts of the museum directors and their supporters to create an "orderly illustration of human history," while emphasizing their intentions and successes and contemplating the social and cultural implications of these projects. This particular reading also merits serious consideration, simply because so much of the current historiography and theoretical postulations about the cultural functions of museums are based on this sort of narrative, which supports the idea that these museums were an explicit extension of the enlightenment project and a potential means of gaining social control. Indeed, it is precisely on this assumption that many scholars have based their arguments about elites' efforts to use museums to control and limit visitors' visions of themselves and the world.[9] Therefore I want to begin this chapter by returning briefly to the museums' more general "histories" and strolling through their pasts with a whiggish perspective, one that will emphasize ethnologists' quest for order and precision and sketch out the progress they made in reorganizing their displays and redesigning their buildings.

These museums' histories typically begin with the division and redistribution of local collections in the 1860s, during which "ethnographic collections" were created or redefined by actively grouping particular kinds of objects together. Conscious decisions about what did and did not belong in ethnographic displays, in other words, defined the museums at their very genesis. In the royal cities of Munich and Berlin, this process stemmed from the deliberate rearranging of the royal collections and their division into artistic and scientific components. As the Munich museum was created, for example, Indian and Chinese collections were removed from the Gemälde Galerie—where they had once "belonged"—and combined with the "ethnographic cabinet" from the academy of sciences building in order to create a new ethnographic collection that would be arranged according to the "different areas of the world and their primary groups of *Kulturvölker*" rather than aesthetics or typologies. As part of the general process of dismantling the older *Kunstkammern* and redistributing their contents, "Eastern art" that once belonged in the art gallery was redefined as material culture, which now belonged in the new ethnographic collection.[10] This new "scientific" museum—like so many others—thus emerged out of a more general attempt to bring the city's collections into a logical and recognizable order.

A similar sort of rearrangement took place in Hamburg and Leipzig as extraneous ethnographic artifacts in their libraries were brought together and combined with new collections to form the nuclei of their ethnographic museums. In Leipzig, for example, the museum was created around the Klemm collection, one of the first "scientifically ordered" ethnographic collections in Europe.[11] Once it arrived in Leipzig in 1870, artifacts that had been held in other places in the city were sent to the newly founded ethnographic museum. The city library, for instance, which had become host to a mishmash of artifacts simply because "there was no where else to put them," quickly sent this new museum thirty-seven items. These included Turkish weapons brought back by Saxon troops after the last siege of Vienna as well as weapons from the Thirty Years War, Chinese clothing, and a mummy with a Latin inscription that dated it to 1703 and which, according to "oral tradition," originated with "a Jesuit from Leiden" who died in Leipzig while taking the mummy to a Jesuit institution in Prague.

When the library's director transferred these items to the new museum, he wrote that he considered it "practically his duty" to insure that such things be "delivered to the place where they belonged." He also explained that he had retained the few "bronze pieces" from Pompeii and the necklace of "cut stones that originated with King Friedrich August of Saxony" for the library, because he considered them "antiquities."[12] Exactly why he defined these later items as antiquities that should remain in the library while an "eighteenth-century wax figure of a woman under glass" and a "collection of old magnifying glasses" were included among the things he felt "belonged" in the ethnographic museum, he did not say. Nevertheless, the point is that the very act of founding ethnographic museums required conscious decisions about what did and did not belong in their collections, beginning a process of inclusion, exclusion, and ordering that would continue to be refined throughout the museums' existence as they became increasingly "scientific."

Once these collections were reassembled and actively broadened, the objects were transformed from "wonders" and "curiosities" to "artifacts" and "specimens." Individual pieces were given meaning through their placement in a constellation of things that represented, and were supposed to articulate, both the variety of humanity and its most essential characteristics. The cultural scientists in charge of these museums expressed this explicitly in countless different forums, and the praise they heaped on any effort to refine collections, bring more order to ethnographic displays, increase their own "scientific" training, and make their methodologies more "scientifically valid," reflected their determination to set themselves and their collections apart from the "curiosity cabinets" of the past and illustrated their desire to assert control over their collections.[13]

Indeed, a director and his assistants' ability to gain and maintain control over their collections essentially defined their museum and their efforts as "scientific." The degree to which they were able to do this was, in fact, often regarded as an accurate measure of their progress. As a result, ethnologists consistently explained the history of their science and of their museums as a story of moving from disorder to order and of achieving a greater degree of precision in their work with their collections. In 1881, Adolf Bastian published perhaps the most influential account of the "prehistory" of ethnology, in which he argued that contemporary efforts to create "ordered collections" began with the French geographer Edmé-François Jomard in the 1830s and found their logical extension in "modern" ethnographic museums and their "scientific" and purposeful arrangements.[14] But this rendition of ethnographic museums' prehistories or their natural, historical development neither began nor ended with Bastian. It was part of the general narrative—or mythos—that defined the purpose and goals of these museums. In Hamburg, for instance, C. W. Lüders, the first director of the Hamburg museum, sketched out this same pedigree in a brief report on the history of his museum in 1891. His successor Karl Hagen followed suit with his own rendition in 1897, and Thilenius repeated these assertions again in his 1916 history of the museum.[15] In each case the *Wunderkammern* or "cabinets of curiosities" from which the ethnographic museum sprang were coded as negative, the polar opposites of what was desirable, and were considered useful only as a point of comparison with which they could rhetorically illustrate their museum's murky origins, the achievements they had made, and the directions in which they needed to be heading as they crafted their modern scientific museums.[16]

Consequently, ethnologists' most important goal within their museums —and, according to the historiography, their most notable efforts—quickly became creating precise and orderly arrangements according to modern scientific principles. Rather than the aesthetic arrangements one might find at world's fairs or the random arrangements common in early collections, these "scientific" institutions demanded catalogued artifacts and well-ordered displays. Thus one of the first things Ferdinand Worlée and Adolph Oberdörffer did as they sought to transform Hamburg's collection of miscellaneous artifacts into an officially recognized "ethnographic collection" in 1867, was to clean the artifacts, order them geographically—each part of the world having its own set of colored numbers —and create a catalog that listed and thus defined the collection's contents.[17] When Lüders became director of the museum in 1877, he also cleaned and ordered the collections and produced new, clearly organized inventories of the museum's geographical sections. He repeated this process again when the museum moved into the upper floor of the building created for the Natural History Museum,[18] and when Thilenius took over the museum in 1904, he immediately began work on a new, more "scientific" *Zettelcatalog* while designing an equally new museum building that would allow him to better organize the collection. Each of these efforts contributed to the process of making the museum more scientific by further bringing the collections under their control, and each effort is listed in the history of this museum as a further step toward a better, more scientific institution.[19] Indeed, when one looks through the institutional history of the Hamburgisches Museum für Völkerkunde, these are precisely the points—together with budgetary changes and major acquisitions— that guide the reader through its first forty years. These are the signposts in the museum's ongoing progression. These are the facts that matter.

One of the markers of scientific progress in German museums was the movement from typological arrangements to geographically-oriented collections. In the Leipzig museum, for instance, from the opening day in 1874 until 1878 artifacts were arranged according to Gustav Klemm's evolutionary ideas, so that "like things" were grouped together. The museum was first set up in part of an old hospital, and occupied a series of oddly-sized, interconnected rooms on a single floor, most of which received natural lighting from two sides. Artifacts were placed on tables, or in glass cabinets, stood freely in the halls and larger rooms, hung from the ceiling, and adorned the walls. As visitors entered the northeast side of the building through a door facing the cemetery, they strolled in a southwesterly direction through the series of rooms. In the first double room they found "the bodily nature of mankind," skeletons, skulls, mummies (the one from Leipzig's library in a special glass case), and "palaeontological finds," as well as various body parts preserved in jars, and "animals that are definitely related to man," such as household pets and domestic animals. The vast majority of the museums' artifacts, however, belonged to the "cultural history section" that filled up the rest of the rooms. There was the "magnificent arsenal of weapons from all peoples and times," the rooms of tools, of different kinds of fishing instruments, and the "already famous" *Garderobe*, filled with a "multicolored" and "complete" collection of clothing. This display included raw materials, an array of tailors' tools, and different sorts of cloth, as well as collections of dress from "essentially all the main groups of people from the old and the new world, from the most primitive . . . to the most complicated clothing of the modern, fancily-dressed [*putzsüchtiger*] *Culturvölker*."[20] From these collections the visitor moved to the museum's "treasure house" of jewelry and bodily ornaments, then into the collections of house hold furniture, and then to a room filled with adults' games and children's toys. Water and land vehicles were spread throughout the museum, while two rooms off to the west contained collections of musical instruments and religious artifacts from Hindu, Christian, Buddhist, and other origins.[21]

After Hermann Obst reordered the collections in 1878 to conform to the dominant geographic mode of arrangement promoted by Bastian and others, visitors were greeted with a different kind of display, one in which each "people's" material culture was grouped together. Rather than skipping from one set of things to another, as Klemm had envisioned, visitors moved through displays that were organized according to continents and regions, just as they would in any other German ethnographic museum at this time. The entire museum was divided according to geographical locations, with different rooms and halls allocated to different regions, and each of these sections were further subdivided into cultural groupings. The amount of materials a visitor might find from any given culture necessarily varied, depending on what the museum's ethnologists had been able to acquire and how much of this material they were able to display. Some areas were better represented than others, but the ethnologists' goal and the measure of their success—in all ethnographic museums—was ultimately to portray each culture as completely as possible in order to facilitate a comparative analysis; and thus visitors might find a vast array of different things in each of the museum's sections.

In 1879, for instance, as visitors entered the Japanese exhibits in the Leipzig museum, they were greeted by "a brightly colored picture constructed of straw" hanging on the first wall, "a masterpiece of the artist Matsmoto" from Omari, near Yedo. As the visitors began to glance around, they would see antiquities from temples, such as "the 200 year old picture of Buddha from the Tokudnidschi temple in Narra." Along the wall that had windows looking out to the courtyard were "three pictures of idols [*Götzenbilder*] crafted from bronze—strange, cowering shapes with curious hair styles and head gear [*Kopfbedekung*], as well as two . . . fabulous lions made from the same metal." In a set of glass cabinets set across the room on the north wall were the "true pearls of the collection" —musical instruments from the imperial minister in Tokyo. Here were an "array" of "strangely shaped" drums, strings and winds, as well as rolls of music laid three by three. In another glass case stood a "giant porcelain vase valued at over 3000 Marks." A number of intricately-made models of Japanese houses were there as well. These finely crafted pieces were incredibly detailed; one included "an adorable birdhouse and a shooting stand with miniature weapons," and another was made with such precision that one commentator noted, "our [Germans'] puppet theaters appear totally clumsy in comparison." There were also samples of Japanese lacquer ware, 107 pieces arranged along one wall, as well as paintings, the finest silk needlework, a room full of the most intricately-detailed porcelain miniatures, and a collection of "Japanese actors' painted wooden masks with their golden eyes, black teeth, grimaces, and any number of devilish horns" hanging from a column. One corner room even held "a forest" of banners on lances, and "three life-sized figures of a knight and his servants, the one mounted on an armored steed." These "fantastically armored men" created from "tin, leather and papier-mâché" were "so orientally medieval," that one was immediately "returned" to the time "of the crusades." "The horse's grotesque costume [was] particularly impressive," and over sixty weapons, enough to "outfit an entire company," were displayed nearby.[22]

The Japanese collection was a typical example of German ethnologists' efforts to produce complete cultural arrangements once they had moved away from typological displays, and Obst's reorganization of the displays along these geographical and cultural lines was considered a critical marker in the museum's history. Ideally, ethnographic museums would be filled with such collections and visitors could easily move from one to another, from Japan over to China, from China down to India, and so on. In reality, however, space limitations made this impossible. These particular Japanese arrangements, for instance, were created following two exceptional acquisitions, and were maintained in this manner only for a short period of time. Because of the limited space within the museum, its ethnologists could not display their next acquisitions and retain this exhibit as it was. As a result, the Japanese exhibits—as well as the museum's other displays—had to be either reduced, removed, or crowded to the side as newer acquisitions were brought into the museum.

Consequently, the quest for order and scientific precision did not end after conscious decisions were made in either Leipzig or the other cities about what did and did not belong in their ethnographic museums, or even after a consensus was reached about the kinds of arrangements the ethnologists wanted to have. Spatial limitations often hindered ethnologists' abilities to fulfill their scientific visions of what an ethnographic museum should be, or to create a sufficient array of displays like those from Japan. Thus these scientists and their supporters worked furiously to try to change their locations and secure better accommodations in bigger and more technically advanced museums. Moreover, each time they gained a bigger location and reorganized their collections, it was hailed—both then and in the institutional histories published today—as another critical step toward achieving their goals.

In both Hamburg and Leipzig the directors and supporters of the museums were engaged in repeated attempts to secure better locations that would allow them to create the kinds of orderly arrangements they desired. While Obst was preparing his Japanese displays in 1878, for example, Lüders moved his collections from Hamburg's city library to a new location in the city's Museum and School Building. Lüders and his supporters had greeted this opportunity with enthusiasm in 1877 because it allowed them to devote an entire room to Africa and Asia and another to the Americas and Australia, and, in fact, their new, much more accessible arrangements, received a favorable review in the city's papers in the following year.[23] This enthusiasm died off rather quickly, however, because after a short time these rooms began to hinder Lüder's ability to expand the museum's holdings and effectively display its collections, and indeed it was precisely this two-room museum that Kristian Bahnson so strongly criticized in 1887 for being "improperly ordered," suffering from cramped conditions, and reflecting the city's disinterest in the arts and sciences.[24] In less than a decade, in other words, the museum's once "new" and liberating accommodations had become its most repressive hindrance, and it was thus with great enthusiasm that Lüders again transferred the ethnographic collections to the more spacious accommodations on the top floor of the Natural History Museum building in 1890 (Fig. 10). More space, he and his supporters continued to be convinced, would allow them to create more orderly, precise, scientific arrangements.

By 1893 Lüders had finished reordering the collections and issued a guide for the museum. The contents were arranged along aisles that conformed to the building's rectangular pattern and followed the scientifically imperative geographical arrangement, essentially achieving what Obst had been hoping to do when he reorganized Leipzig's collections. After ascending the stairs to the fourth floor of the building, visitors walked through the museum's entrance, turned left past Lüders' office and began to follow a series of cabinets filled with numbered artifacts. These began with the museum's collections from Africa, then moved into Asia, then

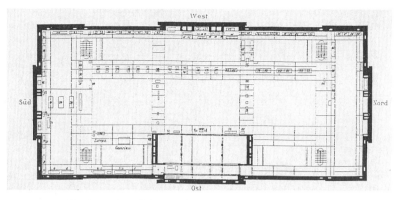

FIGURE 10. The floor plan of the Hamburgisches Museum für Völkerkunde in 1893, when it was located on the top floor of the Naturhistorisches Museum. (Das Hamburgisches Museum für Völkerkunde, *Führer*, 1893)

America, *Ozeanien*, and ended with a small European collection (Figs. 11, 12). Dug-out canoes were set near the walkways, the museum's new intricately-carved ivory tusks from Benin jutted out from support pillars, shields were hung on walls, and in the many glass cabinets that dominated each section, visitors might find everything from Benin bronzes in the African section to leather work, clothing, weaponry, and miniatures in the American cases. Each of the individual sections were geographically organized as well, so that the visitor began, for example, with snowshoes, kayaks and harpoons from North America and then moved progressively south into stone weapons from the Incas, leather saddles from a more contemporary Mexico, silver work from Chile, mummies from Bolivia and Peru, and finally a canoe from the Yahguas Indians near the Magellan Straits.

The museum's new location and Lüders' reorganization were critical markers in its development. The increased space in this new location enabled Lüders to create the kinds of displays and arrangements that were impossible in the museum's previous location. It allowed him to pursue more orderly collections and progress toward more scientific arrangements, and he received what was perhaps the most satisfying vindication of his efforts from Bahnson himself, who wrote Lüders in 1893, congratulating him for having rescued the museum's collections from their earlier "chaos," and assuring him that the museum, "as it is now set up," was finally "living up to its potential." Lüders had gained control over his collections, and the Hamburg museum, or so it would seem, had finally been put in order.[25]

FIGURE 11. Cabinets in the Hamburgisches Museum für Völkerkunde between 1905 and 1910. Note the lack of any aesthetic ordering and the collection of artifacts according to geographical origin. (From Zwernemann, *Hundert Jahre*; copyright © Museum of Ethnology, Hamburg)

FIGURE 12. A view into one area of the permanent display in the Hamburgisches Museum für Völkerkunde between 1905 and 1910. Carved ivory tusks from Benin are mounted on the columns. Benin bronzes are displayed in the cabinets behind them, intermixed with a variety of other things. (From Zwernemann, *Hundert Jahre*; copyright © Museum of Ethnology, Hamburg)

Yet satisfaction was still fleeting. By the time of Lüders' death in 1896, Senator Werner von Melle and his supporters were already condemning the location as an "impossible" and "faulty accommodation," and lamenting its "crushed-together displays,"[26] and when Thilenius arrived in 1904, he noted that he could neither regard the museum as a true "Museum für Völkerkunde" nor a real "scientific institution."[27] Once again, ordered collections had fallen into disarray, Bastian's prophesy continually threatened to be fulfilled, and what was initially considered a "better location" had quickly become a "faulty accommodation."

By the last decade of the nineteenth century, in fact, ethnologists in general were convinced that their science required nothing less than monumental buildings in order to function. Once Thilenius arrived in Hamburg, for instance, he and his supporters immediately began to plan a grand building that they hoped would be as good if not better than those recently created in Leipzig and Berlin. Indeed, after suffering for years from space limitations, the Leipzig museum had gained a commitment from the city government in 1884 for a monumental building funded by a private foundation. Like most of these projects, the Grassi-Museum took over a decade to complete and it was only first opened to the public in 1896. Yet here indeed was an ethnologist's museum, the kind that inspired Thilenius and others to push for ever-bigger accommodations.

The building was essentially divided between the Kunst- und Gewerbemuseum [museum of applied arts] and the Museum für Völkerkunde, the second of which occupied almost twice as much space as the first.[28] It was positioned in the city center, and had a magnificent facade. Large columns separated the high, grand windows that ran across the building above the entrance, and at the base of the columns to either side of the doorway were "allegorical portraits of the continents and of *Kunstgewerbe*," selected during an artistic competition that was held while the museum was being built. On the right side of the building, which housed the Kunst- und Gewerbemuseum, one could see two-meter-high depictions of a painter, a glass worker, a potter, and a goldsmith, and on the left, representations of a Chinese man, an African woman, an American Indian man, and a Polynesian woman, all depicted in classical style (Fig. 13). When visitors entered the museum they walked through a small entryway into the vestibule that held the Japanese guardians that would normally stand at the entrance of a Buddhist temple,[29] and which so enticed the young Alfred Lehmann a decade later. Symmetrically designed stairways opened up on either side of the vestibule, shooting up at clear right angles to the first landing, and then further to the next levels, all of which were lit by the

FIGURE 13. The Grassi-Museum in Leipzig. Note the large windows, the images at the base of the columns, and the division of the building into two museums, devoted to *Völkerkunde* and *Kunst und Gewerbe* (museum of applied arts). (Stadtgeschichtliches Museum, Leipzig)

high, surrounding windows and the magnificent glass roof. The light-gray granite stairs were framed by white walls, arching roofs, gray-green granite pillars, mosaic tiled floors and the yellow marble that was chosen for the landings (Figs. 14, 15). It was, in other words, both a monumental and a majestic building that promised to finally provide Leipzig's ethnologists with the facilities they needed.

Inside, collections that had been sporadically moved from place to place during the previous three decades were finally distributed evenly throughout the new building's four levels: Indonesia and the South Seas on the first floor, Asia on the second, Africa and the Americas on the third floor, and a small prehistory collection on the fourth. As one newspaper explained it on opening day, "quickly moving hands" had been busy "bringing system and order to the inextricable chaos of the thousand upon thousand things" in the museum's collections as the building was completed.[30] From their tight, exiled existence in storage facilities, backroom shelves, and innumerable numbers of boxes, many of these collections saw the light of day for the first time in decades.

The Grassi-Museum was a truly magnificent building. It won an award

FIGURE 14. A view toward the right side of the vestibule in the Grassi-Museum. In addition to the monumental character of the architecture, note the objects from Asian *Kulturvölker*. Like most German ethnographic museums, the Leipzig museum contained objects from all over the world rather than limiting its collections to those from ostensibly primitive peoples. (Museum für Völkerkunde zu Leipzig)

for its design at the Chicago World's Fair in 1893, and it was used by ethnologists in other cities as a model for their own institutions.[31] Yet this museum, as Lehmann ironically noted years later, already appeared to be too small to hold all their collections by 1896, and within a short period of time it began to suffer the same fate as the small and medium-sized mu-

FIGURE 15. The central stairwell in the Grassi-Museum and the magnificent glass ceiling meant to flood the museum with natural light. (Stadtgeschichtliches Museum Leipzig)

seums that preceded it.[32] Even in this monumental new building, display cabinets were soon packed full of artifacts, and by 1909 the museum was suffering under strong public criticism, with one observer remarking that conditions within the museum had made "the careful contemplation of any given area of human activity" a "totally desperate" endeavor.[33] This new building had given Leipzig's ethnologists and their supporters more space than they had ever had, but not even this grand edifice could expand with their radically growing acquisitions.[34] As a result, the extra square footage they gained with the Grassi-Museum failed to offer Leipzig's ethnologists anything more than a temporary solution to the disorder they had been facing, and this museum soon became simply a newer, bigger version of older problems. Ethnologists, in other words, despite repeatedly moving their museums, reordering their displays, and designing new buildings, were ultimately unable to get their collections under control.

The subtext to this whiggish vision of nineteenth-century German ethnographic museums' "development," is the persistent, never-resolved struggle between these ethnologists and their collections. Each of the directors who took charge of the museums—in each of these cities and throughout the entire period of this study—began by attempting to put their institutions into order. Yet each attempt at reordering was quickly followed by even more *dis*order, and then further, more vigorous attempts to gain control. The museums' directors consistently hoped to solve this problem by looking for more space, and each successful attempt to gain it was marked off at that time—and continues to be noted today—as a milestone in that institution's development. However, tracing out these museums' histories from a whiggish perspective is much like crossing a river by jumping from one stone to the next. We remain focused on the stones that guide us along a line from one place to the other without spending too much time examining the currents that actually account for the location of these stones in the first place. The same is true of attempts to map out these museums' development over time by focusing on the "critical moments" in their progressive histories. If we simply string together the key "turning points" in the museums' development from 1868–1914—the major acquisitions, the reorganizations, the reopenings, and the changes of command—we can easily miss the cultural currents in which these points are sitting. In short, we end up paying a great deal of attention to ethnologists' efforts to create a better place for their collections and to gain more space for their arrangements. From this perspective it would be quite easy to argue that it was this lack of space that accounts for ethnologists' inability to gain control over their collections, and we could use this as an explanation for the fact that rather than "sorting the world systematically into drawers, glass-fronted cases, bottles and filing cabinets," many ethnologists found themselves packing as much of the "world" as possible into each of these containers until it finally spilled out all over their floors. Yet in the end, the problem never really lay with the space available for the collections. The problem was inherent in the ethnographic project itself.

Second Walk-Through:
A Peculiar Kind of Stasis

There is another way to read the history of these museums, one that recognizes their development and expansion but does not code their "growth" as progressing toward an ultimate goal. This second reading emphasizes that ethnologists' desires and standards simply expanded with the promise of modern technologies, and that although they continued to believe that they could create a superior informational system, their collections consistently grew much faster than their ability to control them and their needs were only momentarily met by the resources at hand. By the first decade of the twentieth century, despite an ever-increasing number of ethnologists with advanced university degrees, the many technological advances that facilitated their rapidly growing collecting ventures, the relative consensus on arrangements and modes of display, and the successful efforts by ethnologists and their supporters to gain ever-larger buildings, these cultural scientists continually found themselves wedged in between over-crowded glass boxes, forever falling behind in their attempts to catalog their ever-expanding collections, and desperately pursuing the same goals: more space, more money, more collections, more assistants, more recognition, and more order. Their many frenzied actions, in fact, seemed to whirl around a peculiar sort of stasis as they found themselves perpetually overwhelmed by mundane problems that would not go away.

When Bastian wrote the introduction to his 1877 guide to Berlin's ethnographic collection, he began by explaining some of the problems and challenges facing his museum—problems that would ultimately become the bane of all the museums I have discussed here. He noted that the last guide they had issued for the collection was written in 1872, and that although they had long since run out of copies, the museum's changing priorities and the problems created by their limited facilities had forced them to postpone issuing a new guidebook for several years. Indeed, the "terrible conditions" within the museum that had already been mentioned in the 1872 guide, especially the "lack of space" and the "poor lighting," had, with the continual growth of the collection, only gotten worse. As a result, Bastian lamented that the creation of a "detailed and instructive display," was "now even more an impossibility than earlier."[35]

However, not everything he reported was stormy and depressing. Bastian also had some good news. The Prussian Cultural Ministry had committed to creating a new museum, and since 1873 Bastian and his associates had begun planning a new building that was expected to solve their space and lighting problems and allow them to create substantially better displays. Once they acquired more space and better lighting the collections could be properly displayed, and the displays would be "that much more instructive," because of the more complete nature of the collections. Bastian, in other words, began his guide to the museum by both discussing its state of disarray and by arguing that this was a provisional condition that, while it might continue to get worse in the next few years, was legitimated by their preparations for their new museum building and absolved by their anticipation of better things to come.

Unfortunately for Bastian and his counterparts, the provisional state he described in his 1877 guide became a relatively permanent condition for his and other nineteenth-century ethnographic museums.[36] Bastian, for example, was forced to wait more than a decade for his eagerly anticipated new building, spending the entire period in a temporary location crowded in by his provisional displays.[37] During much of this time Bastian declared his museum "inaccessible for scientific studies," and for several years it was completely closed to the public.[38] This situation was anything but exceptional. When Leipzig's city council committed to creating a new building for the city's museum in 1884, the association in charge eagerly began planning its future and anticipating the possibilities for the new museum. But this building, like Bastian's, took more than a decade to complete, slowed down repeatedly by contentions about location, style, size, and funds. During the interim years the museum's collections were shuffled about from one temporary location to the next. First, in 1887, they were moved out of an old hospital building, which itself had been chosen in 1872 as a temporary location, and into storage for a year. Then they were moved into an old book exchange in 1888, and an old conservatory in 1892, before finally moving in 1895 into the new building, which was opened to the public in 1896.[39] For decades then, the museum's provisional arrangements were permanent conditions, and the over-crowded, incomplete, and often ad-hoc temporary displays were the only ones their visitors could know.

Moreover, the market mechanism had pushed ethnologists' collecting at such a pace that almost immediately after their celebrated openings, both of these museums started running out of space in their coveted new buildings, and within a short period of time they were again playing host to an ongoing series of temporary arrangements and provisional displays. In Berlin, this realization hit even before the museum was opened, and proposals for covering the courtyard area with a glass roof in order to gain more space began as early as 1883. Bastian supported these proposals despite the fact that they threatened to delay the opening of his museum even further, because the influx of artifacts had been so tremendous that it was clear that this extra space would be desperately needed. In fact, so many things had come into the museum since they began drawing up the plans for the new building that the museum itself was not only "bursting at its seams" by 1883, but five entire rooms in the basement of the Royal Museums were "packed from floor to ceiling with collections in boxes."[40] The radical pace of acquisitions only increased during the next thirty years.[41] The result was that only a little more than a decade after the new building was opened and hailed as the largest, and only, self-standing museum of its kind, the leaders of its different geographical sections were declaring conditions in the museum "unbearable," and arguing that they simply could not fit all their collections into the cabinets at their disposal, or fit all the cabinets they needed into their hallways and rooms. Felix von Luschan, for example, wrote in a report on the section for Africa and *Ozeanien*, that it contained 14,676 items in seventy-three cabinets when it was opened in 1886. By 1899 the number of artifacts had quadrupled and sixty cabinets had been added to the display areas, but the size of the rooms had obviously remained the same.[42]

Leipzig's collections experienced a similar kind of growth while their museum's supporters created their new building, and they continued to expand rapidly after it was opened in 1896.[43] In fact, they grew so radically, and the museum's arrangements were in such a state of constant flux that both of its directors refused to publish guides to the museum. Only three years after opening the new building, the Leipzig city council began to press Hermann Obst to produce a guide to their collections. He replied, however, that given the constantly changing conditions in the museum, a "printed guide would already be incorrect and useless after a short time," and thus the museum refused to publish one.[44] A decade later, Karl Weule made a similar argument to the city council after he became director, complaining that the constant acquisitions and complete overcrowding of the museum made guiding a pointless task. In fact, it was only in 1913— seventeen years after the museum was opened—that the first guide to the *Völkerkunde* collections in the Grassi-Museum was finally produced at the city council's insistence.[45]

To a certain degree the perplexing conditions in these museums had to do with problems in the museums' designs and the fact that the pace of building simply could not keep up with the pace of acquisitions. Bastian, in fact, seemed to have anticipated this problem, and in the early 1880s recommended to Leipzig's Oberbürgermeister Georgi that he create a museum made of steel and glass, much like the famous Crystal Palace, which could be easily expanded along with its collections.[46] Such plans, however, did not sit well with the monumental designs of the age, the supporters who generally paid the bills, or the architects who created the buildings. In this sense, the Faustian dilemma ethnologists faced when they aligned themselves with local elites also inhibited their abilities to gain control over their collections. As a result of pressure from their supporters, practical concerns about scientific needs were often lost to architectural enthusiasm for the buildings' facades—which received most of the boosters' initial attention and ate up much of the budgeted funds in both Berlin and Leipzig.[47]

The interiors of these early buildings also suffered from the architects' concerns with aesthetics. The Berlin museum, for instance, was composed almost completely of corridors with hardly any wall space; the walls on one side of its hallways were covered with windows that looked outdoors, while the other side was open to the central courtyard—not the ideal situation for creating displays (Fig. 16). Similarly, Leipzig's architects and supporters put so much emphasis on the entryway, the majestic staircases, and the aesthetics of design in their museum, that when their funds grew tight the technical facilities, offices, and workrooms were the first things to be reduced in size or eliminated altogether, while the external niceties were never disturbed.[48] Form and function were often starkly at odds in these museums.

The endlessly provisional character of these museums' locations and the continual growth of their contents also had an understandably great impact on ethnologists' "scientific" efforts within them. Ethnologists in Berlin, for instance, regularly complained that the working conditions in their museum at the turn of the century "made respectable scientific endeavors all but impossible"—evaluations confirmed by disgruntled outside observers.[49] At the same time, the task of cataloguing and ordering these museums' collections were consistently subordinated to the goal of increasing acquisitions. In 1879, for example, the board of directors for Leipzig's museum began asking Obst to "dedicate less of his activity to further collecting" and to "finally begin cataloguing" and ordering the artifacts. Obst, however, refused. Despite the museum's somewhat chaotic condition, he argued that collecting had to remain their top priority, and that it was better to postpone their cataloguing and simply pack their artifacts away in boxes rather than limit their acquisitions. He also explained, in his typically aggressive and sarcastic way that their request was "much easier to make than to follow" because the "scientific ordering" of the

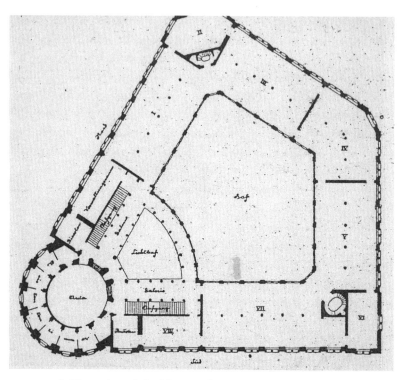

FIGURE 16. Floor plan of the Museum für Völkerkunde Berlin. Note the large number of windows and the virtual absence of interior walls. The design was meant to bring as much natural light as possible into the building and to facilitate scientists' efforts to engage in a comparative analysis of the objects on display. The architecture was supposed to allow scientists to view the collections from multiple vantage points. The lack of wall space, however, later became a subject of much criticism, and the overwhelming number of objects made impossible the kinds of visual comparisons Bastian and his architects initially intended. (From Bastian, *Übersichtlicher Abriß der Sammlungen*)

collection must go "hand in hand" with the cataloguing, a process that would cost an "immense amount of time and money"—both of which he professed to lack.[50] As a result, the board's request was only first met when they hired Karl Weule as directorial assistant in 1899 and gave him the specific assignment of cataloging the museum.[51] This was a daunting task and, according to Weule, a "real museum man" needed to have "incredible patience to avoid becoming an idiot"[52] while sorting through thirty years of acquisitions in which it was "difficult to even determine the origins" of "more than half the things." In short, cataloguing the collections in Leipzig—the action often hailed as the museum's first scientific priority and the feature that most distinguished modern museums from the earlier cabinets of curiosity—was repeatedly postponed until 1900.

As Obst had explained, however, the conditions that greeted Weule's arrival in the museum were a product of necessity and priorities rather than preference; the cycles of accumulation were up and running, the pace was quickening, the market mechanism was pressing them forward, and they simply could not stop for cataloging or ordering their collections. Because the ethnographic project was predicated on possession, collecting was made the overriding priority from the beginning, and as these museums developed over time it remained ethnologists' primary obsession. It was the possession of artifacts that brought these museums their stature in the international community of science and gave their cities and supporters prestige. And indeed, refusals by Obst and Weule to create guidebooks, Obst's refusal to even contemplate cataloguing his collections, as well as Luschan and his co-workers' frustration with the conditions within the Berlin museum, were all vivid articulations of the fact that ethnologists were not in control of the cycles of accumulation that were filling their museums, and that the market mechanism inhibited any break in their incessant flight forward.

Moreover, if cataloguing collections had to be neglected for years at a time, ethnologists generally recognized that maintaining their collections in a proper order was a fanciful dream. The Berlin museum's ethnologists, for example, were consistently struggling with their displays. They were often forced to close different sections, mix their various collections, or remove them altogether. Moreover, many of the collections simply never made it into the museum at all. Bastian, for instance, noted in 1903 that many of the things they had collected before the museum opened in 1886 had still "not even seen the light of day."[53] The non-existent European section is one good example. It was included in the museum's initial plans, but because there was no place for it once their new building was built, it was never created.[54] Similarly, a section devoted to physical anthropology was anticipated in the museum's guidebook in 1881 and promised to visitors in 1888, and again in 1892. By 1895 Berlin's ethnologists removed this promise from the guide, but in 1911 a new announcement appeared in the guidebook explaining that an anthropological collection would be set up in the museum and could be visited by individuals with the director's permission while the displays were being created. The same announcement appeared again in 1914. Evidently it remained in process for quite some time.[55]

Not only were entire collections consistently excluded from the museum but the displays were often shuffled around and regularly closed down, making complete geographical arrangements practically impossible to maintain. By the mid-1890s, in fact, Berlin's guidebooks began including apologies for this situation. The 1895 guide, for example, explained that a large part of the Siberian collection had to be removed from display and was available only to individuals willing to make special appointments to see it.[56] In 1898, the guides began including a disclaimer in reference to their African collections which stated that while "these collections were [meant to be] geographically ordered," their "continual" and "strong growth" had not always permitted their proper distribution within their rooms, and consequently "cabinets containing collections from completely different areas of Africa are often standing next to each other."[57] Already in 1900 this explanation became more general, and the guidebook noted that while their plan was to maintain the museum's arrangements according to geographical principles, such an "arrangement, as a result of the lack of space and the squeezing in [einschieben] of new cabinets, has not been carried out rigorously overall."[58] Indeed, one could argue that it was not "rigorous" at all, and by 1906 the museum's ethnologists began producing a new kind of guide altogether, one that listed the geographical areas at the very beginning, and explained where the different parts of these collections could be found since they were not always kept together or in the most logical places—an arrangement which, of course, was completely contrary to the original vision.[59] By the first decade of the twentieth century, in other words, the Berlin museum's collections were becoming noticeably unruly.

Consequently, by 1905 Berlin's celebrated museum—the world's first self-standing ethnographic museum and by far the largest museum of its kind—had become a spectre in the world of ethnology. Its ability to accumulate tremendous numbers of artifacts continued to be praised and admired across Europe and the United States, but the conditions of its displays were disdained by its scientists and visitors alike. Its fate was seen as a warning and its conditions an outcome to be avoided at all costs. Georg Thilenius made this clear in his proposals for his new building in Hamburg, as did Karl Weule in his correspondence with Leipzig's city fathers and in his papers on the practical uses of museums. Berlin's ethnologists composed stacks of letters lamenting their situation. And already in 1899, the director of the Chicago Field Museum remarked to Bastian that although the Berlin museum's collections were quite probably "the most complete in the world," the "crowded conditions of the cases" were a "great hindrance to study in this museum." In fact, according to him, "many of the collections cannot be seen to advantage by the general visitor; indeed a majority of the collections can leave only a feeling of confusion in the mind of even the most casual observer."[60]

In its own peculiarly exemplary way, the Berlin museum revealed the great paradox inherent in Bastian's ethnographic project. The more successful a museum's ethnologists were at pursuing the first aim of their scientific endeavor—obtaining collections—the more difficulty they had achieving their second and most important aim—bringing the precision of science to bear on their collections and establishing clearly defined, orderly, and accessible displays. As a result, ethnologist's best efforts often created tremendous problems, and Berlin's ethnologists, who appeared to have so excelled beyond their counterparts in other cities, were ironically left with little more than an incredibly large collection of curiosities that ultimately threatened their scientific legitimacy. Thus ethnologists' greatest challenge remained the task of bringing order to their collections, a challenge to which, as is so often pointed out in the general narratives about museums, they occasionally rose. During these infrequent moments, especially the museums' various openings and reopenings, or their exhibitions of temporary displays, their visitors could find well-ordered, accessible collections where they might have the kinds of experiences Bastian envisioned. Yet such moments of clarity were few; more frequently, ethnologists were struggling unsuccessfully to meet the challenge of gaining and maintaining control over their collections. Consequently their visitors were just as likely, or perhaps even more likely, to encounter displays of disorder as the ethnologists engaged in a frenzied attempt to prevent a descent into spectacle.

Displays of Disorder?

Berlin's new Museum für Völkerkunde was opened with considerable fanfare in 1886. Its dedication was, in fact, a carefully orchestrated state occasion. The guest list included individuals from "the highest circles of the political, military, and civil services" as well as the arts and the sciences. Crown Prince Friedrich Wilhelm attended the opening wearing the uniform of his Second Silesian Dragoon regiment. Prince Wilhelm, Princess Victoria, and Otto von Bismarck were present as well. The entryway on Königgrätzer Straße was trimmed with Prussian flags, and the circular vestibule, with its fantastic mosaic ceiling and polished-granite walls, was decorated with large-leafed plants, and wreaths made from the branches of fir trees. The five arching doorways that greeted visitors as they entered

FIGURE 17. The Museum für Völkerkunde Berlin on Königgrätzerstr. 120. (Landesarchiv Berlin)

the vestibule branched off symmetrically into different areas of the building. The outermost led to stairs that went up to the second level, the innermost to the displays on the ground floor, and the central doorway to the museum's interior courtyard [*Lichthof*], where the dedication ceremony took place (Figs. 17, 18).

When guests walked through the middle of the five portals they entered a large open space that resembled a temple of sorts. At the back of the room stood a spectacular, ancient Indian gateway carved out of stone. At its base, a carpeted podium awaited the royalty and state officials who would open the museum. A veritable jungle of palms and other tropical plants framed the scene, stretching out from either side of the gateway. A statue of a Siamese king set against a fantastically painted banner from a temple in Laos glared through its center. An Indian god was nestled in the plants to the right and to the left of the gateway, and two Javanese gods—Siwa and his wife—were set on either side of the podium. Hanging from the walkway above the green vegetation were four bright yellow Chinese banners. And, suspended above the entire room, an enormous flag boasting the Prussian double-headed eagle dominated this otherwise "exotic" scene (Fig. 19).[61]

After the audience was assembled—state officials seated to the left, members of the military and foreign office to the right, Bastian, the ar-

FIGURE 18. Entering the Museum für Völkerkunde Berlin in 1887. Note how the visitors are portrayed by the artist C. Stöving. Clearly middle class (the woodcutting was used in the *Gartenlaube*, a middle-class magazine), the figures are shown strolling through the museum, engaged in a kind of self-edification or *Bildung* that requires them to gaze at length on the collections rather than simply take them in at a glance. This visual experience would change significantly around the turn of the century, as "just looking" became the new mantra in European popular culture. (AKG Berlin)

chitect, and other scientists toward the front, and other guests, including many of the construction workers, toward the back—the royals took their place on the podium. The Crown Prince and Cultural Minister Gustav von Gossler gave eloquent speeches resounding with scientific dedication and patriotism. Gossler, in particular, lauded Bastian, his persistence, and his contributions to science, and portrayed the museum as the material articulation of Bastian's vision. Gossler called the building a "milestone" in the history of the Royal Museums and in the development of the sciences of anthropology, ethnology, and pre-history. He emphasized that Bastian and his associates had transformed the museum's collections from "piles of 'rarities' and 'curiosities'" into a solid "base for scientific disciplines." This new, scientific institution, he explained, would give them critical insights "into the basis of [their] humble past," and provide ethnologists with "indispensable aid in their scientific work" by giving them a space in which they could carefully formulate problems and develop answers through a "complete comparison of their materials."[62]

FIGURE 19. The *Lichthof* on opening day, Museum für Völkerkunde Berlin. Because of the poor quality of this photograph, only a small piece of the giant Prussian flag that hung over the assembly can be seen in the upper right corner of the image. (Staatliche Museen zu Berlin, Ethnologisches Museum)

These state officials, in other words, officially embraced the ethnographic project that had so "enticed" Bastian and others and christened their vision in a public ceremony.

It would be easy to point to these stately proceedings and portray them as indicative of the museum's national importance and somehow characteristic of its existence. Indeed, this moment of official attention and its detailed choreography fit nicely into the first walk-through described above, and historians have held it up as somehow representative of the Berlin museum's existence as the world's first self-standing ethnographic museum.[63] Yet this particular vision of the institution and its place in society is much like the few photographs or sketches that one can find of this and other nineteenth-century museums. They capture exceptional moments, points at which particular presentations—either the entire museum or individual displays—were well-staged. These points in time are important, and we should not ignore what they can tell us about the extent of the museum's state support or the shape that the museum's scientists and supporters ultimately wanted their institution to assume; but we should also bear in mind that these photographs and particularly well-orchestrated moments were meant to be captured and remembered. They are important instances of self-presentation, but they are seldom typical of this or the other museums' existence or the character of their displays. Quite the opposite, these are incongruous visions.

While very few candid photographs of nineteenth-century German ethnographic museums exist, there are many verbal descriptions that throw into question the visions of order and purpose that we might otherwise draw out of ethnologists' descriptions of their plans and intentions, administrative records of official proceedings, and the few surviving sketches and photographs. Indeed, these descriptions give us considerable insight into ethnologists' own realization of the untenable nature of the ethnographic project and provide us with another reason for their desire to abandon it in favor of the pointed educational displays or *Schausammlungen* discussed at the end of Chapter 4.

Max Buchner, for example, complained that his own museum in Munich was placed in a "disgraceful building" (*Schandegebäude*), which illustrated how "criminally bad things in Munich were allowed to be built." During the winter, on the days when it was snowing, visitors left footprints on the floors as they moved through its rooms. "Snow," he recalled, "came though the windows, and even found its way into the cabinets" because of the cracks and holes in their tops. "More than once," he saw "little piles of snow next to artifacts in the apparently closed cabinets," and for years water spots could be seen on the southern wall where the waterlines that had occasionally burst in winter had left their mark. The glass in the poorly constructed windows often rattled in a "humorous" and "sometimes all too humorous" fashion when "a little wind" picked up outside. Only a few of these windows could be regularly opened, and then "always with the danger that they might not close again."

The museum's contents were arranged so that the well-known Siebold-collection from Japan took up most of the room, China and India were given "some space," while the rest of the collections "were miserably pressed together." In addition to the uneven distribution of the various collections, more than a few of the objects seemed completely out of place. A large cork model of the Heidelberg castle, once the private property of King Lüdwig I, was perhaps the most intrusive. But because it took up so much space, the directors of the National Museum refused to take possession of this particular piece of national pride until 1888, and thus for two decades its walls and towers continued to shoot up between the Japanese clothing, porcelains, and masks. Oddities, pressed together artifacts, inadequate cabinets, conditions that "curled the Japanese paintings" and allowed snow to blow up against valuable objects, and arrangements that gave primacy to particularly famous collections at the expense of the others—this is hardly the portrait one might expect of a leading scientific institution.[64]

To be fair, the Munich museum was easily the most neglected of the four museums. During its first forty years it lacked the support of a local association like that which championed the Leipzig museum or the interest groups that embraced Hamburg's institute and lobbied for dramatic improvements at the end of the century. By 1912, once Lucien Sherman had been given the means to change these conditions, the museum was fundamentally altered and the displays were brought under control. Nevertheless, for most of the period 1868–1914 the displays in this museum, like the better-supported museums in Hamburg, Leipzig, and Berlin, suffered from varying degrees of disorder.

The conditions within the Berlin museum are in many ways the most important, precisely because of the fanfare with which it was opened, the strong governmental backing it received, the impressive groups of organized patrons who supported it, its connections to Germany's leading anthropological association, the Berlin Society for Anthropology, Ethnology, and Prehistory, and to the Berlin university, the number of specialists working in its different sections, and its reputation as the leading ethnographic museum in Germany at this time. This museum was considered exemplary, and indeed it was, both in terms of these ethnographic institutions' potential and many of their shortcomings.

Despite Bastian's recognition that his ethnographic project had already gone awry, he went to great lengths to prepare a well-orchestrated opening for his museum so that it communicated the messages that would best legitimate his project and insure its continued support. Bastian wanted to use this public occasion to clearly and "immediately break" with "the character of the ethnological collections connected to the earlier curiosity cabinets," as well as the disheveled state of Berlin's ethnological collections, which had prevailed since at least the mid-1870s. Thus he stressed that the displays must be brought into order for the opening and accompanied by a thorough guidebook that would illustrate the 'scientific' nature and purpose of its collections. In short, he took pains to guarantee that the museum would be celebrated from the moment it opened as a new kind of scientific institution.[65]

While Bastian certainly achieved his short-term goal, historians should not take his successful efforts at self-promotion as representative of the state of his museum. The very conditions Bastian created (or staged) in order to establish his legitimacy and illustrate that his institution was something new—something radically different from the collections that came before it because of the scientific principles that governed its operations—quickly degenerated. Not only did the museum's guidebooks reveal some of the difficulties Berlin's ethnologists had in maintaining their collections, but little more than a decade after the museum opened, its scientists were throwing up their hands in frustration while declaring that their institution was in total disarray.

In 1899 Bastian collected the first of several reports from his directorial assistants on the state of the museum's different sections and sent them, along with his own report, to the director of the Royal Museums. Bastian began by describing the unprecedented influx of materials, the failed attempt to add another floor to the building, the mixed blessing of their monopoly on artifacts from the colonies—which alone could have filled their museum—and sketched out the institution's generally desperate state.[66] Each of his assistants' reports echoed his concerns and painted a bleak picture of impossible overcrowding. Albert Grünwedel, for example, who later revealed that "no oriental collections had been unpacked and put on display since moving [into the new building] in 1885,"[67] wrote that the conditions in the Indian section were simply "impossible," and argued that an "orderly display of the Indian collections" would require the "entire floor" as well as the stairways leading to it;[68] Grünwedel, however, shared his floor with collections from China and Indonesia. Similarly, when suggestions began to circulate again in 1905 about covering the museum's courtyard in an effort to gain space, Felix von Luschan vehemently wrote to the director of the Royal Museums that this stop gap measure would bring little to a museum where he could not "fit a single display cabinet more" into his section, and in which his cabinets had been "packed so full, for such a long time now" that "one could not expect them to have any use for the public."[69]

Indeed, the "public" too was well aware of the museum's "deplorable conditions," in which, as Bastian had put it, the "tightly-packed" cabinets threatened "to explode."[70] In fact public debate about the state of the Berlin museum broke out in the city's papers in 1900, revealing a museum much more akin to the curiosity cabinets from which Bastian had hoped to distance himself in 1886, than the premier scientific institution portrayed in Gossler's speech. One critic, for example, wrote that he had recently visited the museum for the first time in several years and was simply "flabbergasted" by the "strange combination of a gigantic representation of a Japanese god with sacrificial alters and architectural remains from old Mexican cultures" wedged into the vestibule—which created a somewhat different impression than the well-orchestrated scene visitors had experienced on the museum's opening day. But as he walked into the *Lichthof*, "this astonishment gave way to a certain amusement [*Heiterkeit*]" as he took in the mishmashed assemblage of different things that resembled the planned heterogeniety of the *Wunderkammern* more than anything else:[71] "German dug-out canoes were strewn here and there, gateways to Peruvian temples, Mexican gods, Indian *Geschlecterpfeiler*, an Indian *Götterwagen*, yes even a small glass case filled with . . . Damascian wax dolls were there to admire." Gone were the neatly ordered arrangements and calculated aesthetics of the opening ceremonies, and rather than geographical distribution, organizational hierarchies, or scientifically-ordered displays, he was greeted by a strikingly impressionistic vision, a spectacle that might certainly inspire wonder but was completely devoid of order or logical arrangement (Fig. 20).[72]

Given that the *Lichthof*, because of its high ceiling, was generally set aside for items that were too large to fit into other areas of the museum, one might argue that the hodgepodge portrayed in Berlin's papers could not be regarded as characteristic of the rest of the museum. In fact, in the very next week another contributor to this public debate argued just that, claiming that the objects in the rest of the museum were "perfectly ordered according to strict scientific principles."[73] This defensive portrayal, however, agrees with neither the ethnologists' private reports nor the other public responses that appeared in Berlin's papers during this debate. These other responses reveal a museum that was anything but orderly and in which complete chaos seemed to be held only momentarily at bay. One author, for example, portrayed the visitor's odyssey through the museum in this way:

> On the ground floor [of the museum the visitor] finds the *heimische* prehistory and the remains of the Schliemann Iliad. If he is able to pull himself away from the amphora from Troy or the innumerable pieces of pottery from the Prussian administrative region, he will immediately find himself in the middle of a hall, half of which is filled with Inca mummies and earthen vessels, the other half with fur overcoats from the inhabitants of the Amur region and metalwork from the land of the Shah. Naturally only provisionally! He climbs to the second floor of the building; in the Gallery he has the choice of turning from a store of

FIGURE 20. Museum für Völkerkunde Berlin. An orderly display? A cabinet containing materials from Amazonian Indians already well packed in 1886. The crowding escalated dramatically during the next decades, and such displays of disorder became the rule rather than the exception throughout much of the museum. (Staatliche Museen zu Berlin, Ethnologisches Museum)

Papuan idols right to the bronzes out of African Benin or left to the Urns of now extinct Argentineans. He decides for Africa, gadgets in the South Seas, emerges out of New Guinea suddenly among the *Feuerländer* and encounters in the last American hall Asian Tschuktschen with Eskimos, Mexicans, and Chileans united like neighbors. How could he still have the strength and courage to savor the exemplary ordered but overwhelmingly crushed-together treasures from *vorder-* and *Hinterindian*, Indonesia, China, Japan, which are on the third floor? With horror he hears that there is a fourth-floor as well, which is shared by the anthropological collection and American plaster castings. [The author then ends with the question:] Should these scientific collections from throughout the world be permitted to be mixed together like cabbage and turnips?[74]

Perhaps better than any other description, this account of the Berlin museum captures the end-result of an ethnographic project predicated on possession, closely intertwined with international exchange, and governed in many ways by the market mechanism and its ties to a prestige industry which ethnologists helped to create. It vividly illustrates the inadequacy of even the most celebrated museum building, and the rather disconcerting fact that ethnologists were not only unable to realize the promises held out by modern technological advances, but that these very advances complicated their problems as much if not more than they helped to solve them. Indeed, it reveals a museum that was much more akin to the disordered *Wunderkammern* from which Bastian tried to distance his institution in 1886 than the vision that he and Gossler articulated on that opening day—a museum that ultimately threatened the very legitimacy of their scientific project with its disorderly displays.

Moreover, despite ethnologists' official complaints and the sometimes heated public debates around the turn of the century, conditions within the museum hardly improved from 1900–1914; visitors continued to be greeted by displays of disorder. Luschan, for instance, responded to a request by a Dr. W. Greif from the Deutsche Gesellschaft für Volkstümliche Naturkunde, for a tour of the museum's collections in 1905, by stating that although he would, in principle, "welcome" the group's visit, his section suffered from such a "lack of space . . . that one can no longer speak of a guided tour in the usual sense." In fact, he wrote that it would be impossible to take a group of "more than five or six people" through the collections "if they really wanted to see or learn something." As a result, Luschan had long since discontinued the tours he had once eagerly given to groups of workers, and he told Greif that his association would have to wait until the completion of another new building. Of course when he penned this letter Luschan probably did not realize that he was asking them to wait for two decades.[75]

While Luschan and his potential visitors waited for changes throughout the decade prior to World War I, the museum's condition remained a sore subject with ethnologists, the directors of the Royal Museums, the museum's audience, and state officials. At a meeting of Berlin's house of representatives in 1912, for example, one of the representatives, a Dr. Hauptmann, called the museum "a neglected stepchild of the city," noted that they had been debating the state of the museum for over eleven years with no tangible results, and then exclaimed that, given the museum's ever-deteriorating "conditions," it struck him as "rather strange, that . . . 20,000 Marks had been set aside in the budget for 'the restoration and display of the results of the Turfan expedition in the Museum für Völkerkunde'." Although it was certainly a good idea to restore the collection, he found it rather "ridiculous" for them to think of displaying it in the Völkerkundemuseum.[76] Given the museum's condition, he argued, it "would simply be impossible." In a rather sarcastic suggestion that nicely captured both his and the Berlin ethnologists' sense of frustration, he offered an alternative plan: "Perhaps," he suggested, "the 20,000 Marks could be put to good use, if it was applied to procuring rat poison, so that the rats [which were plaguing the museum] would not devour the entire collections." According to the minutes of this meeting, his suggestion was followed by a good amount of laughter, but no concrete decisions.

Unlike the celebrated Pitt-Rivers Museum in Oxford, with its well-ordered displays and prescribed messages, or the many ethnological exhibits temporarily erected at world's fairs, the Berlin museum was unable to maintain a precisely constructed organization. Its ever-growing collections not only inhibited the fulfillment of Bastian's vision, they also threatened the very legitimacy of his project. As the Berlin museum's holdings grew larger and larger, the displays degenerated from disorderly to unfathomable. They became, in essence, a spectacular *tabula rasa* out of which almost anything could be read, or which, for some visitors, might yield nothing at all. This insight provides us with another reason why Berlin's ethnologists chose to move toward the creation of *Schausammlungen* in the first decade of the twentieth century; these displays might have been unscientific and remedial by Bastian's standards, but they appeared much more orderly, scientific, and legitimate to many of their visitors than what Berlin's ethnologists had been able to achieve. Ironically, then, moving toward arrangements they regarded as less scientific was a means of protecting their scientific legitimacy.

Receptions

One simply cannot speak of a museum's reception among its visitors in the singular; indeed, it is misleading to even think of one display in this way. A variety of individuals entered these museums carrying their own cultural baggage—their educational and social backgrounds, their awareness of the non-European world through printed sources or lived experience, their understanding of the science of ethnology, not to mention their familiarity with visual displays inside art museums, department stores, shop windows, and on city streets during fairs, exhibitions, and even the urban commuting that came with streetcars and suburbs. Thus it would be absurd to expect visitors to have received the same messages from any given museum at a particular point in time, let alone from all the museums during the period 1868 to 1914. Moreover, given the prevalent disorder in the museums and the ethnologists' difficulties in fashioning clearly readable displays that could communicate consistently cogent messages, it would be a mistake to focus solely on the intentions of the museums' designers in the hopes of locating their cultural functions. Unfortunately, however, much of the current scholarly work on museums posits their cultural functions based on the intentions of the individuals most closely associated with creating museums and their displays. Indeed, many scholars continue to pursue such analyses despite their recognition that museums functioned simultaneously on several different levels, and that there was not necessarily a causal link between these functions and the intentions of the museums' "creators."[77]

Having spent a good part of this chapter discussing the kinds of displays that awaited visitors when they entered these museums, I would like to turn now to what indeed may have been seen. The cacophony of sights, symbols, and mixed messages that greeted visitors as they arrived in these museums could easily offend the eye of an art critic or museologist who developd his or her own expectations in art and art historical museums.[78] Writing in 1921, Karl Scheffler, who worked for the art journal *Neue Kunstwart* from 1900–1930, laughingly described the Berlin museum as a place that was simply "stuffed full from top to bottom" and which "in the passing of years became an admirable absurdity." Yet humor was only one of his emotional reactions to the museum; he wrote as well that the museum's "unheard of riches" and "costly rarities" were "set so close to, next to, behind, before, and above each other that one almost began to hate them." Indeed, according to Scheffler, one could not help but be both emotionally and even physically affected by the museum's displays.

Walking along the ever-narrowing pathways though the dissonant arti-facts, Scheffler insisted that "the visitor became sick between these over packed cabinets."[79]

Scheffler's response was no doubt owing to his specific personal and professional concerns with the aesthetics of display. Individuals such as Karl Scheffler, who were schooled in museum design and had well-devel-oped artistic sensibilities, visited museums with particular expectations. They were familiar with museum display, the aesthetics of art museums, and had developed conceptions of "effective" modes of organization and methods of exhibition. When visiting these museums they naturally im-ported their own ideas of propriety, using them as points of comparison to distinguish between "orderly" and "disorderly"—or "good" and "bad"—displays. Moreover, because of their experiences, they knew that "good" arrangements could be "read" and used to expand their "knowledge" about particular kinds of art, crafts, sciences or, in this case, humanity. When faced with disorderly or "unreadable" exhibits, however, there was a disruption in this communication that often caused frustration as they searched for messages and meanings that should, and indeed, *must* be there. These individuals went to museums expecting to receive knowl-edge, and when the museums failed to provide it they often voiced their dissatisfaction.

Scheffler is, in fact, only one of many visitors who were familiar with museums and felt they understood the principles of display.[80] The differ-ent kinds of individuals who participated in the public debates over the condition of the Berlin museum in 1900, for instance, regardless of whether or not they were art critics, visiting professors, governmental officials, or more general members of the middle classes, all fall into the same cate-gory. These were all individuals who, based on their own experiences, had learned to expect certain things from museums. These kinds of observers visited all of the museums in this study, and their impressions were valu-able for ethnologists then, and are still valuable for historians today, be-cause they explicitly discussed their reception of the museums' displays. Moreover, because they and the ethnologists shared a similar set of stan-dards, a certain degree of shared subjectivity, and, ideally, the same goals of communication, their criticisms provide us with insight into the degree to which the ethnologists achieved the goals they set out for themselves. In general, they did not.

One public reaction to the Leipzig museum is particularly instructive. It nicely illustrates the critical reception of a visitor who, based on his own experiences, expected the museum's ethnologists to provide him with a coherent narrative, or at least "useful" displays, and, when he recognized that they were failing to do this, expressed his concerns in an effort to assist them. Following the creation of a temporary display in the Leipzig museum in 1909, this author wrote an editorial in a local newspaper that both praised the clarity of the temporary exhibition and condemned the obscurity of the museum's permanent displays. He began his critique by listing the museum's attributes in a way that was clearly meant to legitimate his expectations. He praised the "beautiful building," its tremendous collections, and the "singularity" of many of its individual pieces, and stressed that it "appeared to have *fulfilled all the conditions*, that one generally *expects* from such an institution [my emphasis]"—an institution that was clearly of the first level. The author, in other words, placed the museum rhetorically into a particular category, identifying it as a certain kind of museum that should meet known standards and "fulfill" particular "expectations."

Once he had set the stage, the author drew on his own experiences within the museum to argue that his—commonly recognized—expectations were not being met. He wrote: "the more often one remains in the museum's rooms," the more one begins to wonder "whether despite all these favorable conditions its current arrangements are sufficient." The museum's cabinets, for example, struck him as anything but effective. He asked "whether or not it was right, in *a single* cabinet, to display weapons and toys, pots and jewelry, slippers and religious masks, pieces of cloth and idols," and then argued that "these motley combinations throw the thoughtful contemplation [of the artifacts] out of a single area of human activity and into completely different areas," with the result that "the impressions disturb each other" to such a degree that "only unclear and blurred mental images remain."

As this author underscored the museum's failure to communicate, indeed its fundamental inability to communicate anything but "blurred" images, with its current methods, he also offered an alternative and a warning. He argued that in place of the current displays, the museum should reorganize the cabinets according to "modes of manufacture" or "uses" within particular "cultural areas," and that they should choose a consistent means of exhibition. He also stressed that he and many other visitors regarded it as "necessary" that all the museum's "new materials" be immediately "catalogued and labeled." This contextual information, was critical for the museum's entire project because, according to him, the majority of the museum's visitors were not receiving any messages at all. In his view, "the primary psychological characteristic of the public, which, for example, populate the Grassi-Museum's rooms on Sundays, is a complete lack of comprehension." "Anyone who has fortuitously overheard conversations, questions, and judgments issued in front of the display cabinets," he assured them, "would certainly agree with me." Thus he warned the ethnologists that "if the costly, in part irreplaceable objects in the collections would be more than merely curiosities that delight the eyes of children and adolescents [*Backfischen*]," then much more effort must be made in the way of "definition and explanation."[81]

According to this critic, in other words, neither experienced visitors such as himself nor the more general crowds who wandered through the museum were able to extract any "significant knowledge" from the Leipzig museum's displays; their disorderly arrangements and lack of contextual information simply made this impossible. Moreover, similar reactions from visitors in other cities, as well as ethnologists' own reports, indicate that it was only the rare visitor who encountered clearly articulated messages in these museums or was able to extract "useful" information from their displays.

But what, exactly was this discerning visitor, as well as the more general crowds around him, looking at? He was in the Grassi-Museum, which at this time was organized geographically into sections that should have, from the ethnologists' point of view, provided visitors with overviews of the peoples from a given area—much like a traveler might have gained while venturing there. In the left wing of the first floor, for example, the Godeffroy collections were finally displayed in their entirety. The "Godeffroy hall" was arranged so that visitors would walk down the left side of the long rectangular room to the end of the hall and then return along the right side to the door. A portrait of J. Cesar Godeffroy greeted them as they entered the hall, but it was most likely the giant dance mask set near the entrance from the "little known" Sulka on the south coast of New Pomerania that caught their attention. The collections to their left began with artifacts from Australia, which Weule's 1913 guide to the museum would later argue portrayed a "total cultural picture."[82] Here visitors found the collections of Australian weapons—different shaped boomerangs, small and larger shields, and a variety of different clubs, some of which were tipped with shell, stone or bone—as well as the collections of Australian musical instruments—shells that were strung together to make chimes, and the different drums, whistles, and flutes. The collections were placed primarily in large glass and iron cases, each of which contained items from different geographical areas. The first, for instance, held stone tools and baskets from Tasmania and South-East Australia; the second held shields, spears, stone axes, jewelry and clothing from Queensland and the northern territory.

As visitors circled the room, they came to the island world of the Pacific ocean, known as *Ozeanien*, which included everything in the area framed between the American continents, Australia, and Indonesia. These collections were broken down according to island groupings—Melanesian, Polynesian, and Micronesian sections each holding a number of cabinets devoted to different peoples, and each section containing both rudimentary, everyday items, as well as things that could be counted among the fantastic. In the Melanesian section, for example, visitors would have found simple kava bowls, with samples of the kava roots in them, placed in the cabinets along with explanations of how the roots were ground up in the bowls and later made into a brown concoction that "many drank like coffee." Nearby hung spits, wooden plates, and knives that were allegedly used for cannibalism in the Viti islands, as well as fishing hooks made of bone, nets, arm rings, pottery made of red clay, and a model of a New Caledonian house.[83] In each of the different sections one could find innovative fishing instruments crafted to trap, net, hook, and harpoon fish, as well as the religious artifacts and magical instruments such as the intricately carved idols, staves, knives and the laughing masks adorned with feathers and hair from the Batak near Sumatra (Fig. 21). As visitors completed the circle they moved through Indonesia and returned, finally, to Western and Central Australia. Their progression through the displays mimicked a long, circular voyage of discovery.

From an ethnologist's point of view, these arrangements seemed to make sense, but the very completeness and complexity of the displays as well as the lack of information and clear explanations about the importance of the displays left their critic, who was obviously well-versed in the goals of such museums, with little more than "blurred" images. And if we are to trust his evaluations, the uninitiated visitors around him would have left the Godeffroy hall without any comprehension of what these "costly curiosities" might mean. And indeed, Karl Weule seems to confirm this visitor's point. In his 1910 presentation to the German Anthropological Society, for example, he noted that the number of objects displayed in his museum could be "stifling" for visitors and that many "laymen regard it as absolutely impossible to make sense out of the mass" of things in the Leipzig museum, a complaint his employees heard from visitors again and again.[84] Similarly, Felix von Luschan wrote in a report to the directors of the Royal Museums in 1903 that "the public wanders around completely mindlessly in our halls," and expressed his certainty that 99 out of every

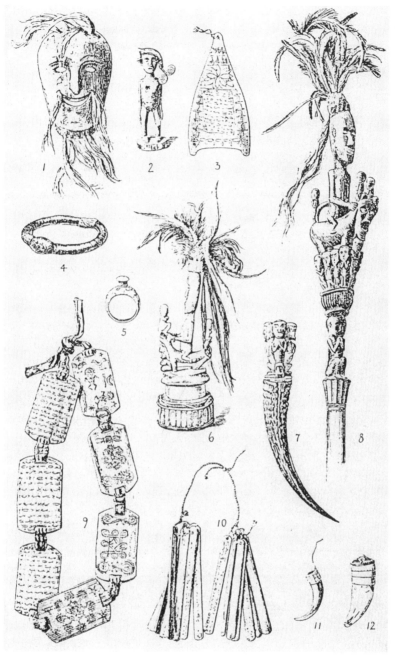

FIGURE 21. Magical implements from the Batak in Sumatra. (From Weule, *Führer durch das Museum für Völkerkunde*)

100 visitors "do not [even] know when they move from one cultural province to the next while strolling through the rooms."[85]

Both public critics and the museums' own ethnologists convincingly argued that the overwhelming number of artifacts and disorganized arrangements in their museums provided visitors with a sea of images but no method for navigating their meanings. The quantity of objects and the lack of order and explanation confused the initiated visitors who expected a certain level of order and explanation. Thus not only did the disorderly displays frustrate ethnologists and reflect their inability to maintain control over their ever-expanding collections, even clear geographical arrangements such as those in the Godeffroy hall proved to be inadequate vehicles for delivering ethnologists' messages to either experienced intellectuals or occasional visitors. In short, despite ethnologists' repeated efforts, their collections generally remained—and were received—as either a disordered mass of potentially instructive artifacts or a collection of delightful curiosities.

Weule, in fact, contended that the "confused and wildly muddled mass" of objects that most visitors encountered in German ethnographic museums often delivered the wrong messages. "In the best case," he argued, such arrangements only led their visitors, to "wonder how these miserable savages, who despite all our teachings are still regarded by popular sentiment as half-animals, could manage to make basic necessities at all, much less in such astonishing diversity and abundance." That these "mountains of objects" were actually the "visual evidence" for the fact that "we whites are only the bearers of one form of culture, and that next to us exist countless other and more often than not different culture forms in the world," is something that "surely only a fraction of the visitors to our ethnographic museums realize" while exploring the display rooms and halls.[86]

Furthermore, during the many well-organized temporary exhibitions, or during periods when museums occupied new buildings and set up carefully organized collections, there is little evidence that even well-educated visitors were able to extract or receive the scientific messages better gained through a close reading of scholarly journals. In an official 1907 report about the current state of ethnographic museums, Thilenius lamented their condition and argued that ethnologists' collections cannot be arranged like magazines if they hope to communicate something: "To the layman, even a well-arranged magazine would easily remain a collection of curiosities which would give him impressions of strangeness, 'amuse' or 'interest' him, but in the end leaves him with a feeling of dissatisfaction. It is quite characteristic that visitors to our museum happily entrust them-

✗ semiotic
commonality

✗   Q: How does narr. cin. replace — or address —
doc./labeling/catalog/"narr. of museum
obj.s?
(immersion,
use,
displays,
...)
narr.
codes,
etc.

selves to guided tours through the collection by one of our overseers; they suspect that the employee knows something about these things, which one cannot begin to understand alone."[87] He noted as well that people visiting the museums enjoyed asking questions, but he also complained that the dominant question was "what does one do with it?" and that the general reaction to any explanation was: "oh, how strange!" Seldom did he hear questions about how things were put together, or why they were fashioned in a certain way.

Strangeness dominated and the museums enticed, but caught up in the spectacle of display, it was often difficult to spark a visitor's interest in the meanings these artifacts might have in other cultures, or for the multiplicity of humanity these artifacts might imply. As Thilenius's report makes clear, even in the best-ordered displays, visitors first had to learn to "read" the taxonomies and to "see" the order before one could discern the messages and take part in the "knowing," and thus many turned to the "knowers" for instructions on how to "see." Without the ethnologists' direct assistance, however, visitors who lacked a familiarity with ethnological terminology, museological methods, or the stakes involved in creating ethnographic displays, were practically incapable of anything but the most "superficial"—and, according to ethnologists, inaccurate—reading of their displays. As the Leipzig critic put it (and as Thilenius would seem to agree) these visitors did little more than "delight" in these "expensive curiosities."

The problem that Thilenius and his counterparts faced was that in order to function as effective means of communication, museums needed to "signify through common codes, and conventions of meaning-making that both producer and reader understood." The objects and the displays needed to be, as Mieke Bal has argued, "inter-subjectively accessible" in order for them to serve as a clear medium for communication.[88] Such shared subjectivity was possible; yet ironically it was probably during the display of seventeenth-century *Wunderkammern* rather than in early twentieth-century science museums that it was best achieved, where both the creators of these collections and their limited number of visitors approached them with a shared set of standards, experiences, and expectations.[89] Much to Thilenius' frustration, however, neither his well-ordered displays nor the less orderly arrangements in most ethnographic museums achieved this fundamental goal. Because of the subjective distance between Thilenius and most of his museum's visitors, even his best displays were unable to communicate effectively his intended messages or receive more substantial comment than "oh, how strange!"[90]

Indeed, the subjective distance between the directors of these muse-

→ yet effect of codes
"ed also render "exotic" mundane, cliché, too familiar
(not only spectacular)

ums and their visitors had only been magnified by the professionalization of ethnology over the last decades of the nineteenth century as well as by the changes in their audiences that occurred during that time. Ethnologists' increasing specialization had served to separate them from audiences that continued to grow larger and more socially diverse, and in many ways it condemned their more "informed" or "scientific" interpretations of the materials to the periphery of general understanding about humanity and human culture. In other words, the more specialized Thilenius and his associates became, the more difficulty they had in understanding how they could communicate with people who did not share their experiences and who, therefore, approached the museums' objects and arrangements in fundamentally different ways. Moreover, the subjective distance between ethnologists and visitors, and the difficulties ethnologists faced communicating with them, only further complicated and frustrated ethnologists' efforts to get around the incoherence of displays brought on by physical and material limitations.

Indeed, if we are to trust Thilenius, Weule, Luschan, and the visitor to the Leipzig museum, most people reacted to these "delightful curiosities" as items that evoked feelings of "strangeness" and "incomprehensibility" that would ultimately and ironically serve to distance them from the non-Europeans represented in the museums rather than, as Bastian had intended, help them to locate similarities, connections, and fundamental truths about a unitary humanity. Furthermore, the intellectual isolation that came with ethnologists' professionalization, an isolation that was perhaps paradigmatic of modernity, left them unable to inhibit the exoticization of these "other" cultures.

Ethnologists' paradoxical difficulties with communication is a particularly important point, because if we accept the relative inability of ethnologists to reach the vast majority of their visitors, then we must also accept that there could only have been a tentative causal connection between the intentions of the ethnologists and their supporters and the broader cultural functions of their museums. We have to recognize that despite the "authority of science," these scientists had little control over how their cultural productions would be appropriated and used, because neither the scientists nor their supporters could dictate the functions or the effects of the kinds of museums they had envisioned once they were opened up to public use. This recognition radically tempers arguments posited by Tony Bennett, Annie Coombes, and others that museums often functioned as political tools which could be purposefully harnessed by social elites to effectively influence the more general public.[91]

In fact, German ethnologists' efforts to control the meaning of their museums' objects and displays make it clear that what Michel Foucault has called "the nomination of the visible" entails much more than simply constructing schemes of classification or the naming and ordering of artifacts. It requires the explicit communication of these systems as well.[92] It is for this reason that Leipzig's critic called for a consistent means of exhibition in their museum and argued that all the museum's "new materials" should be immediately "cataloged and labeled" so that they, the visitors, would know what they were seeing. It was also for this reason that some of the visitors to the Berlin museum became disenchanted with its guidebooks, in some cases "throwing them at the feet of the museums' employees" and demanding that their money be returned because the limited explanations had proved useless for helping them negotiate the displays.[93] The language ethnologists used, either when Thilenius guided visitors through a display and was then frustrated with the responses he received, or when guidebooks and labels simply listed items as "spear," "woodcarving," or "human figure with long nose," often failed to provide ethnologists' visitors with an understanding of their systems of arrangement or the goals of their displays.[94] They failed to communicate the logic of their systems of arrangement even for the displays under their control, and without the system, these visitors were abandoned to the objects— something that many scholars concerned with today's museums have argued can make "museum-going . . . aimless, incoherent, and without measurable impact."[95] Yet in an age that was increasingly awash with such sensational visual stimuli, it is difficult to imagine that the array of unknown shapes and forms in ethnographic museums were without any effect at all.

Even if the museums' displays did not perform exactly as ethnologists intended and instead frustrated many experienced visitors who came to these institutions expecting particular kinds of arrangements, they had a repeated impact on an array of less-experienced visitors and ultimately a more general, and unintended, cultural function: they became displays of spectacular novelty and cultural difference. In this sense Stephen Greenblatt's conception of wonder is helpful. In his work on Europeans' early cultural encounters in the Americas, Greenblatt argued that wonder was "the central figure in the *initial* European response to the New World, the decisive and intellectual experience in the presence of radical difference [my emphasis]."[96] Greenblatt's argument can be extended in part to encompass those first encounters with radical difference that took place centuries later in German ethnographic museums. Alfred Lehmann, for instance, as I mentioned at the beginning of this chapter, described his first journey as a boy through the Leipzig museum as one in which he moved past "wonder after wonder;" this visit occurred precisely during the period in which Karl Weule was concerned that his displays might not be communicating anything at all. Yet Lehmann was clearly affected. He, like Bastian so many decades earlier, was "enticed" and spurred on to learn more. Indeed the wonder of this initial encounter opened up a new world for him and began what turned out to be a rather long journey of exploration. Lehmann, of course, was not a typical visitor, even as a boy; but such first encounters with radical difference on such a massive scale can be considered almost commonplace in these museums. Franz Boas, in fact, observed similar encounters with regard to visitors to American museums,[97] and it seems clear that an initial experience of wonder was shared by most of the individuals who had their first encounters with human diversity and radical forms of difference in these institutions—even if it did not lead them in the same direction as Lehmann. The same spectacle that frustrated ethnologists and led experienced visitors to issue criticisms, often enticed and enchanted other people during their first visit to an ethnographic museum, opening up possibilities for different kinds of receptions among these visitors and providing ethnologists with a possible means for bringing them into a dialogue—something ethnologists such as Boas and Weule recognized as well.

Yet within each individual, reception remained a process rather than a state, and the commonalties of first experiences were fleeting. Other forms of experience soon combined with these moments of wonder, altering each individual visitor's perceptions and preventing the wonder of the first encounter from being easily revisited.[98] As the Leipzig museum's public critic wrote in his editorial, "the more often one remains in the museum's rooms," the more one begins to question the arrangements and look for more meaning in the displays. Through repeated encounters with the displays, in other words, wonder became normalized, and the repeat visitor soon exchanged his or her astonishment for critical inquiry (or perhaps boredom, in which case they probably did not return). The result was that the reception of institutions and displays not only varied from one individual to the next but often changed within these individuals as well.[99] The point, then, is that both the relatively common initial reactions to newness and difference shared by visitors to these museums and the ways in which individuals' responses might change over time illustrate the degree to which reception depended primarily on the context of individual experience. It also helps to further explain why ethnologists—even though they might reach a few individuals—had so much difficulty communicating clear messages to the more general public with even their best exhibits, and how profound difference could be communicated through displays that were not created with this intention.

Ethnologists like Weule consistently attempted to achieve the semiotic commonalty described by Bal through tours, guide books, and even aggressive labeling. Indeed, in many ways this was a significant part of the *Schausammlungen* debate going on at this time, which was focused on communication with a lay public and developing ways of breaching the gap between their subjectivities by creating more pointed, even simplistic, didactic displays. Boas suggested that one method of making this connection in the museums was to place "here and there a striking exhibit intended to arrest [the unguided visitor's] attention," and to create a number of particular displays surrounded with information that would "convey the impression that the visitor, by looking at a single thing, has not grasped all that is conveyed by the collections, and that there is more to study."[100] Weule used similar tactics. He tried to catch visitors as they moved from their initial conditions of wonder to more critical inquiry and to harness their own interests and goals as a way of leading them toward a shared subjectivity.

Ethnologists were willing to take an active, hands-on role in these museums by acting as guides and moving beyond reliance on displays in order to influence their receptions and perhaps even bring their visitors into a dialogue. And this was a role many visitors eagerly encouraged. As an editorial in a Leipzig newspaper noted with regard to a new exhibition in the prehistory section of the museum, visitors surely stroll through the displays "with astonished wonder" and many will "shake their heads" before the array of "unendingly rich things" and say to themselves, "if only we had a specialist here!" In this case, as in many others, a specialist was available to guide them through these new, temporary displays and help them move from astonishment to understanding. Weule himself was holding tours—doing his best to teach people to see.[101] In Hamburg, Berlin, and Munich his counterparts were eager to do the same as they began crafting these temporary displays.

Despite ethnologists' repeated efforts and their many successes, they could not overcome the "interpretive instability" of their displays without abandoning their own purposes and moving to pointed narratives. Nor could they move to the creation of singular, striking exhibits as Boas suggested and continue to pursue their ethnographic project. Scholars have often noted that the museums' visual displays of material culture were meant to be read much like written texts, and a good case could be made that by actively teaching their publics to see, ethnologists could control the meanings in their displays. But as with all texts, new meanings were consistently inscribed on these displays by the visitors themselves and seemingly fixed meanings often proved to be surprisingly fluid.[102] As Boas noted, a well-orchestrated technical display, for example, might be so superb that its impressiveness distracted visitors from the point ethnologists were trying to make with it.[103] Or, as was the case with the Godeffroy hall discussed above, a well-ordered display could easily be open to multiple meanings that stemmed from the individual contexts of each person who viewed them. The Godeffroy hall might simultaneously help a visiting scientist confirm his convictions about the interconnected nature of different sets of peoples in the Pacific, convince a local factory worker of the utter difference between her and the "cannibals" on the Viti islands, and assist a resident member of the Colonial Association in instructing his sons about the primitive nature of non-Europeans, while leaving an art critic distressed. In fact, teaching everyone to see the same things in each display proved to be impossible, and creating displays that were intersubjectively accessible to everyone was ultimately an unrealizable goal. As Thilenius and Weule noted, regardless of what they did with their exhibits, visitors continued to refashion their meanings—not only because of difficulties in communications between the learned scientists and the museums' visitors but also because the visitors consistently appropriated the information for their own uses.[104]

The increasingly broad and socially diverse audiences that were entering German ethnographic museums by the turn of the century were doing so in cities that had changed radically since the 1870s. As a result, they brought considerably more visual information about non-Europeans with them into the museums than had their counterparts some thirty years earlier. Bastian's initial visitors, of course, could always have gained some initial insight into non-Europeans through travel literature, newspapers, scholarly journals, and popular magazines before strolling through his museum. But by 1900, Germans were awash in images and messages about non-Europeans. Not too far from the Berlin museum, for example, the New Guinea Company set up exhibitions of material culture in their storefront on Unter den Linden as part of their advertising campaign.[105] Louis Castan's *Panoptikum* contained plaster casts of "human types" for everyone to see.[106] Images of non-Europeans appeared on postcards that Berliners could purchase at the colonial museum and a range of other lo-

FIGURE 22. "50 wild Congo women, men and children in their model Congo village." The popular exhibition of non-Europeans became increasingly common in Germany during the last third of the nineteenth century and continued even after World War I. These ranged from organized exhibitions that were ostensibly scientific, and at times endorsed by scientific associations, to exhibits such as this one in Castan's Panoptikum, which was meant to be enticing, sexually arousing, and above all entertaining. (Deutsches Historisches Museum, Berlin)

cations in the city (Fig. 22). They also appeared on chocolate wrappers and coffee cans, and in a series of different magazines ranging from popular scientific journals like *Globus* and *Petermann's Mitteilungen*, to more mainstream magazines such as the *Gartenlaube*.[107] Indeed, many of these publications even marketed such images to children.[108] Moreover, it was quite possible for many Germans to have seen non-Europeans in the flesh without ever leaving the country. By 1900, over 100 *Völkerschauen* had circulated through Germany—so many that journalists had begun remarking that these sensational displays no longer offered spectators anything new.[109] Although ethnologists had started to distance themselves from these events during the late nineteenth century, as the *Völkerschauen* became increasingly focused on entertainment, these shows—together with the many printed images and stories about non-Europeans—continued to influence visitors' initial impressions of German ethnographic museums

vgl. Am N.! 1912 !!

FIGURE 23. The Tripoli display at the Munich Oktoberfest in 1912. Such displays had become so common during the decade before World War I that in many ways they were no longer exotic. They were expected parts of world's fairs and municipal festivals. These modes of exhibiting non-Europeans also affected the popular reception of ethnologists' displays. They reinforced common images of non-Europeans that competed with the knowledge ethnologists produced and hoped to transmit. As a result, the popular displays also helped to transform ethnologists' ideas about how to arrange their museums. (Landeshauptstadt München, Stadtarchiv)

FIGURE 24. A "Bedouin show" at the 1901 Oktoberfest in Munich. Dancing, crafts, mock war parties, and such were standard fare at the *Völkerschauen*. These were not static displays of individuals and families; they frequently consisted of groups of entertainers. Note the gender dynamics in this image. The *Völkerschauen* were often meant to be titillating. (Landeshauptstadt München, Stadtarchiv)

and place them increasingly into an overtly colonial context (Figs. 23, 24).[110]

Moreover, if the size of the audiences and their familiarity with images of non-Europeans had changed dramatically since the 1870s, so too had their visual culture. The turn of the century was an age in which the "gaze" had long since given way to the "glance"[111] and "'just looking' described the basic urban encounter."[112] By 1900, social critics commonly characterized modern European cities as disjointedly crowded, full of changing visual images, with cityscapes that seemed to have attained the kind of discontinuous heterogeneity that the creators of sixteenth and seventeenth-century *Wunderkammern* had tried to achieve, and which diminished the impact of the chaos in German ethnographic museums.[113] Such chaos and spectacle could be easily negotiated by educated visitors who browsed more and concentrated less, as well as by the popular classes who grew increasingly visual even as they became more literate, and were at home among crowded, disjointed, and sensational images.[114] Such observers, we can imagine, already presupposed a certain cognitive distance from the displays—a distance that Bastian abhorred as he watched the visitors he had once conceptualized as participants in his ethnographic project be transformed into mere observers whose reception of the displays was tightly linked to their own, non-scientific expectations. The kinds of experiences within the museum that Bastian had initially envisioned, and which visitors such as the Leipzig critic continued to desire, were increasingly pushed aside by the quickened sensations common to urban spectatorship at this time. The efforts by Bastian's successors to reach this new public with pointed, didactic displays were in many ways an attempt to curtail this trend and bridge that divide, but it was an attempt that generally failed.

The result was often miscommunication. Sometimes this was due to the conditions of the displays or the inadequacy of a museum's labels or guides. Indeed, this is what led to most of the criticisms they received from their "educated" audiences. In other instances, however, miscommunication simply resulted from the ethnologists' inability to communicate simultaneously with an array of visitors who were engaging these displays from a variety of different contexts. But while this clearly upset the ethnologists and the minority of visitors who shared their expectations, it evidently had little affect on the other, "uneducated" visitors at all. Approaching the displays with their own sets of interests and concerns, they appeared, as Thilenius, Weule, and Boas observed, to take what they needed from the novel and wondrous objects in these spectacular displays and move undisturbed through the arrangements that so tortured ethnologists and their critics. The majority of these visitors emerged from the spectacle they experienced in these museums with their own worlds in order, untouched by the chaos that left the ethnologists and their critics so "aghast," but which so many of their visitors were unable to see.

The museums I have discussed in this book were first visualized in a Humboldtian world, in which total harmonic projects still seemed possible. The dynamics of professionalization and imperialism combined with the market mechanism to throw these museums into a state of almost continual chaos, while their democratization led to their fundamental transformation. Unfortunately, liberal humanism and democracy, two things that we in the West tend to cherish, do not always or necessarily coexist well together.[1] And what becomes clear through an analysis of the growth and development of Germany's leading ethnographic museums during the late nineteenth and early twentieth centuries is the degree to which an awareness of the world portrayed in these museums became more hierarchical as they became more popular. The democratization of this science combined with its professionalization and the imperialist turn to undermine its initially cosmopolitan character.

There are, of course, a number of practical reasons for this change. It was much easier, for example, for an Alexander von Humboldt, or his follower Adolf Bastian, to be cosmopolitan and open to ideas of grand synthesis and seemingly boundless empirical projects when their jobs and reputations were not tied up in the results, when they had no one to whom they were responsible. For Bastian, who could depend on his own inherited wealth and the authority he ultimately gleaned as the "old master" of German ethnology, this was unquestionably the case. He enjoyed a certain freedom in his "scholarly productions" that younger, more professional generations of ethnologists did not. Moreover ethnology's movement away from Humboldtian visions was not unique to this science. As humanism became disciplinary during the Imperial period, splitting into ever more refined slices of institutionally supported knowledge, a range of natural sciences in Germany followed a similar trajectory. They moved away from Humboldt's penchant for grand syntheses even as their practitioners retained Humboldt himself for iconographic purposes.[2] Indeed, in many ways ethnology was one of the last holdouts in this more general trend.

But the new publics who frequented these museums after the turn of the century—those members of the "uneducated public," or the masses, who were immersed in the new visual culture—also played a critical role in directing this science away from the more gentlemanly kinds of positivism and humanism embraced by Bastian's generation. Even more than the younger generations of ethnologists who succeeded Bastian, this public embraced the imperialist project with much less ambivalence than most of the newly minted professionals like Thilenius—or even Weule. So many other areas of German cultural life were making "exotica" available to their gaze, inculcating these Germans with images and meanings, that everyday stimuli easily succeeded in overwhelming the ethnologists' messages and even usurping their authority within their museums.

Not only did these new publics bring with them the ability to normalize the chaos ethnologists saw in their institutions, they also provided what ultimately became the critical dynamic within these museums: a movement from wonder, to learning, to normalization, and eventually to boredom and complacency. The multiple meanings that each visitor gained in a diachronic sense was the real legacy of these museums, not the intentions of the "museum masters" or their scholarly agendas.[3] Moreover, rather than serving to pull the masses together, to instruct them through some sort of new "universal education" in which everyone might "consume the same product,"[4] these museums, or rather that product within them—the specific arrangements, the scope of the displays, even the science itself—were reshaped by this new public as it learned to voice its interests and desires. Science in this sense was transformed through its consumption, and the ethnology that became comestible after the turn of the century consisted of ideas the masses already found palatable, not those that ethnologists like Bastian, Thilenius, or Luschan had found most intriguing. Indeed, within German ethnographic museums during the first decades of the twentieth century it was the general public that was teaching ethnologists to see, not the other way around.

Furthermore, the transformation of German ethnographic museums around the turn of the century was the end result of a much longer process, one that began as these institutions were first founded. A small number of aspiring ethnologists and their associates first envisioned these museums. But from the moment they set out to build them, they looked to a range of different groups and individuals for assistance. Initially, they gained their greatest support from civic societies in Hamburg, Berlin, Leipzig, and Munich who shared their cosmopolitan visions, as well as people abroad who were interested, enchanted, or enticed by this international science. But as museum directors built up their acquisition networks, and their collections and buildings rapidly expanded, an ever-growing array of allies and supporters were drawn to these institutions. Ethnologists' alliances increased with their expectations, needs, and desires. And every alliance came with a price: municipal, regional, and national governments set their conditions; collectors influenced acquisitions; scientists at home and abroad kept watch over disciplinary boundaries; and patrons and visitors issued demands. There were structural influences as well. An international market in material culture evolved around the museums, shaping and being shaped by the desires of the ethnologists and their supporters. The people who initially founded the museums circumvented the universities and created institutions that would better serve their own needs, but they also engaged in a process of professionalization that led them into a world of conformity and eventually returned them to the university's wings after World War I. All of these factors channeled and reshaped ethnologists' efforts and influenced developments within their museums—setting the stage for their later transformation.

In essence, the museum directors had always been faced with a Faustian dilemma, forced to accept the influence of individuals and groups who were necessary for advancing their project and improving their museums. As a result, the museums served multiple functions from the moment they were created, and their directors were committed from the outset to accommodating their supporters' interests and needs. During the entire period discussed here, neither the directors nor their ever-growing number of supporters wavered from their desire to possess more and larger collections. There was a general conviction that the stature and importance of any ethnographic museum was directly proportional to its size and to the quality and expanse of its collections. But with the growing expense of locating and acquiring increasing numbers of good artifacts came the need for more support—more commitment from groups who championed their own interests, and it was this escalating trend in negotiations between directors and their supporters that led to the dramatic changes in the character of the museums that came with their democratization.

The various individuals and official bodies who supported these museums had always demanded a "useful science." But in the 1870s and 1880s, the very presence of such a scientific institution in a city provided a critical service. It endowed the city that possessed it with the status and prestige that came from supporting and participating in an internationally recognized science; and as long as the museum fulfilled this function—as long as it continued to be recognized internationally as an important institution—the museum's ethnologists were allowed to determine its organization and essentially left to themselves. It is worth noting, for example, that before the turn of the century these museums received very few letters of complaint, concern, or protest from their visitors. As I have argued, however, this was not because the museums I have studied were better organized, more orderly, or more pointedly arranged in the 1870s and 1880s than they were by 1900; disorder abounded throughout the period. Nor can the sudden growth in the size and social diversity of museums' audiences alone account for the increase in these complaints. Rather, it was a combination of visitors' new expectations—resulting from their experiences in other museums, exhibitions, and in their everyday lives—and the isolation that came with ethnologists' professionalization. These factors increased the subjective distance between ethnologists and their ever-growing audiences, and led to the increased confusion and protest from their visitors—as well as from the ethnologists themselves—which became so common by 1900.

Indeed, by the turn of the century, the municipal bodies who supported these museums wanted more than the mere presence of these institutions. They became increasingly interested in public education, and when museums in general began shifting toward educational tasks, they expected their ethnographic museums to follow suit. The scientific needs and efforts of the museums' directors were never completely subverted, abandoned, or disdained, but they were increasingly subordinated to accommodating the expectations and needs of their supporters, which meant accepting external trends toward educational goals and popular audiences—an acceptance that was increasingly regarded as integral to a museum's ability to impart status and prestige to its respective city.

Acceptance of these changes by museum directors and other ethnologists was also encouraged by two internal dilemmas: the recognition that the technological advances they had once assumed were facilitating their efforts had actually created as many difficulties as they had helped to overcome, and the fact that Bastian's grand ethnographic project had proven itself untenable. Despite their radically increased collections and ever-expanding museums, German ethnologists had been unable to construct the kinds of empirical laboratories of inductive science that Bastian had initially envisioned; indeed, the largest museums appeared in many ways to be the least effective tools for pursuing this or any other scientific task.

Moreover, this recognition brought with it two equally critical realizations. Museum directors and ethnologists were not only forced to look for a better means of achieving their scientific or intellectual goals, they were also compelled to quickly locate another source of legitimacy for their institutions and their own professional positions. In this sense the movement toward educational displays allowed ethnologists to do two things at once. These new kinds of displays enabled them to maintain the legitimacy of their scientific institutions (and thus their own positions) by providing public services that were deemed useful and necessary. At the same time, the new displays also allowed directors to avert what they regarded as the museums' descent into places of mere spectacle and sensation—the rather disheartening polar opposite of the sites of intellectual exploration and edification they had once sought to create. Ethnologists' willingness to embrace the shift toward educational displays, in other words, was more of a compromise than a complete abandonment of their initial intentions. It was, in essence, their Faustian bargain.

ПOTES

Abbreviations

AA	Auswärtiges Amt
ASM	Archiv des Staatlichen Museen, Berlin
BAP	Bundesarchiv, Potsdam
BGAEU	Berlin Society for Anthropology, Ethnology, and Prehistory
BHM	Bayerische Hauptstaatsarchiv, Munich
GHM	Geheimes Hausarchiv, Munich
GSA	Geheimes Staatsarchiv, Preußischer Kulturbesitz, Berlin
GVKM	General Administration of the Royal Museums, Berlin
HSA	Staatsarchiv Hamburg
KSG	Königlichen Staatsminister der geistlichen, Unterrichts- und Medizinal-Angelegenheiten
LN	Nachlaß Felix von Luschans, Handschriftenabteilungen, Staatsbibliothek Berlin (Haus II)
LSA	Stadtarchiv Leipzig
MfVB	Archiv des Museum für Völkerkunde, Berlin
MfVH	Archiv des Museum für Völkerkunde, Hamburg
MfVHJA	Nachlaß Adrian Jacobsens, Hamburgisches Museum für Völkerkunde, Hamburg
MfVLB	Archiv des Museum für Völkerkunde zu Leipzig
MfVM	Bibliothek des Staatliches Museum für Völkerkunde, Munich
MSA	Stadtarchiv Munich
NAA	Smithsonian Institution, National Anthropological Archives, Washington D.C.
RSL	Leipzig City Council
SIA	Smithsonian Institution Archives, Washington D.C.

Introduction

1. The terms *Ethnologie* and *Ethnographie* were generally used interchangeably in Germany during the Imperial period. Both referred to the description and comparison of cultures and peoples, both could be used to refer to studies of either non-European or European cultures, and both were set off as distinct from physical anthropology and archeology. Although the current use of the term ethnography is focused more on the description than the comparison of cultures, the nineteenth-century term encompassed all aspects of description and comparison. I have chosen to use the term ethnographic throughout this study with reference to the museums because of its closer association with material culture—the primary focus of *Völkerkunde* museums. I have also decided against using the German term *Völkerkunde* during general discussion, because the term now implies a limited focus on

peoples outside of Europe, while the interests of the ethnologists working in these museums, as well as their publics, were not as limited as this term might lead us to believe. Further discussion of this terminology can be found in Rothfels, "Bring 'em Back Alive"; Staehelin, *Völkerschauen*; W. Smith, *Politics and the Sciences of Culture*; and Stocking, *Bones, Bodies, Behavior*.

2. Dalton, *Report on Ethnographic Museums*.

3. Werner, *Natives of British Central Africa*.

4. On the long history of wonder in science, see especially Daston and Park, *Wonders and the Order of Nature*.

5. See, for example, Bennett, "Exhibitionary Complex," and Rydell, *All the World's a Fair*.

6. On Bastian, see especially Fiedermutz-Laun, *Kulturhistorische Gedanke bei Adolf Bastian*, and Koepping, *Adolf Bastian*.

7. One need only look at George Stocking's excellent series on the history of anthropology published since 1983 by the University of Wisconsin Press. Excluding the many pieces on Boasian anthropology that made cursory reference to Germany, only two of the articles in that series were devoted to questions of German ethnology or anthropology, and the volume on ethnographic museums neglected them entirely. In 1996 a volume focused on Boas and the German anthropological tradition attempted to redress this absence, yet here too the focus was more on Boas than the role of German ethnologists in the history of anthropology. Articles by Matti Bunzl and Benoit Massin were the outstanding exceptions. Similarly, revisionist work on the history of anthropology such as the volume edited by Peter Pels and Oscar Salemink that sought to take the history of anthropology out of the confines of the academy have only repeated clichés about the Germans rather than following them into the field. See Bunzl, "Franz Boas and the Humboldtian Tradition"; Massin, "From Virchow to Fischer"; Pels and Salemink, *Colonial Subjects*; Proctor, "*Anthropologie* to *Rassenkunde*"; and Whitman, "Philology to Anthropology."

8. See, for example, Mühlmann, *Geschichte der Anthropologie*.

9. See, for example, Harms, "historische Verhältnis der deutschen Ethnologie zum Kolonialismus"; Proctor, "From *Anthropologie* to *Rassenkunde*"; and Weindling, *Health, Race and German Science*.

10. For Boas's continued connection to Germany, see Cole, *Franz Boas*.

11. Hinsley, *Savages and Scientists*; Stocking, *After Tylor*.

12. Much of the innovative literature on museums has begun to do just that. See especially the essays in Crane, *Museums and Memory*, and Joachimides et al., *Museumsinszenierungen*.

13. Kirshenblatt-Gimblett, *Destination Culture*, 128.

14. Haraway, "Teddy Bear Patriarchy," 54.

15. Cited in Applegate, *Nation of Provincials*, 26–27.

16. See, for example, Blackbourn, *Long Nineteenth Century*; Koshar, *Germany's Transient Pasts*; Ladd, *Urban Planning*; and Penny, "Fashioning Local Identities."

17. See, for example, David, *Scientist's Role in Society*, 133–34; Johnson, *Kaiser's Chemists*; and Nyhart, "Civic and Economic Zoology."

18. Jeffrey Allan Johnson has argued something similar in his work on the Kaiser Wilhelm Society, but because he remained focused on Berlin, the tensions he

identified were limited to the national and the international. See Johnson, *Kaiser's Chemists*.

19. Several scholars have begun to engage this issue directly. See, for example, the essays in Eley, *Society, Culture, and the State*.

20. The now standard work on regional identity during the Imperial period is Applegate, *Nation of Provincials*. See also Confino, *Nation as a Local Metaphor*, and Retallack, *Saxony in German History*.

21. This competition did not just turn around science museums, but many other things as well. See, for example, Ladd, *Urban Planning*, and Lenman, *Artists and Society*.

22. Beyerchen, "On the Stimulation of Excellence," 139.

23. See, for example, Bracken, *Potlach Papers*; Cole, *Captured Heritage*; Price, *Primitive Art in Civilized Places*; and Wade, "Ethnic Art Market."

24. See, for example, Harms, "Historische Verhältnis"; Marchand, "Leo Frobenius," 154; and most recently, Zimmerman, *Anthropology and Anti-humanism*.

25. The lack of enthusiasm for colonialism in Germany has been noted by many. See, for example, Blackbourn, *Long Nineteenth Century*, 335; Brunn, *Deutschland und Brasilien*; Mitchell, *Danger of Dreams*, 159; W. Smith, "Colonialism and Colonial Empire;" W. Smith, *German Colonial Empire*; and Winkelmann, "Bürgerliche Ethnographie."

26. For explication of the terms imperialism and colonialism, see Said, *Culture and Imperialism*, 9.

27. See, for example, Stocking, *Colonial Situations*.

28. Stocking, "Maclay, Kubary, Malinowski," 10.

29. See, for example, Zantop, *Colonial Fantasies*, and many of the essays in Friedrichsmeyer et al., *Imperialist Imagination*. For an impressive alternative that pays close attention to multiple contexts and the variety of colonial situations, see Wildenthal, *German Women for Empire*.

30. This too is not surprising. Ambiguity is often at the heart of colonial encounters. See, for example, Hermannstädter, "Karl von den Steinen"; Pratt, *Imperial Eyes*; Probst, "Beobachtung und Methode"; Stocking, "Maclay, Kubary, Malinowski"; Stoler and Cooper, *Tensions of Empire*; Wolfe, *Settler Colonialism*. See also the comment in Bruckner, "Tingle-Tangle of Modernity," 72.

31. For comments on this, see Thomas, *Colonialism's Culture*.

32. For an example of this argument, see Schwartz, *Spectacular Realities*.

33. Latour, *Science in Action*.

Chapter One

1. The Godeffroy collection, created by the owner of a Hamburg trading firm, was perhaps the best collection in Germany at the time. Municipal museums were quite limited. See Bastian, *Vorgeschichte der Ethnologie*.

2. The classic account of these associations is Nipperdey, *Gesellschaft, Kultur, Theorie*, 174–205. See also Dann, *Vereinswesen und bürgerliche Gesellschaft*.

3. Blackbourn, *Long Nineteenth Century*, 278.

4. Daum, "Naturwissenschaften und Öffentlichkeit," 67.

5. Blackbourn, *Long Nineteenth Century*, 274; fourteen new zoological gardens

alone were founded across Germany from 1840 to 1870. Dittrich and Rieke-Müller, *Der Löwe Brüllt Nebenan*, 7, 264.

6. On Humboldt's impact in Germans' popular imagination, see Daum, *Wissenschaftspopularisierung*.

7. Tylor, "Professor Adolf Bastian," 138.

8. For testaments to Bastian's broad influence by his students and others, see, for example, Ankermann, "Entwicklung der Ethnologie"; Bahnson, "Ueber ethnographische Museen," 112; Graebner, "Adolf Bastians 100. Geburtstag;" Heger, "Zukunft der ethnographischen Museen"; Preuss, "Adolf Bastian"; and von den Steinen, "Gedächtnisrede auf Adolf Bastian."

9. Rupke, "Introduction," vii

10. Bunzl, "Franz Boas and the Humboldtian Tradition," 43–52; Fiedermutz-Laun, *Kulturhistorische Gedanke bei Adolf Bastian*, 7.

11. Bastian, *Alexander von Humboldt*; Bastian, *Mensch in der Geschichte*. See also Fiedermutz-Laun, *Kulturhistorische Gedanke bei Adolf Bastian*, 7–12.

12. Bastian, *Alexander von Humboldt*, 25.

13. For details of these ventures see Fiedermutz-Laun, *Kulturhistorische Gedanke bei Adolf Bastian*, 9–12.

14. Von den Steinen, "Gedächtnisrede auf Adolf Bastian," 243. Karl von den Steinen was educated as a medical doctor specializing in psychiatry when he met Bastian during a trip to Hawaii in 1880. Bastian convinced him to turn toward ethnology, and von den Steinen became one of the most respected ethnologists in Germany during the Imperial period.

15. Bastian, *Alexander von Humboldt*, 23–25.

16. Massin, "Virchow to Fischer." See also Boas, "Rudolf Virchow's Anthropological Work," 39, and Cole, *Franz Boas*, 285.

17. Daum, *Wissenschaftspopularisierung*, 66–71.

18. Bastian, "Darwin, The Descent of Man," 138.

19. Bastian, "Offner Brief an Prof. Dr. E. Haeckel," 8. See also Fiedermutz-Laun, "Aus der Wissenschaftsgeschichte."

20. Bastian, *Alexander von Humboldt*, 23–25.

21. Bastian, "Ethnologische Erörterung," 183, excerpted and translated in Koepping, *Adolf Bastian*, 176.

22. Koepping, "Enlightenment and Romanticism," 86.

23. Bastian, *Rechtsverhältnisse bei verschiedenen Völkern*.

24. Graebner, "Adolf Bastians 100. Geburtstag," x.

25. Bastian, *Zur Lehre von den geographischen Provinzen*. His conception of the geographical provinces was well recognized during his lifetime as a seminal part of his thought. See, for example, Tylor, "Professor Adolf Bastian," and von den Steinen, "Gedächtnisrede auf Adolf Bastian."

26. Bastian, *Geographische und ethnologische Bilder*, 324. See also Fiedermutz-Laun, *Kulturhistorische Gedanken bei Adolf Bastian*, 147–93.

27. The term *Halbkulturvölker* (half-cultured peoples) was also posited as a term for people who had no written language but possessed "a distinct and highly developed culture." However, this was a term Bastian seldom employed. Fiedermutz-Laun, *Kulturhistorische Gedanke bei Adolf Bastian*, 114.

28. Ibid., 114 n. 36. Franz Heger made the same point about Bastian in 1896: Heger, "Zukunft der ethnographischen Museen."

29. Bastian, "Alexander von Humboldt," 15–16. Translations based on Koepping, *Adolf Bastian*, 161.

30. Tylor, *Primitive Culture*. Boas made the differences between Bastian and Tylor's conceptions of "the psychic unity of mankind" explicit in several cases. See, for example, Boas, "Methods of Ethnology," and "Limitations of the Comparative Method."

31. Bastian, *Alexander von Humboldt*, translation taken in this case from Koepping, *Adolf Bastian*, 161.

32. See, for example, Coombes, *Reinventing Africa*.

33. Richards, *Commodity Culture*.

34. van Keuren, "Cabinets and Culture," 26. See also Bennett, *Birth of the Museum*, and Rydell, *All the World's a Fair*.

35. Displays set up by Willy Foy and Fritz Graebner in Cologne after a new museum was opened there in 1906 are the most striking example. Foy, *Führer*.

36. van Keuren, "Cabinets and Culture," 32.

37. Hochreiter, *Musuemtempel zum Lernort*, 58–86. See also Marchand, *Down from Olympus*.

38. Marchand, "Rhetoric of Artifacts," 109.

39. Trail, *Schliemann of Troy*. Cf. Crane, *Museums and Memory*, 11, and Marchand, *Down from Olympus*, 116–24.

40. van Keuren, "Cabinets and Culture," 28.

41. The ethnologists in Berlin's *Völkerkunde* museum, for example, referred explicitly to the connection between archeology and ethnology in the introduction to their collections: Königliche Museen zu Berlin, *Führer*, 7th ed., 55. See also Bahnson, "Ueber ethnographische Museen," 112.

42. Pickstone, "Museological Science?" 111–17; Jenkins, "Object Lessons," 249.

43. Karl Ritter also pushed the idea of such a collection before Bastian took over the royal ethnographic collection in 1868. Essner, "Berlins Völkerkunde Museum," 65–66.

44. See, for example, Barkan and Bush, *Prehistories of the Past*, 10.

45. Findlen, *Possessing Nature*, 3–4, 22–3, 49–50, 71; Pomian, *Collectors and Curiosities*, 49.

46. Blackbourn, *Long Nineteenth Century*, 192.

47. Essner, *Deutsche Afrikareisende*, 57.

48. Bastian, *Heilige Sage der Polynesier*, excerpted and translated in Koepping, *Adolf Bastian*, 216.

49. Ibid., 216.

50. Bastian, *Führer*, 3.

51. Cited in Westphal-Hellbusch, "Geschichte des Museums," 4.

52. Königliche Museen zu Berlin, *Führer*, 2nd ed., 7.

53. Fiedermutz-Laun, *Kulturhistorische Gedanke bei Adolf Bastian*, 70.

54. "Ueber die Bedeutung ethnographischer Museen: mit besonderer Beziehung auf die vor zehn Jahren erfolgte Gründung eines solchen in Leipzig," dated 23 May 1883 and issued by Geh. Reg-Rath von Seckendorff als Vorsitzender des Aufsicht-

srathes des Verein des Museum für Völkerkunde in Leipzig, in LSA: kap. 31, no. 12, vol. I (1873–95), pp. 160–61. This *Denkschrift* was sent to the city government and reprinted in Leipzig's city newspapers.

55. On *Bildung* see Assmann, *Arbeit am Nationalen Gedächtnis*, and Bollenbeck, *Bildung und Kultur*. For a definitive discussion of *Kultur*, see Fischer, "Zivilization, Kultur."

56. My use of the term modernist draws on the following: Berman, *All That Is Solid Melts into Air*, 5; Eksteins, *Rites of Spring*; Fritzsche, "Landscape of Danger"; Fritzsche, "Nazi Modern." For further discussion of the link between modernism and ethnology, see Barkan and Busch, *Prehistories of the Past*.

57. Cited in Liss, "German Culture and German Science," 165.

58. Bastian and BGAEU to Adalbert Falk, 2 July 1872, in MfVB: "Die Gründung des Museums," vol. 1 (1872–93), 1214/73.

59. Ibid.

60. Years later, Preuss credited Bastian with having inspired the creation of "the first *Rettungsasyl* on European soil for the products of humanity." The terminology was not meant to be ironic. Preuss, "Adolf Bastian," 3.

61. Bastian, "Vortrage in der Sitzung der Berliner Anthropologischen Gesellschaft"; Bastian, "Erwerbungen der Ethnographischen Abtheilung"; and Bastian, *Führer*, 3.

62. Bahnson, "Ueber ethnographische Museen," 113; Richter, "Über die Idealen und Praktischen Aufgaben," 202.

63. Northoff to Rat der Stadt Leipzig, 20 Nov. 1896, in LSA: "Das Deutsche Centralmuseum für Völkerkunde betr.," kap. 31, no. 12, vol. 2 (1896–1902), pp. 48–59.

64. Karl Hagen, "Grundriß der Entstehungsgeschichte des Museums," 14 Dec. 1897, in HSA: 361-5 I, Hochschulwesen I, CII, a16, bd. I, "Bau eines Museums für Völkerkunde" (1896–1907).

65. Thilenius to Hamburg Senat, "Report on Budget Increases, 1905," in HSA: 111-1, Senat, CL. VII, Lit. He nr. 1, vol. 54, FSC 3.

66. Meier to Weule, 27 July 1904, in MfVLB: no. 08757-8.

67. Luschan to the General Administration of the Royal Museums, 12 October 1903, in MfVB: "Erweiterungsbau des Königlichen Museums für Völkerkunde," vol. 2, 1286/1903.

68. W. Smith, *Politics and the Sciences of Culture*, 113.

69. Thurnwald, "Über Völkerkundemuseen," 199.

70. Weule, "50 Jahre Völkerkundemuseum!" 5.

71. Hinsley, *Savages and Scientists*, 7, 22.

72. Ibid., 83. See also Conn, *Museums and American Intellectual Life*, 15.

73. Hinsley, *Savages and Scientists*, 84.

74. Both of these phrases appear repeatedly in the official and private correspondence, publications, and government documents generated by German ethnologists.

75. W. Smith, *Politics and the Sciences of Culture*, 109–10, 119.

76. Kalmar, "Völkerpsychologie of Lazarus and Steinthal," 682.

77. Bastian, *Führer*. These principles remain essentially consistent throughout the

period. See also Bunzl, "Franz Boas and the Humboldtian Tradition," 51; and Koepping, *Adolf Bastian*, 17, 52–53.

78. Hinsley, *Savages and Scientists*, 98.

79. Stocking, *Shaping of American Anthropology*, 1–20.

80. Eksteins, *Rites of Spring*, 69–73.

81. Ibid., 69.

82. Reulecke, *Geschichte der Urbanisierung*, 203.

83. Eksteins, *Rites of Spring*, 72–73.

84. Ringer, *Decline of the German Mandarins*.

85. Bastian explicitly discussed the advantages ethnology had over other fields because its students were able to move beyond written texts: Königliche Museen zu Berlin, *Führer*, 2nd ed., 9–10.

86. A number of different kinds of research institutes outside of the universities were being created as alternatives at this time. See, for example, David, *Scientist's Role in Society*, 133–34; Johnson, *Kaiser's Chemists*; Nyhart, "Civic and Economic Zoology."

87. Bunzl, "Franz Boas and the Humboldtian Tradition"; Fiedermutz-Laun, *Kulturhistorische Gedanke bei Adolf Bastian*; Kalmar "Völkerpsychologie of Lazarus and Steinthal"; W. Smith, *Politics and the Sciences of Culture*.

88. W. Smith, *Politics and the Sciences of Culture*, 3.

89. Smolka, *Völkerkunde in München*, 54.

90. Ibid., 77–78.

91. Wagner's only titles were an honorary doctorate from Erlangen University that he received following his 1838 publications about Africa, and an honorary professor title at the University of Munich that he gained in 1862. The museum provided him with the means for gaining a foothold on the Munich university, yet his honorary titles were not well respected and he consistently felt himself on the fringes. Ibid., 80–82.

92. Beck, "Moritz Wagner"; Ganslmayr, "Moritz Wagner"; and Ratzel, *Anthropogeographie*, vii.

93. Gareis, *Exotik in München*, 46–47.

94. Smolka, *Völkerkunde in München*, 49.

95. See, for example, Bastian, *Heilige Sage der Polynesier*, 63–66.

96. E. Haberland, *Leo Frobenius*.

97. This was true outside of Germany as well. See, for example, Harris, *Cultural Excursions*, 135; Forgan, "Architecture of Display," 141; and Kohlstedt, "Museums," 152.

98. See David, *Scientist's Role in Society*.

99. See, for example, Assmann, *Arbeit am Nationalen Gedächtnis*; Hammer, "Preußische Musemspolitik," 256; Hochreiter, *Musuemtempel zum Lernort*, 33, 68; Kuntz, *Museum als Volksbildungsstätte*, 43; Marchand, "Orientalism as Kulturpolitik."

100. See, for example, Ditt, "Konservative Kulturvorstellungen und Kulturpolitik," 231; and Findlen, *Possessing Nature*, 396.

101. Pretzell, "75 Jahre Museum für Deutsche Volkskunde"; Hochreiter, *Musuemtempel zum Lernort*, 58–87.

102. A. Voss, "Untitled Gutachten" 3 Nov. 1899, in MfVB: "Erweiterungsbau des Königlichen Museums für Völkerkunde," vol. 1, 1134/99.

103. Königliche Museen zu Berlin, *Führer*, 7th ed., 199. Cf. Steinmann, "Gründer," 72.

104. Jahn, "neubegründete Museum für deutsche Volkstrachten," 336; Steinmann, "Entwicklung des Museums für Volkskunde," 13.

105. Steinmann, "Entwicklung des Museums für Volkskunde," 16.

106. Steinmann, "Gründer," 90.

107. Ibid., 73.

108. Ibid., 97–98. See also Oskar Scheindrazheim, "Erinnerungen," in HSA: 622-1.5: 27–28.

109. Virchow, Bartels, Schwarz, von Kaufmann, and von Heyden, "Die Vorgeschichtliche Abteilung des königl.: Museums für Völkerkunde und die vorgeschichtliche Forschung," 18 Feb. 1893, in MfVB: "Gründung," vol. 1, 203/93.

110. See, for example, A. Voss, "Untitled Gutachten," 3 Nov. 1899, in MfVB: "Erweiterungsbau des Königlichen Museums für Völkerkunde." vol. 1, 1134/99; Voss to Dir. Assis. Herrn Dr. Goetze, Königl. MfV., 9 June 1906, in MfVB:"Den Umzug und die Aufstellung der Sammlungen des Museums," vol. 8, 1064/1906. For examples from the press, see *Vossische Zeitung,* 12 June, 3 July, and 6 July 1900.

111. von Bode, "Denkschrift betreffend Erweiterungs- und Neubauten bei den Königlichen Museen in Berlin," Feb. 1907, in MfVB: "Erweiterung," vol. 3, 441/07.

112. Steinmann, "Entwicklung des Museums für Volkskunde," 32.

113. Schneider, "Deutsche Kolonialmuseum."

114. Schöne to the Cultural Ministerium, 13 Jan. 1888, in GSA: Rep. 76, Ve., Sekt. 15, Abt. XI, nr. 2, bd. 7. See also Essner, "Berlins Völkerkunde Museum," 81.

115. Schneider, "Deutsche Kolonialmuseum," 163.

116. *Deutsches Kolonialblatt* 10 (1899): 73, cited in Schneider, "Deutsche Kolonialmuseum," 172.

117. That the kaiser actually participated in the opening of this museum illustrates that simply gaining his presence and interest for a moment was no recipe for success. Schneider, "Deutsche Kolonialmuseum," 177.

118. Dirks to Thilenius, 31 Jan. 1905, in MfVH: M.B.10, bd. 1, "Deutsches Kolonial-Museum Berlin." Luschan had rejected the collection a few days earlier, MfVB: "Die Übernahme des deutschen Kolonial-Museums," 225/05.

119. Three months after the outbreak of the war, the museum was again up for sale, this time, however, not even Thilenius would consider the collections. Dirks to Thilenius, 3 March 1915, and Dirks to Thilenius, 31 Jan. 1905, in MfVH: M.B.10, bd. 1, "Deutsches Kolonial-Museum Berlin."

120. Ultimately, both of these museums were focused on an internal audience, and their presentations (proposed or realized) lacked the cosmopolitan or international appeal of the successful *Völkerkunde* museums.

121. Ladd, *Urban Planning*, 14.

122. Ibid., 240.

123. Lenman, *Artists and Society*, 125.

124. For an intriguing look at the potential for natural history to help groups of

people cultivate a certain cosmopolitanism, see Nyhart, "Civic and Economic Zoology," 615.

125. This was not only recognized in Germany. Indeed this was a central concern of patrons in the United States as well. See, for example, Cole, *Franz Boas*, 189; Kohlstedt, "Museums," 151–66; Winsor, *Reading the Shape of Nature*.

126. Staehelin, *Völkerschauen*, 136.

127. Thode-Arora, *Für fünfzig Pfennig um die Welt*.

128. Evans, *Death in Hamburg*.

129. Bahnson, "Ueber ethnographischen Museen," 117.

130. *Hamburg Correspondent*, 1 Nov. 1887. Other articles appeared in the *Hamburg Fremdenblatt* on 17 Nov. 1887.

131. "Mittheilungen der Bürgerschaft an den Senat," from 29 Feb. 1888, in HSA: 361-5, Hochschulwesen I, CII, b10.

132. Melle, *Dreizig Jahre Hamburger Wissenschaft*, 5.

133. "Mitteilung des Senats an die Bürgerschaft," 29 July 1907, in HSA: 361-5 I, Hochschulwesen I, CII, b15, bd. 3: 1904–08. This concerned the purchase of the Thomannschen collection from Burma, gathered by a Hamburg resident and offered for sale to other European and American cities as well. The central argument in the debate was that the failure to purchase this collection would also be recognized as the inability to understand its value.

134. F. Jagor, W. Reih, Simon to Robert von Puttkamer, 11 Dec. 1879, in GSA: I. HA, Rep. 76, Ve. Sekt. 15, Abt. III, nr. 2, bd. 2.

135. Similar public arguments were made in *Vossische Zeitung*, 3 July 1900; *Berliner Tageblatt*, 17 Feb. 1901; and *Tägliche Rundschau*, 18 Feb. 1901.

136. *Dresdener Zeitung*, 5 Sept. 1874. This sort of rhetoric appeared again and again when discussing the particularity of Leipzig's municipal landscape.

137. Smolka, *Völkerkunde in München*, 153.

138. Despite his focus on the high art of India and Asia, Sherman was not an artist but a dedicated scientist who specialized in an area of ethnology that was particularly suitable for Munich. Sherman was the first professional museum man to take over this collection. He had a Ph.D. and a *Habilitation*, was an excellent organizer, and a sound if not brilliant scientist. His work was very well respected by other scientists in and outside of Munich, and it was his qualifications as a scientist that enabled him to become the first director to gain a university professorship. All these factors contributed to his and the museum's success, but it was the link to the art complex of the *Kulturstadt* that allowed this to happen.

139. Once they entered into this competition, they, like their counterparts in Hamburg, Leipzig, and Berlin, were driven forward by the constant comparisons and rivalries between the cities. See, for example, Heigel to Cultural Ministry, 24 March 1910, in BHM: MK 19455.

Chapter Two

1. Bastian, "Heilige Sage der Polynesier."

2. Otto Georgi, *Vortrag das Grassi-Museums betreffend*, 11 April 1884, in LSA: kap. 31, no. 14: 40–63.

3. Bayern, *Meine Reisen*, 350. While the museum did not take this turn, a similar rhetoric was nevertheless adopted with regard to the museum's emphasis on eastern art.

4. See, for example, the debates in LSA: "Die Protokolle des gemischten Verwaltungsausschusses für das Museum für Völkerkunde," 5 June 1907, kap. 31, no. 33, bd. 1: 30–36.

5. Baudrillard, "System of Collecting," 18.

6. This policy had its critics. See, for example, Marchand, "Orientalism as Kulturpolitik," 331.

7. Bahnson, "Ueber ethnographischen Museen," 143.

8. Dietrich in particular has gained considerable scholarly attention. See, for example, Sumner, *Woman in the Wilderness*.

9. Panning, "Beiträge zur Geschichte des Zoologischen Staatsinstituts."

10. Bastian, "Untitled report on the Godeffroy collection," 3 June 1881, in GSA: Rep. 76, Ve., Sekt. 15., Abt. XI, nr. 2, bd. 2.

11. For details on the negotiations and more information on Godeffroy, see Penny, "Science and the Marketplace."

12. The report issued by the committee organized to try to retain the museum in Hamburg contained over four pages of signatures from the most well known members of Hamburg's scientific and artistic associations. HSA: 361-5 I, Hochschulwesen I, C IX, a39, bd. 1.

13. *Leipziger Zeitung*, 21 May 1882.

14. See, for example, the *Hamburger Fremdenblatt*, 9 Oct. 1885.

15. See, for example, *Leipziger Zeitung*, 9 Oct. 1885.

16. Deutsches Committee to Obst, 12 Oct. 1885, in MfVLB: no. 02467. After Godeffroy's death on 9 Feb. 1885, the collection was sold for a reduced price of 95,000 Marks. The reasoning for the sale appears to have been that Godeffroy had sent a letter to Leipzig before his death in which he stated that he would be pleased to have the collection stay in Germany, and if possible in Leipzig. Leipzig's association used this to push the sale. It is unclear why Gustav Godeffroy (the brother of Johann Caesar) agreed on the low price. G. Godeffroy to Northoff, 2 May 1885, in MfVLB: no. 02437.

17. Indeed, some of these were even from Kubary, Godeffroy's former employee. See Probst, "Beobachtung und Methode."

18. Bastian calculated the monetary value of the items in the Godeffroy museum that were not represented in his collections (300,000 Marks) using an average price. "Beschluß der Kommission," in the "Protokoll der Sitzung der Sachverständigen-Kommission der ethnologischen und nordischen Abteilung am 29 Nov. 1882," in GSA: Rep. 76, Ve., Sekt. 15., Abt. XI, nr. 2, bd. 4.

19. Bastian to Obst, unclear date 1882, in MfVLB: no. 01873; Bastian to Obst, n.d., in MfVLB: no. 01877. Bastian to Obst, 13 Oct. 1882, in MfVLB: no. 01874; Bastian to Obst, 20 Dec. 1882, in MfVLB: no. 01875.

20. Bastian could have purchased this collection by 1883; by that time, Godeffroy was offering the ethnographic section to Leipzig for 300,000 Marks, the same sum Bastian had designated six months earlier. Godeffroy to Obst, 20 June 1883, in MfVLB: no. 01957.

21. Kirchenpauer, untitled report on the sale of the Godeffroy collection, 9 Oct. 1885, in HSA: 361-5 I, Hochschulwesen I, CIX a, nr. 39 a, bd. 1. See also *Leipziger Zeitung*, 9 Oct. 1885.

22. *Leipziger Tageblatt*, 24 April 1882; *Leipziger Tageblatt*, 25 April 1882; *Leipziger Zeitung*, 21 May 1882.

23. *Hamburger Fremdenblatt*, 9 Oct. 1885.

24. *Hamburger Correspondent*, 1 Nov. 1887. This controversy is discussed in detail in Chapter 1.

25. Thilenius, "Proposed Budget for 1905," in HSA: 111-1, Senat, DL. VII, Lit. He, nr. 1, vol. 54.

26. Thilenius, Untitled proposal for a South-Seas Expedition, accompanying a letter from Moritz Warburg, dated 4 March 1905, in MfVH: SSE 1. See also "Denkschrift über ein hamburgische Expedition nach der Südsee," in 1907, in MfVH: SSE 1.

27. Melle, *Dreizig Jahre Hamburger Wissenschaft*, 511.

28. See, for example, Coombes, *Reinventing Africa*; Rydell, *All the World's a Fair*.

29. Lehmann, "85 Jahre."

30. Ibid., 21. A number of other donors are also listed on the shipping invoices. MfVLB: vol. 1 (no catalog numbers), dated 1874.

31. Gossler to Kaiser, 27 Aug. 1904, in GSA: Rep. 89 H, 20491.

32. Deutsches Committee to Obst, 12 Oct. 1885, in MfVLB: no. 02467.

33. Obst to Museum für Völkerkunde zu Leipzig, 4 Oct. 1883, in MfVLB: no. 02192.

34. Jacobsen, "Ausstellung in Chicago, 1888–1893," and an unpublished biographical manuscript for the years 1884–1920, in MfVHJA. See also W. Haberland, "Remarks on the 'Jacobsen Collections'," 191.

35. Schöne to Puttkamer, 27 April 1881, in GSA: I. HA, Rep. 76, Ve., Sekt. 15, Abt. III, nr. 2, bd. 2.

36. MfVLB: no. 01280–1. These documents list 100 consulates and 32 consuls. MfVLB: no. 01289-2 contains similar letters addressed to ships' captains and officers.

37. See, for example, correspondence with the Kaiserliches Consul in Melbourne, and the first officer of the Nautilus. 2 Oct. 1879, in MfVB: no. 01530 and no. 01428.

38. By the end of the century, the Leipzig museum was engaged in a standing exchange of publications with 55 German institutions and associations, as well as various organizations in the European nations of Belgium, Denmark, Finland, France, Great Britain, Italy, the Netherlands, Norway, Austria-Hungary, Portugal, Russia, Spain, Sweden, Switzerland, and numerous ports and towns in Africa, Asia, Australia, North and South America, and the Melanesian and Polynesian Islands. Museum für Völkerkunde zu Leipzig, *Bericht des Museum* (1900).

39. This document accompanied a letter from Abbot Gatsche, Dept. of Interior (Geog. and Geogaph. Survey) to Spencer Baird, 21 June 1879, in SIA: RU 28, pp. 3380–81.

40. Schweinfurth, *Heart of Africa*; Essner, *Deutsche Afrikareisende*, 81–86.

41. Schweinfurth to Obst, 5 March 1877, in MfVLB: no. 00534.

42. Herrings to Obst, 1 Oct. 1884, in MfVLB: no. 02830. Rohlfs to Obst, 29 April 1885, in MfVLB: no. 02613.

43. Wolff to Obst, 10 Dec. 1888, in MfVLB: no. 03112–13; and Wolff to Obst, 16 Jan. 1890, in MfVLB: no. 03520–23.

44. Andrews to Obst, 28 Nov. 1891, in MfVLB: no. 03589; and Andrews to Obst, 14 May 1892, in MfVLB: no. 03595.

45. On the importance of reputation in science, see Luhmann, *Wissenschaft der Gesellschaft*.

46. Obst to Henry, June 30 1873, in SIA: RU 26, vol. 138, pp. 134–36. Henry's response was positive. Henry to Obst, 22 Dec. 1873, in SIA: RU 33, vol. 37, p. 55.

47. See, for example, the letter Obst sent on 3 July 1877, to a series of powerful men, ranging from the Herzog von Baden and the king of Bavaria to the prince of Wales and the king of the Netherlands, in MfVLB: no. 00621. A second, similar set of letters was sent out in 1878, in MfVLB: no. 00899–00931.

48. *Bevollmächtigte, Ehrenmitglieder, Förderer,* and *Protektoren.*

49. Wolff to Obst, 16 Jan. 1890, in MfVLB: no. 03520–23.

50. Vice-consulate to Obst, 3 Aug. 1893, in MfVLB: no. 04263.

51. Hamburg was the exception. The Hanseatic city-states had a general policy that eschewed the honor system. See Thompson, "Honors Uneven." In Munich, however, the policy of "Titel gegen Mittel" was taken to extremes. See Schumann, *Bayerns Unternehmer in der Gesellschaft und Staat,* 250–77.

52. Bastian, "Untitled report to the GVKM on the state of ethnography and the ethnographic museum," 1 June 1881, in GSA: Rep. 76, Ve., Sekt. 15., Abt. XI., nr. 2, bd. 3.

53. GVKM to KSG, 8 July 1897, in GSA: Rep. 76, Ve., Sekt. 15., Abt. XI., nr. 2, bd. 10. The Roten Adler Ordnen 2nd, 3rd, or 4th class was also a special favorite.

54. For details, see Penny, "Cosmopolitan Visions and Municipal Displays," 111–12.

55. Thilenius to Hamburg Senat, "Report on budget increases," 1905, in HSA: 111-1, Senat, CL. 7, Lit. He nr. 1, vol. 54, FSC 3.

56. "Auszug aus dem Protokolle der Kommission," 26 January 1911, includes a report by Thilenius about how to make the international connections of the city work better for them, and discusses methods of rewarding donors, such as honoring them with plaques in the museum, in HSA: 361-5 I, Hochschulwesen I, CII, a25.

57. Thilenius, "Lebenslauf," 30 July 1926, in HSA: 361-6 Hochschulwesen Dozenten- u. Personalakten IV 1030.

58. His efforts had mixed success. Stuttgart purchased them, but Dorsey bought his Benin items, sight unseen, through a Dr. Forbes in Liverpool. Luschan to Dorsey, 23 Nov. 1898; Dorsey to Luschan, 14 Dec. 1898; telegraphs from Linden to Luschan, 23 Nov. 1898; Luschan to Lamprect, 28 Nov. 1898; Luschan to Linden, 28 Nov. 1898, in MfVB: "Die Erwerbung ethnologischer Gegenstände aus der Benin-Expedition," vol. 2, 1151/98.

59. In 1900, for example, they concluded a transaction with Gustav Diehl in Wiesbaden for his well-known African collection and then quickly divided out a third of the 3,000 objects for sale. Weule to Vorstand des Museum für Völkerkunde zu Leipzig, 12 Aug. 1900, in MfVLB: no. 07176; Weule to Meyer, 18 Nov. 1900, in MfVLB: Kopiebuch 1900, no. 884.

60. Weule to Vorstand, 31 May 1899, MfVLB: no. 06824.

61. Bastian to Obst, 8 Jan. 1885, in MfVLB: no. 02378.

62. Ribbe to Obst, 10 Feb. 1885, in MfVLB: no. 02597. Ribbe to Obst, 1 April 1887, in MfVLB: no. 02983; and Ribbe to Obst, 9 June 1896, in MfVLB: no. 05263. There are many similar stories.

63. Mengelbier to Obst, 1 Dec. 1900, in MfVLB: no. 07019.

64. Mengelbier to Obst, 11 Dec. 1900, in MfVLB: no. 07467; Mengelbier to Obst, 18 Dec. 1900, in MfVLB: no. 07461.

65. Mengelbier to Vorstand, 8 Jan. 1901, in MfVLB: no. 07464. The collection was returned to Mengelbier that same month. Mengelbier to Obst, 23 Jan. 1901, in MfVLB: no. 07460.

66. Indeed, after initial transactions, the market could also affect what was produced by non-Europeans, just as the European art markets affected what was produced at home. The best known work is Price, *Primitive Art in Civilized Places*. For nineteenth-century ethnographica, see, for example, Cole, *Captured Heritage*, 295.

67. Cole, *Captured Heritage*, 290.

68. Thode-Arora, "Umlauff," 150.

69. Thomas, *Entangled Objects*, 31 provides us with a nice example.

70. Appadurai, *Social Life of Things*.

71. The estimate is from Museum für Völkerkunde zu Leipzig, *Kunst aus Benin*, 43. On violence and the Benin expedition, see Coombes, *Reinventing Africa*; Harms, "Ethnographische Kunstobjekte."

72. Berlin possessed 580 pieces in 1919, and 594 by 1945, making this the largest collection of all museums. Krieger, "Das Schicksal der Benin-Sammlung." Large collections were also acquired by the museums in Leipzig, Dresden, Stuttgart, and Vienna.

73. See, for example, Luschan, *Altertümer von Benin*. For the limited British context, see Coombes, *Reinventing Africa*.

74. Coombes, *Reinventing Africa*, 59.

75. One-third of the bronzes were sold for this purpose in 1897. Coombes, *Reinventing Africa*, 59. The merchants who bought them also failed to recognize their importance at first. See Luschan to Grünwedel, 25 July 1897, and Luschan to Hans Meyer, 31 July 1897, in MfVB: "Benin," vol. 1, 937/97.

76. Meyer to Luschan, 26 March 1898, in LN. According to O. M. Dalton at the British Museum, Meyer's conclusion was essentially correct. Dalton, *Report on Ethnographic Museums*.

77. Luschan to Grünwedel, 25 July 1897, in MfVB: "Benin," vol. 1, 937/97.

78. Meyer to Luschan, 27 July 1897, in MfVB: "Benin," vol. 1, 937/97.

79. Grünwedel to Luschan, 28 July 1897, and Luschan to Meyer, 31 July 1897, in MfVB: "Benin," vol. 1, 937/97.

80. Luschan also left with a pledge of funds from Heger in Vienna, who, without having seen any of the items, had already commissioned Luschan to purchase 1,500 Marks' worth of whatever was being offered for sale. Meyer to Luschan, 27 July 1897, and Heger to Luschan, 14 Aug. 1897, in MfVB: "Benin," vol. 1, 937/97.

81. Luschan to Brinkmann, 13 Aug. 1897, in MfVB: "Benin," vol. 1, 937/97.

82. Webster to Luschan, 22 April 1898, in MfVB: "Benin," vol. 2, 429/98. Similar letters were also received by Weule in Leipzig: Webster to Weule, 30 May 1899, in

MfVLB: no. 06793; Webster to Weule, 9 Jan. 1899, in MfVLB: no. 06795; Webster to Weule, 12 June 1899, in MfVLB: no. 06792.

83. Webster to Luschan, 18 July 1898, in MfVB: "Benin," vol. 2, 682/98; Webster to Luschan, 29 July 1898, and Luschan to Grünwedel, 10 August 1898, in MfVB: "Benin," vol. 2, 909/98. After a while almost no one who was not involved in selling or buying these things on a daily basis could know their value. When Weule was offered a collection from someone in Breslau in July 1900, for example, he simply could not decide on their value and was forced to contact Meyer, who had recently been at an auction in London. Obst to Meyer, 23 July 1900, in MfVLB: Kopiebuch 1900, no. 753.

84. Luschan to Baessler, 9 Nov. 1899, and Baessler to Luschan, 11 Dec. 1899, in MfVB: "Benin," vol. 3, 21041/99.

85. One unfortunate traveler, for example, enthusiastically returning from Africa to Hamburg with a small collection in the winter of 1903, was unable to sell his Benin items to either Berlin or Leipzig, even after reducing the prices in some cases by half. S. Stumpf to Obst, 2 Dec. 1903, in MfVLB: no. 08455; Strumpf to Zehn, 4 Dec. 1903, in MfVLB: no. 08449; Zehn to Stumpf, 5 Dec. 1903, in MfVLB: Kopiebuch 1903, no. 392; Strumpf to Obst, 8 Dec. 1903, in MfVLB: no. 08454; Strumpf to Obst, 18 Jan. 1904, in MfVLB: no. 8450.

86. "Die Forschungsreise von L. Frobenius nach Nigerien," vol. 1, 303/11, MfVB.

87. Baudrillard, "System of Collecting," 13.

88. Jenkins does not take an absolute stand on this shift, but notes, "natural history museums abandoned *many* of the aesthetic and mystical criteria that had previously determined the arrangement of objects [my emphasis]." Jenkins, "Object Lessons," 242–43.

89. Pomian, *Collectors and Curiosities*, 21, 46, 71.

90. Bahnson, "Ueber ethnographischen Museen," 113.

91. Ibid., 123.

92. Ibid., 126.

93. Beauty remained a critical characteristic for collection, regardless of professionalization. See, for example, Weule to Rath der Stadt Leipzig, 22 Feb. 1909, in LSA: kap. 31, no. 12, vol. 5, pp. 267–69.

94. Cole, *Captured Heritage*, 63–65.

95. Schöne to Gossler, 10 June 1884, in GSA: Rep. 76, Ve., Sekt. 15., Abt. 11., nr. 2, bd. 5.

96. W. Haberland, "Remarks on the 'Jacobsen Collections'."

97. Similar comments about the value of the Jacobsen collection can be found in discussions by Bastian, Boas, and Virchow as well.

98. Jacobsen himself recognized the potential for similar problems, and in several cases noted that he was concerned because he had been forced to decide what and how to collect without any assistance or guidance. Jacobsen to Bastian, 11 July 1883, in MfVB: "Jacobsen," vol. 2.

99. Indeed, Boas's descriptions and interpretations of the objects found their way into the museum's guidebooks as well. Königlichen Museen zu Berlin, *Führer*, 2nd ed., 213–14, 221.

100. Cole, *Captured Heritage*, 294.

101. Cited in Bunzl, "Franz Boas and the Humboldtian Tradition," 57. As Bunzl notes, this is essentially an extension of Bastian's argument.

102. Boas to Seler, 9 May 1893, in MfVB: "Jacobsen," vol. 1, 685/93.

103. Directors of museums constantly asked for better information. Grünwedel to Zengen, 2 Aug. 1905, in MfVB: "Reise des H. von Zengen," 1330/05.

104. Thurnwald, "Über Völkerkundemuseen," 206.

105. See, for example, the July 1907 contracts between Frobenius and the Hamburg and Leipzig museums in LSA: kap. 31, no. 12, bd. 5, pp. 119–20.

106. Frobenius to Thilenius, 29 Oct. 1904. Cited in Zwernemann, "Leo Frobenius und das Hamburgische Museum," 113.

107. This had always been true. See, for example, the debate in Strubel to Bastian, 19 July 1881, in GSA: Rep. 76, Ve., Sekt. 15., Abt. XI., nr. 2, bd. 3.

108. Guido von Usedom, "Plan zu einer Ethnographischen Museum in Berlin," 6 Aug. 1873, in GSA: Rep. 76, Ve., Sekt. 15., Abt. XI., nr. 2, bd. 1, pp. 46–48.

109. Bastian, *Führer*, 13.

110. Bahnson, "Ueber ethnographischen Museen," 115.

111. Essner, *Deutsche Afrikareisende*, 42.

112. Thilenius, "Denkschrift über ein hamburgische Expedition nach der Südsee," 1907, in MfVH: SSE 1.

113. This was the standard wage offered to collectors while working in the museum, and a standard tactic. Bastian liked to keep collectors around in case another venture came up. After many complaints, Jacobsen received a short-term raise to 120 Marks per month, which was difficult for Bastian to obtain. Bastian to GVKM, 17 June 1889, in MfVB: "Umzug," vol. 1, 579/89.

114. Jacobsen to his wife, 6 April 1889, in MfVHJA; and Gossler to GVKM, 20 March 1889, in MfVB: "Umzug," vol. 1, 286/89.

115. Jacobsen to Kaiser, 27 Aug. 1890, in MfVB: "Umzug," vol. 1, 933/90. The kaiser did make inquiries in response to this letter, but the museum refused to give Jacobsen a permanent position, and by 1891 he left to work at an exhibition in Köln.

116. The BGAEU, for example, termed Jacobsen "a very exceptionally talented collector and observer" in their official correspondence: BGAEU to GVKM, 25 May 1884, in MfVB: "Jacobsen," 869/84.

117. The exact reason is never stated. Grünwedel simply stated that he could "in no way" support Jacobsen to be employed in such a capacity in the museum, "because he is absolutely *untauglich* [unsuitable] for such work." Grünwedel to Müller, 1 Oct. 1890, in MfVB: "Umzug," vol. 1, 782/90.

118. The same was true of many other collectors as well. See, for example, Probst, "Beobachtung und Methode."

119. Jenkins, "Object Lessons," 248; Appadurai, *Social Life of Things*, 20.

120. Pomian, *Collectors and Curiosities*, 125.

121. Kuklick, "After Ishmael"; and Kuklick, *Savage Within*.

122. Kuklick, "After Ishmael."

123. Essner, *Deutsche Afrikareisende*, argues a similar point for geographers.

124. These included several circumnavigations of the world as well as extended

trips to Africa, Persia, India, South America, Asia, and Australia. Considering Bastian's role in shaping ethnology in Germany, this is a critical exception.

125. Indeed, von den Steinen's fieldwork earned him notice from the otherwise highly critical Paul Radin. Radin, *Method and Theory of Ethnology*, 76.

126. Consider the enthusiasm with which Bastian greeted Boas's trip to Baffin Island. Liss, "German Culture and German Science," 176.

127. See, for example, Fischer, *Hamburger Südsee-Expedition*, 13. The Jesup North Pacific Expedition (1897–1902), organized by Boas, was the first of the bigger expeditions. It drew on Jacobsen's example and set the next trend.

128. Weule to RSL, 19 Feb. 1906, in LSA: kap. 31, no. 12, vol. 4, pp. 31–34.

129. Weule, "Vorschlag des Museums für Völkerkunde für des Jahr 1910," 26 March 1909, in LSA: kap. 31, no. 12, vol. 6, pp. 55–62.

130. Thilenius, "Proposed Budget for 1905," in HSA: 111-1, Senat, DL. 7, Lit. He nr. 1, vol. 54.

131. Weule, "Vorschlag des Museums für Völkerkunde für des Jahr 1910," 26 March 1909, in LSA: kap. 31, no. 12, vol. 6, pp. 55–62. The American he is referring to in this citation is Dorsey, from the Chicago Field Museum. See also Weule to RSL, 3 March 1910, in LSA: 31, no. 12, vol. 6, pp. 148.

132. Thilenius made the same arguments, noting, for example, that in only a few years, baskets from American Indians had increased in price from 0.50 Marks to 20–25 Marks a piece. Thilenius, "Erläuterung zu dem Budget-Entwurf, 1906," in HSA: 361-5 I, Hochschulwesen I, CII a, nr. 15, bd. 2.

133. Weule, "Vorschlag des Museums für Völkerkunde für des Jahr 1910," 26 March 1909, in LSA: kap. 31, no. 12, vol. 6, pp. 55–62.

134. Thilenius, "Erläuterung zu dem Budget-Entwurf, 1906," in HSA: 361-5 I, Hochschulwesen I, CII a, nr. 15, bd. 2.

135. Ibid.

136. This same conviction is actually what prompted Bastian to send Jacobsen to the northwest coast of the United States and Canada at the time he did. He feared that ethnologists from Bremen would get there first and snatch up all the best pieces. MfVHJA: Jacobsen, "Wie ich in Verbindung mit Hagenbeck kahm!"

137. Thilenius, "Antrag auf einmalige Nachbewilligung von M 4500 für die Bibliothek des Museums für Völkerkunde," in HSA: 361-5 I, Hochschulwesen I, CII a, nr. 15, bd. 2.

138. Thilenius, "Denkschrift über eine hamburgische Expedition nach der Südsee," in MfVH: SSE 1. Thilenius noted years later that much to his pleasure, this goal was essentially achieved. Thilenius, "Lebenslauf," 30 July 1926, in HSA: 361-6 Hochschulwesen Dozenten- u. Personalakten IV 1030. From 1904 to 1908, Thilenius produced at least five similar proposals, MfVH: SSE 1. See also Fischer, *Hamburger Südsee-Expedition*.

Chapter Three

1. During the first decade of the twentieth century, the directors of the Hamburg (1904), Berlin (1905), Leipzig (1907), and Munich (1907) museums were all replaced

by younger men with a completely different stance toward colonialism than that shared by Bastian and Virchow.

2. This was common across many of the sciences. See Home and Kohlstedt, *International Science*, 1–17.

3. Baird's efforts to create and maintain such exchanges are recorded in his papers in SIA: RU 33.

4. Bastian to Dall, 8 July 1881, in SIA: RU 7073, Box 6, folder 25.

5. Bastian, "Vorbemerkungen," v.

6. Bastian's support of the museum was publicly noted as early as 1870. See *Leipziger Tageblatt*, 14 April 1870. He is also listed as one of their first *Förderer* and *Ehrenmitglieder* [supporter and honorary member] in the museum's reports. Museum für Völkerkunde zu Leipzig, *Bericht des Museum*, 1875.

7. Weule to Obst, 23 Jan. 1899, in MfVLB: no. 06825.

8. German Gesandschaft in Mexico in Vertretung Paul Kosidowski Kaiserlicher Consul to Bastian, 3 June 1896, in BAP: AA, R901, 37868: 82–83.

9. Kuklick, "After Ishmael," 47–65.

10. Thurnwald noted as late as 1912 that, despite their inability to maintain the desired standards of collection, "gifts from amateurs must naturally always be received with thanks." Thurnwald, "Über Völkerkundemuseen," 204.

11. Gerhard, "Die Sammlung der Nordwestküsten-Indianer," 18; W. Haberland, "Remarks on the 'Jacobsen Collections'." This division is not a product of the nineteenth century, but has a long tradition. See Thomas, *Entangled Objects*, 141.

12. Cited in Massin, "From Virchow to Fischer," 96.

13. Cited in Koepping, "Enlightenment and Romanticism," 75–91.

14. Von Luschan, "Vortrag auf dem VII Internationalen Geographen-Kongress in Berlin im Jahr 1899" in MfVB: "Erweiterungsbau des Königlichen Museums für Völkerkunde" vol. 2, 1286/1903. Similar arguments about the "contemptible," "misguided," or "uneducated" attitudes and actions by Europeans were repeated often by ethnologists as they argued for the utility of their science. See, for example, Thilenius, "Arbeiterfrage in der Südsee."

15. Jenkins, "Object Lessons," 252.

16. Cole, *Captured Heritage*, 307–11. Jacobsen to Luschan? (addressed only to "Herr Doktor"), 16 Jan. 1896, in MfVB: "Erwerbung der Sammlungen Jacobsen," vol. 2.

17. Fischer, *Hamburger Südsee-Expedition*; see also Dörfel and Carstensen, "Wie Ethnographica und Großwildtrophäen," and Harms, "Ethnographische Kunstobjekte."

18. Some ethnologists held stronger to these tenets than others. See, for example, Gareis on Lucian Shermann: Gareis, *Exotik in München*, 89.

19. Fischer, *Hamburger Südsee-Expedition*, 123–24.

20. Jacobsen to Bastian, 15 May 1883, in MfVB: "Jacobsen," vol. 2.

21. Memorandum, British Embassy to AA, 6 June 1900, in BAP: AA, R901, 37869: 66.

22. Kaiserlich Konsulat in Calcutta to Reichzkanzler Bülow, 18 Jan. 1901, in BAP: AA, R901, 37870: 6–10.

23. KSG to Bülow, 5 Nov. 1901, in BAP: AA, R901, 37869: 25–27.

24. Cole recounts Boas as having said that stealing from graves was "'repulsive work' but 'someone had to do it'." Someone working under the guise of scientific legitimacy, that is. Cole, *Captured Heritage*, 308.

25. Bastian to AA, n.d. (follows a similar letter dated 23 Jan. 1901), in BAP: AA, R901, 37869: 103–4; Bastian to GVKM, 21 July 1900, in MfVB: "Müller," 1008/1900.

26. Königliche Generalconservatorium des wissenschaftlichen Sammlung des Staates to Königliche Staats-Ministerium des Innern für Kirchen- und Schulangelegenheiten, 17 Sept. 1895, in BHA: MK 19454.

27. Thilenius to Luschan, 13 Jan. 1906, in LN.

28. Herr Geheimrath Prof. Dr. Wislicenus, discussing the purchase of a collection from Umlauff during the "Öffentliche Verhandlungen der Stadtverordneten," on 9 Nov. 1898, in LSA: kap. 31, no. 12, vol. 2, p. 181.

29. Corbey, *Tribal Art Traffic*.

30. Museum für Völkerkunde zu Leipzig, *Bericht des Museum* (1877), 10.

31. The best account is in Bruckner, "Tingle-Tangle of Modernity."

32. Rothfels, "Bring 'em Back Alive," 143–45, 190–91, 194, 208–12.

33. See, for example, Königlichen Museen zu Berlin, *Führer*, 3rd ed., 78.

34. Rothfels "Bring 'em Back Alive," 190–91. This happened in other museums as well. Thilenius to Hagenbeck, 24 June 1908, and Hagenbeck to Thilenius, 25 June 1908, in MfVH: D3, 184 "Hagenbecks Tierpark."

35. See, for example, *Beilage der Leipziger Nachrichten*, 4 April 1872, and *Leipziger Tageblatt*, 14 May 1876; *Verzeichnis, Hamburgisches Museum für Völkerkunde*, 1881, Abteilung Africa, in HSA: 361-5 I, Hochschulwesen I, CII, bd. 1; and Museum für Völkerkunde zu Leipzig, *Berichte des Museum* (1876), 5.

36. There are many examples. See, for example, Lehmann, "85 Jahre," 25.

37. Ibid., 26; Umlauff to Obst, 30 Nov. 1876, in MfVLB: no. 0453.

38. *Hamburger Nachricht*, 3 Dec. 1906; *Hamburger Correspondent*, 3 Dec. 1906.

39. Weule to Umlauff, 18 April 1912, in MfVLB: Kopiebuch 1912, no. 458.

40. Thode-Arora, "Umlauff," 147.

41. Ibid., 151.

42. Indeed, J. M. Ita notes that Benin set new standards for collecting actions in many ways, arguing, for example, that Leo Frobenius used Benin as a point of comparison for his own activities and methods in Africa. See Ita, "Frobenius in West African History," 673–88.

43. Forces eventually included contingents from Britain, France, Russia, Italy, Germany, Austria-Hungary, and the United States.

44. Bastian to GVKM, 21 July 1900, in MfVB: "Die Reise des Dr. Müller nach China, Erwerbungen durch das Expeditions-Corps,""Müller," 1008/1900.

45. Goltz to Bastian, 12 Oct. 1900, in MfVB: "Müller," 1008/1900. Goltz wrote in response to a letter from Bastian from 3 Aug. 1900. They received similar reports from other sources.

46. Ibid.

47. Bastian to GVKM, 23 Jan. 1901, in MfVB: "Müller," 1008/1900.

48. Ibid.

49. Bastian to Goltz, 21 Jan. 1901, in MfVB: "Müller," 92/01.

50. KSG to Bülow, 13 Feb. 1901, in BAP: AA, R901, 37869: 99.

51. KSG to Bastian, 5 Feb. 1901, in MfVB: "Müller," 141/01.

52. Friedrich Wilhelm Karl Müller's title was *wissenschaftlicher Hilsarbeiter* in the East-Asian section of the museum.

53. GVKM to F. W. K. Müller, 14 Feb. 1901. Müller initially received 18,000 Marks to cover his expenses and acquisitions. His final report, however, notes that he spent 20,000 Marks on acquisitions and 6,500 Marks on expenses. "Gesamtübersicht," 14 March 1902, in MfVB: "Müller," 305/02.

54. Müller, "Reisebericht," 15 May 1902, in MfVB: "Müller," 682/12.

55. Müller to Bastian, 29 April 1901, in MfVB: "Müller," 715/01.

56. Massin, "From Virchow to Fischer," 95.

57. The literature on this aspect of the relationship between colonialism and anthropology and ethnology is extensive. For Germany, see Essner, "Berlins Völkerkunde Museum"; for Britain, see Kuklick, *Savage Within*, 182.

58. Hope, "Naturwissenschaftliche und zoologische Forschungen in Afrika," 197.

59. Lustig, "'Außer ein paar zerbrochenen Pfeilen nichts zu verteilen'." See also the correspondence in MfVH: D2, 23.

60. Teogbert Maler to Bastian, 1 May 1896, in BAP: AA, R901, 37868: 92. The situation in Mexico was repeated as other countries closed their borders to ethnographica at the end of the nineteenth century.

61. Vorstand des Museum für Völkerkunde zu Leipzig to RSL, 18 Aug. 1894, in LSA: kap. 31, no. 12, vol. 1, pp. 345–46. C.f. "Auszug aus dem Protokolle des Senats," in HSA: 361-5 I, Hochschulwesen I, CII b, nr. 15, bd. 5.

62. Zengen, "Lebenslauf," 15 Sept. 1904, in MfVB: "Reise des H. von Zengen," 1371/04.

63. Grünwedel to Fenkel (Hilfcomitté), 15 Sept. 1904, in MfVB: "Zengen," 1371/04.

64. On Frobenius and his place in German ethnology, see, for example, Durham, "Leo Frobenius," and E. Haberland, *Leo Frobenius.*

65. Frobenius participated in six major expeditions as leader of the Deutschen Innerafrikanischen Forschungsexpedition from 1904 to 1914, which included a foray into the Congo in 1904, a trip from Senegal through Mali, over Togo, and to the coast in 1907–8, a trip in North Africa in 1910, which included Algiers and Kabylia, another in 1910–11 through Nigeria and Cameroon, an expedition from the Red Sea to Khartoum and Kordofan in 1912, and excavations in Morocco and a trip through the Sahara in 1913–14 (during this last he was not connected to the museums). I am concerned here with his fourth trip in 1910–11 through Nigeria and Cameroon.

66. Frobenius's own version of events can be found in Frobenius, *Und Afrika sprach*, 66–126.

67. Ifé was a particularly important city, since the Oni (king) had the right of crowning all the rulers of the various Yoruba kingdoms, including the king of Benin.

68. Memorandum concerning the Olokun Affair from the British Foreign Office, 15 April 1911, and a letter of protest from the British Foreign Office to the German

secretary of state, 4 May 1911, in LSA: kap. 31, no. 12, bd. 7. See *Berliner Tageblatt*, 31 May 1911. E.g., *Berliner Tageblatt*, 5 Feb. 1911; *Berliner Zeitung*, 2 Feb. 1911; *Deutsche Tageszeitung*, 21 May 1912.

69. Frobenius, *Und Afrika sprach*, 102.

70. Frobenius often used the words "Habgier," "Intrigen," "Intrigenlust," and "Verlogenhiet" in reference to Partridge.

71. Partridge was a fellow of the Royal Anthropological Society and author of *Cross River Natives: being some notes on the primitive pagans of Obubra Hill district, Southern Nigeria; including a description of the circle of upright stones on the left bank of the Aweyong River* (London: Hutchinson, 1905).

72. Frobenius, *Und Afrika sprach*, 81–82, 89, 102, 107.

73. Ibid., 68, 105, 110.

74. Ibid., 83, 90, 100, 102.

75. Ibid., 112, 119, 123.

76. Ibid., 117, 118, 126.

77. *Berliner Zeitung*, 2 Feb. 1911.

78. Frobenius, *Und Afrika sprach*, 126.

79. Thilenius to Senat, 24 June 1911, in MfVH: L. F. 5.

80. Weule to RSL, 14 July 1911, in LSA: kap. 31, no. 24, bd. 7; Weule to Ankermann, 13 July 1911, in MfVLB: Kopiebuch 1911, no. 218; Weule to Thilenius, 7 July 1911, in MfVLB: Kopiebuch 1911, no. 642; Weule to Frobenius, 31 Aug. 1911, in MfVLB: Kopiebuch 1911, no. 811–13.

81. By using the term *Auch-Gelehrten*, Weule is referring to Partridge, who had done some ethnographic work and belonged to the Royal Anthropological Society, and ridiculing the idea that these qualifications might make Partridge his own, or Frobenius's, intellectual equal.

82. Weule to Ankermann, 13 July 1911, in MfVLB: Kopiebuch 1911, no. 218. See also Frobenius, *Und Afrika sprach*, 105.

83. Weule to Ankermann, 13 July 1911, in MfVLB: Kopiebuch 1911, no. 218.

84. Thilenius to Ankermann, 21 July 1911, in MfVB: "Die Forschungsreise von L. Frobenius nach Nigerien," vol. 1, 1215/11.

85. C. H. Read, "Plato's 'Atlantis' Re-Discovered," in *Burlington Magazine* 18, no. 96 (March 1911): 330–35.

86. Even Weule, who had once sought to go into the colonial service, and who was perhaps the staunchest supporter of German colonialism among the directors of German museums, wrote, following his own expedition to Africa: "Are those the savages, or are we?" Cited in Winkelmann, "Bürgerliche Ethnographie," 161.

87. The term is from Pratt, *Imperial Eyes*.

88. The same was true even in the American Midwest. See Goldstein, "Yours for Science."

89. Frič undertook four trips to South America from 1900 to 1913. For an uncritical discussion of Frič's ventures, see Kandert, "Alberto Vojtěch Frič."

90. Frič to Thilenius, 20 Nov. 1906, in MfVH: D2, 36. Frič, "Sambaqui-Forschungen."

91. See Frič to Thilenius, 6 Feb. 1907, in MfVH: D2, 36.

92. Frič to GVKM, 1 July 1907, in BAP: AA, R901, 37874: 11–14.

93. "Pacificacao dos Botocudos," in *Odia* 7, no. 1808 (Florianopolis, 7 March 1907); "Pobres Indios," *Diario Tarde* 10, no. 2449 (Coritiba, 13 March 1907); "Catechese em Blumenau," *Novidades* 3, no. 147 (Santa Catharina, 24 March 1907); "Pobres Indios," *O Livre Pensador* 4, no. 158 (Sao Paulo, 7 April 1907).

94. At this time the south Brazilian states of San Paulo, Paraná, and Santa Catharina had over 300,000 German-speaking inhabitants. *Vossische Zeitung*, 17 May 1907.

95. Frič focused specifically on the actions of German settlers, while Gensch implied that participants "from all lands" were at the root of the problem: Gensch, "Die Erziehung eines Indianerkindes."

96. Gensch to Kaiserlich Deutschen Konsulat in Blumenau, 1 Aug. 1907, in BAP: AA, R901, 37874: 39–48.

97. See also Gustav Salinger the Königliche Consul in Blumenau to Kaiserliche Gesandschaft Petropolis, 25 March 1907, in BAP: AA, R901, 37873: 73.

98. As Gensch retold this story in a second letter, he also claimed that Frič had photographs of naked Indian women as well as naked photos of himself wearing Indian masks while standing next to these women. Gensch to Kaiserlich Deutschen Konsulat in Blumenau, 1 Aug. 1907, in BAP: AA, R901, 37874: 39–48.

99. Thilenius to Seler, 23 Oct. 1907 in MfVH: M. B. 10, bd. 3, "Kgl. Museen Berlin;" and Seler to Thilenius, 24 Oct. 1907, in MfVB: "Frič," 1943/07.

100. Frič to Thilenius, 19 July 1907, in MfVH: D2, 36. These moralistic arguments increased in tone over time. Frič to GVKM, 1 July 1907, in BAP: AA, R901, 37874: 11–14. Frič, "Offener Brief and die 'Vossische Zeitung,' Berlin," *Argentinisches Tageblatt*, 6 July 1907 (Buenos Aires). Salinger to AA, 7 Aug. 1907, in BAP: AA, R901, 37874: 37. Frič to GVKM, 12 Aug. 1907, in BAP: AA, R901, 37874: 21–7.

101. Seler to Thilenius, 24 Oct. 1907, in MfVB: "Die Reise des Adalbert Frich nach Südamerika," vol. 1, "Frič," 1943/07.

102. Thilenius to Frau Baronin v. Malsen, 22 July 1907, in MfVH: D2, 36. Thilenius to Seler, 23 Oct. 1907, in MfVH: M.B.10, bd. 3-4.

103. Bode to KSG, 13 June 1907, in BAP: AA, R901, 378673: 55–56. KSG to GVKM, 21 June 1907, in MfVB: "Frič," 1200/07. Museum für Völkerkunde, Berlin to Frič, 22 June 1907, in BAP: AA, R901, 378673: 66. Hamburgisches Völkerkunde Museum to Frič, 29 June 1907, in MfVH: D2, 36. Thilenius to GVKM, 10 July 1907, in MfVH: D2, 36. The degree to which this decision was precipitated by the AA was confirmed by Seler in a later letter as well: Seler to Herrn Jarosalv Brázda in Prague, 29 Dec. 1908, in MfVB: "Frič," 2801/08.

104. Frič, "Völkerwanderung."

105. *Neue Freie Presse* (NFP), 15 Sept. 1908. This part of the NFP's coverage is confirmed by the general reports in other papers. See, for example, *Der Tag*, 15 Sept. 1908.

106. Indeed, as von den Steinen later lamented, it gained far more public attention than the conference proceedings themselves. Von den Steinen, "Frič und keine Ende," *Berliner Tageblatt*, Erste Beiblatt, 7 Oct. 1908.

107. Von den Steinen, "Frič und keine Ende." Cf. Eduard Seler, "Ein letztes Wort zur Frič -Sache," *Berliner Tageblatt*, 20 Oct. 1908.

108. *Berliner Tageblatt*, 15 Sept. 1908.

109. Frič, "Eine Pilcomayo-Reise," and Frič and Radin, "Contribution to the Study of the Bororo Indians."

110. Hartmann, *Xingú*, 14.

Chapter Four

1. The influence of public enthusiasm on museums has been acknowledged by a number of scholars. See, for example, Frese, *Anthropology and the Public*, and Kohlstedt, "Museums." For more general reflections on the public and science see Cooter and Pumfrey, "Separate Spheres," 240, 250–51.

2. In Hamburg, Leipzig, and Berlin, the decisions to build new buildings were immediately followed by a series of survey trips by architects and staff members. See HSA: 361-5 I, Hochschulwesen I, CII, a16, bd. 1 & 2; LSA: cap. 31, no. 11, vol. 2; GSA: I. HA, Rep. 76, Ve., Sekt. 15, Abt. 3, nr. 2, bd. 1.

3. Thilenius, "Besichtigung verschiedener auswärtiger Museen," 8–16 Sept. 1908, in HSA: Hochschulwesen I, CII, a16, bd. 2. Thilenius, "Beobachtungen und Überlegungen für die Aufstellung der Sammlungen des Museums für Völkerkunde," May 1912, in HSA: Hochschulwesen I, CII, a1.

4. Circular from Bode to all section directors of the Museum für Völkerkunde, Berlin, 4 Jan. 1912, in MfVB: "Erweiterungsbau des Königlichen Museums für Völkerkunde," vol. 4, 124/12.

5. See, for example, William Henry Holmes, "Report of Studies of European Museums Made during the Summer of 1904," in *Random Records of a Lifetime*, vol. 9, sec. 2, 1904: 42–59, in SIA: RU 7084.

6. He apologized at great lengths to both of them and promised to include their museums in his next publication. Goode to Obst, 23 Jan. 1883, in SIA: RU 112, L 45, pp. 384–85.

7. Giglioli visited museums in Germany, Denmark, Bohemia, and Austria in 1880. His essay appeared in *Archivo per l'Antropologia e la Etnologia* 11, no. 2 (1881) and excerpts were reprinted in the *Leipziger Tageblatt*, 17 June 1882.

8. Lehmann, "85 Jahre," 27.

9. *Leipziger Tageblatt*, 31 May 1883.

10. More contention did take place in the following year. Museum für Völkerkunde zu Leipzig Vorstand to RSL, 29 Oct. 1883, in LSA: kap. 31, no. 14, pp. 34–38.

11. Otto Georgi, *Vortrag das Grassi-Museums betreffend*, 11 April 1884, in LSA: kap. 31, no. 14, pp. 40–63.

12. These critiques and evaluations were often solicited and then put to use by the museums' supporters who recognized the power of the "scientific" voice. See, for example, efforts by Hamburgers to gain Friedrich Ratzel's criticisms: Brinckmann to Ratzel, 30 Nov. 1898, in HSA: 361-5 I, Hochschulwesen I, CII, a16, bd. 1.

13. Königliche Museen zu Berlin, *Führer*, 7th ed., 12–16.

14. For example, the name of the collector was written in red ink and attached to *each item* in the Indian section of the Berlin museum. Ibid., 153.

15. This is made clear in the exchange of letters between Schliemann, Virchow,

and the kaiser in Meyer, *Briefe von Heinrich Schliemann*. See also Trail, *Schliemann of Troy*, especially 186–95.

16. Puttkamer to kaiser, 21 Jan. 1881, in GSA: Rep. 89 H, 20489, pp. 52–60.

17. Königliche Museen zu Berlin, *Führer*, 3rd ed., 56.

18. Lehmann, "85 Jahre," 30.

19. RSL to Stübel, Oct. 1891, in LSA: kap. 31, no. 12, vol. 1, p. 309.

20. Stübel to Obst, 12 Feb. 1894, in MfVLB: 04579.

21. Licht to RSL, 5 Sept. 1894, in LSA: kap. 31, no. 11, vol. 2, p. 302, cited in Mannschatz, "Grassi," 34.

22. Stübel to RSL, 25 April 1896, in LSA: kap. 31, no. 25, vol. 1, pp. 7–8.

23. Stübel to Zehn, 27 July 1900, in MfVLB: 07133–41.

24. "Protokolle des gemischten Verwaltungsausschusses für das Museum für Völkerkunde," 11 April 1908, in LSA: kap. 31, no. 33, bd. 1.

25. Obst to Stübel, 9 Jan. 1899, in MfVB: Kopiebuch 1898&1899, 380; Stübel to Obst, 10 Jan. 1899, in MfVB: 06736.

26. New Guinea Company to Gossler, 24 Sept. 1885, in GSA: I. HA, Rep. 76, Ve. Sekt. 15., Abt. XI., nr. 2, bd. 6, pp. 83–87; and Gossler to GVKM, 16 Oct. 1885, in MfVB: "Die Erwerbung ethnologischer Gegenstände durch Vermittlung der Neu-Guinea-Compagnie," 216/85. New Guinea Company to Gossler, 3 Aug. 1886, in GSA: I. HA, Rep. 76, Ve. Sekt. 15., Abt. XI., nr. 2, bd. 6, pp. 241–44.

27. Frhrr. v. Hammerstein to kaiser, 3 April 1902, in BAP: AA, R901, 37870, bd. 6, pp. 49–53.

28. In 1899, for example, Baessler offered to give the museum both collections from South America and financial assistance for further ventures there in return for his conditions. Foreign Minister von Bulow termed these demands "cheap." Von Bulow to kaiser, 30 Oct. 1899, in BAP: AA, R901, 37870, bd. 5, pp. 41–44.

29. See Penny, "Municipal Displays."

30. F. Jagor, R. Virchow, and W. Reiss to Robert von Puttkamer, 11 Dec. 1879, in GSA: I. HA, Rep. 76 Ve. Sekt. 15. Abt. III. nr. 2, bd. 2.

31. Weule to RSL, 22 Sept. 1909, "Bericht über die Spezialausstellung über die Wirtschaft der Naturvölker und aussereuropäischen Kulturvölker im Juni und Juli 1909," in LSA: kap. 31, no. 12, vol. 6, p. 80.

32. Göring to Obst, n.d. [1896], in MfVLB: 05063.

33. Schneider to Königlich Bayerischen Staats-Ministerium des Innern für Kirchen- und Schulengelegenheiten, 16 May 1904, in BHA: MK 19454.

34. Despite Buchner's protest, many of the museums were organized in this way. In the African Hall of the Berlin museum in 1877, for example, visitors moved through collections that were essentially organized according to geography and donor; many of the items even included their approximate monetary value. Bastian, *Führer*, 22–24, 30–31. Entire walls devoted to particular collectors were still common in 1892. Königliche Museen zu Berlin, *Führer*, 5th ed., 66.

35. Buchner to KGK, 16 July 1904, in BHA: MK 19454.

36. On the development of this new aesthetic, see Crane, *Museums and Memory*; Joachimedies et al., *Museumsinszenierungen*; and especially, Sheehan, *Museums in the German Art World*.

37. This was common across Europe and the United States. See, for example,

Sherman, *Worthy Monuments*. For reactions to specific complaints about closing procedures and dress, see circular by Schöne, 4 March 1898, in MFVB: "Dienstbestimmungen," vol. 1, 261/98; and circular from von Bode, 27 Feb. 1909, in MFVB: "Dienstbestimmungen," vol. 7, 503/09.

38. E. Prölss to GVKM, 8 July 1890, in MFVB: "Die Eröffnung des Museums und die Besichtigung der Sammlungen durch das Publikum," vol. 1, 747/90.

39. "Das Völkerkunde Museum und die Kinder," *Leipziger Neueste Nachrichten*, 22 Nov. 1909, signed simply, "a father."

40. Circular by Schöne, 16 Dec. 1901, in MFVB: "Dienstbestimmungen," vol. 1, 1453/01.

41. Buchner, *Orientalische Reise*, 151.

42. Weule to Frobenius, 30 Dec. 1909, in MfVLB: Kopiebuch 1909, p. 1127.

43. H. H., "Das Stiefkind des Leipziger Völkermuseums," *Leipziger Nachrichten*, 2 Dec. 1904.

44. "Das Stiefkind des Leipziger Museums für Völkerkunde," *Leipziger Nachrichten*, 10 Dec. 1904.

45. Jacob, "Eröffnung der vorgeschichtlichen Abteilung der Museums für Völkerkunde," *Leipziger Neueste Nachrichten*, 26 Sept. 1910.

46. Richter, "Über die Idealen."

47. For discussions of trends toward education in Britain and the United States, see, for example, Coombes, "Museums," 63, and Kirshenblatt-Gimblet, "Objects of Ethnography," 395.

48. Dr. med. Fritze to Oberschulbehörde, 4 March 1904, in HSA: 361-5 I, Hochschulwesen I, CII, a17.

49. Hagen to Oberschulbehörde, 15 March 1904, in HSA: 361-5 I, Hochschulwesen I, CII, a17.

50. Gottsche to Oberschulbehörde, March 1904, in HSA: 361-5 I, Hochschulwesen I, CII, a17.

51. By the turn of the century, museums, along with many other public institutions, were being harnessed by local elites for, as George Brown Goode put it, "the increase of knowledge and for the culture and enlightenment of the people." See Goode *Principles of Museum Administration*, 3.

52. This was an international trend as well. See, for example, the British debates in Yanni, *Nature's Museums*.

53. "Mitteilungen des Senats an die Bürgerschaft," no. 109, in HSA: CIIa, nr. 16, bd. 1. See also "Bericht des von der Bürgerschaft am 22 June 1904," Nov. 1904, nr. 38, in HSA: CIIa, nr. 16, bd. 1; and "42 Sitzung der Bürgerschaft," 14 Dec. 1904, in HSA: CIIa, nr. 16, bd. 1.

54. *Neue Hamburger Zeitung* (Abend Ausgabe), 14 June 1904.

55. For a precise rendition of what this entailed, see Thilenius, *Hamburgische Museum*.

56. Richter did continue to agree that the museums should be primarily designed for educated visitors [*Gelehrter*], but he also advocated bringing a much broader public into the museum. Richter, "Über die Idealen," 190–99.

57. Bastian to GVKM, 17 Nov. 1900, in MfVB: "Erweiterungsbau des Königlichen Museums für Völkerkunde," vol. 1, 985/1900.

58. See the extensive discussion in MfVB: "Erweiterungsbau des Königlichen Museums für Völkerkunde," vol. 1.

59. There had been some earlier exchange on this point as well. See Boas to Grünwedel, Jan. 1897, in MfVB: "Umzug," vol. 3, 8/97.

60. Their private evaluations were even stronger than their published condemnations. See Boas, "Some Principles," and Dorsey, "Anthropological Exhibits."

61. Boas to Luschan, 18 Oct. 1909; Dorsey to Luschan 14 Nov. 1909; and Luschan to GVKM, 24 Nov. 1909, all in MfVB: "Umzug," vol. 10, 2124/09.

62. Indeed, the displays were not actually reorganized until 1924. See "Die Neuordnung des Museums für Völkerkunde," in *Berliner Tageblatt*, 26 Oct. 1924.

63. Following the 1918 revolutions, the "elite" focus of Prussian museums came under heavy attack. See Scheffler, *Berliner Museumskrieg*, 22.

64. Weule, *Führer durch das Museum für Völkerkunde*, 1909; Weule, *Illustrierter Führer*, 1910.

65. Weule, "Bericht über die Spezialausstellung über die Wirtschaft der Naturvölker und aussereuropäischen Kulturvölker im Juni und Juli 1909," 22 July 1909, in LSA: kap. 31, no. 12, vol. 6, pp. 79–80; *Leipziger Tageblatt*, 25 July 1909.

66. [*reger und stärker*].

67. Weule, "Bericht über die Spezialausstellung," 79–80 (see n. 65).

68. Two lecture series organized under the title, "The Essentials of Völkerkunde, and Instructions for a Useful Visit to the Völkerkundemuseum," were held in the Winter of 1909–10. Weule's report on these lectures also reflected his strong interest in reaching, and showing that he had reached, a broad public. Weule to RSL, "Bericht über die Museumskurse 1909/1910," 3 March 1910, in LSA: kap. 31, no. 12, vol 6.

69. Krause, "Bericht über die Sonderausstellung über Verkehrs- und Transportmittel im Museum für Völkerkunde," 24 Sept. 1910, in LSA: kap. 31, no. 12, vol. 6, pp. 185–86.

70. Weule, "Der volkserzieherische Wert des Leipziger Völkermuseums," *Leipziger Tageblatt*, 5 Aug. 1910.

71. Arrangements made by Berlin following Weule's talk, for example, were noted by Krause, "Bericht über die Sonderausstellung," 24 Sept. 1910 (see n. 69).

72. A particularly important example is Willy Foy's museum in Cologne.

73. Schlör (Royal secretary) to director of Munich's Polytechnical Schools, 29 Sept. 1868, in BHA: MK 14423. See also "Das neue ethnographische Museum in München," in *Beilage zur Allgemeine Zeitung*, 8–11 Jan. 1868.

74. Smolka, *Völkerkunde in München*, 94; Gareis, *Exotik in München*, 153.

75. Smolka, *Völkerkunde in München* 89; Gareis, *Exotik in München*, 56–61.

76. "Das neue ethnographische Museum in München," in *Beilage zur Allgemeine Zeitung*, 8–11 Jan. 1868. Cited in Gareis, *Exotik in München*, 56.

77. Smolka, *Völkerkunde in München*, 93–94, 108.

78. Ibid., 89–92.

79. Ibid., 154.

80. Buchner, *Orientalische Reise*, 21.

81. Smolka, *Völkerkunde in München*, 124, 141.

82. Gareis, *Exotik in München*, 86. Smolka, *Völkerkunde in München*, 93.

83. This had actually been initiated by Buchner. Lucian Sherman, "K. Ethnographisches Museum, Jahres Bericht 1909," *Münchener Jahrbuch der Bildenden Kunst* (1909): 79.

84. Gareis, *Exotik in München*, 97.

85. From 1908 to 1909 alone, the figures grew from 9,101 to 15,518. Walter Lehmann, "K. Ethnographisches Museum, Jahres Bericht 1910," *Münchener Jahrbuch der Bildenden Kunst* (1910): 144.

86. This, in fact, is ultimately Smolka's argument. Smolka, *Völkerkunde in München*, 292–96.

87. These nine candidates, who ranged from self-educated travelers with limited experience in museums, to well-known museum men such as Willy Foy and well-credentialed scientists such as Sherman—who had both a doctorate and a *Habilitation* (second doctoral degree) and was the editor of the *Orientalische Bibliographie*—are described in detail in Smolka, *Völkerkunde in München*, 170–74.

88. Prinz Rupprecht von Bayern also showed a particular interest in the museum and became a critical patron. Gareis, *Exotik in München*, 90.

89. Smolka, *Völkerkunde in München*, 180.

90. For a good discussion of these artists, see Gareis, *Exotik in München*, 94–98.

91. Germer, "Vorgeschichte der Gründung."

92. The lectures for 1872, for example, are listed in *Leipziger Zeitung*, 14 Dec. 1871, and the individual lectures were covered in a series of articles in both this paper and the *Leipziger Tageblatt* under the title "Vorlesungen zum Besten des Deutschen Centralmuseums für Völkerkunde." These ran from January through March 1872.

93. This remained consistent through the entire run of the museum's reports from 1873 to 1900. See Museum für Völkerkunde zu Leipzig, *Bericht des Museum*.

94. The fact that the Museum für Völkerkunde zu Leipzig archive has six large volumes of news clippings for this period of the museum's history, is the best indication of the breadth of coverage the museum received in local papers.

95. For budget details, see Lehmann, "85 Jahre," 24.

96. For a more complete comparison of these two museums' histories, see Zwernemann, "Aus den frühen Jahren."

97. Zwernemann, *Hundert Jahre*, 3–4.

98. Ibid., 4.

99. The initial budget was minimalist. 2,000 Marks for Lüders, 1,000 for his assistant, and 2,000 for maintenance and acquisitions. Zwernemann, *Hundert Jahre*, 10.

100. Lüders, in fact, essentially gained his position because he contributed a substantial collection from his travels to the museum. Zwernemann, *Hundert Jahre*, 10–11.

101. And like Sherman he was given the funds. The total budget of the museum rose from 21,870 Marks in 1904 to 112,150 Marks in 1910. See Melle, *Dreizig Jahre Hamburger Wissenschaft*, 509.

102. These differences, of course, are ones of emphasis. I do not mean to imply that either museum was completely void of the kinds of collections most coveted by the other, only that because of each museum's particular focus, its audiences had necessarily different visual experiences.

103. Compare, for example, Königlichen Museen zu Berlin, *Führer*, 2nd ed. and

8th ed. There were also no attempts at this time to record who visited the museum. Luschan to Otto Finsch, Braunschweig, 31 Oct. 1904, in MFVB: "Die Eröffnung des Museums und die Besichtigung der Sammlungen durch das Publikum," vol. 1, 1723/04.

Chapter Five

1. Bastian uses the term "instructive" here in the sense of being useful or helpful. He is not focused on their use as tools of instruction. Bastian, *Führer*, 3–4.

2. Bastian, *Heilige Sage der Polynesier*, exerpted and translated in Koepping, *Adolf Bastian*, 216–17.

3. Alfred Lehmann, "85 Jahre," 10. See also Westphal-Hellbusch, "Zur Geschichte des Museums," and Zwernemann, *Hundert Jahre*.

4. Compare Hagen, "Grundriß der Entstehungsgeschichte des Museums," 14 Dec. 1897, in HSA: Hochschulwesen I, CIIa, nr. 16, bd. 1; and Thilenius, *Hamburgische Museum*, with Zwernemann, *Hundert Jahre*.

5. See, for example, Hog, *Ziele und Konzeptionen*.

6. Frese, *Anthropology and the Public*, 8.

7. Jenkins, "Object Lessons," 242.

8. Coombes, *Reinventing Africa*, 118. These assertions continue to be reproduced in more general works on museums. See, for example, Bennett, *Birth of the Museum*.

9. The most widely cited is Bennett, *Birth of the Museum*.

10. Director of the Central-Gemälde Galerie to king of Bavaria, 17 Jan. 1868, in BHA: MK 14423. *Außerordentliche Beilage zur Allgemeinen Zeitung*, nr. 119, 29 April 1870.

11. Obst to Wüttke, 28 Nov. 1868, in MfVLB: vol. 1, no inventory number.

12. Stadtsbibliothek to Dr. Naumann, 4 Jan. 1872, in LSA: kap. 31, no. 12, vol. 1, p. 1; and Naumann to RSL, 8 Jan. 1872, in LSA: kap. 31, no. 12, vol. 1, p. 2.

13. In Britain, "curiosity cabinet" was essentially a term for a bad collection used among nineteenth-century ethnologists. Coombes, *Reinventing Africa*, 113.

14. Bastian, *Vorgeschichte der Ethnologie*.

15. C. W. Lüders, "Museum für Völkerkunde," 17 Sept. 1891, in HSA: 361-5 I, Hochschulwesen I, CII, b1; Hagen, "Grundriß der Entstehungsgeschichte des Museums," 14 Dec. 1897, in HSA: CIIa, nr. 16, bd. 1; Thilenius, *Hamburgische Museum*. This was common in all the museums. See also "Ueber die Bedeutung ethnographisher Museen: mit besonderer Beziehung auf die zehn Jahren erfolgte Gründung eines solchen in Leipzig," 23 May 1883, in LSA: kap. 31, no. 12., vol. 1, pp. 160–61.

16. These contentions, explanations, and juxtapositions were reiterated in the popular press as well: *National Zeitung* (Morgen Ausgabe, Berlin), 10 Jan. 1890.

17. Worlée and Oberdörffer, *Ethnographische oder Sammlung für Völkerkunde*.

18. "Auszug aus dem Protocolle der Oberschulbehörde Erste Section," 20 Dec. 1877, and the news clipping (probably from the *Hamburg Correspondent*) that follows, in HSA: 361-5 I, Hochschulwesen I, CII, b1. Hamburgisches Museum für Völkerkunde, *Führer durch das Museum*.

19. Zwernemann, *Hundert Jahre*, 4–5, 8–9, 15, 19, 30–34.

20. *Leipziger Tageblatt*, 14 May 1874.

21. For an itemized listing of what could be found in each of these groupings, see Mason, "Leipsic 'Museum of Ethnology'."

22. *Leipziger Tageblatt*, 25 March 1879.

23. *Hamburger Correspondent*, Feb. 1878, in HSA: 361-5 I, Hochschulwesen I, CII, b1.

24. Bahnson, "Ueber ethnographischen Museen."

25. Bahnson to Lüders, 8 Oct. 1893, in HSA: 361-5 I, Hochschulwesen I, CII, b1.

26. Zwernemann, *Hundert Jahre*, 24.

27. Thilenius, "Lebenslauf," in HSA: 361-6, Hochschulwesen Dozenten- u. Personalakten IV, 1030.

28. The Museum für Völkerkunde occupied 3,611 square meters, the Kunst- und Gewerbemuseum 1,924 square meters, the Verein für Erdkunde 124 square meters, and there was also a lecture hall and side room that took up 227 square meters. Lehmann, "85 Jahre," 32.

29. *Leipziger Tageblatt*, 5 Feb. 1896.

30. *General-Anzeiger*, 5 Feb. 1896.

31. The National Museum in Copenhagen, for example, asked for complete sketches and photos of the museum to use in redesigning their own institution. MfVLB: no. 05685, 11 August 1897.

32. Lehmann, "85 Jahre," 32.

33. *Leipziger Tageblatt*, 25 July 1909.

34. From 1899 to 1909 they generally gained more than one collection per week, 91 in 1907 alone, and during these eleven years they acquired over 57,000 objects. Karl Weule, "Die nächsten Aufgaben," 163.

35. Bastian, *Führer*, 3–4.

36. Ibid., 3–4.

37. For protests, see Bastian to GVKM, 19 Dec. 1879, in MfVB: "Die Gründung des Museums," vol. 1, 777/83.

38. Bastian to GVKM, Sept. 1883, in MfVB: "Die Gründung des Museums," vol. 1, 2835/83.

39. Director des Central Museums für Völkerkunde/RSL, 16 July 1872, in MfVLB: bd. 1, no catalog number.

40. By 1884 they were expecting to acquire a further 10,000 per year. Bastian to GVKM, 24 July 1884, in MfVB: "Die Gründung des Museums," vol. 1, 27/85.

41. Bastian to GVKM, 12 July 1899, in MfVB: "Erweiterungsbau des Königlichen Museums für Völkerkunde," vol. 1, 712/99.

42. Bastian to GVKM, 31 Oct. 1899, in MfVB: "Erweiterungsbau des Königlichen Museums für Völkerkunde," vol. 1, 1134/99.

43. From 1884 to 1889, for example, while preparations were being made for building the museum, the estimated space required rose from 3,890 square meters to 5,755 square meters, based on the increase in collections. Manschatz, *Grassi*, 23, 32.

44. Northoff, Obst to RSL, 8 March 1899, in LSA: kap. 31, no. 12, bd. 2, pp. 189–90.

45. "Sitzung des gemischten Verwaltungsausschusses für das Museum für Völkerkunde," 30 June 1908, in LSA: kap. 31, no. 12, bd. 5, p. 185.

46. Otto Georgi, *Vortrag das Grassi-Museums betreffend*, 11 April 1884, in LSA: kap. 31, no. 14, pp. 40–63. See also Bastian to GVKM, 24 July 1884, in MfVB, "Die Gründung des Museums," vol., 27/85; Mannschatz, *Grassi*, 13.

47. See Mannschatz, *Grassi*, 38, and Scheffler, *Berliner Museumskrieg*, 20.

48. Mannschatz, *Grassi*, 38.

49. See, for example, Hambruch to Thilenius, 2 June 1908, in HSA: 361-5 I, Hochschulwesen I, CII, a12, bd. 2.

50. MfVL Vorstand to Obst, n.d., in MfVLB: no. 01221–2; Obst to MfVL Vorstand, 2 Feb. 1879, in MfVLB: no. 01223.

51. "Instruction für den Zweiter Director Herrn Dr. Karl Weule," n.d., in LSA: kap. 31, no. 12, vol. 2, p. 1.

52. He also noted that Obst was "not born for such real work." Weule to Luschan, 3 Jan. 1900, in LN.

53. Bastian to Wirklichen Geheimen Rat, Geheimen Kabinet Rat Seiner Majestät des Kaisers und Königs, Kapitular des Domstifts Merseburg, Herrn Dr. jur. u. md. v. Lucanus, 25 Nov. 1903, in GSA: Rep. 89 H, 20491, pp. 49–51.

54. Königlichen Museen zu Berlin, *Führer*, 7th ed., 199.

55. There was a very small physical anthropology collection belonging to the Berlin Anthropological Society on the fourth floor, but this is not the section promised in the guides.

56. Königlichen Museen zu Berlin, *Führer*, 6th ed., 192.

57. Königlichen Museen zu Berlin, *Führer*, 7th ed., 61–2.

58. Königlichen Museen zu Berlin, *Führer*, 8th ed.

59. Königlichen Museen zu Berlin, *Führer*, 13th ed.

60. Cited by Bastian in an undated letter from 1899 to the GVKM, in MfVB: "Erweiterungsbau," vol. 1, 1134/99.

61. *Deutscher Reichs- und Königlich-Preußischer Staatsanzeiger*, 18 Dec. 1886.

62. *Vossische Zeitung*, 19 Dec. 1886.

63. See Cole, *Captured Heritage*, 56, and Westphal-Hellbusch, "Zur Geschichte des Museums," 1–20.

64. Buchner, *Orientalische Reise*.

65. Bastian to GVKM, 29 Sept. 1886, in GSA: I. HA, Rep. 76 Ve., Sekt. 15., Abt. III., nr. 2, bd. 5.

66. Bastian to GVKM, 12 July 1899, in MfVB: "Erweiterungsbau," vol. 1, 712/99 & 1134/99.

67. Grünwedel to GVKM, 10 July 1903, in MfVB: "Erweiterungsbau," vol. 2, 878/03.

68. Grünwedel to GVKM, 18 Oct. 1899, in MfVB: "Erweiterungsbau," vol. 1, 1134/99.

69. Luschan to MfVB, 12 Jan. 1901, in MfVB: "Erweiterungsbau," vol. 1, 73/01.

70. Bastian to Wirklichen Geheimen Rat, Geheimen Kabinet Rat Seiner Majestät des Kaisers und Königs, Kapitular des Domstifts Merseburg, Herrn Dr. jur. u. md. v. Lucanus, 25 Nov. 1903, in GSA: Rep. 89 H, 20491, pp. 49–51. See also *Vossisches Zeitung*, 24 Jan. 1901.

71. Daston and Park, *Wonders and the Order of Nature*, 273.

72. *Vossische Zeitung*, 26 June 1900.

73. Ibid., 3 July 1900.

74. Ibid., 6 July 1900. This article was one of a series in a public debate about the future of the museum.

75. Luschan to Greif, 12 July 1905, in MfVB: "Die Eröffnung des Museums und die Besichtigung der Sammlungen durch das Publikum," vol. 2, 1298/05.

76. 46. Sitzung, Haus der Abgeordneten, 27 March 1912, in MfVB: "Erweiterungsbau," vol. 4, 133/12.

77. For example, Tony Bennett, one of the most well known scholars interested in theorizing the cultural functions of museums and exhibitions, notes at the beginning of his oft-cited book on museums: "My concern in this book is largely with museums, fairs and exhibitions as envisioned in the plans and projections of their advocates, designers, directors and managers. The degree to which such plans and projections were and are successful in organizing and framing the experience of the visitor or, to the contrary, the degree to which such planned effects are evaded, sidestepped or simply not noticed raises different questions which, important though they are, I have not addressed here." *Birth of the Museum*, 11.

78. On visitors' expectations in general, see Crane, "Memory, Distortion, and History."

79. Scheffler, *Berliner Museumskrieg*, 21–22.

80. See Crane, "Memory, Distortion, and History," and Joachimides et al., "The Museum's Discourse on Art."

81. *Leipziger Tageblatt*, 25 July 1909.

82. Weule, *Führer durch das Museum für Völkerkunde*, 1913, 15.

83. *Leipziger Tageblatt*, 8 Nov. 1896.

84. Ibid., 5 Aug. 1910.

85. Luschan to GVKM, 12 Oct. 1903, in MfVB: "Erweiterungsbau," vol. 2, 1286/03.

86. Weule, "nächsten Aufgaben und Ziele," 155.

87. Thilenius's official report on the creation of a *Schausammlung* from 3 May 1907, in HSA: 361-5 I, Hochschulwesen I, CII, a1.

88. Bal, "Telling Objects," 98.

89. Daston and Park, *Wonders and the Order of Nature*, 265–66.

90. Guidebooks written as "study books" that contained short explanations of the science of ethnology as well as the displays, and which could be taken home and studied and then brought back to a museum again and again were one means ethnologists later used to try to reduce this subjective distance. The best examples are those produced by Willy Foy in Cologne in 1906, and Weule in Leipzig in 1913. Thilenius, *Hamburgische Museum*, 69.

91. Coombes, *Reinventing Africa*, 4. See also Bennett, *Birth of the Museum*; Hooper-Greenhill, *Museums*; Rydell, *All the World's a Fair*; and Sherman, *Worthy Monuments*. The tendency to take such efforts at face value with little inquiry into their reception can also be found in histories of anthropology as well. See, for example, Kuklick, *Savage Within*, 108. This criticism has also been aimed at more general work on popular receptions of the sciences by Cooter and Pumfrey in their "Separate Spheres," 243.

92. Foucault, *Order of Things*, 132.

93. Circular, 1 March 1898, in MfVB: "Berliner Anthrop. Gesellschaft," vol. 1, 232/98. Cf. Weule, "Nächsten Aufgaben und Ziele," 164.

94. Indeed, these guides often provided little more than a listing of objects and a general geographical place of origin, such as "North coast of New Guinea." See, for example, Königlichen Museen zu Berlin, *Führer*, 2nd ed., 132.

95. Harris, *Cultural Excursions*, 146.

96. Greenblatt, *Marvelous Possessions*, 14.

97. Boas, "Some Principles," 921–33.

98. Second encounters are by their very nature less enticing. Boas, for example, noted that repetitive experiences with newness and strangeness made each new encounter somewhat *less* strange. Over time, even the magnificent Crystal Palace—which had excited so many—lost its allure, and an attempt to reenact the event eleven years after its initial opening in 1851 was a flop. Boas, "Some Principles," 922, and Richards, *Commodity Culture*, 56.

99. This was Franz Boas's contention as well, and the reason for his interest in supporting museums as forms of entertainment. Boas, "Some Principles."

100. Boas, "Some Principles," 923. See also Pomian, *Collectors and Curiosities*, 21.

101. *Leipziger Volkszeitung*, 26 June 1914.

102. On the fluidity of language, see Assmann and Harth, *Kultur als Lebenswelt*, 181–99.

103. See Boas, "Some Principles," 923.

104. As Cooter and Pumpfrey emphasize with respect to science in general, it would be a mistake to forget what Natalie Zemon Davis has called "the creative competence of the lower orders." Cited in Cooter and Pumpfrey, "Separate Spheres," 249.

105. Bruckner, "Tingle-Tangle of Modernity," 82.

106. Letkemann, "Berliner Panoptikum."

107. Bruckner, " Tingle-Tangle of Modernity," 89. See also Grasskamp, *Triviale Negerbilder*, and Wiener, *Ikonographie des Wilden*.

108. Belgum, *Popularizing the Nation*.

109. Bruckner, "Tingle-Tangle of Modernity," 11.

110. Ibid., 274, 369, 423; Belgum, *Popularizing the Nation*, 153–60.

111. Williams, *Viewing Positions*, 12.

112. Fritzsche, *Reading Berlin*, 185.

113. The classic account is Simmel, "Metropolis and Mental Life."

114. Fritzsche, *Reading Berlin*, 130, 155; Schwartz, *Spectacular Realities*, 2.

Conclusion

1. I am grateful to Suzanne Marchand for this and many other insights.

2. Daum, "Naturwissenschaften und Öffentlichkeit," 86.

3. Many thanks to Susan Crane for helping me see this.

4. Schwartz, *Spectacular Realities*, 202.

BIBLIOGRAPHY

Archival Collections

Berlin, Germany
Archiv des Museum für Völkerkunde Berlin
Archiv der Staatlichen Museen
Geheimes Staatsarchiv, Preußischer Kulturbesitz
Nachlaß Felix von Luschans, Handschriftenabteilungen, Staatsbibliothek Berlin
  (Haus II)

Hamburg, Germany
Archiv des Museum für Völkerkunde Hamburg
Nachlaß Adrian Jacobsens, Hamburgisches Museum für Völkerkunde
Staatsarchiv Hamburg

Leipzig, Germany
Archiv des Museum für Völkerkunde zu Leipzig
Stadtarchiv Leipzig

Munich, Germany
Bayerische Hauptstaatsarchiv
Bibliothek des Staatliches Museum für Völkerkunde
Geheimes Hausarchiv
Stadtarchiv Munich

Potsdam, Germany
Bundesarchiv, Potsdam

Washington, D.C.
Smithsonian Institution Archives
Smithsonian Institution, National Anthropological Archives

Periodicals

American Anthropologist, 1888−1915
Anthropos, 1906−15
Berichte des Museum für Völkerkunde zu Leipzig, 1873−1900
Centralblatt für Anthropologie, Ethnologie, und Urgeschichte, 1873−1918
Correspondenz-Blatt der Deutschen Anthropologischen Gesellschaft, 1873−1918
Ethnologisches Notizblatt, 1894−1901
Das Ausland, 1880−93
Die Gartenlaube, 1860−1914

Globus, 1862–1910

Jahrbuch des Städtischen Museums für Völkerkunde zu Leipzig, 1906–18

Museumskunde, 1905–18

Münchener Jahrbuch der bildenden Kunst, 1909–14

Petermanns Mitteilungen, 1868–1918

Zeitschrift für Ethnologie, 1869–1930

Printed Sources

Ackerknecht, Erwin H. *Rudolf Virchow: Doctor, Statesman, Anthropologist.* Madison: University of Wisconsin Press, 1953.

Ames, Michael M. *Cannibal Tours and Glass Boxes: The Anthropology of Museums.* Vancouver: University of British Columbia Press, 1992.

Anderson, Benedict. *Imagined Communities: Reflections on the Origin and Spread of Nationalism.* New York: Verso, 1983, 1989.

Ankermann, Bernhard. "Die Entwicklung der Ethnologie seit Adolf Bastian." *Zeitschrift für Ethnologie* 58 (1926): 221–30

————. "Kulturkreise und Kulturschichten in Afrika." *Zeitschrift für Ethnologie* 37 (1905): 54–84.

Appadurai, Arjun, ed. *The Social Life of Things: Commodities in Cultural Perspective.* Cambridge: Cambridge University Press, 1986.

Applegate, Celia. *A Nation of Provincials: The German Idea of Heimat.* Berkeley: University of California Press, 1990.

Asad, Talal, ed. *Anthropology and the Colonial Encounter.* New York: Humanities Press, 1973.

Assmann, Aleida. *Arbeit am Nationalen Gedächtnis: Eine kurze Geschichte der deutschen Bildungsidee.* Frankfurt am Main: Pandora, 1993.

Assmann, Aleida, and Dietrich Harth, eds. *Kultur als Lebenswelt und Monument.* Frankfurt am Main: Fischer, 1991.

Assmann, Jan. *Das kulturelle Gedächtnis: Schrift, Erinnerung und politische Identität in frühen Hochkulturen.* Munich: C. H. Beck, 1997.

Bahnson, Kristian. "Ueber ethnographischen Museen Mit besonderer Berücksichtigung der Sammlungen in Deutschland, Oesterreich und Italien." *Mittheilungen der Anthropologischen Gesellschaft in Wien* 18 (1888): 109–64.

Bal, Mieke. "Telling Objects: A Narrative Perspective on Collecting." In *The Culture of Collecting*, edited by John Elsner and Roger Cardinal, 97–115. London: Reaktion Books, 1994.

Barkan, Elazar. "Post-colonial Histories: Representing the Other in Imperial Britain." *Journal of British Studies* 33 (1994): 180–203.

Barkan, Elazar, and Ronald Bush, eds. *Prehistories of the Past: The Primitivist Project and the Culture of Modernism.* Stanford: Stanford University Press, 1995.

Bastian, Adolf. *Alexander von Humboldt: Festrede.* Berlin: Wiegandt and Hempel, 1869.

————. *Das Beständige in den Menschenrassen und die Spielweite ihrer Veränderlichkeit. Prolegomena zu einer Ethnologie der Culturvölker.* Berlin: Reimer, 1868.

———. *Der Buddhismus als religions-philosophisches System.* Berlin: Weidmannsche Buchhandlung, 1893.

———. "Darwin, The Descent of Man, 1871." *Zeitschrift für Ethnologie* 3 (1871): 133–43.

———. "Erwerbungen der Ethnographischen Abtheilung des Berliner kgl. Museums von der Nordwestküste Nordamerikas." *Globus* 45, no. 1 (1884): 8–11, 24–29.

———. *Führer durch die Ethnographische Abtheilung.* Berlin: W. Spemann, 1877.

———. *Geographische und ethnologische Bilder.* Jena: H. Costenoble, 1873.

———. *Die heilige Sage der Polynesier; Kosmogonie und Theogonie.* Leipzig: F. A. Brockhaus, 1881.

———. "Meine Reise um und durch die Welt." *Illustrirte Zeitung* 35 (1860): 219–22.

———. *Der Mensch in der Geschichte: Zur Begründung einer psychologischen Weltanschauung.* Osnabrück: Biblioverlag, 1860.

———. *Offner Brief an Prof. Dr. E. Haeckel, Verfasser der 'Natürlichen Schöpfungsgeschichte'.* Berlin: Wiegandt, Hempel and Parey, 1874.

———. "Randglossen zur musealen Ethnologie." *Ethnologisches Notizblatt* 1, no. 1 (1894): 1–19.

———. *Die Rechtsverhältnisse bei verschiedenen Völkern der Erde: Ein Beitrag zur vergleichenden Ethnologie.* Berlin: G. Reimer, 1872.

———. "Über Methoden in der Ethnologie." *Petermanns Mitteilungen* 39 (1893): 186–91.

———. *Übersichtler Abriß der Sammlungen in Königlichen Museum für Völkerkunde.* Berlin: Museum für Völkerkunde, 1889.

———. "Ueber Ethnologische Sammlungen." *Zeitschrift für Ethnologie* 17 (1885): 38–42.

———. "Vorbemerkungen." *Ethnologisches Notizblatt* 1, no. 1 (1894): 5.

———. *Die Vorgeschichte der Ethnologie: Deutschlands Denkfreunden gewidmet für eine Mussestunde.* Berlin: Ferd. Dümmlers Verlagsbuchhandlung, 1881.

———. "Vortrage in der Sitzung der Berliner Anthropologischen Gesellschaft vom 22. April 1882." In *Verhandlungen der Berliner Anthropologische Gesellschaft,* in *Zeitschrift für Ethnologie* 14.

———. *Zur Lehre von den geographischen Provinzen: Aufgenommen in die Controversen.* Berlin: 1886.

Baudrillard, Jean. "The System of Collecting." In *The Culture of Collecting,* edited by John Elsner and Roger Cardinal, 7–24. London: Reaktion, 1994.

Bayern, Theresa von. *Meine Reisen in den brasilianischen Tropen.* Berlin: Dietrich Reimer Verlag, 1897.

Beck, Hanno. "Moritz Wagner in der Geschichte der Geographie." Ph.D. diss., University of Marburg, 1951.

Belgum, Kirsten. *Popularizing the Nation: Audience, Representation, and the Production of Identity in Die Gartenlaube, 1853–1900:* Lincoln: Univesity of Nebraska Press, 1998.

Bennett, Tony. *Birth of the Museum: History, Theory, Politics.* London: Routledge, 1995.

———. "The Exhibitionary Complex." *New Formations* 4 (1988): 73–102.

———. "The Shaping of Things to Come: Expo '88." *Cultural Studies* 5, no.1 (1991): 30–51.

———. "Useful Culture." *Cultural Studies* 6, no. 3 (1992): 395–423.

Benninghoff-Lühl, Sibylle. "Völkerschauen—Attraktionen und Gefahr des Exotischen." *SOWI—Sozialwissenschaftliche Informationen* 15, no. 4 (1986): 41–48.

Bergt, Walter. "Dr. Hermann Obst." *Jahrbuch des Städtischen Museums für Völkerkunde zu Leipzig* 1 (1906): 7–14.

Berman, Marshall. *All That Is Solid Melts into Air: The Experience of Modernity.* New York: Simon and Schuster, 1982

Bernal, Martin. *Black Athena.* Vol. 1. New Brunswick: Rutgers University Press, 1987.

Beyerchen, Alan. "On the Stimulation of Excellence in Wilhelmian Science." In *Another Germany: A Reconsideration of the Imperial Era,* edited by Jack R. Dukes and Joachim Remak, 139–68. Boulder: Westview Press, 1988.

Blackbourn, David. *The Long Nineteenth Century: A History of Germany, 1780–1918.* New York: Oxford University Press, 1998.

Blackbourn, David, and Geoff Eley. *The Peculiarities of German History: Bourgeois Society and Politics in Nineteenth-Century Germany.* Oxford: Oxford University Press, 1985.

Blackbourn, David, and Richard J. Evans, eds. *The German Bourgeoisie: Essays on the Social History of the German Middle Class from the Late Eighteenth to the Early Twentieth Century.* London: Routledge, 1991.

Blesse, Giselher. "'Negerleben in Ostafrika'—Karl Weule als Feldforscher. Zur wissenschaftlichen Expeditionstätigkeit Karl Weules in Südost-Tansania 1906." *Jahrbuch des Museums für Völkerkunde zu Leipzig* 40 (1994): 153–67.

Bode, Wilhelm von. *Mein Leben.* Vol. 2. Berlin: Hermann Reckendorf, 1930. Reprint, Berlin: Nicolai, 1997.

Boas, Franz. "The Limitations of the Comparative Method of Anthropology." *Science,* n.s., 4 (1896): 901–8.

———. "The Methods of Ethnology" *American Anthropologist,* n.s., 22 (1920): 311–22.

———. *Race, Language, and Culture.* Chicago: University of Chicago Press, 1982.

———. "Rudolf Virchow's Anthropological Work." In *The Shaping of American Anthropology, 1883–1911,* edited by George W. Stocking Jr., 36–41. New York: Basic Books, 1974.

———. "Some Principles of Museum Administration." *Science,* n.s., 25 (1907): 921–33.

Bollenbeck, Georg. *Bildung und Kultur: Glanz und Elend eines deutschen Deutungsmusters.* Frankfurt am Main: Suhrkamp, 1996.

Bracken, Christopher. *The Potlach Papers: A Colonial History.* Chicago: University of Chicago Press, 1997.

Brednich, Rolf W., ed. *Grundriss der Volkskunde.* Berlin: Reimer, 1988.

Bruckner, Sierra Ann. "The Tingle-Tangle of Modernity: Popular Anthropology and the Cultural Politics of Identity in Imperial Germany." Ph.D. diss., University of Iowa, 1999.

Brunn, Gerhard. *Deutschland und Brasilien (1889–1914)*. Köln: Böhlau, 1971.

Buchner, Max. *Eine orientalische Reise und ein Königliches Museum. Rücksichtslose Erin-nerungen*. Munich: Piloty and Loehle, 1919.

Buck-Morss, Susan. *The Dialectics of Seeing: Walter Benjamin and the Arcades Project*. Cambridge: MIT Press, 1989.

Bunzl, Matti. "Franz Boas and the Humboldtian Tradition: From *Volksgeist* and *Nationalcharakter* to an Anthropological Concept of Culture." In *Volksgeist as Method and Ethic: Essays on Boasian Ethnography and the German Anthropological Tradition*, edited by George W. Stocking Jr., 17–78. Madison: University of Wisconsin Press, 1995.

Camerini, Jane R. "Wallace in the Field." *Osiris* 11 (1996): 44–65.

Chartier, Roger. *Cultural History: Between Practices and Representations*. Cambridge: Cambridge University Press, 1988.

Chickering, Roger, ed. *Imperial Germany: A Historiographical Companion*. London: Greenwood, 1996.

Clark, T. J. *The Painting of Modern Life: Paris in the Art of Manet and His Followers*. New York: Alfred A. Knopf, 1985.

Clifford, James. *The Predicament of Culture: Twentieth-Century Ethnography, Literature, and Art*. Cambridge: Harvard University Press, 1988.

Cocks, Geoffrey, and Konrad H. Jarausch. *German Professions, 1800–1950*. New York: Oxford University Press, 1990.

Cohn, Bernard S. "Representing Authority in Victorian England." In *The Invention of Tradition*, edited by Eric Hobsbawm and Terence Ranger, 165–210. Cambridge: Cambridge University Press, 1983.

Cole, Douglas. *Captured Heritage: The Scramble for Northwest Coast Artifacts*. Seattle: University of Washington Press, 1985.

———. *Franz Boas: The Early Years, 1858–1906*. Seattle: University of Washington Press, 1999.

Confino, Alon. *The Nation as a Local Metaphor: Württemberg, Imperial Germany, and National Memory, 1871–1918*. Chapel Hill: University of North Carolina Press, 1997.

Conn, Steven. *Museums and American Intellectual Life, 1876–1926*. Chicago: University of Chicago Press, 1998.

Coombes, Annie E. "Museums and the Formation of National and Cultural Iden-tities." *Oxford Art Journal* 11, no. 2 (1988): 57–68.

———. *Reinventing Africa: Museums, Material Culture, and Popular Imagination in Late Victorian and Edwardian England*. New Haven: Yale University Press, 1994.

Cooter, Rodger, and Stephen Pumfrey. "Separate Spheres and Public Spaces: Reflections on the History of Science Popularization and Science in Popular Culture." *History of Science* 32 (1994): 237–67.

Corbey, Raymond. *Tribal Art Traffic: A Chronicle of Taste, Trade and Desire in Colonial and Post-colonial Times*. Amsterdam: Royal Tropical Institute, 2000.

Crane, Susan A. *Collecting and Historical Consciousness in Early Nineteenth-Century Ger-many*. Ithaca, N.Y.: Cornell University Press, 2000.

———. "Memory, Distortion, and History in the Museum." *History and Theory* 36, Theme Issue (1997): 44–63.

―――, ed. *Museums and Memory*. Stanford: Stanford University Press, 2000.

Dalton, O. M. *Report on Ethnographic Museums in Germany*. London: Her Majesty's Stationery Office, 1898.

Dann, Otto. *Nation und Nationalismus in Deutschland 1770–1990*. Munich: C. H. Beck, 1993.

―――. *Vereinswesen und bürgerliche Gesellschaft in Deutschland*. Munich: R. Oldenbourg, 1984.

Daston, Lorraine, and Katherine Park. *Wonders and the Order of Nature, 1150–1750*. New York: Zone Books, 1998.

Daum, Andreas. "Naturwissenschaften und Öffentlichkeit in der bürgerlichen Gesellschaft: Zu den Anfängen einder 'Populärwissenschaft' nach der Revolution von 1848." *Historische Zeitschrift* 257 (August 1998): 57–90.

―――. "Naturwissenschaftler Journalismus im Dienst der darwinistischen Weltanschauung: Ernst Krause alias Carus Sterne, Ernst Haeckel und die Zeitschrift Kosmos." *Mauritiana* 15, no. 2 (1995): 227–45.

―――. "Das versöhnende Element in der neuen Weltanschauung: Entwicklungsoptimismus, Naturästhetik und Harmoniedenken im populärwissenschaftlichen Diskurs der Naturkunde um 1900." In *Vom Weltbildwandel zur Weltanschauungsanalyse: Krisenwahrnehmung und Krisenbewältigung um 1900*, edited by Volker Drehsen and Walter Sparn, 203–15. Berlin: Akademie Verlag, 1996.

―――. *Wissenschaftspopularisierung im 19. Jahrhundert: Bürgerliche Kultur, naturwissenschaftliche Bildung und die deutsche Öffentlichkeit, 1848–1914*. Munich: R. Oldenbourg, 1998.

David, Joseph Ben. *The Scientist's Role in Society: A Comparative Study*. Englewood Cliffs, N.J.: Prentice-Hall, 1971.

Ditt, Karl. "Konservative Kulturvorstellungen und Kulturpolitik vom Kaiserreich bis zum Dritten Reich." *Neue Politische Literatur* 41 (1996): 230–59.

Dittrich, Lothar, and Annelore Rieke-Müller. *Der Löwe Brüllt Nebenan: Die Gründung Zoologischer Gärten im deutschsprachigen Raum, 1833–1869*. Cologne: Böhlau Verlag, 1998.

Dörfel, Andrea, and Christian Carstensen. "Wie Ethnographica und Großwildtrophäen in Museen gelangten." In *Andenken an den Kolonialismus: Eine Ausstellung des Völkerkundlichen Instituts der Universität Tübingen*, edited by Volker Harms, 95–113. Tübingen: ATTEMPTO Verlag, 1984.

Dorsey, George A. "The Anthropological Exhibits at the American Museum of Natural History." *Science*, n.s., 25 (1907): 584–89.

Douglas, Mary. *How Institutions Think*. Syracuse: Syracuse University Press, 1986.

Durham, Dewitt Clinton. "Leo Frobenius and the Reorientation of German Ethnology, 1890–1930." Ph.D. diss., Stanford University, 1985.

Eksteins, Modris. *Rites of Spring: The Great War and the Birth of the Modern Age*. Boston: Houghton Mifflin, 1989.

Eley, Geoff. *From Unification to Nazism: Reinterpreting the German Past*. Boston: Allen and Unwin, 1986.

―――. *Reshaping the German Right: Radical Nationalism and Political Change after Bismarck*. New Haven: Yale University Press, 1980.

———, ed. *Society, Culture, and the State in Germany, 1870–1930*. Ann Arbor: University of Michigan Press, 1996.

Elsner, John, and Roger Cardinal, eds. *The Cultures of Collecting*. London: Reaktion Books, 1994.

Essner, Cornelia. "Berlins Völkerkunde Museum in der Kolonialära: Anmerkungen zum Verhältnis von Ethnologie und Kolonialismus in Deutschland." In *Berlin in Geschichte und Gegenwart: Jahrbuch des Landesarchivs Berlin*, edited by Hans J. Reichhardt, 65–94. Berlin: Siedler Verlag, 1986.

———. *Deutsche Afrikareisende im neunzehnten Jahrhundert: Zur Sozialgeschichte des Reisens*. Stuttgart: Steiner Verlag, 1985.

Evans, Richard J. *Death in Hamburg: Society and Politics in the Cholera Years: 1830–1910*. New York: Penguin, 1987.

Fiedermutz-Laun, Annemarie. "Aus der Wissenschaftsgeschichte: Adolf Bastian und die Deszendenztheorie." *Paideuma* 16 (1970): 1–26.

———. *Der Kulturhistorische Gedanke bei Adolf Bastian: Systematisierung und Darstellung der Theorie und Methode mit dem Versuch einer Bewertung des Kulturhistorischen Gehaltes auf dieser Grundlage*. Wiesbaden: Franz Steiner Verlag, 1970.

Findlen, Paula. *Possessing Nature: Museums, Collecting, and Scientific Culture in Early Modern Italy*. Berkeley: University of California Press, 1994.

Fink, Karl J. "Storm and Stress Anthropology." *History of the Human Sciences* 6, no. 1 (1993): 51–71.

Fischer, Hans. *Die Hamburger Südsee-Expedition: Über Ethnographie und Kolonialismus*. Frankfurt am Main: Syndikat, 1981.

———. *Völkerkunde im Nationalsozialismus: Aspekte der Anpassung, Affinität und Behauptung einer wissenschaftlichen Disziplin*. Berlin: Reimer, 1990.

Fischer, Jörg. "Zivilisation, Kultur." In vol. 7 of *Geschichtliche Grundbegriffe: historisches Lexikon zur politisch-sozialen Sprache in Deutschland*, edited by Otto Brunner, Werner Conze, and Reinhart Koselleck, 679–774. Stuttgart: E. Klett, 1972.

Forgan, Sophie. "The Architecture of Display: Museums, Universities and Objects in Nineteenth-Century Britain." *History of Science* 32 (1994): 139–62.

Forster-Hahn, Françoise. "The Politics of Display or the Display of Politics?" *Art Bulletin* (June 1995): 174–79.

Foucault, Michel. *The Archeology of Knowledge*. Translated by A. M. Sheridan Smith. New York: Pantheon Books, 1972.

———. *Discipline and Punish: The Birth of the Prison*. Translated by Alan Sheridan. New York: Vintage Books, 1975.

———. *The Order of Things: An Archeology of the Human Sciences*. New York: Random House, 1970.

Foy, Willy. "Ethnologie und Kulturgeschichte." *Petermanns Geographische Mitteilungen* 1, no. 3 (1911): 230–33.

———. *Führer durch das Rautenstrauch-Josef-Museum der Stadt Cöln*. Cöln: M. Dumont Schauberg, 1906.

———. "Das städtische Rautenstrauch-Joest-Museum für Völkerkunde in Cöln." *Ethnologia* 1 (1909): 1–70.

Frese, Hermann Heinrich. *Anthropology and the Public: The Role of Museums*. Leiden: E. J. Brill, 1960.

Frič, Alberto Votěch. "Eine Pilcomayo-Reise in den Chaco Central." *Globus* 89, no. 14 (12 April 1906): 213–20, 229–34.

———. "Sambaqui-Forschungen im Hafen von Antonina (Paraná)." *Globus* 91, no. 8 (28 February 1907): 117–22.

———. "Völkerwanderung, Ethnographie und Geschichte der Konquita in Südbrasilien." In *Verhandlungen des XVI Internationalen Amerikanisten-Kongresses*, 63–7. Vienna: 1909.

Frič, Alberto Votěch, and Paul Radin. "Contribution to the Study of the Bororo Indians." *Journal of the Royal Anthropological Institute* 36: 382–406.

Friedberg, Anne. *Window Shopping: Cinema and the Postmodern*. Berkeley: University of California Press, 1993.

Friedrichsmeyer, Sara, Sara Lennox, and Susanne Zantop, eds. *The Imperialist Imagination: German Colonialism and Its Legacy*. Ann Arbor: University of Michigan Press, 1998.

Fritzsche, Peter. "Landscape of Danger, Landscape of Design: Crisis and Modernism in Weimar Germany." In *Dancing on the Volcano: Essays on the Culture of the Weimar Republic*, edited by Thomas W. Kniesche and Stephen Brackmann, 29–46. Columbia, S.C.: Camden House, 1994.

———. "Nazi Modern." *Modernism/Modernity* 3, no. 1 (1996): 1–21.

———. *Reading Berlin, 1900*. Cambridge: Harvard University Press, 1996.

Frobenius, Leo. *Und Afrika sprach*. Vol. 1 of *Auf den Trümmern des klassischen Atlantis*. Berlin: Vita, 1912.

Fülleborn, Susanne. "Die ethnographischen Unternehmungen des Hamburger Handelshauses Gödeffroy." Master's thesis, Universität Hamburg, 1985.

Gall, Lothar. "Zur politischen und gesellschaftlichen Rolle der Wissenschaften in Deutschland um 1900." In *Wissenschaftsgeschichte seit 1900*, edited by Helmut Coing et. al., 9–28. Frankfurt am Main: Suhrkamp Traschenbuch Verlag, 1992.

Ganslmayr, Helmut. "Moritz Wagner und seine Bedeutung für die Ethnologie." In vol. 4 of *Verhandlungen des 38. Internationalen Amerikanistenkongresses*, 459–70. Munich: 1972.

Gareis, Sigrid. *Exotik in München: Museumsethnologische Konzeptionen im historischen Wandel*. Munich: Anacon, 1990.

Gensch, Hugo. "Die Erziehung eines Indianerkindes." *Beilage: Verhandlungen des 16. Internationalen Amerikanistenkongresses*. Berlin: Gebr. Unger, 1908.

Gerhard, Thomas. "Die Sammlung der Nordwestküsten-Indianer im Kölner Rautenstrauch-Joest-Museum: Ihre Entstehungs- und Verkaufsgeschichte." Master's thesis, Rheinischen Friedrich-Wilhelms-Universität zu Bonn, 1992.

Germer, Ernst. "Völkerkundliche Museen und Sammlungen in der Demokratischen Republik." *Abhandlungen und Berichte des Staatlichen Museums für Völkerkunde Dresden* 39 (1982): 7–54.

———. "Die Vorgeschichte der Gründung des Museums für Völkerkunde zu Leipzig 1868–1869." *Jahrbuch des Museums für Völkerkunde zu Leipzig* 26 (1969): 5–40.

Gillis, John R., ed. *Commemorations: The Politics of National Identity*. Princeton, N.J.: Princeton University Press, 1994.

Glaser, Herman. *Bildbürgertum und Nationalismus.* Deutsche Geschichte der neuesten Zeit. Munich: Deutscher Taschenbuch Verlag, 1993.

Goldmann, Stefan. "Wilde in Europa." In *Wir und die Wilden: Einblicke in eine kannibalische Beziehung,* edited by Thomas Theye, 243–69. Reinbeck bei Hamburg: Rowohlt, 1985.

Goldstein, Daniel. "Yours for Science: The Smithsonian Institution's Correspondents and the Shape of Scientific Community in Nineteenth-Century America." *Isis* 85 (1994): 573–99.

Goode, George Brown. *The Principles of Museum Administration.* New York: Coultas and Volans, 1895.

Goschler, Constantin, ed. *Wissenschaft und Öffentlichkeit in Berlin, 1870–1930.* Stuttgart: Franz Steiner Verlag, 2001.

Gothsch, Manfred. *Die deutsche Völkerkunde und ihr Verhältnis zum Kolonialismus: Ein Beitrag zur kolonialideologischen und kolonialpraktischen Bedeutung der deutschen Völkerkunde in der Zeit von 1870 bis 1945.* Hamburg: Institut für Internationale Angelegenheiten der Universität Hamburg, 1983.

Graebner, Fritz. "Adolf Bastians 100. Geburtstag." *Ethnologica* 3 (1927): ix–xii.

———. "Kulturkreise und Kulturschichten in Ozeanien." *Zeitschrift für Ethnologie* 37 (1905): 28–53.

———. *Methode der Ethnologie.* Heidelberg: Carl Winter, 1911.

———. "Prof. Haberlands Kritik der Lehre von den Kulturschichten und Kulturkreisen." *Petermanns Geographische Mitteilungen* 1, no. 3 (1911): 228–30.

Grahammer, Veronika. "Eskimos in Wien." In *Am Nordrand der Welt: Eskimo,* edited by Christian F. Feest. Vienna: Museum für Völkerkunde Wien, 1991.

Grasskamp, Walter. *Museumsgründer und Museumsstürmer: Zur Sozialgeschichte des Kunstmuseums.* Munich: C. H. Beck, 1981.

———. *Triviale Negerbilder in europäischer Werbung und Illustration.* Cologne: Vista Point, 1978.

Green, Nicholas. *The Spectacle of Nature: Landscape and Bourgeois Culture in Nineteenth-Century France.* Manchester: Manchester University Press, 1990.

Greenblatt, Stephen. *Marvelous Possessions: The Wonder of the New World.* Oxford: Clarendon Press, 1988.

Gregory, Frederick. *Scientific Materialism in Nineteenth Century Germany.* Boston: D. Reidel, 1977.

Griffiths, Tom. *Hunters and Collectors: The Antiquarian Imagination in Australia.* Cambridge: Cambridge University Press, 1996.

Gupta, Akhil, and James Ferguson, eds. *Anthropological Locations: Boundaries and Grounds of a Field Science.* Berkeley: University of California Press, 1997.

Gupta, Tapan Kumar Das. *Von Kant zu Bastian: Ein Beitrag zum Verständnis des Wissenschaftlichen Konzepts von Adolf Bastian mit vier kleinen Schriften von demselben.* Hamburg: Selbstverlag, 1990.

Haberland, Elke, ed. *Leo Frobenius 1873–1973: An Anthology.* Wiesbaden: Franz Steiner Verlag, 1973.

Haberland, Wolfgang. "'Diese Indianer sind Falsch,' Neun Bella Coola im Deutschen Reich 1885/6." *Archiv für Völkerkunde* 42 (1988): 3–67.

————. "Nine Bella Coolas in Germany." In *Indians in Europe: An Interdisciplinary Collection of Essays*, edited by Christian F. Feest, 337–82. Aachen: Rader, 1987.

————. "Remarks on the 'Jacobsen Collections' from the Northwest Coast." In *Culturas de La Costa Noroeste de América*, edited by José Luis Peset, 183–94. Madrid: Turner, 1989.

Haberlandt, M. "Zur Kritik der Lehre von den Kulturschichten und Kulturkreisen." *Petermanns Geographische Mitteilungen* 1, no. 3 (1911): 113–18.

Habermas, Jürgen. *The Structural Transformation of the Public Sphere: An Inquiry into a Category of Bourgeois Society.* Translated by Thomas Burger. Cambridge: MIT Press, 1989.

Das Hamburgisches Museum für Völkerkunde. *Fuhrer durch das Museum für Völkerkunde zu Hamburg.* Hamburg: Ferdinand Schlotke, 1893.

Hammer, Karl. "Preußische Museumspolitik im 19. Jahrhundert." In *Bildungspolitik in Preußen zur Zeit des Kaiserreiches*, edited by Peter Baumgarten, 256–77. Stuttgart: Klett-Cota, 1980.

Haraway, Donna. "Teddy Bear Patriarchy: Taxidermy in the Garden of Eden, New York City, 1908–1936." *Social Text* 11 (1984–1985): 20–64.

Hardtwig, Wolfgang. "Bürgertum, Staatsymbolik und Staatsbewußtsein in Deutschen Kaiserreich 1871–1914." *Geschichte und Gesellschaft* 3 (1990): 269–95.

Harms, Volker. "The Aims of the Museum for Ethnology: Debate in the German-Speaking Countries." *Current Anthropology* 31, no. 4 (1990): 457–63.

————. "Ethnographische Kunstobjekte als Beute des europäischen Kolonialismus." *Kritische Berichte* 23, no. 2 (1995): 15–31.

————. "Das Historische Verhältnis der deutschen Ethnologie zum Kolonialismus." *Zeitschrift für Kulturaustausch* 4 (1984): 401–16.

————. "Ist die Darstellung des Fremden im Museum möglich? Das Beispiel der ständigen Afrika-Ausstellung im Linden-Musem für Völkerkunde in Stuttgart." *SOWI—Sozialwissenschaftliche Informationen* 15, no. 4 (1986): 49–53.

————. "Kolonialhandel und Völkerkundemuseen: Nützlichkeit von ethnographischen Museen in den Staaten, die Kolonien besitzen." In *Übersee: Seefahrt und Seemacht im Deutschen Kaiserreich*, edited by Volker Plagemann, 355–59. Munich: C. H. Beck, 1988.

Harrer, Cornelia Andrea. *Das Ältere Bayerische Nationalmuseum an der Maximilianstraße in München.* Munich: Tuduv, 1993.

Harris, Neil. *Cultural Excursions: Marketing Appetites and Cultural Tastes in Modern America.* Chicago: University of Chicago Press, 1990.

Hartmann, Günther. *Xingú: Unter Indianern in Zentral-Brasilien.* Berlin: D. Reimer, 1986.

Harvey, David. *The Urban Experience.* Baltimore: Johns Hopkins University Press, 1989.

Harwood, Jonathan. "Mandarins and Outsiders in the German Professoriat, 1890–1933: A Study of the Genetics Community." *European History Quarterly* 23 (1993): 485–511.

Heger, Franz. "Die Zukunft der ethnographischen Museen." In *Festschrift für A. Bastian zu seinem 70. Geburtstag, 26. Juni 1896*, 585–93. Berlin: Reimer, 1896.

Hermannstädter, Anita. "Karl von den Steinen und die Zingu-Bevölkerung. Zur

Wahrnehmung und Darstellung Fremder Kulturen in der Ethnographie des 19. Jahrhunderts." *Baessler-Archiv*, n.s., 44, no. 2 (1996): 1–26.

Hinsley, Curtis M., Jr. *Savages and Scientists: The Smithsonian Institution and the Development of American Anthropology 1846–1910*. Washington D.C.: Smithsonian Institution Press, 1981.

Hobsbawm, Eric. "Mass-Producing Traditions: Europe, 1870–1914." In *The Invention of Tradition*, edited by Eric Hobsbawm and Terence Ranger, 263–308. Cambridge: Cambridge University Press, 1983.

———. *Nations and Nationalism since 1780: Program, Myth, Reality*. 2nd ed. New York: Canto, 1992.

Hochreiter, Walter. *Vom Musuemtempel zum Lernort: Zur Sozialgeschichte deutscher Museen 1800–1914*. Darmstadt: Wissenschaftliche Buchgesellschaft, 1994.

Hog, Michael. *Ethnologie und Öffentlichkeit: Ein entwicklungsgeschichtlicher Überblick*. Frankfurt am Main: Peter Lang, 1990.

———. *Ziele und Konzeptionen der Völkerkundemuseen in ihrer historischen Entwicklung*. Frankfurt am Main: Rit G. Fischer Verlag, 1981.

Home, R. W., and S. G. Kohlstedt, eds. *International Science and National Scientific Identity*. Boston: Kluwer, 1991.

Honigsheim, Paul. "Adolf Bastian und die Entwicklung der ethnologischen Soziologie." *Kölner Vierteljahrshefte für Soziologie* 6, no. 1 (1926): 59–76.

Hooper-Greenhill, Eilean. *Museums and the Shaping of Knowledge*. London: Routledge, 1992.

Hope, Brigitte. "Naturwissenschaftliche und zoologische Forschungen in Afrika während der deutschen Kolonialbewegung bis 1914." *Berichte zur Wissenschaftsgeschichte* 13 (1990): 193–206.

Ita, J. M. "Frobenius in West African History." *Journal of African History* 13, no. 4 (1972): 673–88.

Jacobsen, Adrian. *Reise in die Inselwelt des Banda-Meers*. Berlin: Mitscher and Röstell, 1896.

———. *Die Weiße Grenze: Abenteuer eines alten Seebären rund um den Polarkreis*. Leipzig: Brockhaus, 1931.

Jahn, Janheinz. "Nochmals Frobenius: Ein Geist über den Erdteilen." *Internationales Afrika-Forum* 9, no. 9/10 (September 1973): 524–36.

Jahn, Ulrich. "Das neubegründete Museum für deutsche Volkstrachten und Erzeugnisse des Hausgewerbes zu Berlin." *Zeitschrift für Völkerpsychologie und Sprachwissenschaft* 19 (1889): 334–43.

Jenkins, David. "Object Lessons and Ethnographic Displays: Museum Exhibitions and the Making of American Anthropology." *Comparative Studies in Society and History* 36, no. 2 (1994): 242–70.

Joachimides, Alexis. "The Museum's Discourse on Art: The Formation of Curatorial Art History in Turn-of-the-Century Berlin." In *Museums and Memory*, edited by Susan A. Crane, 200–217. Stanford: Stanford University Press, 2000.

———, et al. *Museumsinszenierungen: Zur Geschichte der Institution des Kunstmuseums: Die Berliner Museumslandschaft 1830–1990*. Dresden: Basen, 1995.

Johnson, Jeffrey Allan. *The Kaiser's Chemists: Science and Modernization in Imperial Germany*. Chapel Hill: University of North Carolina Press, 1990.

Kaeselitz, Hella, ed. *Die verhinderte Weltausstellung: Beiträge zur Berliner Gewerbeausstellung 1896*. Berlin: Berliner Debatte, 1996.

Kalmar, Ivan. "The Völkerpsychologie of Lazarus and Steinthal and the Modern Concept of Culture." *Journal of the History of Ideas* 48 (1987): 671–90.

Kandert Josef. "Alberto Votěch Frič—On the Centenary of His Birth." In *Annals of the Naprstek Museum* 11 (1983): 111–46.

Kaplan, Flora E. S., ed. *Museums and the Making of Ourselves: The Role of Objects in National Identity*. London: Leicester University Press, 1994.

Karasek, Erika. *Die Volkskundlich-kulturhistorischen Museen in Deutschland: Zur Rolle der Volkskunde in der bürgerlich-imperialistischen Gesellschaft*. Berlin: Institut für Museumswesen, 1984.

Karp, Ivan, and Steven D. Lavine, eds. *Exhibiting Cultures: The Poetics and Politics of Museum Display*. Washington: Smithsonian Institution Press, 1991.

Karp, Ivan, Christine Mullen Kreamer, and Steven D. Lavine, eds. *Museums and Communities: The Politics of Public Culture*. Washington: Smithsonian Institution Press, 1992.

Kaschuba, Wolfgang. "Kulturalismus: Kultur statt Gesellschaft." *Geschichte und Gesellschaft* 21 (1995): 80–95.

———. "Nationalismus und Ethnozentrismus: Zur Kulturellen Ausgrenzung ethnischer Gruppen in (deutscher) Geschichte und Gegenwart." In *Grenzfälle: Über neuen und alten Nationalismus*, edited by Michael Jeismann and Henning Ritter, 239–73. Leipzig: Reclam, 1993.

Kavanagh, Gaynor, ed. *Museum Languages: Objects and Texts*. London: Leicester University Press, 1991.

Kelly, Alfred. *The Descent of Darwin: The Popularization of Darwinism in Germany, 1860–1914*. Chapel Hill: University of North Carolina Press, 1981.

Keuren, David K. van. "Cabinets and Culture: Victorian Anthropology and the Museum Context." *Journal of the History of the Behavioral Sciences* 25 (1989): 26–39.

———. "Museums and Ideology: Augustus Pitt Rivers, Anthropological Museums, and Social Change in Later Victorian England." *Victorian Studies* 28 (1984): 171–89.

Kirshenblatt-Gimblett, Barbara. *Destination Culture: Tourism, Museums, and Heritage*. Berkeley: University of California Press, 1998.

———. "Objects of Ethnography." In *Exhibiting Cultures: The Poetics and Politics of Museum Display*, edited by Ivan Karp and Steven D. Lavine, 384–443. Washington D.C.: Smithsonian Institution Press, 1991.

Klueting, Harm, ed. *Nation, Nationalismus, Postnation: Beiträge zur Identitätsfindung der Deutschen im 19. und 20. Jahrhundert*. Löln/Vienna: Böhlau, 1992.

Koepping, Klaus-Peter. *Adolf Bastian and the Psychic Unity of Mankind: The Foundations of Anthropology in Nineteenth Century Germany*. London: Queensland Press, 1983.

———. "Enlightenment and Romanticism in the Work of Adolf Bastian: The Historical Roots of Anthropology in the Nineteenth Century." In *Fieldwork and Footnotes: Studies in the History of European Anthropology*, edited by Han F. Vermeulen and Arturo Alvarez Roldán, 75–94. New York: Routledge, 1995.

Kohlstedt, Sally Gregory. "Museums: Revisiting Sites in the History of the Natural Sciences." *Journal of the History of Biology* 28 (1995): 151–66.

Königlichen Museen zu Berlin. *Führer durch die Ethnologische Sammlung, mit Einschluss der Nordischen Alterthümer.* Berlin: W. Spemann, 1881.

———. *Führer durch das Museum für Völkerkunde.* 2nd ed. Berlin: W. Spemann, 1887.

———. *Führer durch das Museum für Völkerkunde.* 3rd ed. Berlin: W. Spemann, 1888.

———. *Führer durch das Museum für Völkerkunde.* 5th ed. Berlin: W. Spemann, 1892.

———. *Führer durch das Museum für Völkerkunde.* 6th ed. Berlin: W. Spemann, 1895.

———. *Führer durch das Museum für Völkerkunde.* 7th ed. Berlin: W. Spemann, 1898.

———. *Führer durch das Museum für Völkerkunde.* 8th ed. Berlin: W. Spemann, 1900.

———. *Führer durch das Museum für Völkerkunde.* 10th ed. Berlin: W. Spemann, 1903.

———. *Führer durch das Museum für Völkerkunde.* 13th ed. Berlin: W. Spemann, 1906.

Korff, Gottfried, and Martin Roth, eds. *Das historische Museum: Labor, Schaubühne, Identitätsfabrik.* Frankfurt am Main: Campus, 1990.

Koshar, Rudy. "Altar, Stage and City: Historic Preservation and Urban Meaning in Nazi Germany." *History and Memory* 3, no. 1 (1991): 30–59.

———. "Building Pasts: Historic Preservation and Identity in Twentieth-Century Germany." In *Commemorations: The Politics of National Identity,* edited by John R. Gillis, 215–38. Princeton, N.J.: Princeton University Press, 1994.

———. *Germany's Transient Pasts: Preservation and National Memory in the Twentieth Century.* Chapel Hill: University of North Carolina Press, 1998.

———. "The *Kaiserreich's* Ruins: Hope, Memory, and Political Culture in Imperial Germany." In *Society, Culture, and the State in Germany, 1870–1930,* edited by Geoff Eley, 487–512. Ann Arbor: University of Michigan Press, 1996.

Kramer, Fritz. *Verkehrte Welten: Zur imaginären Ethnographie des 19. Jahrhunderts.* Frankfurt am Main: Syndikat, 1977.

Krause, Fritze. "Dem Andenken Karl Weules." *Jahrbuch des Städtischen Museums für Völkerkunde zu Leipzig* 9 (1922/1925): 7–33.

Krieger, Kurt. "Das Schicksal der Benin-Sammlung des Berliner Museums für Völkerkunde." *Baessler-Archiv,* n.s., 5 (1957): 225–29.

Kubach Reutter, Ursula. *Überlegungen zur Ästhetik in der Ethnologie und zur Rolle der Ästhetik bei der Präsentation völkerkundlicher Ausstellungsgegenstände.* Nürnberg: Gesellschaft für Sozialwissenschaftliche Forschung und Praxisberatung, 1985.

Kuhn, Thomas S. *The Structure of Scientific Revolutions.* Chicago: University of Chicago Press, 1970.

Kuklick, Henrika. "After Ishmael: The Fieldwork Tradition and Its Future." In *Anthropological Locations: Boundaries and Grounds of a Field Science,* edited by James Ferguson and Akhil Gupta, 47–65. Berkeley: University of California Press, 1997.

———. *The Savage Within: The Social History of British Anthropology.* Cambridge: Cambridge University Press, 1991.

Kuntz, Andreas. *Das Museum als Volksbildungsstätte: Museumskonzeptionen in der Volksbildungs Bewegung in Deutschland zwischen 1871–1918.* Vol. 7. Marburger Studien zur vergleichenden Ethnosoziologie. Marburg: Marburger Studienkreis für Europäische Ethnologie, 1976.

Ladd, Brian. *Urban Planning and Civic Order in Germany, 1860–1914.* Cambridge: Harvard University Press, 1990.

Latour, Bruno. *Science in Action: How to Follow Scientists and Engineers through Society.* Cambridge: Harvard University Press, 1987.

Lebovics, Herman. *True France: The Wars over Cultural Identity 1900–1945.* Ithaca, N.Y.: Cornell University Press, 1992.

Lehmann, Alfred. "85 Jahre Museum für Völkerkunde zu Leipzig." *Jahrbuch des Museums für Völkerkunde zu Leipzig* 12 (1953): 10–51.

Lenman, Robin. *Artists and Society in Germany 1850–1914.* Manchester: University of Manchester Press, 1997.

Letkemann, Peter. "Das Berliner Panoptikum: Namen, Häuser, Schicksale." *Mitteilungen des Vereins für die Geschichte Berlins* 69, no. 11 (1973): 319–26.

Levin, David Michael, ed. *Modernity and the Hegemony of Vision.* Berkeley: University of California Press, 1993.

Liebersohn, Harry. *Aristocratic Encounters: European Travelers and North American Indians.* Cambridge: Cambridge University Press, 1998.

———. "Discovering Indigenous Nobility: Tocqueville, Chamisso, and Romantic Travel Writing." *American Historical Review* 99, no. 3 (1994): 746–66.

Lincoln, Bruce. *Discourse and the Construction of Society.* New York: Oxford University Press, 1989.

Liss, Julia E. "German Culture and German Science in the Bildung of Franz Boas." In *Volksgeist As Method and Ethic: Essays on Boasian Ethnography and the German Anthropological Tradition*, edited by George W. Stocking Jr., 155–84. Madison: University of Wisconsin Press, 1996.

Löfgren, Orvar, and Jonas Frykman. *Culture Builders: A Historical Anthropology of Middle-Class Life.* Translated by Alan Crozier. New Brunswick, N.J.: Rutgers University Press, 1987.

Lowie, Robert H. *The History of Ethnological Theory.* New York: Farrar and Rinehart, 1937.

Luhmann, Niklas. *Die Wissenschaft der Gesellschaft.* Frankfurt am Main: Suhrkamp, 1994.

Lumley, Robert, ed. *The Museum Time Machine: Putting Cultures On Display.* London: Routledge, 1988.

Luschan, Felix von. *Die Altertümer von Benin.* 3 vols. Berlin: Staatliche Museen zu Berlin, 1919.

Lustig, Wolfgang. "'Außer ein paar zerbrochenen Pfeilen nichts zu verteilen'— Ethnographische Sammlungen aus den deutschen Kolonien und ihre Verteilung an Museen 1889 bis 1914." *Mitteilungen aus dem Museum für Völkerkunde Hamburg* n.s., 18 (1988): 157–78.

Mai, Ekehard, Hans Pohl, and Stephan Waetzoldt, eds. *Kunst, Kultur und Politik im Deutschen Kaiserreich.* Vol. 2 of *Kunstpolitik und Kunstförderung im Kaiserreich: Kunst im Wandel der Sozial- und Wirtschaftsgeschichte.* Berlin: Mann Verlag, 1982.

Mannschatz, Hans-Christian. *Mit Grassi auf dem Dach und Klinger im Hof—100 Jahre Wilhelm-Leuschner-Platz 10/11: Die Geschichte eines Hauses.* Leipzig: Leipzig Stadtsbibliothek, 1996. Unpublished paper.

Marchand, Suzanne L. "Archeology and Cultural Politics in Germany, 1800–1965." Ph.D. diss., University of Chicago, 1992.

————. *Down from Olympus: Archeology and Philhellenism in Germany, 1750–1970.* Princeton, N.J.: Princeton University Press, 1996.

————. "Leo Frobenius and the Revolt against the West." *Journal of Contemporary History* 32, no. 2 (1997): 153–70.

————. "Orientalism as Kulturpolitik: German Archeology and Cultural Imperialism in Asia Minor." In *Volksgeist as Method and Ethic: Essays on Boasian Ethnography and the German Anthropological Tradition*, edited by George W. Stocking Jr., 298–336. Madison: University of Wisconsin Press, 1996.

————. "The Quarrel of the Ancients and the Moderns in the German Museums." In *Museums and Memory*, edited by Susan A. Crane, 179–99. Stanford: Stanford University Press, 2000.

————. "The Rhetoric of Artifacts and the Decline of Classical Humansim: The Case of Josef Strzygowski." *History and Theory* 33 (1994): 106–30.

Martin, Rudolf. *Anthropologie als Wissenschaft und Lehrfach: Eine akademische Antrittsrede.* Jena: Gustav Fischer, 1901.

Marx, Karl. *Capital: A Critique of Political Economy.* 3rd ed., vol. 1. Translated by Samuel Moore and Edward Aveling. Edited by Frederick Engels. Chicago: Charles H. Kerr and Company, 1912.

Mason, Otis T. "The Leipsic 'Museum of Ethnology'." *Smithsonian Report* (1875): 390–410.

Mason, Peter, and Florike Egmond. "Skeletons on Show: Learned Entertainment and Popular Knowledge." *History Workshop Journal* 41 (1996): 92–116.

Massin, Benoit. "From Virchow to Fischer: Physical Anthropology and 'Modern Race Theories' in Wilhelmine Germany." In *Volksgeist as Method and Ethic: Essays on Boasian Ethnography and the German Anthropological Tradition*, edited by George W. Stocking Jr., 79–154. Madison: University of Wisconsin Press, 1996.

Mauss, Marcel. *The Gift: Forms and Functions of Exchange in Archaic Societies.* Translated by Ian Cunnison. London: Cohen and West, 1969.

McClelland, Charles E. *The German experience of Professionalization: Modern Learned Professions and Their Organizations from the Early Nineteenth Century to the Hitler Era.* New York: Cambridge University Press, 1991.

Meek, Ronald L. *Social Science and the Ignoble Savage.* Cambridge: Cambridge University Press, 1976.

Melle, Werner von. *Dreizig Jahre Hamburger Wissenschaft 1891–1921.* Hamburg: Hamburger Wissenschaft Stiftung, 1924.

Meyer, Ernst. *Briefe von Heinrich Schliemann: Gesammelt und mit einer Einleitung in Auswahl Herausgegeben.* Berlin: Walter de Gruyter, 1936.

Mitchell, Nancy. *The Danger of Dreams: German and American Imperialism in Latin America.* Chapel Hill: University of North Carolina Press, 1999.

Mitchell, Timothy. *Colonizing Egypt.* New York: Cambridge University Press, 1985.

Moore, Anneliese. "Harry Maitey: From Polynesia to Prussia." *The Hawaiian Journal of History* 11 (1977): 125–61.

Mosse, George L. *The Nationalization of the Masses: Political Symbolism and Mass Movements in Germany from the Napoleonic Wars through the Third Reich.* New York: Howard Fertig, 1975.

Mühlmann, Wilhelm E. *Geschichte der Anthropologie.* Frankfurt am Main: Athenaum Verlag, 1968.

Müller, Anett. *Der Leipziger Kunstverein und das Museum der bildenden Künste—Materialen einer Geschichte 1836–1886/87,* Der Leipziger Vereins-Anzeiger Band 5, edited by Jörg Asshoff and Gaby Kirchhof. Leipzig: Nouvelle Alliance, 1995.

Müller, Heidi. "Die Sammlungskonzeption des Museums für Deutsche Volkskunde von der Gründung 1889 bis zum Ersten Weltkrieg." *Jahrbuch der Berliner Museen* 34 (1992): 185–95.

Museum für Völkerkunde zu Leipzig. *Bericht des Museum für Völkerkunde zu Leipzig.* Vols. 1–24. Leipzig: Museum für Völkerkunde zu Leipzig, 1874–1900.

———. *Jahrbuch des Städtischen Museums für Völkerkunde.* Vols. 1–6. Leipzig: Museum für Völkerkunde zu Leipzig, 1906–1914.

———. *Kunst aus Benin: Afrikanische Meisterwerke aus der Sammlung Hans Meyer.* Leipzig: Müseum für Völkerkunde zu Leipzig, 1994.

Nipperdey, Thomas. *Gesellschaft, Kultur, Theorie, Gesammelte Aufsätze zur neueren Geschichte.* Göttingen: Vandenhoeck und Ruprecht, 1976.

———. *Nachdenken über die deutsche Geschichte.* Munich: C. H. Beck, 1986, 1991.

Nyhart, Lynn K. *Biology Takes Form: Animal Morphology and the German Universities, 1800–1900.* Chicago: University of Chicago Press, 1995.

———. "Civic and Economic Zoology in Nineteenth-Century Germany: The 'Living Communities' of Karl Möbius." *Isis* 89 (1998): 605–30.

———. "Natural History and the 'New' Biology." In *Cultures of Natural History,* edited by J. A. Secord, N. Jardine, and E. C. Spray, 426–43. Cambridge: Cambridge University Press, 1996.

Olesko, Kathryn M. *Physics As a Calling: Discipline and Practice in the Königsberg Seminar for Physics.* Ithaca, N.Y.: Cornell University Press, 1991.

Palmowski, Jan. *Urban Liberalism in Imperial Germany: Frankfurt am Main, 1866–1914.* Oxford: Oxford University Press, 1999.

Panning, Albert. "Beiträge zur Geschichte des Zoologischen Staatsinstituts und Zoologischen Museums in Hamburg, 2. Teil." *Mitteilungen des Hamburgisches Zoologisches Museum und Institut* 54 (December 1956): 1–20.

Paret, Peter. *Art As History: Episodes in the Culture and Politics of Nineteenth-Century Germany.* Princeton, N.J.: Princeton University Press, 1988.

———. *The Berlin Secession: Modernism and Its Enemies in Imperial Germany.* Cambridge, Mass.: Belknap, 1980.

Pels, Peter. "The Anthropology of Colonialism: Culture, History, and the Emergence of Western Governmentality." *Annual Review of Anthropology* 26 (1997): 163–83.

Pels, Peter, and Oscar Salemink, eds. *Colonial Subjects: Essays on the Practical History of Anthropology.* Ann Arbor: University of Michigan Press, 1999.

Penny, H. Glenn. "'Beati possedentes:' Die Aneignung materieller Kultur und die Anschaffungspolitik des Leipziger Völkerkundemuseums." *Comparativ: Leipziger Beiträge zur Universalgeschichte und vergleichenden Gesellschaftsforschung* 10, no. 5/6 (2000): 68–103.

———. "The Civic Uses of Science: Ethnology and Civil Society in Imperial Germany." *Osiris* 17 (2002): 228–52.

————. "Cosmopolitan Visions and Municipal Displays: Museums, Markets, and the Ethnographic Project in Germany, 1868–1914." Ph.D. diss., University of Illinois at Urbana-Champaign, 1999.

————. "Fashioning Local Identities in an Age of Nation-Building: Museums, Cosmopolitan Traditions, and Intra-German Competition." *German History* 17, no. 4 (1999): 488–504.

————. "Municipal Displays: Civic Self-Promotion and the Development of German Ethnographic Museums, 1870–1914." *Social Anthropology* 6, no. 2 (1998): 157–68.

————. "The Museum für Deutsche Geschichte and German National Identity." *Central European History* 28, no. 3 (1995): 343–72.

————. "Science and the Marketplace: The Creation and Contentious Sale of the Museum Godeffroy." *Pacific Arts* 21/22 (July 2000): 1–18.

Pickering, Andrew, ed. *Science As Practice and Culture*. Chicago: University of Chicago Press, 1992.

Pickstone, John V. "Museuological Science? The Place of the Analytical/Comparative in Nineteenth-Century Science, Technology and Medicine." *History of Science* 32 (1994): 111–38.

Plessen, Marie-Louise von. *Die Nation und Ihre Museen*. Frankfurt am Main: Campus, 1992.

Pomian, Krzysztof. *Collectors and Curiosities: Paris and Vienna, 1500–1800*. Translated by Elizabeth Wiles-Portier. Cambridge: Polity Press, 1990.

Pratt, Mary Louise. *Imperial Eyes: Travel Writing and Transculturation*. New York: Routledge, 1992.

Pretzell, Lothar. "75 Jahre Museum für Deutsche Volkskunde." *Rheinisch-Westfälische Zeitschrift für Volkskunde* 11 (1964): 74–78.

Preuss, K. Th. "Adolf Bastian und die Heutige Völkerkunde." *Baessler-Archiv* 10 (1936): 1–15.

Price, Sally. *Primitive Art in Civilized Places*. Chicago: University of Chicago Press, 1989.

Probst, Peter. "Beobachtung und Methode Johann Stanislaus Kubary als Reisender und Ethnograph im Spiegel seiner Briefe an Adolf Bastian." *Baessler-Archiv*, n.s., 31 (1983): 23–56.

Proctor, Robert. "From *Anthropologie* to *Rassenkunde* in the German Anthropological Tradition." In *Bones, Bodies, Behavior: Essays on Biological Anthropology*, edited by George W. Stocking Jr., 138–79. Madison: University of Wisconsin Press, 1985.

————. *Value-Free Science? Purity and Power in Modern Knowledge*. Cambridge: Harvard University Press, 1991.

Radin, Paul. *The Method and Theory of Ethnology: An Essay in Criticism*. New York: Basic Books, 1933.

Ratzel, Friedrich. *Anthropogeographie*. 2 vols. Stuttgart: J. Engelhorn, 1882–1891.

Read, C. H. "Plato's 'Atlantis' Re-Discovered." *Burlington Magazine*, 18, no. 96 (March 1911): 330–35.

Reinhard, Wolfgang. *Imperialistische Kontinuität und nationale Ungeduld im 19. Jahrhundert*. Frankfurt am Main: Fischer, 1991.

Retallack, James. *Germany in the Age of Kaiser Wilhelm II*. New York: St. Martin's Press, 1996.

———. *Saxony in German History: Culture, Society, and Politics, 1830–1933.* Ann Arbor: University of Michigan Press, 2000.

Reulecke, Jurgen. *Geschichte der Urbanisierung in Deutschland.* Frankfurt am Main: Suhrkamp, 1985.

Richards, Thomas. *The Commodity Culture of Victorian England: Advertising and Spectacle, 1851–1914.* Stanford: Stanford University Press, 1990.

Richter, Oswald. "Über die Idealen und Praktischen Aufgaben der Ethnographischen Museen." *Museumskunde* 2–6 (1906–1910).

Ringer, Fritz K. *The Decline of the German Mandarins.* Cambridge: Harvard University Press, 1969.

Roth, Martin. *Heimatmuseum: Zur Geschichte einer deutschen Institution.* Berlin: Gebr. Mann Verlag, 1990.

Rothfels, Nigel T. "Bring 'em Back Alive: Carl Hagenbeck and Exotic Animal and People Trades in Germany, 1848–1914." Ph.D. diss., Harvard University, 1994.

Rupke, Nicholaas A. Introduction to *Cosmos: A Sketch of a Physical Description of the Universe,* vol. 1, by Alexander von Humboldt, translated by E. C. Otté. Baltimore: Johns Hopkins University Press, 1997.

Rydell, Robert W. *All the World's a Fair: Visions of Empire at American International Expositions, 1876–1916.* Chicago: University of Chicago Press, 1984.

Ryding, James N. "Alternatives in Nineteenth-Century German Ethnology: A Case Study in the Sociology of Science." *Sociologicus* 25 (1975): 1–28.

Sabean, David Warren. *Power in the Blood: Popular Culture and Village Discourse in Early Modern Germany.* Cambridge: Cambridge University Press, 1984.

Said, Edward W. *Culture and Imperialism.* New York: Aldine Publishing Company, 1993.

———. *Orientalism.* New York: Pantheon Books, 1978.

Scheffler, Karl. *Berliner Museumskrieg.* Berlin: Cassirer, 1921.

Scherer, Valentin. *Deutsche Museen: Entstehung und Kulturgeschichtliche Bedeutung unserer öffentlichen Kunstsammlungen.* Jena: Diederichs, 1913.

Schieder, Theodor. *Das Deutsche Kaiserreich von 1871 als Nationalstaat.* Göttingen: Vandenhoeck and Ruprecht, 1992.

Schmidt-Herwig, Angelika, and Gerhard Winter, eds. *Museumsarbeit und Kulturpolitik.* Frankfurt am Main: Brandes and Apsel, 1992.

Schildkrout, Enid, and Curtis A. Heim, eds. *The Scramble for Art in Central Africa.* Cambridge: Cambridge University Press, 1998.

Schneider, Gerhard. "Das Deutsche Kolonialmuseum Berlin und seine Bedeutung im Rahmen der preußischen Schulreform um die Jahrhundertwende." In *Die Zukunft beginnt in der Vergangenheit: Museumsgeschichte und Geschichtsmuseum,* 155–99. Frankfurt am Main: Historisches Museum der Stadt Frankfurt am Main, 1982.

Schumann, Dirk. *Bayerns Unternehmer in der Gesellschaft und Staat 1834–1914.* Göttingen: Vandenhoeck and Ruprecht, 1992.

Schwartz, Vanessa R. *Spectacular Realities: Early Mass Culture in Fin-de-Siècle Paris.* Berkeley: University of California Press, 1998.

Schwartz, Vanessa R., and Leo Charney, eds. *Cinema and the Invention of Modern Life.* Berkeley: University of California Press, 1995.

Schweinfurth, Georg. *The Heart of Africa*. Translated by Ellen E. Frewer. New York: Drallop Publishing Company, 1896.

Seidensticker, W. "Das Konzept der Ethnologie im Werk Adolf Bastians." *Sonderausdruck aus dem Jahrbuch der Wittheit zu Bremen* 13 (1969): 25.

Shapin, Steven. "Discipline and Bounding: The History and Sociology of Science as Seen Through the Externalism-Internalism Debate." *History of Science* 30 (1992): 333–69.

Sheehan, James J. "From Princely Collections to Public Museums: Toward a History of the German Art Museum." In *Rediscovering History*, edited by Michael S. Roth, 169–82. Stanford: Stanford University Press, 1994.

———. *German Liberalism in the Nineteenth Century*. Chicago: University of Chicago Press, 1978.

———. "Liberalism and the City in Nineteenth-Century Germany." *Past and Present* 51 (May 1971): 116–37.

———. *Museums in the German Art World: From the End of the Old Regime to the Rise of Modernism*. New York: Oxford University Press, 2000.

———. "What is German History? Reflections on the Role of the Nation in German History and Historiography." *Journal of Modern History* 53, no. 1 (March 1981): 1–23.

Sheets-Pyenson, Susan. *Cathedrals of Science: The Development of Colonial Natural History Museums during the Late Nineteenth Century*. Kingston, Quebec: McGill-Queen's University Press, 1988.

Sherman, Daniel J. "The Bourgeoisie, Cultural Appropriation, and the Art Museum in Nineteenth-Century France." *Radical History Review* 38 (1987): 38–58.

———. *Worthy Monuments: Art Museums and the Politics of Culture in Nineteenth-Century France*. Cambridge: Harvard University Press, 1989.

Sherman, Daniel J., and Irit Rogoff, eds. *Museum Culture: Histories, Discourses, Spectacles*. Minneapolis: University of Minnesota Press, 1994.

Simmel, Georg. "The Metropolis and Mental Life." In *The Sociology of Georg Simmel*, edited by Kurt Wolff, translated by H. H. Gerth. New York: Free Press, 1950.

———. *The Philosophy of Money*. Translated by Tom Bottomore and David Frisby. Boston: Routledge and Kegan Paul, 1978.

Smith, Bernard. *European Vision and the South Pacific*. 2nd ed. New Haven: Yale University Press, 1985.

Smith, Woodruff D. "Colonialism and Colonial Empire." In *Imperial Germany: A Historiographical Companion*, edited by Roger Chickering, 430–53. London: Greenwood, 1996.

———. *The German Colonial Empire*. Chapel Hill: University of North Carolina Press, 1978.

———. *Politics and the Sciences of Culture in Germany 1840–1920*. New York: Oxford University Press, 1991.

Smolka, Wolfgang J. *Völkerkunde in München: Voraussetzungen, Möglichkeiten und Entwicklungslinien ihrer Institutionalisierung (ca. 1850–1933)*. Berlin: Dunker and Humboldt, 1994.

Sperber, Jonathan. "*Bürger, Bürgertum, Bürgerlichkeit, Bürgerliche Gesellschaft*: Studies of the German (Upper) Middle Class and Its Sociocultural World." *Journal of Modern History* 69, no. 2 (1997): 271–97.

Staehelin, Balthasar. *Völkerschauen im Zoologischen Garten Basel 1879–1935*. Basel: Basler Afrika Bibliographien, 1993.

Steedman, Carolyn. "Inside, Outside, Other: Accounts of National Identity in the Late 19th Century." *History of the Human Sciences* 8, no. 4 (1995): 59–76.

Steinberg, Michael P. *The Meaning of the Salzburg Festival: Austria as Theater and Ideology, 1890–1938*. Ithaca, N.Y.: Cornell University Press, 1990.

Steinen, Karl von den. "Gedächtnisrede auf Adolf Bastian." *Zeitschrift für Ethnologie* 37, no. 2 (1905): 236–49.

———. *Unter den Naturvölker Zentral-Brasiliens: Reiseschilderung und Ergebnisse der Zweiten Schingú-Expedition 1887–1888*. Berlin: Reimer, 1984.

Steinmann, Ulrich. "Die Entwicklung des Museums für Volkskunde von 1889 bis 1964." In *75 Jahre Museum für Volkskunde zu Berlin*, 7–47. Berlin: Staatliche Museen zu Berlin, 1964.

———. "Gründer und Förderer des Berliner Volkskunde-Museums." *Staatliche Museen zu Berlin-Forschung und Berichte* 9 (1967): 71–111.

———. "Die Volkskundemuseen in Wien und Berlin." *Österreichische Zeitschrift für Volkskunde* 66 (1963): 6.

Sternberger, Dolf. *Panorama of the Nineteenth Century*. Translated by Joachim Neugroschel. New York: Urizon, 1977.

Stewart, Susan. *On Longing: Narratives of the Miniature, the Gigantic, the Souvenir, the Collection*. Baltimore: Johns Hopkins University Press, 1984.

Stocking, George W., Jr. *After Tylor: British Social Anthropology, 1881–1951*. Madison: University of Wisconsin Press, 1996.

———. "Maclay, Kubary, Malinowski: Archetypes from the Dreamtime of Anthropology." In *Colonial Situations: Essays on the Contextualization of Ethnographic Knowledge*, edited by George W. Stocking Jr. Madison: University of Wisconsin Press, 1991.

———. *Race, Culture, and Evolution: Essays in the History of Anthropology*. Chicago: University of Chicago Press, 1968.

———. *Victorian Anthropology*. New York: Free Press, 1987.

———, ed. *Bones, Bodies, Behavior: Essays on Biological Anthropology*. Madison: University of Wisconsin Press, 1988.

———, ed. *Colonial Situations: Essays on the Contextualization of Ethnographic Knowledge*. Madison: University of Wisconsin Press, 1991.

———, ed. *Functionalism Historicized: Essays on British Social Anthropology*. Madison: University of Wisconsin Press, 1984.

———, ed. *Objects and Others: Essays on Museums and Material Culture*. Madison: University of Wisconsin Press, 1985.

———, ed. *The Shaping of American Anthropology, 1883–1911: A Franz Boas Reader*. New York: Basic Books, 1974.

———, ed. *Volksgeist as Method and Ethic: Essays on Boasian Ethnography and the German Anthropological Tradition*. Madison: University of Wisconsin Press, 1996.

Stoler, Ann Laura, and Frederick Cooper, eds. *Tensions of Empire: Colonial Cultures in a Bourgeois World*. Berkeley: University of California Press, 1997.

Sumner, Ray. *A Woman in the Wilderness: The Story of Amalie Dietrich in Australia*. Kensington: New South Wales University Press, 1993.

Taussig, Michael. "Culture of Terror—Space of Death: Roger Casement's Putumayo Report and the Explanation of Torture." *Comparative Studies in Society and History* (1984): 467–97.

———. *The Devil and Commodity Fetishism in South America*. Chapel Hill: University of North Carolina Press, 1980.

———. *Shamanism, Colonialism, and the Wild Man: A Study in Terror and Healing*. Chicago: University of Chicago Press, 1987.

Termer, Franz, and Thomas Georg Theye, eds. *Der Geraubte Schatten: Die Photographie als ethnographisches Dokument*. Munich: Münchener Stadtmuseum, 1989.

Thilenius, Georg. "Die Arbeiterfrage in der Südsee." *Globus* 77, no. 5 (1900): 69–72.

———. *Das Hamburgische Museum für Völkerkunde*. Vol. 14, Museumskunde. Berlin: Reimer, 1916.

———. "Museum und Völkerkunde." *Mitteilungen aus dem Museum für Völkerkunde in Hamburg* 12/13 (1928): 1–39.

———. "Plan der Expedition." In *Ergebnisse der Südsee-Expedition 1908–1910*, edited by Georg Thilenius, 1–41. Hamburg: L. Friederichsen, 1927.

———. "Vortrag über Volkskunde und Völkerkunde." *Mitteilungen des Verbandes deutscher Vereine für Volkskunde (Korrespondenzblatt)* 3 (1906): 14–18.

———, ed. *Ergebnisse der Südsee-Expedition 1908–1910*. Hamburg: L. Friederichsen, 1927.

Thode-Arora, Hilke. "Die Familie Umlauff und ihre Firmen—Ethnographica-Händler in Hamburg." *Mitteilungen aus dem Museum für Völkerkunde Hamburg*, n.s., 22 (1992): 143–58.

———. *Für fünfzig Pfennig um die Welt: Die Hagenbeckschen Völkerschauen*. Frankfurt: Campus, 1989.

———. Völkerschauen als Kulturkontakt." Master's thesis, University of Hamburg, 1985.

Thomas, Nicholas. *Colonialism's Culture: Anthropology, Travel and Government*. Cambridge: Polity, 1994.

———. *Entangled Objects: Exchange, Material Culture, and Colonialism in the Pacific*. Cambridge: Harvard University Press, 1991.

———. "Licensed Curiosity: Cook's Pacific Voyages." In *The Cultures of Collecting*, edited by John Elsner and Roger Cardinal, 116–36. London: Reaktion Books, 1994.

Thompson, Alastair. "Honors Uneven: Decorations, the State and Bourgeois Society in Imperial Germany." *Past and Present* 144 (1994): 171–204.

Thurnwald, Richard. "Über Völkerkundemuseen, Ihre Wissenschaftlichen Bedingungen und Ziele." *Museumskunde* 8, no. 4 (1912): 197–214.

Trail, David A. *Schliemann of Troy: Treasures and Deceit*. New York: St. Martin's Press, 1995.

Tucker, Jennifer. "Science Illustrated: Photographic Evidence and Social Practice in England, 1870–1920." Ph.D. diss., Johns Hopkins University, 1996.

Tylor, Edward B. *Primitive Culture: Researches into the Development of Mythology, Philosophy, Religion, Language, Art, and Custom.* 2 vols. London: John Murray, 1873.

———. "Professor Adolf Bastian." *Man* 75–76 (1905): 138–43.

Vermeulen, Han F., and Arturo Alvarez Roldán, eds. *Fieldwork and Footnotes: Studies in the History of European Anthropology.* New York: Routledge, 1995.

Vincent, Joan. *Anthropology and Politics: Visions, Traditions, and Trends.* Tucson: University of Arizona Press, 1990.

Virchow, Rudolf. "Das Museum für deutsche Volkstrachten und Erzeugnisse des Hausgewerbes in Berlin." *Die Gartenlaube* 26 (1889): 435–36.

Wade, Edwin L. "The Ethnic Art Market in the American Southwest, 1880–1980." In *Objects and Others: Essays on Museums and Material Culture,* edited by George W. Stocking Jr., 167–91. Madison: University of Wisconsin Press, 1985.

Walton, Whitney. *France at the Crystal Palace: Bourgeois Taste and Artisan Manufacture in the Nineteenth Century.* Berkeley: University of California Press, 1992.

Washausen, Helmut. *Hamburg und die Kolonialpolitik des Deutschen Reiches 1880–1890.* Hamburg: Hans Christians, 1968.

Wehler, Hans-Ulrich. *Bismarck und der Imperialismus.* 2nd ed. Frankfurt am Main: Suhrkamp, 1985.

———. *The German Empire.* Translated by Kim Traynor. Providence, R.I.: Berg, 1985.

Weindling, Paul. *Health, Race and German Politics between National Unification and Nazism, 1870–1945.* New York: Cambridge University Press, 1989.

Weingart, Peter. *The Social Production of Scientific Knowledge.* Boston: D. Reidel, 1977.

Werner, Alice. *The Natives of British Central Africa.* London: Archibald Constable and Company, 1906.

Westphal-Hellbusch, Sigrid. "Zur Geschichte des Museums." In *Hundert Jahre Museum für Völkerkunde Berlin,* edited by K. Krieger and G. Koch, 1–100. Berlin: Reimer, 1973.

Weule, Karl. "50 Jahre Völkerkundemuseum!" *Jahrbuch des Städtischen Museums für Völkerkunde zu Leipzig* 8 (1918/1921): 5–10.

———. "Aufgaben, Grundlagen und Einteilung der Völkerkunde." *Jahrbuch des Städtischen Museums für Völkerkunde zu Leipzig* 9 (1922–25): 46–55.

———. *Führer durch das Museum für Völkerkunde zu Leipzig.* Leipzig: Museum für Völkerkunde zu Leipzig, 1913.

———. *Führer durch die Sonderausstellung über die Wirtschaft der Naturvölker.* Leipzig: Museum für Völkerkunde zu Leipzig, 1909.

———. *Illustrierter Führer durch die Sonderausstellung über Transport-und Verkehrsmittel der Naturvölker und der außereuropäischen Kulturvölker.* Leipzig: Museum für Völkerkunde zu Leipzig, 1910.

———. "Das Museum für Völkerkunde zu Leipzig." *Jahrbuch des Städtischen Museums für Völkerkunde zu Leipzig* 6 (1913/1914): 23–28.

————. "Die nächsten Aufgaben und Ziele des Leipziger Völkermuseums." *Jahrbuch des Städtischen Museums für Völkerkunde zu Leipzig* 3 (1908/1909): 151–74.

White, Dan S. "Regionalism and Particularism." In *Imperial Germany: A Historiographical Companion*, edited by Roger Chickering, 131–55. London: Greenwood, 1996.

Whitman, James. "From Philology to Anthropology in Mid-nineteenth Century Germany." In *Functionalism Historicized: Essays on British Social Anthropology*, edited by George W. Stocking Jr., 214–29. Madison: University of Wisconsin Press, 1984.

Wiener, Michael. *Ikonographie des Wilden: Menschen-Bilder in Ethnographie und Photographie zwischen 1850 und 1918*. Munich: Trickster Verlag, 1990.

Wildenthal, Lora. *German Women for Empire, 1884–1945*. Durham, N.C.: Duke University Press, 2001.

Williams, Elizabeth. "The Science of Man: Anthropological Thought and Institutions in Nineteenth-Century France." Ph.D. diss., Indiana University, 1983.

Williams, Linda, ed. *Viewing Positions: Ways of Seeing Film*. New Brunswick, N.J.: Rutgers University Press, 1995.

Winkelmann, Ingeburg. "Die Bürgerliche Ethnographie im Dienste der Kolonialpolitik des Deutschen Reiches (1870–1918)." Ph.D. diss., Humboldt-Universität zu Berlin, 1966.

Winsor, Mary P. *Reading the Shape of Nature: Comparative Zoology at the Agassiz Museum*. Chicago: University of Chicago Press, 1991.

Witt, Ruth. "Georg Thilenius in seiner Bedeutung für die Ethnologie." Master's thesis, University of Hamburg, 1995.

Wolfe, Patrick. *Settler Colonialism and the Transformation of Anthropology: The Politics and Poetics of an Ethnographic Event*. New York: Cassell, 1999.

Worlée, Ferdinand, and A. Oberdörffer. *Die Ethnographische oder Sammlung für Völkerkunde im Anschluß an das Naturhistorisches Museum in Hamburg*. Hamburg: Herbst, 1867.

Wörner, Martin. "Bauerhaus und Nationalpavillion: Die architektonische Selbstdarstellung Österreich-Ungarns auf den Weltausstellung des 19. Jahrhunderts." *Österreichisches Zeitschrift für Volkskunde* 48/97 (1994): 395–424.

Yanni, Carla. *Nature's Museums: Victorian Science and the Architecture of Display*. Baltimore: Johns Hopkins University Press, 1999.

Zantop, Susanne. *Colonial Fantasies: Conquest, Family, and Nation in Precolonial Germany, 1770–1870*. Durham, N.C.: Duke University Press, 1997.

Zimmerman, Andrew. *Anthropology and Anti-humanism in Imperial Germany*. Chicago: University of Chicago Press, 2001.

————. "Anthropology and the Place of Knowledge in Imperial Berlin." Ph.D. diss., University of California at San Diego, 1998.

————. "Anti-Semitism as Skill: Rudolf Virchow's Schulstatistik and the Racial Composition of Germany." *Central European History* 32, no. 4 (1999): 409–29.

————. "Science and Schaulust in the Berlin Museum of Ethnology." In *Wissenschaft und Öffentlichkeit in Berlin, 1870–1930*, edited by Constantin Goschler, 65–88. Stuttgart: Franz Steiner Verlag, 2000.

Zwernemann, Jürgen. "Aus den frühen Jahren des Museum für Völkerkunde zu

Leipzig." In *Festansprache aus Anlaß der 125—Jahrfeier am 24. November 1994.* Un-published manuscript in the library of the Museum für Völkerkunde zu Leip-zig, 1994.

————. *Culture History and African Anthropology: A Century of Research in Germany and Austria.* Stockholm: Uppsala, 1983.

————. *Hundert Jahre Hamburgisches Museum für Völkerkunde.* Hamburg: Museum für Völkerkunde Hamburg, 1980.

————. "Leo Frobenius und das Hamburgische Museum für Völkerkunde." *Mit-teilungen aus dem Museum für Völkerkunde Hamburg* 17 (1987): 111–27.

ing monopolies while, 67, 73, 113–
60; and creating sets, 77–79, 94; and
collectors, 86–88, 136–40; moral
parameters for, 95–98, 100–102,
118, 121–22, 128. *See also* Networks
of communication and exchange
Colonialism, German, 11–13, 17,
41, 107–24, 127, 213–14. *See also*
Colonial Museum, German; Ethnology, German: and colonialism;
Imperialism
Colonial Museum, German, 42–43
Competition: intra-German, 9–10,
40–49, 52, 54–58; international scientific, 10, 51–53, 109–11, 116–23
Coombes, Annie, 206
Cosmopolitanism, 2, 6, 9–11, 18, 40,
44–49, 64, 111–12, 115, 129, 215–16
Crystal Palace, 183
Cultural pluralism, 35–36
Curiosities and curiosity cabinets, 13,
15, 17, 80–81, 149–50, 164, 165,
168, 185, 192–95, 200, 204, 205,
207–8. See also *Wunderkammern*
Cushing, Frank Hamilton, 100–101

Dall, William H., 97
Dalton, O. M., 1, 9
Darwin, Charles, 21, 26
Dealers in artifacts, 73–79, 102–6,
108–10
Dietrich, Amalie, 5, 55
Difference, human, 23
Displays, 2–3, 4–5, 16, 24, 136–38,
148, 156–58, 169, 173, 176–81,
187–214
Dorsey, George A., 67, 100, 148–49,
186
Doubles of artifacts, 5, 67

Elementargedanken, 22
Empiricism, 2, 21–22, 25–26, 30;
some limits of, 180, 196. *See also*
Induction
Ethnology, German: and colonialism,
1, 3, 32, 41–102, 107–23, 128–30,

206; characteristics of, 2–3, 5, 12,
221 (n. 1); and National Socialism, 3;
impact of public on, 14, 55, 138–51;
professionalization of, 14–15, 19,
30, 79, 88–94, 95–96, 102, 104, 130,
138–39, 144–61, 184, 206, 215, 218;
and international community of science, 14–15, 32, 45, 59–69, 96–102,
132–35, 151, 157, 160, 161, 217; vs.
Anglo-American anthropology, 23,
34–35, 117–18, 148–49; and natural
science, 28; and civic society, 44–49,
141–61, 217–18; impact of, on non-
European cultures, 93, 100, 121–22,
126, 130; and authority of science,
96–102, 117–23, 128–30; and dealers in artifacts, 109, 176–79; and international borders, 112–23; and nationalism, 115–23. *See also* Bastian,
Adolf; Materialism and markets: and
impact on ethnology; Museums,
German ethnographic
Evans, Richard, 45
Expeditions, 28, 39, 90–94. *See also*
South Seas Expedition; Jesup
North Pacific Expedition; Turfan
Expedition

Field work, 88–90
Forster, Georg, 12
Foucault, Michel, 207
Foy, Willy, 246 (n. 87)
Frič, Alberto Vojtěch, 123–30
Frobenius, Leo, 39, 67, 78, 86, 142;
and Olokun affair, 115–23

Garret, Andrew, 55
Gemälde Galerie, Munich, 166
Gensch, Hugo, 124–26
Geographical provinces, 22
Georgi, Otto, 157
German Anthropological Society, 67,
151, 202
"German Sciences," 9–11, 40–41, 152
Germany, Imperial: character of, 9–11,
18, 33, 35–36, 40, 43–45, 210–15

Giglioli, Enrico Hillner, 134
Godeffroy, Johann Cesar, 54, 201
Godeffroy collection, 5–6, 54–58, 69,
    91, 134, 201–2, 204, 210
Goode, G. Brown, 17, 133
Göring, H., 139
Gossler, Gustav von, 41, 88, 188–89,
    193, 196
Gottsche, Carl, 145
Graebner, Fritz, 22
Grassi-Museum, Leipzig, 4–5, 175–79,
    201–2
Greenblatt, Stephen, 207
Greif, W., 196
Grünwedel, Albert, 75, 76, 115, 193

Haeckel, Ernst, 21
Hagen, Karl, 32, 144–46, 168
Hagenbeck, Carl, 44, 61, 103–5
Hamburg, 44–46, 56–58, 158–61,
    172–75
Haraway, Donna, 7
Heigel, Theodore von, 155
Hellwig collection, 93
Herrings, Hermann, 64–65
Hinsley, Curtis M., 4, 34
Historicism, 4, 22–23
Honors. See *Orden*
Humanism, 2, 15, 25, 127
Humboldt, Alexander von, 2, 18–21,
    37–38, 137, 215

Ifé, 116–23
Imperialism, 13, 15, 41–43, 49, 96,
    107–12, 116–30
Indian hunters in Brazil, 124–30
Induction, 21–23, 26, 29, 52
International Congress of American-
    ists XVI, 128–29
International expositions. *See* World's
    fairs

Jacob, Karl, 143
Jacobsen, Adrian, 56, 60–61, 70,
    81–85, 88, 89, 91, 99, 100, 101
Jagor, Feodor, 47–48

Jenkins, David, 80
Jesup North Pacific Expedition,
    91
Jomard, Edmé-François, 168

Klee, Paul, 155
Klemm, Gustav, 167, 169
Krause, Fritz, 150–51
Kubary, Johann Stanislaus, 55
Kucklick, Henrika, 88–89, 98
Kultur, 30, 35–36
Kulturvölker, 23, 107, 159–60, 166

Latour, Bruno, 14
Lehmann, Alfred, 164–65, 175, 177,
    207–8
Leipzig, 47–48, 56–58, 59, 62–66,
    156–58, 164–65, 167–72, 175–
    79, 199–204
Licht, Hugo, 136
Linden Museum, Stuttgart, 67
Lüders, Carl Wilhelm, 158–59, 168–
    69, 172–75
Luschan, Felix von, 33, 67, 75–79, 99,
    103, 148–49, 182, 193, 196–97,
    202–4, 216

Mason, Otis T., 4
Mass culture, 144–62 passim, 216
Material culture: ethnologists' uses of,
    5–6, 24, 27–28, 52–53; and unset-
    tling impact on university hierar-
    chies, 25–26; intersecting values of,
    53–54, 57–58, 67–71, 79–81, 84–
    94, 138–40; monopolies on, 67, 79,
    113, 160; commodification of, 79–
    81, 84–94 passim
Materialism and markets, 8, 14–15, 24,
    51–94 passim, 129; and impact on
    ethnology, 15, 52, 79, 88–91, 152,
    185. *See also* Collecting; Dealers in
    artifacts; Museums, German
    ethnographic
Meier, Joseph, 32
Melle, Werner von, 46, 58, 159, 175
Mengelbier, Oscar, 68–69

Schliemann, Heinrich, 25, 136, 137
Schmeltz, J. D. E., 5, 55
Schneider, Herman, 139–40
Schöne, Richard, 61, 83–84
Schweinfurth, Georg, 63–64
Science, spaces of, 91, 127–29, 141–51 passim
Sciences, German. *See* "German Sciences"
Seler, Eduard, 60, 124, 127, 128, 130
Sherman, Lucien, 49, 154–55, 159, 229 (n. 138)
Smithsonian Institution, 34–35, 60, 63, 97
Société Khedivale de Geographie, Cairo, 63
South Seas Expedition, 93–94, 100–101
Steinen, Karl von den, 20, 89, 124, 126, 128, 129–30
Stocking, George W. Jr., 4, 12, 222 (n. 7)
Strebel, Hermann, 114
Stübel, Alphons, 136–37

Thilenius, Georg, 32, 58, 66–67, 86, 91–94, 95, 99, 100, 103, 113, 118–23, 124, 126, 127, 130, 133, 147, 159–60, 169, 204–6, 210, 213, 216
Thomann-Gillis, W., 101–2, 106–7
Thomas, Northcote W., 1
Thurnwald, Richard, 33, 85, 148
Travel and travel literature, 2, 19–20, 22, 27–28, 37–39, 55, 89–90
Turfan Expedition, 197
Tylor, Edward B., 4, 23

Umlauff (family firm), 61, 67, 70, 75, 103–5
Universities, 19, 30, 36, 38, 40, 44, 89–90, 150, 159, 192; and intellectual counter culture, 18, 25–26, 36, 38–39, 49

Virchow, Rudolf, 21, 41, 86, 89, 99, 104, 136, 138
Visitors. *See also* Audiences; Reception
Visual culture, 24, 132, 135, 140–41, 198–214, 216
Völkergedanken, 22
Völkerschauen, 44, 103–4, 211–13
Volkskunde Museum, 41–42

Wagner, Mortiz, 37–38, 139, 153–54, 159, 227 (n. 91)
Webster, W. D., 77–78
Weule, Karl, 67, 90, 92, 97, 105, 113, 118–23, 139, 142–43, 148–49, 156–58, 165, 182, 184–85, 201–2, 209–10, 213, 216
Wissmann, Hermann von, 87, 135
Wolff, Paul Eugen, 64–65, 103
Wonder. *See* Curiosity and curiosity cabinets; *Wunderkammern*
World's fairs, 24–25, 56, 59–61, 85, 177
Worlée, Ferdinand, 168
Wunderkammern, 2, 165, 167, 194, 196, 204, 205, 208, 213

Zengen, H., 114–15